New Perspectives on

MICROSOFT® EXCEL 2000

Introductory

JUNE JAMRICH PARSONS

DAN OJA

ROY AGELOFF
University of Rhode Island

PATRICK CAREY
Carey Associates, Inc.

APPROVED COURSEWARE

COURSE
TECHNOLOGY

Thomson Learning™

ONE MAIN STREET, CAMBRIDGE, MA 02142

New Perspectives on Microsoft Excel 2000—Introductory is published by Course Technology.

Senior Editor	Donna Gridley
Senior Product Manager	Rachel A. Crapser
Acquisitions Editor	Christine Guivernau
Product Manager	Catherine V. Donaldson
Associate Product Manager	Karen Shortill
Editorial Assistant	Melissa Dezotell
Developmental Editor	Joan Kalkut
Production Editor	Catherine G. DiMassa
Text Designer	Meral Dabcovich
Cover Designer	Douglas Goodman

© 2000 by Course Technology, a division of Thomson Learning

Course Technology
1 Main Street
Cambridge, MA 02142
Or find us on the World Wide Web at: http://www.course.com

For permission to use material from this text or product, contact us by:
Web: www.thomsonrights.com
Phone: 1-800-730-2214
Fax: 1-800-730-2215

Trademarks

Disclaimer

ISBN 0-7600-7086-5

Printed in the United States of America

6 7 8 9 10 BM 03 02 01

PREFACE

The New Perspectives Series

About New Perspectives

Course Technology's **New Perspectives Series** is an integrated system of instruction that combines text and technology products to teach computer concepts, the Internet, and microcomputer applications. Users consistently praise this series for innovative pedagogy, use of interactive technology, creativity, accuracy, and supportive and engaging style.

How is the New Perspectives Series different from other series?

The **New Perspectives Series** distinguishes itself by **innovative technology**, from the renowned Course Labs to the state-of-the-art multimedia that is integrated with our Concepts texts. Other distinguishing features include **sound instructional design, proven pedagogy**, and **consistent quality**. Each tutorial has students learn features in the context of solving a realistic case problem rather than simply learning a laundry list of features. With the **New Perspectives Series**, instructors report that students have a complete, integrative learning experience that stays with them. They credit this high retention and competency to the fact that this series incorporates critical thinking and problem-solving with computer skills mastery. In addition, we work hard to ensure accuracy by using a multi-step quality assurance process during all stages of development. Instructors focus on teaching and students spend more time learning.

Choose the coverage that's right for you

New Perspectives applications books are available in the following categories:

Brief
2-4 tutorials

Brief: approximately 150 pages long, two to four "Level I" tutorials, teaches basic application skills.

Introductory
6 or 7 tutorials, or Brief + 2 or 3 more tutorials

Introductory: approximately 300 pages long, four to seven tutorials, goes beyond the basic skills. These books often build out of the Brief book, adding two or three additional "Level II" tutorials. The book you are holding is an Introductory book.

Comprehensive
Introductory + 4 or 5 more tutorials. Includes Brief Windows tutorials and Additional Cases

Comprehensive: approximately 600 pages long, eight to twelve tutorials, all tutorials included in the Introductory text plus higher-level "Level III" topics. Also includes two Windows tutorials and three or four fully developed Additional Cases.

Advanced
Quick Review of basics + in-depth, high-level coverage

Advanced: approximately 600 pages long, cover topics similar to those in the Comprehensive books, but offer the highest-level coverage in the series. Advanced books assume students already know the basics, and therefore go into more depth at a more accelerated rate than the Comprehensive titles. Advanced books are ideal for a second, more technical course.

Office
Quick Review of basics + in-depth, high-level coverage

Office: approximately 800 pages long, covers all components of the Office suite as well as integrating the individual software packages with one another and the Internet.

Custom Books: The New Perspectives Series offers you two ways to customize a New Perspectives text to fit your course exactly: *CourseKits*™ are two or more texts shrink-wrapped together, and offer significant price discounts. *Custom Editions*®, offer you flexibility in designing your concepts, Internet, and applications courses. You can build your own book by ordering a combination of topics bound together to cover only the subjects you want. There is no minimum order, and books are spiral bound. Contact your Course Technology sales representative for more information.

What course is this book appropriate for?

New Perspectives on Microsoft Excel 2000—Introductory can be used in any course in which you want students to learn some of the most important topics of Excel 2000, including creating, editing, and formatting worksheets and charts, working with Excel lists and pivot tables, and integrating worksheet data with various programs and the World Wide Web. It is particularly recommended for a short-semester course on Microsoft Excel 2000. This book assumes that students have learned basic Windows navigation and file management skills from Course Technology's *New Perspectives on Microsoft Windows 95—Brief*, or the equivalent book for Windows 98 or NT.

What is the Microsoft Office User Specialist Program?

The Microsoft Office User Specialist Program provides an industry-recognized standard for measuring an individual's mastery of an Office application. Passing one or more MOUS Program certification exam helps your students demonstrate their proficiency to prospective employers and gives them a competitive edge in the job marketplace. Course Technology offers a growing number of Microsoft-approved products that cover all of the required objectives for the MOUS Program exams. For a complete listing of Course Technology titles that you can use to help your students get certified, visit our Web sit at **www.course.com**.

   New Perspectives on Microsoft Excel 2000—Introductory has been approved by Microsoft as courseware for the Microsoft Office User Specialist (MOUS) Program. After completing the tutorials and exercises in this book, students may be prepared to take the MOUS exam for Microsoft Excel 2000. For more information about certification, please visit the MOUS program site at **www.mous.net**.

Proven Pedagogy

CASE

Tutorial Case Each tutorial begins with a problem presented in a case that is meaningful to students. The case turns the task of learning how to use an application into a problem-solving process.

45-minute Sessions Each tutorial is divided into sessions that can be completed in about 45 minutes to an hour. Sessions allow instructors to more accurately allocate time in their syllabus, and students to better manage their own study time.

1.
2.
3.

Step-by-Step Methodology We make sure students can differentiate between what they are to *do* and what they are to *read*. Through numbered steps—clearly identified by a gray shaded background—students are constantly guided in solving the case problem. In addition, the numerous screen shots with callouts direct students' attention to what they should look at on the screen.

TROUBLE?

TROUBLE? Paragraphs These paragraphs anticipate the mistakes or problems that students may have and help them continue with the tutorial.

"Read This Before You Begin" Page Located opposite the first tutorial's opening page for each level of the text, the Read This Before You Begin Page helps introduce technology into the classroom. Technical considerations and assumptions about software are listed to save time and eliminate unnecessary aggravation. Notes about the Student Disks help instructors and students get the right files in the right places, so students get started on the right foot.

QUICK CHECK

RW

TASK REFERENCE

REVIEW

CASE

INTERNET

LAB

Explore

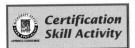

Certification Skill Activity

Quick Check Questions Each session concludes with meaningful, conceptual Quick Check questions that test students' understanding of what they learned in the session. Answers to the Quick Check questions are provided at the end of each tutorial.

Reference Windows Reference Windows are succinct summaries of the most important tasks covered in a tutorial and they preview actions students will perform in the steps to follow.

Task Reference Located as a table at the end of the book, the Task Reference contains a summary of how to perform common tasks using the most efficient method, as well as references to pages where the task is discussed in more detail.

End-of-Tutorial Review Assignments, Case Problems, Internet Assignments and Lab Assignments Review Assignments provide students with additional hands-on practice of the skills they learned in the tutorial using the same case presented in the tutorial. These Assignments are followed by three to four Case Problems that have approximately the same scope as the tutorial case but use a different scenario. In addition, some of the Review Assignments or Case Problems may include Exploration Exercises that challenge students encourage them to explore the capabilities of the program they are using, and/or further extend their knowledge. Finally, if a Course Lab accompanies a tutorial, Lab Assignments are included after the Case Problems.

File Finder Chart This chart, located in the back of the book, visually explains how a student should set up their data disk, what files should go in what folders, and what they'll be saving the files as in the course of their work.

MOUS Certification Chart In the back of the book, you'll find a chart that lists all the skills for the Microsoft Office User Specialist Exam on Excel 2000. With page numbers referencing where these skills are covered in this text and where students get hands-on practice in completing the skills, the chart can be used as an excellent study guide in preparing for the Excel MOUS exam.

The Instructor's Resource Kit for this title contains:

- Electronic Instructor's Manual
- Data Files
- Solution Files
- Course Labs
- Course Test Manager Testbank
- Course Test Manager Engine
- Figure Files

These teaching tools come on CD-ROM. If you don't have access to a CD-ROM drive, contact your Course Technology customer service representative for more information.

The New Perspectives Teaching Tools

Electronic Instructor's Manual. Our Instructor's Manuals include tutorial overviews and outlines, technical notes, lecture notes, solutions, and Extra Case Problems. Many instructors use the Extra Case Problems for performance-based exams or extra credit projects. The Instructor's Manual is available as an electronic file, which you can get from the Instructor Resource Kit (IRK) CD-ROM or download it from **www.course.com**.

Data Files Data Files contain all of the data that students will use to complete the tutorials, Review Assignments, and Case Problems. A Readme file includes instructions for using the files. See the "Read This Before You Begin" page/pages for more information on Student Files.

Solution Files Solution Files contain every file students are asked to create or modify in the tutorials, Tutorial Assignments, Case Problems, and Extra Case Problems. A Help file on the Instructor's Resource Kit includes information for using the Solution files.

Course Labs: Concepts Come to Life These highly interactive computer-based learning activities bring concepts to life with illustrations, animations, digital images, and simulations. The Labs guide students step-by-step, present them with Quick Check questions, let them explore on their own, test their comprehension, and provide printed feedback. Lab icons at the beginning of the tutorial and in the tutorial margins indicate when a topic has a corresponding Lab. Lab Assignments are included at the end of each relevant tutorial. The Labs available with this book and the tutorials in which they appear are:

Tutorial 1

Figure Files Many figures in the text are provided on the IRK CD-ROM to help illustrate key topics or concepts. Instructors can create traditional overhead transparencies by printing the figure files. Or they can create electronic slide shows by using the figures in a presentation program such as PowerPoint.

Course Test Manager: Testing and Practice at the Computer or on Paper Course Test Manager is cutting-edge, Windows-based testing software that helps instructors design and administer practice tests and actual examinations. Course Test Manager can automatically grade the tests students take at the computer and can generate statistical information on individual as well as group performance.

Online Companions: Dedicated to Keeping You and Your Students Up-To-Date Visit our faculty sites and student sites on the World Wide Web at **www.course.com**. Here instructors can browse this text's password-protected Faculty Online Companion to obtain an online Instructor's Manual, Solution Files, Student Files, and more. Students can also access this text's Student Online Companion, which contains Student files and all the links that the students will need to complete their tutorial assignments.

More Innovative Technology
Course CBT

Enhance your students' Office 2000 classroom learning experience with self-paced computer-based training on CD-ROM. Course CBT engages students with interactive multimedia and hands-on simulations that reinforce and complement the concepts and skills covered in the textbook. All the content is aligned with the MOUS (Microsoft Office User Specialist) program, making it a great preparation tool for the certification exams. Course CBT also includes extensive pre- and post-assessments that test students' mastery of skills. These pre- and post-assessments automatically generate a "custom learning path" through the course that highlights only the topics students need help with.

Course Assessment

How well do your students really know Microsoft Office? Course Assessment is a performance-based testing program that measures students' proficiency in Microsoft Office 2000. Previously known as SAM, Course Assessment is available for Office 2000 in either a live or simulated environment. You can use Course Assessment to place students into or out of courses, monitor their performance throughout a course, and help prepare them for the MOUS certification exams.

WebCT

WebCT is a tool used to create Web-based educational environments and also uses WWW browsers as the interface for the course-building environment. The site is hosted on your school campus, allowing complete control over the information. WebCT has its own internal communication system, offering internal e-mail, a Bulletin Board, and a Chat room. Course Technology offers pre-existing supplemental information to help in your WebCT class creation, such as a suggested Syllabus, Lecture Notes, Figures in the Book/ Course Presenter, Student Downloads, and Test Banks in which you can schedule an exam, create reports, and more.

Acknowledgments

We would like to thank the many people whose invaluable contributions made this book possible. Our reviewers were Greg Lowry, Macon Technical Institute; Rick Wilkerson, Dyersburg State Community College; Mary Dobranski, College of St. Mary; Suzanne Tomlinson, Iowa State University; and Barbara Miller, Indiana University. At Course Technology, we would like to thank Donna Gridley, Senior Editor; Rachel Crapser, Senior Product Manger; Catherine Donaldson, Product Manager; Karen Shortill, Associate Product Manager; Melissa Dezotell, Editorial Assistant; Greg Bigelow, QA Supervisor; John Bosco, John Freitas, Nicole Ashton, Quality Assurance testers; and Catherine DiMassa, Senior Production Editor. A special thanks to Joan Kalkut, Developmental Editor, for her helpful suggestions and dedication to completing the text.

June Jamrich Parsons
Dan Oja
Roy Ageloff
Patrick Carey

BRIEF CONTENTS

TABLE OF CONTENTS

Reference **Windows List**

Tutorial **Tips**

These tutorials will help you learn about Microsoft Excel 2000. The tutorials are designed to be worked through at a computer. Each tutorial is divided into sessions. Watch for the session headings, such as Session 1.1 and Session 1.2. Each session is designed to be completed in about 45 minutes, but take as much time as you need. It's also a good idea to take a break between sessions.

To use the tutorials effectively you, read the following questions and answers before you begin.

Where do I start?
Each tutorial begins with a case, which sets the scene for the tutorial and gives you background information to help you understand what you will be doing. Read the case before you go to the lab. In the lab, begin with the first session of a tutorial.

How do I know what to do on the computer?
Each session contains steps that you will perform on the computer to learn how to use Microsoft Excel 2000. Read the text that introduces each series of steps. The steps you need to do at a computer are numbered and are set against a shaded background. Read each step carefully and completely before you try it.

How do I know if I did the step correctly?
As you work, compare your computer screen with the corresponding figure in the tutorial. Don't worry if your screen display is somewhat different from the figure. The important parts of the screen display are labeled in each figure. Check to make sure these parts are on your screen.

What if I make a mistake?
Don't worry about making mistakes—they are part of the learning process. Paragraphs labeled "TROUBLE?" identify common problems and explain how to get back on track. Follow the steps in a TROUBLE? paragraph only if you are having the problem described. If you run into other problems:

- Carefully consider the current state of your system, the position of the pointer, and any messages on the screen.

- Complete the sentence, "Now I want to…" Be specific, because identifying your goal will help you rethink the steps you need to take to reach that goal.

- If you are working on a particular piece of software, consult the Help system.

- If the suggestions above don't solve your problem, consult your technical support person for assistance.

How do I use the Reference Windows?
Reference Windows summarize the procedures you will learn in the tutorial steps. Do not complete the actions in the Reference Windows when you are working through the tutorial. Instead, refer to the Reference Windows while you are working on the assignments at the end of the tutorial.

How can I test my understanding of the material I learned in the tutorial?
At the end of each session, you can answer the Quick Check questions. The answers for the Quick Checks are at the end of that tutorial.

After you have completed the entire tutorial, you should complete the Review Assignments and Case Problems. They are carefully structured so that you will review what you have learned and then apply your knowledge to new situations.

What if I can't remember how to do something?
You should refer to the Task Reference at the end of the book; it summarizes how to accomplish tasks using the most efficient method.

Before you begin the tutorials, you should know the basics about your computer's operating system. You should also know how to use the menus, dialog boxes, Help system, and My Computer.

How can I prepare for MOUS Certification?
The Microsoft Office User Specialist (MOUS) logo on the cover of this book indicates that Microsoft has approved it as a study guide for Excel 2000 MOUS exam. At the back of this text, you'll see a chart that outlines the specific Microsoft certification skills for Excel 2000 that are covered in the tutorials. You'll need to learn these skills if you're interested in taking a MOUS exam. If you decide to take a MOUS exam, or if you just want to study a specific skill, this chart will give you an easy reference to the page number on which the skill is covered. To learn more about the MOUS certification program refer to the preface in the front of the book or go to *http://www.mous.net*.

Now that you've read Tutorial Tips, you are ready to begin.

New Perspectives on

MICROSOFT®
EXCEL 2000

Read This Before You Begin

To the Student

Data Disks

To complete the Level I tutorials, Review Assignments, and Case Problems, you need 2 Data Disks. Your instructor will either provide you with these Data Disks or ask you to make your own.

If you are making your own Data Disks, you will need 2 blank, formatted high-density disks. You will need to copy a set of folders from a file server or standalone computer or the Web onto your disks. Your instructor will tell you which computer, drive letter, and folders contain the files you need. You could also download the files by going to www.course.com, clicking Data Disk Files, and following the instructions on the screen.

The following table shows you which folders go on each of your disks, so that you will have enough disk space to complete all the tutorials, Review Assignments, and Case Problems:

Data Disk 1

Write this on the disk label:
Data Disk 1: Tutorials 1-3

Put these folders and all subfolders on the disk:
Tutorial.01, Tutorial.02, Tutorial.03

Data Disk 2

Write this on the disk label:
Data Disk 2: Tutorial 4

Put these folders and all subfolders on the disk:
Tutorial.04

When you begin each tutorial, be sure you are using the correct Data Disk. Refer to the "File Finder" Chart at the back of this text for more detailed information on which files are used in which tutorials. See the inside front or inside back cover of this book for more information on Data Disk files, or ask your instructor or technical support person for assistance.

Course Labs

The Excel Level I tutorials feature an interactive Course Lab to help you understand spreadsheet concepts. There are Lab Assignments at the end of Tutorial 1 that relate to this Lab.

To start a Lab, click the **Start** button on the Windows taskbar, point to **Programs**, point to **Course Labs**, point to **New Perspectives Course Labs**, and click the name of the Lab you want to use.

Using Your Own Computer

If you are going to work through this book using your own computer, you need:

- **Computer System** Microsoft Windows 95, 98, NT, or higher must be installed on your computer. This book assumes a typical installation of Microsoft Excel.

- **Data Disk** You will not be able to complete the tutorials or exercises in this book using your own computer until you have your Data Disks.

- **Course Labs** See your instructor or technical support person to obtain the Course Lab software for use on your own computer.

Visit Our World Wide Web Site

Additional materials designed especially for you are available on the World Wide Web. Go to http://www.course.com.

To the Instructor

The Data files and Course Labs are available on the Instructor's Resource Kit for this title. Follow the instructions in the Help file on the CD-ROM to install the programs to your network or standalone computer. For information on creating Data Disks or the Course Labs, see the "To the Student" section above.

You are granted a license to copy the Data Files and Course Labs to any computer or computer network used by students who have purchased this book.

OBJECTIVES

In this tutorial you will:

- Start and exit Excel

- Discover how Excel is used in business

- Identify the major components of the Excel window

- Navigate an Excel workbook and worksheet

- Open, save, print, and close a worksheet

- Enter text, numbers, formulas, and functions

- Correct mistakes

- Perform what-if analyses

- Clear contents of cells

- Use the Excel Help system

LABS

Spreadsheets

USING WORKSHEETS TO MAKE BUSINESS DECISIONS

Evaluating Sites for an Inwood Design Group Golf Course

CASE

Inwood Design Group

Golf is big business in Japan. Spurred by the Japanese passion for the sport, golf enjoys unprecedented popularity in Japan. But because the country is small and mountainous, the 12 million golfers have fewer than 2,000 courses from which to choose. Fees for 18 holes on a public course average between $200 and $300; golf club memberships are bought and sold like stock shares. The market potential is phenomenal, but building a golf course in Japan is expensive because of inflated property values, difficult terrain, and strict environmental regulations.

Inwood Design Group plans to build a world-class golf course, and one of the four sites under consideration is Chiba Prefecture, Japan. Other possible sites are Kauai, Hawaii; Edmonton, Canada; and Scottsdale, Arizona. You and Mike Nagochi are members of the site selection team for Inwood. The team is responsible for collecting information on the sites, evaluating that information, and recommending the best site for the new golf course.

Your team identified five factors likely to determine the success of a golf course: Climate, Competition, Market Size, Topography, and Transportation. The team has already collected information on these factors for three of the four potential golf course sites. Mike has just returned from visiting the last site in Scottsdale, Arizona.

Using Microsoft Excel 2000 for Windows, Mike has created a worksheet that the team can use to evaluate the four sites. He needs to complete the worksheet by entering the data for the Scottsdale site. He then plans to bring the worksheet to the group's next meeting so that the team can analyze the information and recommend a site to management.

In this tutorial you will learn how to use Excel as you work with Mike to complete the Inwood site selection worksheet and with the Inwood team to select the best site for the golf course.

SESSION 1.1

In this session you will learn what a spreadsheet is and how it is used in business. You will learn what Excel is and about the Excel window and its elements, how to move around a worksheet using the keyboard and the mouse, and how to open a workbook.

What Is Excel?

Spreadsheets

Excel is a computerized spreadsheet. A **spreadsheet** is an important business tool that helps you analyze and evaluate information. Spreadsheets are often used for cash flow analysis, budgeting, decision making, cost estimating, inventory management, and financial reporting. For example, an accountant might use a spreadsheet like the one in Figure 1-1 for a budget.

Figure 1-1	BUDGET SPREADSHEET

Cash Budget Forecast

	January Estimated	January Actual
Cash in Bank (Start of Month)	$1,400.00	$1,400.00
Cash in Register (Start of Month)	100.00	100.00
Total Cash	$1,500.00	$1,500.00
Expected Cash Sales	$1,200.00	$1,420.00
Expected Collections	400.00	380.00
Other Money Expected	100.00	52.00
Total Income	$1,700.00	$1,852.00
Total Cash and Income	$3,200.00	$3,352.00
All Expenses (for Month)	$1,200.00	$1,192.00
Cash Balance at End of Month	$2,000.00	$2,160.00

To produce the spreadsheet in Figure 1-1, you could manually calculate the totals and then type your results, or you could use a computer and spreadsheet program to perform the calculations and print the results. Spreadsheet programs are also referred to as electronic spreadsheets, computerized spreadsheets, or just spreadsheets.

In Excel 2000, the document you create is called a **workbook**. Each workbook is made up of individual **worksheets**, or **sheets**, just as a spiral-bound notebook is made up of sheets of paper. You will learn more about using multiple sheets later in this tutorial. For now, just keep in mind that the terms *worksheet* and *sheet* are often used interchangeably.

Starting Excel

Mike arrives at his office early because he needs to work with you to finish the worksheet and get ready for your meeting with the design team.

Start Excel and complete the worksheet that Mike will use to help the design team decide about the golf course site.

To start Microsoft Excel:

1. Make sure Windows is running on your computer and the Windows desktop appears on your screen.

2. Click the **Start** button on the taskbar to display the Start menu, and then point to **Programs** to display the Programs menu.

3. Point to **Microsoft Excel** on the Programs menu. See Figure 1-2.

Figure 1-2	STARTING MICROSOFT EXCEL

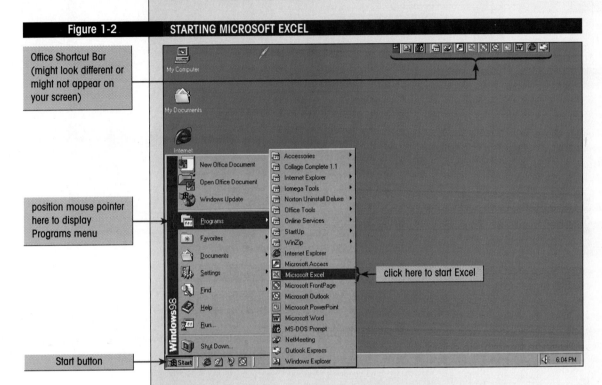

Office Shortcut Bar (might look different or might not appear on your screen)

position mouse pointer here to display Programs menu

click here to start Excel

Start button

TROUBLE? Don't worry if your screen differs slightly. Although figures in this book were created while running Windows 98 in its default setting, these operating systems share the same basic user interface and Microsoft Excel runs equally well using Windows 95, Windows 98 in Web style, Windows NT, and Windows 2000.

TROUBLE? If the Office Shortcut Bar, which appears along the top border of the desktop in Figure 1-2, looks different on your screen or does not appear at all, your system may be set up differently. The steps in these tutorials do not require that you use the Office Shortcut Bar; therefore, the remaining figures do not display it.

4. Click **Microsoft Excel**. After a short pause, the Microsoft Excel copyright information appears in a message box and remains on the screen until the Excel program window and a blank worksheet appear. See Figure 1-3.

TROUBLE? If the Office Assistant (see Figure 1-3) window opens when you start Excel, click Help on the menu bar then click Hide the Office Assistant. You'll learn more about the Office Assistant later in this tutorial.

Figure 1-3

EXCEL PROGRAM WINDOW WITH BLANK WORKSHEET

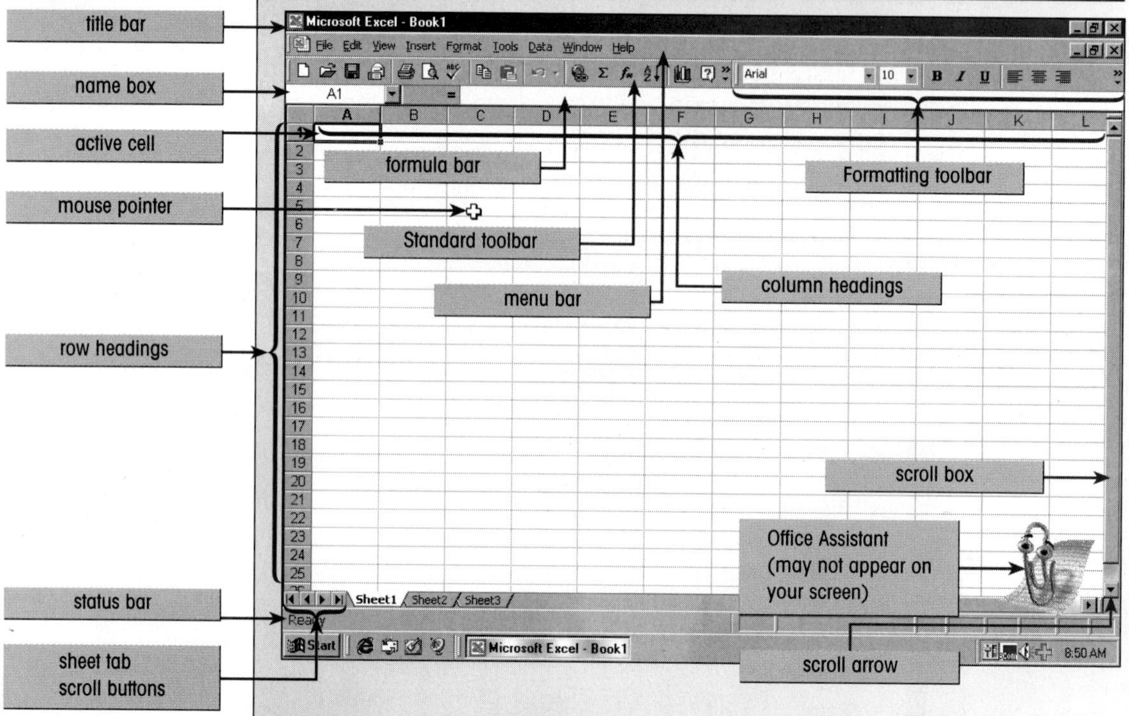

title bar

name box

active cell

mouse pointer

formula bar

Standard toolbar

menu bar

Formatting toolbar

column headings

row headings

scroll box

Office Assistant
(may not appear on
your screen)

status bar

sheet tab
scroll buttons

scroll arrow

5. If the Microsoft Excel program window does not fill the entire screen as in Figure 1-3, click the **Maximize** button ▢ in the upper-right corner of the program window. If the Book1 window is not maximized, click ▢ in the upper-right corner of the Book1 window. Your screen should now resemble Figure 1-3.

The Excel Window

The Excel window layout is consistent with the layout of other Windows programs. It contains many common features, such as the title bar, menu bar, scroll bars, and taskbar. Figure 1-3 shows these elements as well as the main components of the Excel window. Take a look at each of these Excel components so you are familiar with their location and purpose.

Toolbars

Toolbars allow you to organize the commands in Excel. The menu bar is a special toolbar at the top of the window that contains menus such as File, Edit, and View. The Standard toolbar and the Formatting toolbar are located below the menu bar. The **Standard** toolbar contains buttons corresponding to the most frequently used commands in Excel. The **Formatting** toolbar contains buttons corresponding to the commands most frequently used to improve the appearance of a worksheet.

Formula Bar

The **formula bar**, located immediately below the toolbars, displays the contents of the active cell. A **cell's contents** is the text, numbers, and formulas you enter into it. As you type or edit data, the changes appear in the formula bar. The **name box** appears at the left end of the formula bar. This area displays the cell reference for the active cell.

Workbook Window

The document window, usually called the **workbook window** or **worksheet window**, contains the sheet you are creating, editing, or using. Each worksheet consists of a series of columns identified by lettered column headings and a series of rows identified by numbered row headings. Columns are assigned alphabetic labels from A to IV (256 columns). Rows are assigned numeric labels from 1 to 65,536 (65,536 rows).

A **cell** is the rectangular area where a column and a row intersect. Each cell is identified by a **cell reference**, which is its column and row location. For example, the cell reference B6 indicates the cell where column B and row 6 intersect. The column letter is always first in the cell reference. B6 is a correct cell reference; 6B is not. The **active cell** is the cell in which you are currently working. Excel identifies the active cell with a dark border that outlines one cell. In Figure 1-3, cell A1 is the active cell. Notice that the cell reference for the active cell appears in the name box of the formula bar. You can change the active cell when you want to work elsewhere in the worksheet.

Pointer

The **pointer** is the indicator that moves on your screen as you move your mouse. The pointer changes shape to reflect the type of task you can perform at a particular location. When you click a mouse button, something happens at the pointer's location. In Figure 1-3, the pointer looks like a white plus sign ✚.

Sheet Tabs

Each worksheet has a **sheet tab** that identifies the name of the worksheet. The name on the tab of the active sheet is bold. The sheet tabs let you move quickly between the sheets in a workbook; you can simply check the sheet tab of the sheet you want to move to. By default, a new workbook consists of three worksheets. If your workbook contains many worksheets, you can use the **sheet tab scroll buttons** to scroll through the sheet tabs that are not currently visible to find the sheet you want.

Moving Around a Worksheet

Before entering or editing the contents of a cell, you need to select that cell to make it the active cell. You can select a cell using either the keyboard or the mouse.

Using the Mouse

Using the mouse, you can quickly select a cell by placing the mouse pointer on the cell and clicking the mouse button. If you need to move to a cell that's not currently on the screen, use the vertical and horizontal scroll bars to display the area of the worksheet containing the cell you are interested in, and then select the cell.

Using the Keyboard

In addition to the mouse, Excel provides you with many keyboard options for moving to different cell locations within your worksheet. Figure 1-4 shows some of the keys you can use to select a cell within your worksheet.

Figure 1-4	KEYS TO MOVE AROUND THE WORKSHEET
KEYSTROKE	**ACTION**
↑, ↓, ←, →	Moves up, down, left, or right one cell
PgUp	Moves the active cell up one full screen
PgDn	Moves the active cell down one full screen
Home	Moves the active cell to column A of the current row
Ctrl + Home	Moves the active cell to cell A1
F5 (function key)	Opens Go To dialog box, in which you enter cell address of cell you want to make active cell

Now, try moving around the worksheet using your keyboard and mouse.

To move around the worksheet:

1. Position the mouse pointer ✛ over cell E8, then click the **left mouse** button to make it the active cell. Notice that the cell is surrounded by a black border to indicate that it is the active cell and that the name box on the formula bar displays E8.

2. Click cell **B4** to make it the active cell.

3. Press the → key to make cell C4 the active cell.

4. Press the ↓ key to make cell C5 the active cell. See Figure 1-5.

Figure 1-5	CELL C5 AS ACTIVE CELL

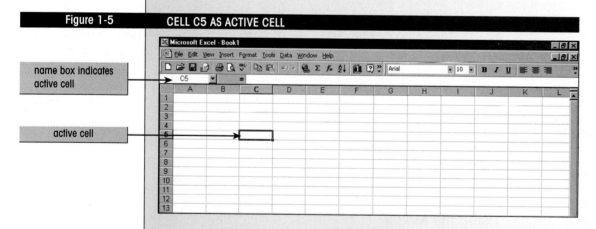

name box indicates active cell

active cell

5. Press the **Home** key to move to cell A5, the first cell in the current row.

6. Press **Ctrl + Home** to make cell A1 the active cell. The shortcut key Ctrl + Home can be used at any time to move to the beginning of the worksheet. Normally this is cell A1.

So far you've moved around the portion of the worksheet you can see. Many worksheets can't be viewed entirely on one screen. Next, you'll use the keyboard and mouse to bring other parts of the worksheet into view.

To bring other parts of the worksheet into view:

1. Press the **Page Down** key to move the display down one screen. The active cell is now cell A26 (the active cell on your screen may be different). Notice that the row numbers on the left side of the worksheet indicate you have moved to a different area of the worksheet. See Figure 1-6.

| Figure 1-6 | WORKSHEET SCREEN AFTER MOVING TO DIFFERENT AREA OF WORKSHEET |

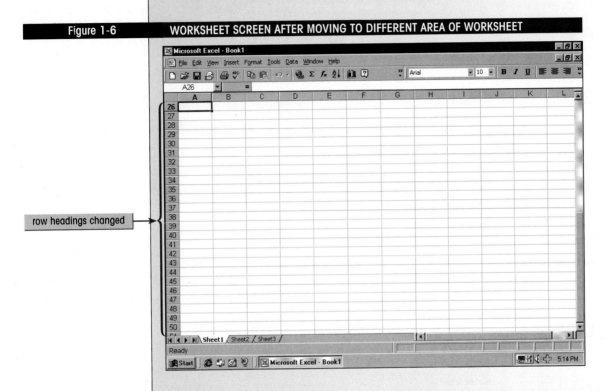

row headings changed

2. Press the **Page Down** key again to move the display down one screen. Notice that the row numbers indicate that you have moved to a different area of the worksheet.

3. Press the **Page Up** key to move the display up one screen. The active cell is now cell A26 (the active cell on your screen may be different).

4. Click the **vertical scroll bar up arrow** button until row 12 is visible. Notice that the active cell is still A26 (the active cell on your screen may be different). Using the scroll bar changes the portion of the screen you can view without changing the active cell.

5. Click cell **C12** to make it the active cell.

6. Click the blank area above the vertical scroll box to move up a full screen.

7. Click the blank area below the vertical scroll box to move down a full screen.

8. Click the **scroll box** and drag it to the top of the scroll area to again change the area of the screen you're viewing. Notice that the ScrollTip appears telling you the current row location.

9. Press **F5** to open the Go To dialog box.

10. Type **K55** in the Reference box and then click **OK**. Cell K55 is now the active cell.

11. Press **Ctrl + Home** to make cell A1 the active cell. Now click cell **E6**.

As you know, a workbook can consist of one or more worksheets. Excel makes it easy to switch between them. Next, try moving from worksheet to worksheet.

Navigating in a Workbook

The sheet tabs let you move quickly among the different sheets in a workbook. If you can see the tab of the sheet you want, click the tab to activate the worksheet. You can also use the sheet tab scroll buttons to see sheet tabs hidden from view. Figure 1-7 describes the four tab scrolling buttons and their effects.

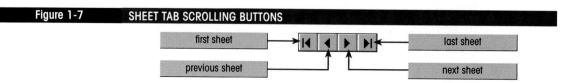

| Figure 1-7 | SHEET TAB SCROLLING BUTTONS |

first sheet
previous sheet
last sheet
next sheet

Next, try moving to a new sheet.

To move to Sheet2:

1. Click the **Sheet2** tab. Sheet2, which is blank, appears in the worksheet window. Notice that the Sheet2 sheet tab is white and the name is bold, which means that Sheet2 is now the active sheet. Cell A1 is the active cell in Sheet2.

2. Click the **Sheet3** tab to make it the active sheet.

3. Click the **Sheet1** tab to make it the active sheet. Notice that cell E6 is still the active cell.

Now that you have some basic skills navigating a worksheet and workbook, you can begin working with Mike to complete the golf site selection worksheet.

Opening a Workbook

When you want to use a workbook that you previously created, you must first open it. Opening a workbook transfers a copy of the workbook file from the hard drive or 3½-inch disk to the random access memory (RAM) of your computer and displays it on your screen. When the workbook is open, the file is both in RAM and on the disk.

After you open a workbook, you can view, edit, print, or save it again on your disk.

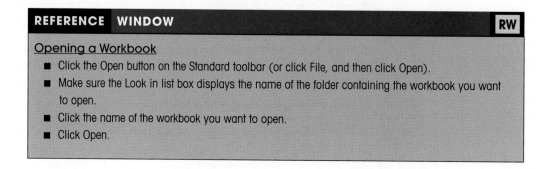

REFERENCE WINDOW **RW**

Opening a Workbook
- Click the Open button on the Standard toolbar (or click File, and then click Open).
- Make sure the Look in list box displays the name of the folder containing the workbook you want to open.
- Click the name of the workbook you want to open.
- Click Open.

Mike created a workbook to help the site selection team evaluate the four potential locations for the golf course. The workbook, Inwood, is on your Data Disk.

To open an existing workbook:

1. Place your Excel Data Disk in the appropriate drive.

TROUBLE? If you don't have a Data Disk, you need to get one before you can proceed. Your instructor or technical support person will either give you one or ask you to make your own by following the instructions on the "Read This Before You Begin" page before this tutorial. See your instructor or technical support person for information.

2. Click the **Open** button 🖼 on the Standard toolbar. The Open dialog box opens. See Figure 1-8.

Figure 1-8	OPEN DIALOG BOX

names and files specified here (yours may differ)

click here to specify drive and folder

enter filename here

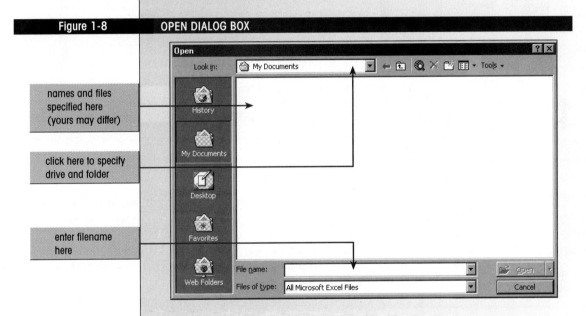

3. Click the **Look in** list arrow to display the list of available drives. Locate the drive containing your Data Disk. In this text, we assume your Data Disk is a 3½-inch disk in drive A.

4. Click the drive that contains your Data Disk. A list of documents and folders on your Data Disk appears in the list box.

5. In the list of document and folder names, double-click **Tutorial.01,** double-click **Tutorial** to display that folder in the Look in list box, then click **Inwood**.

6. Click the **Open** button 🖼. (You could also double-click the filename to open the file.) The Inwood workbook opens and the first sheet in the workbook, Documentation, appears. See Figure 1-9. Notice the filename, Inwood, appears on the title bar at the top of your screen.

Figure 1-9   **DOCUMENTATION SHEET IN INWOOD WORKBOOK**

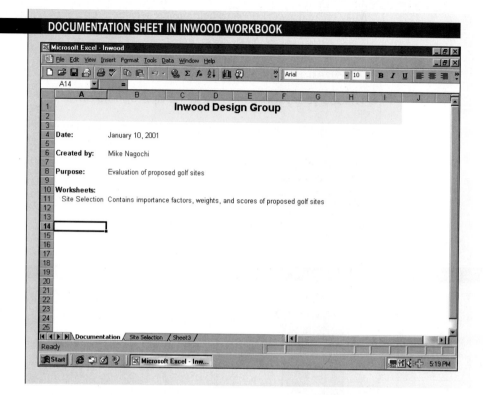

Layout of the Inwood Workbook

The first worksheet, Documentation, contains information about the workbook. The Documentation sheet shows who created the workbook, the date when it was created, its purpose, and a brief description of each sheet in the workbook.

Mike explains that whenever he creates a new workbook he makes sure he documents it carefully. This information is especially useful if he returns to a workbook after a long period of time (or if a new user opens it) because it provides a quick review of the workbook's purpose.

After reviewing the Documentation sheet, Mike moves to the Site Selection worksheet.

To move to the Site Selection worksheet:

1. Click the **Site Selection** sheet tab to display the worksheet Mike is preparing for the site selection team. See Figure 1-10.

Figure 1-10 **SITE SELECTION WORKSHEET**

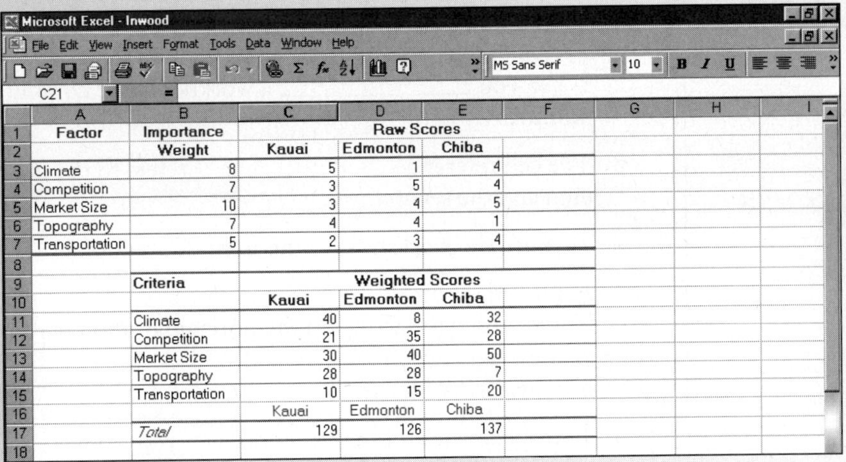

	A	B	C	D	E
1	Factor	Importance		Raw Scores	
2		Weight	Kauai	Edmonton	Chiba
3	Climate	8	5	1	4
4	Competition	7	3	5	4
5	Market Size	10	3	4	5
6	Topography	7	4	4	1
7	Transportation	5	2	3	4
8					
9		Criteria		Weighted Scores	
10			Kauai	Edmonton	Chiba
11		Climate	40	8	32
12		Competition	21	35	28
13		Market Size	30	40	50
14		Topography	28	28	7
15		Transportation	10	15	20
16			Kauai	Edmonton	Chiba
17		*Total*	129	126	137
18					

Mike explains the general layout of the Site Selection worksheet to you. He reminds you that to this point he has only entered data for three of the four sites. He will provide the missing Scottsdale information to you. Cells C2 through E2 list three of the four sites for which he has data. Cells A3 through A7 contain the five factors on which the team's decision will be based: Climate, Competition, Market Size, Topography, and Transportation. They assign scores for Climate, Competition, Market Size, Topography, and Transportation to each location. The team uses a scale of 1 to 5 to assign a raw score for each factor. Higher raw scores indicate strength; lower raw scores indicate weakness. Cells C3 through E7 contain the raw scores for the first three locations. For example, the raw score for Kauai's Climate is 5; the two other locations have scores of 1 and 4, so Kauai, with its warm, sunny days all year, has the best climate for the golf course of the three sites visited so far. Edmonton, on the other hand, has cold weather and only received a Climate raw score of 1.

The raw scores, however, do not provide enough information for the team to make a decision. Some factors are more important to the success of the golf course than others. The team members assigned an *importance weight* to each factor according to their knowledge of what factors contribute most to the success of a golf course. The importance weights are on a scale from 1 to 10, with 10 being most important. Mike entered the weights in cells B3 through B7. Market size, weighted 10, is the most important factor. The team believes the least important factor is Transportation, so Transportation is assigned a lower weight. Climate is important but the team considers Market Size most important. They do not use the raw scores to make a final decision; instead, they multiply each raw score by its importance weight to produce a weighted score. Which of the three sites already visited has the highest weighted score for any factor? If you look at the scores in cells C11 through E15, you see that Chiba's score of 50 for Market Size is the highest weighted score for any factor.

Cells C17 through E17 contain the total weighted scores for the three locations. With the current weighted and raw scores, Chiba is the most promising site, with a total score of 137.

Session 1.1 QUICK CHECK

1. A(n) _____ is the rectangular area where a column and a row intersect.

2. When you _____ a workbook, the computer copies it from your disk into RAM.

3. The cell reference _____ refers to the intersection of the fourth column and the second row.

4. To move the worksheet to the right one column:

   a. press the Enter key
   b. click the right arrow on the horizontal scroll bar
   c. press the Esc key
   d. press Ctrl + Home

5. To make Sheet2 the active worksheet, you would _____.

6. What key or keys do you press to make cell A1 the active cell?

You have now reviewed the layout of the worksheet. Now, Mike wants you to enter the data on Scottsdale. Based on his meeting with local investors and a visit to the Scottsdale site, he has assigned the following raw scores: Climate 5, Competition 2, Market Size 4, Topography 3, and Transportation 3. To complete the worksheet, you must enter the raw scores he has assigned to the Scottsdale site. You will do this in the next session.

SESSION 1.2

In this session you will learn how to enter text, values, formulas, and functions into a worksheet. You will use this data to perform what-if analyses using a worksheet. You'll also correct mistakes and use the online Help system to determine how to clear the contents of cells. Finally, you'll learn how to print a worksheet and how to close a worksheet and exit Excel.

Text, Values, Formulas, and Functions

As you have now observed, an Excel workbook can hold one or more worksheets, each containing a grid of 256 columns and 65,536 rows. The rectangular areas at the intersections of each column and row are called cells. A cell can contain a value, text, or a formula. To understand how the spreadsheet program works, you need to understand how Excel manipulates text, values, formulas, and functions.

Text (Label)

Text entries include any combination of letters, symbols, numbers, and spaces. Although text is sometimes used as data, it is more often used to describe the data contained in a worksheet. Text is often used to label columns and rows in a worksheet. For example, a projected monthly income statement contains the months of the year as column headings and income and expense categories as row labels. To enter text in a worksheet, you select the cell in which you want to enter the text by clicking the cell to select it, then typing the text. Excel automatically aligns the text on the left in a cell.

Mike's Site Selection worksheet contains a number of column heading labels. You need to enter the label for Scottsdale in the Raw Scores and Weighted Scores sections of the worksheet.

To enter a text label:

1. If you took a break after the last session, make sure Excel is running and make sure the Site Selection worksheet of the Inwood workbook is showing.

2. Click cell **F2** to make it the active cell.

3. Type **Scottsdale**, then press the **Enter** key.

   TROUBLE? If you make a mistake while typing, you can correct the error with the Backspace key. If you realize you made an error after you press the Enter key, retype the entry by repeating Steps 2 and 3.

4. Click cell **F10** and type **S**. Excel completes the entry for you based on the entries already in the column. If your data involves repetitious text, this feature, known as **AutoComplete**, can make your data entry go more quickly.

5. Press the **Enter** key to complete the entry.

6. Click cell **F16**, type **S**, and press the **Enter** key to accept Scottsdale as the entry in the cell. See Figure 1-11. Next, you need to enter the raw scores Mike assigned to Scottsdale.

| Figure 1-11 | WORKSHEET AFTER TEXT HAS BEEN ENTERED |

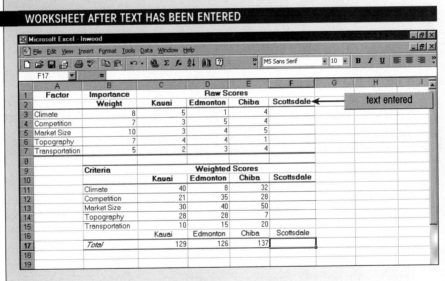

Values

Values are numbers that represent a quantity of some type: the number of units in inventory, stock price, an exam score, and so on. Examples of values are 378, 25.275, and -55. Values can also be dates (11/29/99) and times (4:40:31). As you type information in a cell, Excel determines whether the characters you're typing can be used as values. For example, if you type 456, Excel recognizes it as a value and it is right-justified in the cell. On the other hand, Excel treats some data commonly referred to as "numbers" as text. For example, Excel treats a telephone number (1-800-227-1240) or a Social Security number (372-70-9654) as text that cannot be used for calculations.

You need to enter the raw scores for Scottsdale.

To enter a value:

1. If necessary, click the scroll arrow so row 2 is visible. Click cell **F3**, type **5** and then press the **Enter** key. The active cell is now cell F4.

2. With cell F4 as the active cell, type **2** and press the **Enter** key.

3. Enter the value **4** for Market Size in cell F5, the value **3** for Topography in cell F6, and the value **3** for Transportation in cell F7. See Figure 1-12.

| Figure 1-12 | WORKSHEET AFTER NUMBERS HAVE BEEN ENTERED |

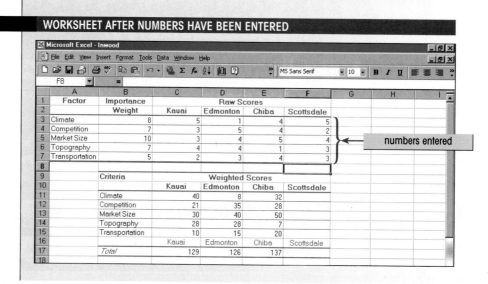

Next, you enter the formulas to calculate Scottsdale's weighted score in each category.

Formulas

When you need to perform a calculation in Excel you use a formula. A **formula** is the arithmetic used to calculate values appearing in a worksheet. You can take advantage of the power of Excel by using formulas in worksheets. If you change one number in a worksheet, Excel recalculates any formula affected by the change.

An Excel formula always begins with an equal sign (=). Formulas are created by combining numbers, cell references, arithmetic operators, and/or functions. An **arithmetic operator** indicates the desired arithmetic operations. Figure 1-13 shows the arithmetic operators used in Excel.

| Figure 1-13 | ARITHMETIC OPERATORS USED IN FORMULAS |

ARITHMETIC OPERATIONS	ARITHMETIC OPERATOR	EXAMPLE	DESCRIPTION
Addition	+	=10+A5	Adds 10 to value in cell A5
		=B1+B2+B3	Adds the values of cells B1, B2, and B3
Subtraction	–	=C9–B2	Subtracts the value in cell B2 from the value in cell C9
		=1–D2	Subtracts the value in cell D2 from 1
Multiplication	*	=C9*B9	Multiplies the value in cell C9 by the value in cell B9
		=E5*.06	Multiplies the value in E5 by the constant .06
Division	/	=C9/B9	Divides the value in cell C9 by the value in cell B9
		=D15/12	Divides the value in cell D15 by 12
Exponentiation	^	=B5^3	Raises the value stored in cell B5 to 3
		=3^B5	Raises 3 to the value stored in cell B5

The result of the formula appears in the cell where you entered the formula. To view the formula that has been entered in a cell, you must first select the cell, then look at the formula bar.

REFERENCE WINDOW   **RW**

Entering a Formula
- Click the cell where you want the result to appear.
- Type = and then type the rest of the formula.
- For formulas that include cell references, such as B2 or D78, you can type the cell reference or you can use the mouse or arrow keys to select each cell.
- When the formula is complete, press the Enter key.

You need to enter the formulas to compute the weighted scores for the Scottsdale site. The formula multiples the raw score for a factor by the importance weight assigned to the factor. Figure 1-14 displays the formulas you need to enter into the worksheet.

Figure 1-14	FORMULAS TO CALCULATE SCOTTSDALE'S WEIGHTED SCORES	
CELL	**FORMULA**	**EXPLANATION**
F11	=B3*F3	Multiplies importance weight by raw score for Climate
F12	=B4*F4	Multiplies importance weight by raw score for Competition
F13	=B5*F5	Multiplies importance weight by raw score for Market Size
F14	=B6*F6	Multiplies importance weight by raw score for Topography
F15	=B7*F7	Multiplies importance weight by raw score for Transportation

To enter the formulas to calculate each weighted score for the Scottsdale site:

1. Click cell **F11** to make it the active cell. Type **=B3*F3** to multiply the weight assigned to the Climate category by the raw score assigned to Scottsdale for the Climate category. Press the **Enter** key. The value 40 appears in cell F11.

   TROUBLE? If you make a mistake while typing, you can correct the error with the Backspace key. If you realize you made an error after you press the Enter key, repeat Step 1 to retype the entry.

2. Click cell **F11** to make it the active cell again. See Figure 1-15. Notice, the results of the formula appear in the cell, but the formula you entered appears on the formula bar.

Figure 1-15	WORKSHEET DISPLAYS VALUE IN CELL AND FORMULA IN FORMULA BAR

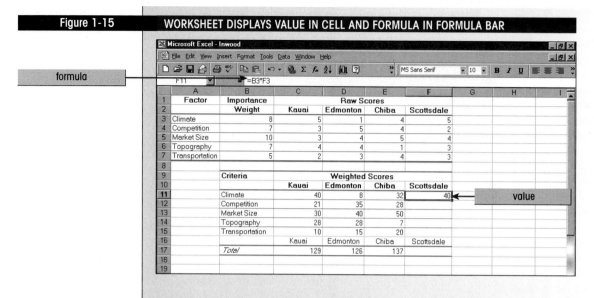

3. Click cell **F12**, type **=B4*F4**, and then press the **Enter** key. This formula multiplies the weight assigned to Competition (the contents of cell B4) by Scottsdale's raw score for Competition (cell F4). The value 14 appears in cell F12.

4. Enter the remaining formulas from Figure 1-14 into cells F13, F14, and F15. When completed, your worksheet will contain the values 40, 14, 40, 21, and 15 in cells F11 to F15.

TROUBLE? If any value in cells F11 through F15 differs, retype the formula for that cell.

You now have to enter the formula to calculate the total weighted score for Scottsdale into the worksheet. You can use the formula *=F11+F12+F13+F14+F15* to calculate the total score for the Scottsdale site. As an alternative, you can use a function to streamline this long formula.

Functions

A **function** is a predefined or built-in formula that's a shortcut for commonly used calculations. For example, the SUM function is a shortcut for entering formulas that total values in rows or columns. You can use the SUM function to create the formula =SUM(F11:F15) instead of typing the longer *=F11+F12+F13+F14+F15*. The SUM function in this example adds the range F11 through F15. A **range** is a group of cells, either a single cell or a rectangular block of cells. The range reference F11:F15 in the function SUM(F11:F15) refers to the rectangular block of cells beginning in the upper-left corner (F11) and ending in the lower-right corner (F15) of the range. The colon separates the upper-left corner and lower-right corner of the range. Figure 1-16 shows several examples of ranges.

Figure 1-16   **EXAMPLES OF RANGES**

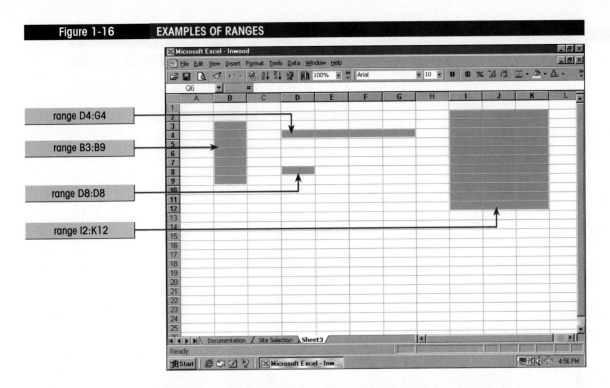

range D4:G4

range B3:B9

range D8:D8

range I2:K12

REFERENCE   WINDOW   **RW**

<u>Entering the SUM Function</u>
- Type = to begin the function.
- Type SUM in either uppercase or lowercase letters, followed by an opening left parenthesis. Do not put a space between "SUM" and the parenthesis.
- Type the range of cells you want to sum, separating the first and last cells in the range with a colon, as in B9:B15, or drag the pointer to outline the cells you want to sum.
- Press the Enter key.

You use the SUM function to compute the total score for the Scottsdale site.

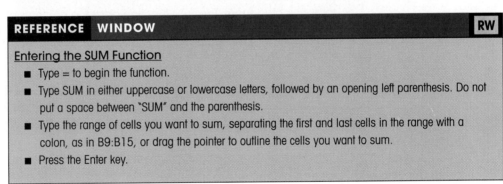

To enter the formula using a function:

1. Click cell **F17** to make it the active cell.

2. Type **=SUM(F11:F15)**. Notice that the formula appears in the cell and the formula bar as you enter it. See Figure 1-17.

Figure 1-17	VIEWING THE SUM FUNCTION BEFORE COMPLETING THE ENTRY

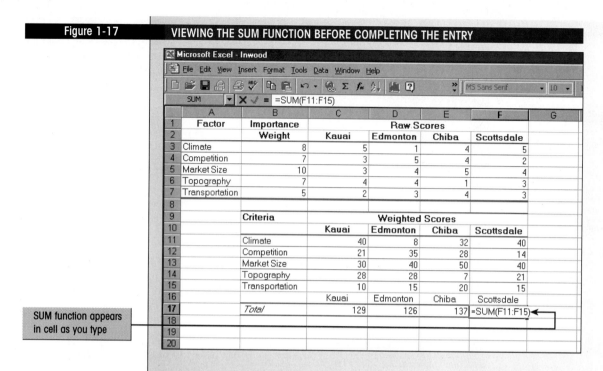

SUM function appears
in cell as you type

3. Press the **Enter** key to complete the formula entry and display 130, Scottsdale's total weighted score. The SUM function adds the contents of cells F11 through F15.

TROUBLE? If 130 is not displayed in cell F17, return to Step 1 and retype formula.

The Site Selection worksheet is now complete. Mike's worksheet contains columns of information about the site selection and a chart displaying the weighted scores for each potential site. To see the chart, you must scroll the worksheet.

To scroll the worksheet to view the chart:

1. Click the **scroll arrow** button on the vertical scroll bar until the section of the worksheet containing the chart appears. See Figure 1-18.

| Figure 1-18 | SCROLLING THE WORKSHEET TO VIEW THE CHART |

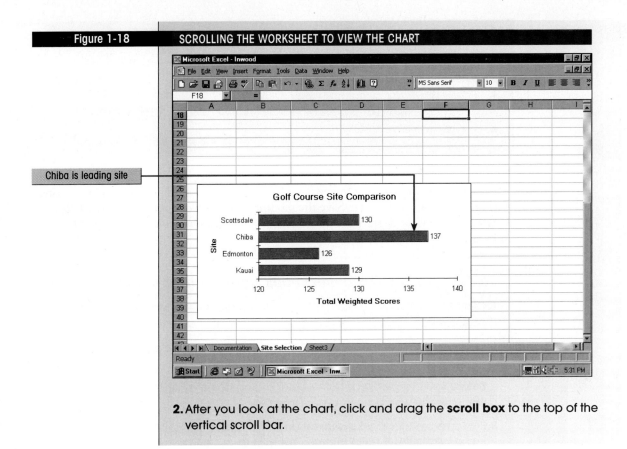

Chiba is leading site

2. After you look at the chart, click and drag the **scroll box** to the top of the vertical scroll bar.

You have completed the worksheet; Mike decides to save it before showing it to the site selection team.

Saving the Workbook

To store a workbook permanently so you can use it again without having to reenter the data and formulas, you must save it as a file on a disk. When you save a workbook, you copy it from RAM onto your disk. You'll use either the Save or the Save As command. The Save command copies the workbook onto a disk using its current filename. If a version of the file already exists, the new version replaces the old one. The Save As command asks for a filename before copying the workbook onto a disk. When you enter a new filename, you save the current file under that new name. The previous version of the file remains on the disk under its original name.

As a general rule, use the Save As command the first time you save a file or whenever you modify a file and want to save both the old and new versions. Use the Save command when you modify a file and want to save only the current version.

It is a good idea to save your file often. That way, if the power goes out or the computer stops working, you're less likely to lose your work. Because you use the Save command frequently, the Standard toolbar has a Save button, a single mouse-click shortcut for saving your workbook.

REFERENCE WINDOW   RW

Saving a Workbook with a New Filename
- Click File and then click Save As.
- Change the workbook name as necessary.
- Make sure the Save in box displays the folder in which you want to save your workbook.
- Click the Save button.

Mike's workbook is named Inwood. The version of Inwood that you modified during this work session is on your screen. Save the modified workbook under the new name Inwood 2. This way if you want to start the tutorial from the beginning, you can open the Inwood file and start over.

To save the modified workbook under a new name:

1. Click **File** on the menu bar, and then click **Save As**. The Save As dialog box opens with the current workbook name in the File name text box.

2. Click at the end of the current workbook name, press the **spacebar**, and then type **2**. (Do not press the Enter key.)

   Before you proceed, check the other dialog box specifications to ensure that you save the workbook on your Data Disk.

3. If necessary, click the **Save in** list arrow to display the list of available drives and folders. Click the Tutorial folder in **Tutorial.01**.

4. Confirm that the Save as type text box specifies "Microsoft Excel Workbook."

5. As the number of saved worksheets begins to accumulate, you can create new folders or subfolders to store related files. You can create a new folder by clicking the New Folder button. See Figure 1-19.

6. If you need to save an Excel file in an earlier Excel format, or another format such as Lotus 1-2-3, click the drop-down area next to the Save as type box and then select the file type from the list shown.

7. When your Save As dialog box looks like the one in Figure 1-19, click the **Save** button to close the dialog box and save the workbook. Notice that the new workbook name, Inwood 2, now appears in the title bar.

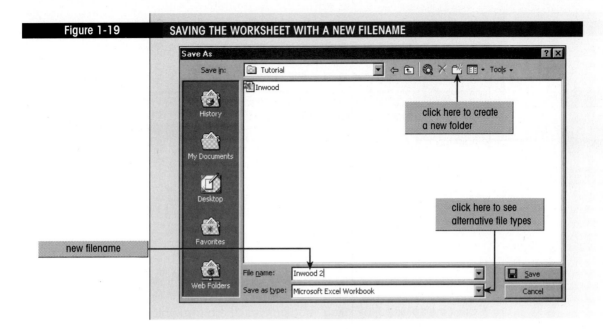

Figure 1-19   **SAVING THE WORKSHEET WITH A NEW FILENAME**

You now have two versions of the workbook: the original file—Inwood—and the modified workbook—Inwood 2.

What-if Analysis

The worksheet for site selection is now complete. Mike is ready to show it to the group. As the team examines the worksheet, you ask if the raw scores take into account recent news that a competing design group has announced plans to build a $325-million golf resort just 10 miles away from Inwood's proposed site in Chiba. Mike admits that he assigned the values before the announcement, so the raw scores do not reflect the increased competition in the Chiba market. You suggest revising the raw score for the Competition factor to reflect this market change in Chiba.

When you change a value in a worksheet, Excel automatically recalculates the worksheet and displays updated results. The recalculation feature makes Excel an extremely useful decision-making tool because it lets you quickly and easily factor in changing conditions. When you revise the contents of one or more cells in a worksheet and observe the effect this change has on all the other cells, you are performing a **what-if analysis**. In effect, you are saying, what if I change the value assigned to this factor? What effect will it have on the outcomes in the worksheet?

Because another development group has announced plans to construct a new golf course in the Chiba area, the team decides to lower Chiba's Competition raw score from 4 to 2.

To change Chiba's Competition raw score from 4 to 2:

1. Click cell **E4**. The black border around cell E4 indicates that it is the active cell. The current value of cell E4 is 4.

2. Type **2**. Notice that 2 appears in the cell and in the formula bar, along with a formula palette of three new buttons. The buttons shown in Figure 1-20—the Cancel button ☒, the Enter button ☑, and the Edit Formula button ▣ offer alternatives for canceling, entering, and editing data and formulas.

Figure 1-20	CHANGING A CELL'S CONTENTS

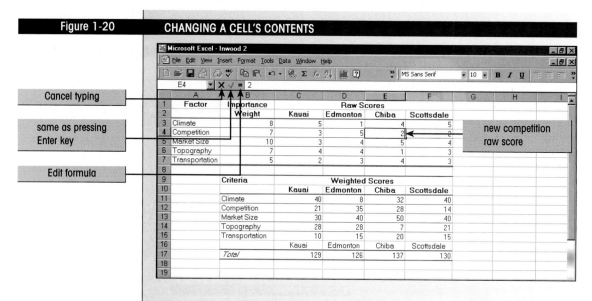

3. Click the **Enter** button. Excel recalculates Chiba's weighted score for the Competition factor (cell E12) and the total score for Chiba (cell E17). If necessary, click the **vertical scroll** arrow until row 17 is visible on your screen. The recalculated values are 14 and 123. See Figure 1-21.

Figure 1-21	WORKSHEET AFTER FORMULAS ARE RECALCULATED

The team takes another look at the total weighted scores in row 17. Scottsdale is now the top-ranking site, with a total weighted score of 130, compared to Chiba's total weighted score of 123.

As the team continues to discuss the worksheet, several members express concern over the importance weight used for Transportation. In the current worksheet, Transportation is weighted 5 (cell B7). You remember that the group agreed to use an importance weight of 2 at a previous meeting. You ask Mike to change the importance weight for Transportation.

To change the importance weight for Transportation:

1. Click cell **B7** to make it the active cell.

2. Type **2** and press the **Enter** key. Cell B7 now contains the value 2 instead of 5. Cell B8 becomes the active cell. See Figure 1-22. Notice that the weighted scores for Transportation (row 15) and the total weighted scores for each site (row 17) have all changed.

Figure 1-22	WORKSHEET AFTER CHANGE MADE TO THE TRANSPORTATION IMPORTANCE WEIGHT

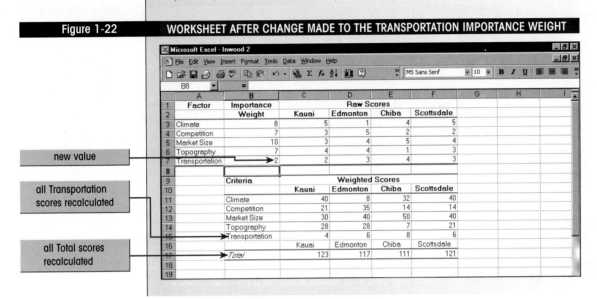

new value

all Transportation scores recalculated

all Total scores recalculated

The change in the Transportation importance weight puts Kauai ahead as the most favorable site, with a total weighted score of 123.

As you enter and edit a worksheet, there are many data entry errors that can occur. The most commonly made mistake on a worksheet is a typing error. Typing mistakes are easy to correct.

Correcting Mistakes

It is easy to correct a mistake as you are typing information in a cell, before you press the Enter key. If you need to correct a mistake as you are typing information in a cell, press the Backspace key to back up and delete one or more characters. If you want to start over, press the Esc key to cancel all changes. When you are typing information in a cell, *don't* use the cursor arrow keys to edit because they move the cell pointer to another cell. One of the team members suggests changing the label "Criteria" in cell B9 to "Factors." The team members agree and you make the change to the cell.

To correct a mistake as you type:

1. Click cell **B9** to make it the active cell.

2. Type **Fak**, intentionally making an error, but don't press the Enter key.

3. Press the **Backspace** key to delete "k".

4. Type **ctors** and press the **Enter** key.

Now the word "Factors" is in cell B9. Mike suggests changing "Factors" to "Factor." The team agrees. To change a cell's contents after you press the Enter key, you use a different method. You can either retype the contents of a cell, or enter Edit mode to change the contents of a cell on the formula bar. Double-clicking a cell or pressing the F2 key puts Excel into **Edit** mode, which lets you use the Home, End, Delete, Backspace keys and the ← and → keys, and the mouse to change the text in the formula bar.

REFERENCE WINDOW   **RW**

Correcting Mistakes Using Edit Mode
- Double-click the cell you want to edit to begin Edit mode. The contents of the cell appear directly in the cell as well as the formula bar (or click the cell you want to edit, then press F2).
- Use Home, End, Delete, Backspace, ←, → or the mouse to edit the cell's contents either in the cell or in the formula bar.
- Press the Enter key when you finish editing.

You use Edit mode to change "Factors" to "Factor" in cell B9.

To change the word "Factors" to "Factor" in cell B9:

1. Double-click cell **B9** to begin Edit mode. Note that "Edit" appears in the status bar, reminding you that Excel is currently in Edit mode.

2. Press the **End** key if necessary to move the cursor to the right of the word "Factors," then press the **Backspace** key to delete the "s".

3. Press the **Enter** key to complete the edit.

You ask if the team is ready to recommend a site. Mike believes that, based on the best information they have, Kauai should be the recommended site and Scottsdale the alternative site. You ask for a vote, and the team unanimously agrees with Mike's recommendation.

Mike wants to have complete documentation to accompany the team's written recommendation to management, so he wants to print the worksheet.

As he reviews the worksheet one last time, he thinks that the labels in cells C16 through F16 (Kauai, Edmonton, Chiba, Scottsdale) are unnecessary and decides he wants you to delete them before printing the worksheet. You ask how to delete the contents of a cell or a group of cells. Mike is not sure, so he suggests using the Excel Help system to find the answer.

Getting Help

If you don't know how to perform a task or forget how to carry out a particular task, Excel provides an extensive on-screen help. The Excel Help system provides the same options as the Help system in other Office programs—asking help from the Office Assistant, getting help from the Help menu, and obtaining help information from Microsoft's web site. If you are not connected to the Web, you only have access to the Help files stored on your computer.

One way to get help is to use the Office Assistant, which you may have seen on your screen when you first started Excel, and which you closed earlier in this tutorial. The Office Assistant, an animated object, pops up on the screen when you click the Microsoft Excel

Help button on the Standard toolbar. The Office Assistant answers questions, offers tips, and provides help for a variety of Excel features. In addition to the Office Assistant, Figure 1-23 identifies several other ways you can get Help.

Figure 1-23	ALTERNATIVE WAYS TO USE MICROSOFT EXCEL HELP
ACTION*	**RESULTS IN**
A. Right-click Office Assistant, click Options from short-cut menu and then click Use the Office Assistant checkbox to remove check	Office Assistant no longer in use
B. On Help menu, click Microsoft Excel Help, then click Contents tab	Displays an outline of topics and subtopics on which you can get information
C. On Help menu, click Microsoft Excel Help, then click Index tab	Displays alphabetical listing of topics; enter words or phrases to scroll to an entry
D. On Help menu, click Microsoft Excel Help, then click Answer Wizard tab	Displays a Help window where a question can be entered. After clicking Search button, Excel displays a selected list of Help topics
E. Press F1	Displays Microsoft Excel Help window
F. Press Shift + F1	Pointer changes to What's This [?] which you click when positioned over any object or menu option on the screen to see a description of the object or option

*(Alternatives B–F assume that alternative A has been implemented.)

REFERENCE WINDOW   **RW**

Using the Office Assistant
- Click the Microsoft Excel Help button on the Standard toolbar (or choose Microsoft Excel Help from the Help menu) to display the Office Assistant.
- Click Options to change the Office Assistant features you want to use.
  or
- Type an English-language question on a topic where you need help, and then click Search.
- Click the suggested Help topic.
- To hide the Office Assistant, right-click the Office Assistant, then click Hide.

Use the Office Assistant to get information on how to clear the contents of cells.

To get Help using the Office Assistant:

1. Click **Help** from the menu bar, then click **Show the Office Assistant** to display an animated object. If necessary, click the **Office Assistant** to display the Information Box next to the Office Assistant. See Figure 1-24.

Figure 1-24   OFFICE ASSISTANT WITH INFORMATION BOX

enter question here
(yours may look different)

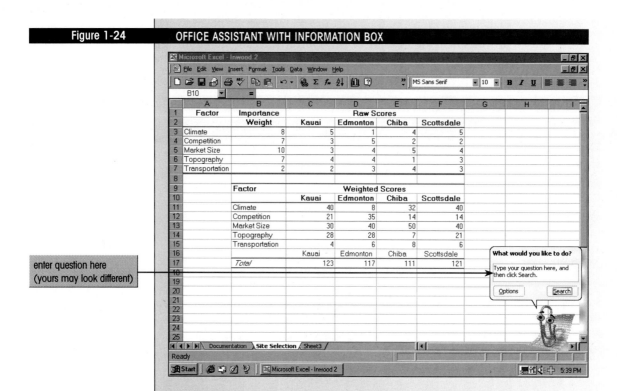

The Office Assistant can respond to an English-language question.

2. Type **how do I clear cells** in the box for your question, then click **Search** to display several possible Help topics. See Figure 1-25.

Figure 1-25   OFFICE ASSISTANT WITH SEVERAL SUGGESTED HELP TOPICS

suggested Help topics

click this topic

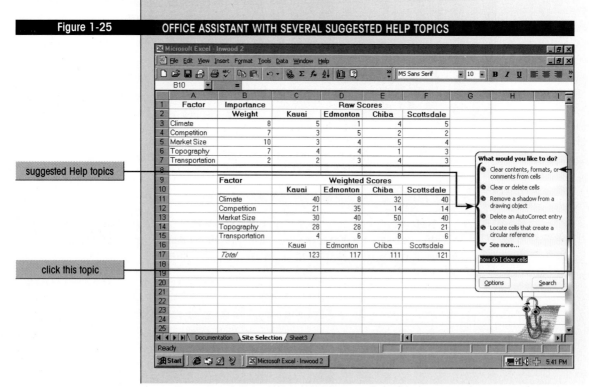

3. Click **Clear contents, formats, or comments from cells**, to display information on this topic. See Figure 1-26.

| Figure 1-26 | EXCEL HELP DISPLAYS INFORMATION ON CLEARING CELL CONTENTS |

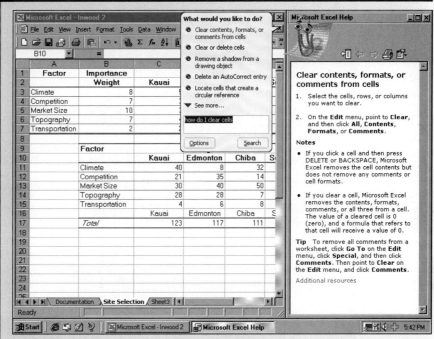

You can print the information on the topic, or you can keep the window on the screen where you can refer to it as you go through each step.

4. After reviewing the information, click the **Close** button ☒ on the Microsoft Excel Help window.

Hide the Office Assistant.

5. Move the mouse pointer over the Office Assistant, right-click the **mouse pointer**, then click **Hide**.

After reviewing the information from the Office Assistant, you are ready to remove the labels from the worksheet.

Clearing **Cell Contents**

As you are building or modifying your worksheet, you may occasionally find that you have entered a label, number, or formula in a cell that you want to be empty. To erase the contents of a cell, you use either the Delete key or the Clear command on the Edit menu. Removing the contents of a cell is known as clearing a cell. Do not press the spacebar to enter a blank character in an attempt to clear a cell's contents. Excel treats a blank character as text, so even though the cell appears to be empty, it is not.

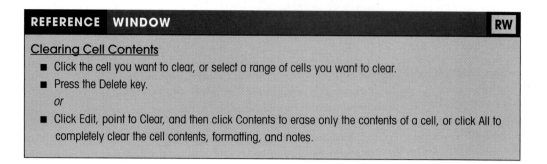

You are ready to clear the labels from cells C16 through F16.

To clear the labels from cells C16 through F16:

1. Click cell **C16**. This will be the upper-left corner of the range to clear.

2. Position the cell pointer over cell C16. With the cell pointer the shape of ✛, click and drag the cell pointer to F16 to select the range C16:F16. If your pointer changes to a crosshair ✛, or an arrow ⬉, do not drag the cell pointer to F16 until the pointer changes to ✛. Note that when you select a range, the first cell in that range, cell C16 in this example, remains white and the other cells in the range are highlighted. See Figure 1-27.

| Figure 1-27 | SELECTED RANGE |

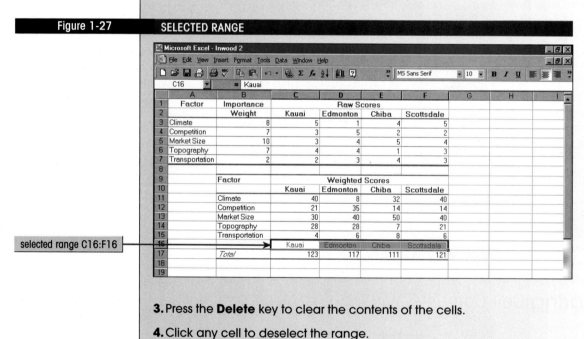

selected range C16:F16

3. Press the **Delete** key to clear the contents of the cells.

4. Click any cell to deselect the range.

Now that you have cleared the unwanted labels from the cells, Mike wants you to print the Site Selection worksheet.

Printing the Worksheet

You can print an Excel worksheet using either the Print command on the File menu, the Print button on the Standard toolbar, or the Print Preview command on the File menu. If you use the Print command, Excel displays a dialog box where you can specify which worksheet pages you want to print, the number of copies you want to print, and the print quality (resolution). If you use the Print button, you do not have these options; Excel prints one copy of the entire worksheet using the current print settings. If you use the Print Preview command, you can see a preview of your printout before printing the worksheet.

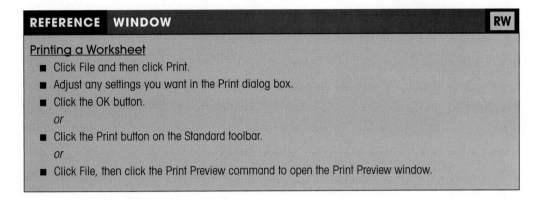

REFERENCE WINDOW   **RW**

Printing a Worksheet
- Click File and then click Print.
- Adjust any settings you want in the Print dialog box.
- Click the OK button.
  or
- Click the Print button on the Standard toolbar.
  or
- Click File, then click the Print Preview command to open the Print Preview window.

If you are printing to a shared printer, many other people may be printing documents there as well. To avoid confusion finding your printed output in an office or computer lab environment, you should first set up a method to know which document is yours. You will enter your name as the person who prepared the work in a cell on the worksheet.

To enter your name as the person who prepared the Site Selection worksheet:

1. Click **Edit**, then click **Go To** to open the Go To dialog box. If necessary, click ⏬ to display Go To on the menu.

2. Type **A40** in the Reference box and click **OK**. The active cell is now A40.

3. Type **Prepared by** *(enter your name here)*.

4. Press **Ctrl + Home** to return to cell A1.

Mike wants a printout of the entire Site Selection worksheet. You decide to select the Print command from the File menu instead of using the Print button so you can check the Print dialog box settings.

To check the print settings and then print the worksheet:

1. Make sure your printer is turned on and contains paper.

2. Click **File** on the menu bar, and then click **Print** to open the Print dialog box. See Figure 1-28.

Figure 1-28   **PRINT DIALOG BOX**

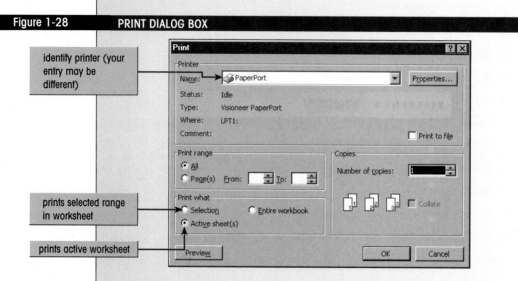

identify printer (your entry may be different)

prints selected range in worksheet

prints active worksheet

Now you need to select what to print. You could print the complete workbook, which would be the Documentation sheet and the Site Selection sheet. To do this, you would click the Entire workbook option button. You could also choose to print just a portion of a worksheet. For example, to print only the weighted scores data of the Site Selection worksheet, first select this range with your mouse pointer, and then select the Selection option button in the Print dialog box. In this case, Mike needs just the Site Selection worksheet.

3. If necessary, click the **Active sheet(s)** option button in the Print what section of the dialog box to print just the Site Selection worksheet, and not the Documentation sheet.

4. Make sure "1" appears in the Number of copies text box, as Mike only needs to print one copy of the worksheet.

5. Click the **OK** button to print the worksheet. See Figure 1-29.

TROUBLE? If the worksheet does not print, see your instructor or technical support person for help.

Figure 1-29   **PRINTED WORKSHEET**

Factor	Importance Weight	Raw Scores			
		Kauai	Edmonton	Chiba	Scottsdale
Climate	8	5	1	4	5
Competition	7	3	5	2	2
Market Size	10	3	4	5	4
Topography	7	4	4	1	3
Transportation	2	2	3	4	3

Factor	Weighted Scores			
	Kauai	Edmonton	Chiba	Scottsdale
Climate	40	8	32	40
Competition	21	35	14	14
Market Size	30	40	50	40
Topography	28	28	7	21
Transportation	4	6	8	6
Total	123	117	111	121

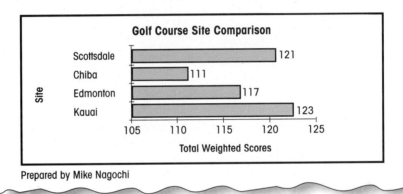

Golf Course Site Comparison

Prepared by Mike Nagochi

Mike volunteers to put together the report with the team's final recommendation, and the meeting adjourns. You and Mike are finished working with the worksheet and are ready to close the workbook.

Closing the Workbook

Closing a workbook removes it from the screen. If a workbook contains changes that have not been saved, Excel asks if you want to save your modified worksheet before closing the workbook. You can now close the workbook.

To close the Inwood 2 workbook:

1. Click **File** on the menu bar, and then click **Close**. A dialog box displays the message "Do you want to save the changes you made to 'Inwood 2.xls'?" Click Yes, if you want to save the changes you made since last saving the workbook. Click No, if you do not want to keep the changes you've made to the workbook.

2. Click **Yes** to save the Inwood 2 workbook before closing it.

The Excel window stays open so you can open or create another workbook. You do not want to, so your next step is to exit Excel.

Exiting **Excel**

To exit Excel, you can click the Close button on the title bar, or you can use the Exit command on the File menu.

To exit Excel:

1. Click the **Close** button [X] on the title bar. Excel closes and you return to the Windows desktop.

The Inwood site selection team has completed its work. Mike's worksheet helped the team analyze the data and recommend Kauai as the best site for Inwood's next golf course. Although the Japanese market was a strong factor in favor of locating the course in Japan's Chiba Prefecture, the mountainous terrain and competition from nearby courses reduced the site's desirability.

Session 1.2 **Q**UICK **C**HECK

1. Indicate whether Excel treats the following cell entries as a value, text, or a formula:

   a. 11/09/2001   **e.** 200-19-1121
   b. Net Income   **f.** D1-D9
   c. 321   **g.** 44 Evans Avenue
   d. =C11*225

2. You type a character and Excel finishes the entry based on entries already in the column. This feature is known as _____.

3. The formula =SUM(C3:I3) adds how many cells? Write an equivalent formula without using the SUM function.

4. What cells are included in the range D5:G7?

5. Why do you need to save a worksheet? What command do you use to save the worksheet?

6. Explain the term *what-if analysis*.

7. You can get Excel Help in any of the following ways except:

   a. clicking Help on the menu bar
   b. clicking the Help button on the Standard toolbar
   c. closing the program window
   d. pressing the F1 key

8. What key do you press to clear the contents of an active cell?

9. To print a copy of your worksheet, you use the _____ command on the _____ menu.

REVIEW ASSIGNMENTS

The other company that had planned a golf course in Chiba, Japan, has run into financial difficulties. Rumors are that the project may be canceled. A copy of the final Inwood Design Group workbook is on your Data Disk. Do the Tutorial Assignments to change this worksheet to show how the cancellation of the other project will affect your site selection.

1. If necessary, start Excel and make sure your Data Disk is in the appropriate disk drive. Open the **Inwood 3** file in the Review folder for Tutorial.01 on your Data Disk.

2. Use the Save As command to save the workbook as **Inwood 4** in the Review folder for Tutorial 1. That way you won't change the original workbook.

3. In the Site Selection worksheet, change the competition raw score for Chiba from 2 to 4. What site is ranked first?

4. The label "Topography" in cell A8 was entered incorrectly as "Topogriphy." Use Edit mode to change the "i" to "a".

5. Enter the text "Scores if the competing project in Chiba, Japan, is canceled" in cell A1.

6. Remove the raw scores for Chiba, cells E5 through E9.

7. Type your name in cell A42, then save the worksheet.

8. Print the worksheet.

9. Print the worksheet data without the chart. (*Hint*: Select the worksheet data before checking out the options in the Print dialog box.)

10. Use the What's This button ![What's This button]. Learn more about the following Excel window components:
    a. Name box
    b. Sheet tabs
    c. Tab scrolling button (*Hint*: Click ![What's This button], then click each item with the Help pointer.)

11. Use the Office Assistant to learn how to delete a sheet from a workbook. Write the steps to delete a sheet. Delete Sheet3.

12. In addition to the Office Assistant, Excel offers a Help window with three sections of Help: Contents, Index, and Answer Wizard. Use the Contents tab from Microsoft Excel Help window to learn how to insert an additional worksheet into your workbook. (*Hint*: Choose Working in workbooks.) Write the steps to insert a worksheet.

13. Close the workbook and exit Excel without saving the changes.

CASE PROBLEMS

Case 1. Enrollments in the University   You work 10 hours a week in the provost's office at your college. The assistant to the provost has a number of meetings today and has asked you to complete a worksheet she needs for a meeting with college deans this afternoon.

1. Open the workbook **Enroll** in the Cases folder for Tutorial.01 on your Data Disk.

2. Use the Save As command to save the workbook as **Enrollment**.

3. Complete the workbook by performing the following tasks:
   a. Enter the title "Enrollment Data for University" in cell A1.
   b. Enter the label "Total" in cell A9.
   c. Calculate the total enrollment in the University for 2001 in cell B9.
   d. Calculate the total enrollment in the University for 2000 in cell C9.
   e. Calculate the change in enrollments from 2000 to 2001. Place the results in column D. Label the column heading "Change" and use the following formula:

   Change = 2001 enrollment – 2000 enrollment

4. Type "Prepared by [your name]" in cell A12.

5. Save the workbook.

6. Print the worksheet.

Case 2. Cash Budgeting at Halpern's Appliances   Fran Valence, the business manager for Halpern's Appliances, a retail appliance store, is preparing a cash budget for January. The store has a loan that must be paid the first week in February. Fran wants to determine whether the business will have enough cash to make the loan payment to the bank.

Fran sketches the projected budget so that it will have the format shown in Figure 1-30.

Figure 1-30

```
         Halpern's Appliances Cash Budget
      Projected Cash Receipts and Disbursements
      January 1, 2001
      Cash balance, January 1, 2001                          xxxx
      Projected receipts during January:
              Cash sales during month           xxxx
              Collections from credit sales      xxxx
                     Total cash receipts                      xxxx
      Projected disbursements during January:
              Payments for goods purchased      xxxx
              Salaries                          xxxx
              Rent                              xxxx
              Utilities                         xxxx
                     Total cash disbursements                 xxxx
      Cash balance, January 31, 2001                          xxxx
```

1. Open the workbook **Budget** in the Cases folder for Tutorial.01. Save as **BudgetSol**.

2. Enter the following formulas in cells C8, C14, and C15 of your worksheet:
   a. Total cash receipts = Cash receipts during month + Collections from credit sales
   b. Total cash disbursements = Payments for goods purchased + Salaries + Rent + Utilities
   c. Cash Balance, January 31, 2001 = Cash Balance, January 1, 2001 + Total cash receipts – Total cash disbursements

3. Enter the data in Figure 1-31 into the worksheet.

4. Type "Prepared by [your name]" in a cell two rows below the last line of the budget.

Figure 1-31

BUDGET ITEM	AMOUNT	BUDGET ITEM	AMOUNT
Cash balance at beginning of month	32000	Salaries	4800
Cash receipts during month	9000	Rent	1500
Collection from credit sales	17500	Utilities	800
Payments for goods purchased	15000		

5. Save the worksheet.

6. Print the projected cash budget.

7. After printing the budget, Fran remembers that in January the monthly rent increases by $150. Modify the projected cash budget. Print the revised cash budget.

Case 3. Selecting a Hospital Laboratory Computer System for Bridgeport Medical Center David Choi is on the Laboratory Computer Selection Committee for the Bridgeport Medical Center. After an extensive search, the committee has identified three vendors whose products appear to meet its needs. The Selection Committee has prepared an Excel worksheet to help evaluate the strengths and weaknesses of the three potential vendors. The formulas and raw scores for two of the vendors, LabStar and Health Systems, have already been entered. Now the formulas and raw scores must be entered for the third vendor, MedTech. Which vendor's system is best for the Bridgeport Medical Center? Complete these steps to find out which system is best.

1. Open the workbook **Medical** in the Cases folder for Tutorial.01.

2. Use the Save As command to save the workbook as **Medical 2** in the Cases folder for Tutorial 1. That way you won't change the original workbook for this case.

3. Examine the LAB worksheet, and type the following raw scores for MedTech: Cost = 6, Compatibility = 5, Vendor Reliability = 5, Size of Installed Base = 4, User Satisfaction = 5, Critical Functionality = 9, Additional Functionality = 8.

4. Enter the formulas to compute the weighted scores for MedTech in cells E17 to E23. See Figure 1-32.

Figure 1-32

CELL	FORMULA	CELL	FORMULA	CELL	FORMULA
E17	=B6*E6	E20	=B9*E9	E22	=B11*E11
E18	=B7*E7	E21	=B10*E10	E23	=B12*E12
E19	=B8*E8				

5. Enter the formula to compute MedTech's total weighted score.

6. In cell A2 type "Prepared by [your name]".

7. Activate the Documentation worksheet and enter information such as the name of the case, your name, date created, and purposes on this sheet.

8. Use the Save command to save the modified worksheet.

9. Print the worksheet and Documentation sheet.

10. Based on the data in the worksheet, which vendor would you recommend? Why?

11. Assume you can adjust the value for only one importance weight (cells B6 through B12). Which factor would you change and what would its new weight be in order for LabStar to have the highest weighted score? (*Hint*: Remember that the value assigned to any importance weight cannot be higher than 10.)

12. Print the modified worksheet. Close the workbook without saving it.

Case 4. Cash Counting Calculator   Rob Stuben works at a local town beach in Narragansett where a fee is collected for parking. At the end of each day, the parking attendants turn in the cash they have collected, with a statement of the daily total. Rob is responsible for receiving the daily cash from each attendant, checking the accuracy of the total, and making the cash deposit to the bank.

Rob wants to set up a simple cash counter using Excel, so that he can insert the number of bills of each denomination into a worksheet and have the total cash automatically computed. By using this method he only has to count and enter the number of one-dollar bills, the number of fives, and so on.

1. Set up this worksheet for Rob. First, list all currency denominations (1, 2, 5, 10, 20, 50, 100) in the first column of your worksheet. The next column will be used to enter the count of the number of bills of each denomination (initially blank). In the third column, enter formulas to calculate totals for each denomination. That is, the number of bills multiplied by the denomination of the bill. Below this total column, enter a formula to calculate the grand total received.

   Next, you want to compare the grand total with the amount reported by an attendant. In the row below the grand total, enter the cash reported by the attendant.

   Finally, below the cash reported amount, enter the formula to calculate the difference between the grand total (calculated amount) and the cash reported by the attendant. The difference should equal zero.

2. On a separate worksheet, create a Documentation sheet. Include the title of the case, your name, date created, and the purpose of the worksheet.

3. On Rob's first day using the worksheet, the cash reported by an attendant was $1,560. Rob counted the bills and entered the following: five 50s, twenty-three 20s, forty-one 10s, sixty-five 5s, and one hundred and twenty 1s. Enter these amounts in your worksheet.

4. Type "Prepared by [your name]" in a cell two rows below the cash calculator worksheet.

5. Save the workbook in the Cases folder of Tutorial.01 using the name **CashCounter**.

6. Print the worksheet.

7. On the second day, the cash reported by an attendant was $1,395. Rob counted the bills and entered the following: two 100s, four 50s, seventeen 20s, thirty-four 10s, forty-five 5s, and ninety 1s. Delete the previous day's count and replace it with the new data.

8. Print the worksheet using the data for the second day.

9. Print the Documentation sheet.

10. Close the workbook without saving changes.

Spreadsheets

LAB ASSIGNMENTS

The New Perspectives Labs are designed to help you master some of the key computer concepts and skills presented in each chapter of the text. If you are using your school's lab computers, your instructor or technical support person should have installed the Labs software for you. If you want to use the Labs on your home computer, ask your instructor for the appropriate software. See the Read This Before You Begin page for more information on installing and starting the Lab.

Each Lab has two parts: Steps and Explore. Use Steps first to learn and review concepts. Read the information on each page and do the numbered steps. As you work through the Lab, you will be asked to answer Quick Check questions about what you have learned. At the end of the Lab, you will see a Summary Report of your answers to the Quick Checks. If your instructor wants you to turn in this Summary Report, click the Print button on the Summary Report screen.

When you have completed Steps, you can click the Explore button to complete the Lab Assignments. You can also use Explore to practice the skills you learned and to explore concepts on your own.

SPREADSHEETS Spreadsheet software is used extensively in business, education, science, and humanities to simplify tasks that involve calculations. In this Lab you will learn how spreadsheet software works. You will use spreadsheet software to examine and modify worksheets, as well as to create your own worksheets.

1. Click the Steps button to learn how spreadsheet software works. As you proceed through the Steps, answer all of the Quick Check questions that appear. After you complete the Steps, you will see a Quick Check Summary Report. Follow the instructions on the screen to print this report.

2. Click the Explore button to begin this assignment. Click OK to display a new worksheet. Click File, then click Open to display the Open dialog box. Click the file **Income.xls**, then press the Enter key to open the **Income and Expense Summary** worksheet. Notice that the worksheet contains labels and values for income from consulting and training. It also contains labels and values for expenses such as rent and salaries. The worksheet does not, however, contain formulas to calculate Total Income, Total Expenses, or Profit. Do the following:

   a. Calculate the Total Income by entering the formula =sum(C4:C5) in cell C6.
   b. Calculate the Total Expenses by entering the formula =sum(C9:C12) in C13.
   c. Calculate Profit by entering the formula =C6-C13 in cell C15.
   d. Manually check the results to make sure you entered the formulas correctly.
   e. Print your completed worksheet showing your results.

3. You can use a spreadsheet to keep track of your grade in a class. In Explore, click File, then click Open to display the Open dialog box. Click the file **Grades.xls** to open the Grades worksheet. This worksheet contains the labels and formulas necessary to calculate your grade based on four test scores. You receive a score of 88 out of 100 on the first test. On the second test, you score 42 out of 48. On the third test, you score 92 out of 100. You have not taken the fourth test yet. Enter the appropriate data in the **Grades.xls** worksheet to determine your grade after taking three tests. Print out your worksheet.

4. Worksheets are handy for answering "what if" questions. Suppose you decide to open a lemonade stand. You're interested in how much profit you can make each day. What if you sell 20 cups of lemonade? What if you sell 100? What if the cost of lemons increases?

   In Explore, open the file **Lemons.xls** and use the worksheet to answer questions a through d, then print the worksheet for question e:

   a. What is your profit if you sell 20 cups a day?
   b. What is your profit if you sell 100 cups a day?
   c. What is your profit if the price of lemons increases to $.07 and you sell 100 cups?
   d. What is your profit if you raise the price of a cup of lemonade to $.30? (Lemons still cost $.07 and assume you sell 100 cups.)
   e. Suppose your competitor boasts that she sold 50 cups of lemonade in one day and made exactly $12.00. On your worksheet adjust the cost of cups, water, lemons, and sugar, and the price per cup to show a profit of exactly $12.00 for 50 cups sold. Print this worksheet.

5. It is important to make sure the formulas in your worksheet are accurate. An easy way to test this is to enter 1's for all the values on your worksheet, then check the calculations manually. In Explore, open the worksheet **Receipt.xls**, which calculates sales receipts. Enter 1 as the value for Item 1, Item 2, Item 3, and Sales Tax %. Now, manually calculate what you would pay for three items that cost $1.00 each in a state where sales tax is 1% (.01). Do your manual calculations match those of the worksheet? If not, correct the formulas in the worksheet and print out a *formula report* of your revised worksheet.

6. In Explore, create your own worksheet showing your household budget for one month. You may make up numbers. Put a title on the worksheet. Use formulas to calculate your total income and expenses for the month. Add another formula to calculate how much money you were able to save. Print a formula report of your worksheet. Also, print your worksheet showing realistic values for one month.

INTERNET ASSIGNMENTS

The purpose of the Internet Assignments is to challenge you to find information on the Internet that you can use to create effective documents. The actual assignments are updated and maintained on the Course Technology Web site. Log on to the Internet and use your Web browser to go to the Student Online Companion to accompany this text at **www.course.com/NewPerspectives/office2000**. Click the Excel link, and then click the link for Tutorial 1.

QUICK CHECK ANSWERS

Session 1.1

1. cell
2. open
3. D2

4. b
5. click the "Sheet2" sheet tab
6. press Ctrl + Home

Session 1.2

1. a. value
   b. text
   c. value
   d. formula

   e. text
   f. text
   g. text

2. AutoComplete
3. 7; C3+D3+E3+F3+G3+H3+I3
4. D5,D6,D7,E5,E6,E7,G5,G6,G7
5. When you exit Excel, the workbook is erased from RAM. So if you want to use the workbook again, you need to save it to disk. Click File, then click Save As.
6. revising the contents of one or more cells in a worksheet and observing the effect this change has on all other cells in the worksheet
7. c
8. press the Delete key; click Edit, point to Clear, and then click Contents; click Edit, point to Clear, and then click All.
9. Print, File

OBJECTIVES

In this tutorial you will:

- Plan, build, test, document, preview, and print a worksheet

- Enter labels, values, and formulas

- Calculate a total using the AutoSum button

- Copy formulas using the fill handle and Clipboard

- Learn about relative, absolute, and mixed references

- Use the AVERAGE, MAX, and MIN functions to calculate values in the worksheet

- Spell check the worksheet

- Insert a row

- Reverse an action using the Undo button

- Move a range of cells

- Format the worksheet using AutoFormat

- Center printouts on a page

- Customize worksheet headers

CREATING A WORKSHEET

Producing a Sales Comparison Report for MSI

CASE

Motorcycle Specialties Incorporated

Motorcycle Specialties Incorporated (MSI), a motorcycle helmet and accessories company, provides a wide range of specialty items to motorcycle enthusiasts throughout the world. MSI has its headquarters in Atlanta, Georgia, but it markets products in North America, South America, Australia, and Europe.

The company's marketing and sales director, Sally Caneval, meets regularly with the regional sales managers who oversee global sales in each of the four regions in which MSI does business. This month, Sally intends to review overall sales in each region for the last two fiscal years and present her findings at her next meeting with the regional sales managers. She has asked you to help her put together a report that summarizes this sales information.

Specifically, Sally wants the report to show total sales for each region of the world for the two most recent fiscal years. Additionally, she wants to see the percentage change between the two years. She also wants the report to include the percentage each region contributed to the total sales of the company in 2001. Finally, she wants to include summary statistics on the average, maximum, and minimum sales for 2001.

SESSION 2.1

In this session you will learn how to plan and build a worksheet; enter labels, numbers, and formulas; and copy formulas to other cells.

Developing Worksheets

Effective worksheets are well planned and carefully designed. A well-designed worksheet should clearly identify its overall goal. It should present information in a clear, well-organized format and include all the data necessary to produce results that address the goal of the application. The process of developing a good worksheet includes the following planning and execution steps:

- determine the worksheet's purpose, what it will include, and how it will be organized
- enter the data and formulas into the worksheet
- test the worksheet
- edit the worksheet to correct any errors or make modifications
- document the worksheet
- improve the appearance of the worksheet
- save and print the completed worksheet

Planning the Worksheet

Sally begins to develop a worksheet that compares global sales by region over two years by creating a planning analysis sheet. Her planning analysis sheet helps her answer the following questions:

1. What is the goal of the worksheet? This helps to define the problem to solve.

2. What are the desired results? This information describes the output—the information required to help solve the problem.

3. What data is needed to calculate the results you want to see? This information is the input—data that must be entered.

4. What calculations are needed to produce the desired output? These calculations specify the formulas used in the worksheet.

Sally's completed planning analysis sheet is shown in Figure 2-1.

Figure 2-1   PLANNING ANALYSIS SHEET

Planning Analysis Sheet

My Goal:
To develop a worksheet to compare annual sales in each region for the last two fiscal years

What results do you want to see?
Sales by region for 2001, 2000
Total Sales for 2001, 2000
Average sales for 2001, 2000
Maximum sales for 2001, 2000
Minimum sales for 2001,2000
Percentage change for each region
Percentage of 2001 sales for each region

What information do I need?
Sales for each region in 2001
Sales for each region in 2000

What calculations do I perform?
Percentage change = (Sales in 2001 – Sales in 2000)/ Sales in 2000
Percentage of 2001 sales = Sales in a region for 2001/Total sales 2001
Total sales for year = Sum of sales for each region
Average sales in 2001
Maximum sales in 2001
Minimum sales in 2001

Next Sally makes a rough sketch of her design, including titles, column headings, row labels, and where data values and totals should be placed. Figure 2-2 shows Sally's sketch. With these two planning tools, Sally is now ready to enter the data into Excel and build the worksheet.

Figure 2-2	SKETCH OF WORKSHEET

Motorcycle Specialties Incorporated
Sales Comparison 2001 with 2000

Region	Year 2001	Year 2000	% Change	% of 2001 Sales
North America	365000	314330	0.16	0.28
South America	354250	292120	0.21	0.28
Australia	251140	262000	-0.04	0.19
Europe	310440	279996	0.11	0.24
Total	1280830	1148446	0.12	

Average	320207.5
Maximum	365000
Minimum	251140

Building the Worksheet

You use Sally's planning analysis sheet, Figure 2-1, and the rough sketch shown in Figure 2-2 to guide you in preparing the sales comparison worksheet. You begin by establishing the layout of the worksheet by entering titles and column headings. Next you work on inputting the data and formulas that will calculate the results Sally needs.

To start Excel and organize your desktop:

1. Start Excel as usual.

2. Make sure your Data Disk is in the appropriate disk drive.

3. Make sure the Microsoft Excel and Book1 windows are maximized.

Entering Labels

When you build a worksheet, it's a good practice to enter the labels before entering any other data. These labels help you identify the cells where you will enter data and formulas in your worksheet. As you type a label in a cell, Excel aligns the label at the left side of the cell. Labels that are too long to fit in a cell spill over into the cell or cells to the right, if those cells are empty. If the cells to the right are not empty, Excel displays only as much of the label as fits in the cell. Begin creating the sales comparison worksheet for Sally by entering the two-line title.

To enter the worksheet title:

1. If necessary, click cell **A1** to make it the active cell.

2. Type **Motorcycle Specialties Incorporated**, and then press the **Enter** key. Since cell A1 is empty, the title appears in cell A1 and spills over into cells B1, C1, and D1. Cell A2 is now the active cell.

TROUBLE? If you make a mistake while typing, remember that you can correct errors with the Backspace key. If you notice the error only after you have pressed the Enter key, then double-click the cell to activate Edit mode, and use the edit keys on your keyboard to correct the error.

3. In cell A2 type **Sales Comparison 2001 with 2000**, and then press the **Enter** key.

Next you enter the column headings defined on the worksheet sketch in Figure 2-2.

To enter labels for the column headings:

1. If necessary, click cell **A3** to make it the active cell.

2. Type **Region** and then press the **Tab** key to complete the entry. Cell B3 is the active cell.

3. Type **Year 2001** in cell B3, and then press the **Tab** key.

   Sally's sketch shows that three more column heads are needed for the worksheet. Enter those next.

4. Enter the remaining column heads as follows:

   Cell C3: **Year 2000**

   Cell D3: **% Change**

   Cell E3: **% of 2001 Sales**

   See Figure 2-3.

   TROUBLE? If any cell does not contain the correct label, either edit the cell or retype the entry.

| Figure 2-3 | WORKSHEET AFTER TITLES AND COLUMN HEADINGS HAVE BEEN ENTERED |

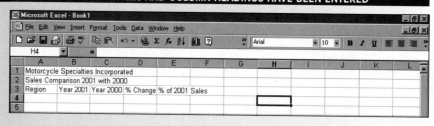

Recall that MSI conducts business in four different regions of the world, and the spreadsheet needs to track the sales information for each region. So Sally wants labels reflecting the regions entered into the worksheet. Enter these labels next.

To enter the regions:

1. Click cell **A4**, type **North America**, and then press the **Enter** key.

2. In cell **A5** type **South America**, and then press the **Enter** key.

3. Type **Australia** in cell A6, and then **Europe** in cell A7.

The last set of labels entered identifies the summary information that will be included in the report.

To enter the summary labels:

1. In cell A8 type **Total**, and then press the **Enter** key.

2. Type the following labels into the specified cells:

Cell A9: **Average**

Cell A10: **Maximum**

Cell A11: **Minimum**

See Figure 2-4.

| Figure 2-4 | WORKSHEET AFTER ALL LABELS HAVE BEEN ENTERED |

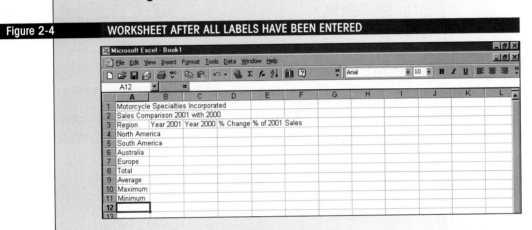

The labels that you just entered into the worksheet will help to identify where the data and formulas need to be placed.

Entering Data

Recall that values can be numbers, formulas, or functions. The next step in building the worksheet is to enter the data, which in this case are the numbers representing sales in each region during 2000 and 2001.

To enter the sales values for 2000 and 2001:

1. Click cell **B4** to make it the active cell. Type **365000** and then press the **Enter** key. See Figure 2-5. Notice that the region name, North America, is no longer completely visible in cell A4 because cell B4 is no longer empty. Later in the tutorial you will learn how to increase the width of a column in order to display the entire contents of cells.

| Figure 2-5 | WORKSHEET WITH LABEL TRUNCATED IN CELL |

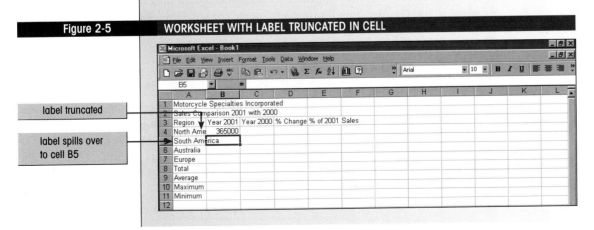

label truncated

label spills over to cell B5

2. In cell B5 type **354250**, and then press the **Enter** key.

3. Enter the values for cells B6, **251140**, and B7, **310440**.

Next, type the values for sales during 2000.

4. Click cell **C4**, type **314330**, and then press the **Enter** key.

5. Enter the remaining values in the specified cells as follows:

Cell C5: **292120**

Cell C6: **262000**

Cell C7: **279996**

Your screen should now look like Figure 2-6.

Figure 2-6	WORKSHEET AFTER SALES FOR 2001 AND 2000 HAVE BEEN ENTERED

Now that you have entered the labels and data, you need to enter the formulas that will calculate the data to produce the output, or the results. The first calculation Sally wants to see is the total sales for each year. To determine total sales for 2001, you would simply sum the sales from each region for that year. In the previous tutorial you used the SUM function to calculate the weighted total score for the Scottsdale golf site by typing that function into the cell. Similarly, you can use the SUM function to calculate total sales for each year for MSI's comparison report.

Using the AutoSum Button

Since the SUM function is used more often than any other function, Excel includes the AutoSum button on the Standard toolbar. This button automatically creates a formula that contains the SUM function. To do this, Excel looks at the cells adjacent to the active cell, makes an assumption as to which cells you want to sum, and displays a formula based on its best determination about the range you want to sum. You can press the Enter key to accept the formula, or you can select a different range of cells to change the range in the formula. You want to use the AutoSum button to calculate the total sales for each year.

To calculate total sales in 2001 using the AutoSum button:

1. Click cell **B8** because this is where you want to display the total sales for 2001.

2. Click the **AutoSum** button Σ on the Standard toolbar. Excel enters a SUM function in the selected cell and determines that the range of cells to sum is B4:B7, the range directly above the selected cell. See Figure 2-7. In this case, that's exactly what you want to do.

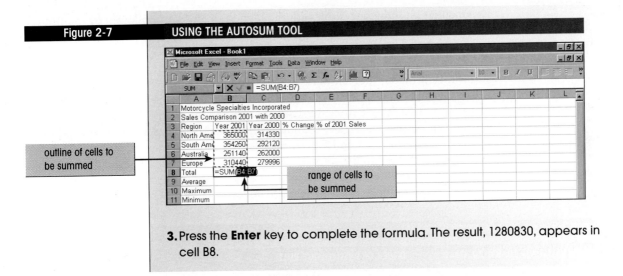

Figure 2-7 USING THE AUTOSUM TOOL

outline of cells to be summed

range of cells to be summed

3. Press the **Enter** key to complete the formula. The result, 1280830, appears in cell B8.

Now use the same approach to calculate the total sales for 2000.

To calculate total sales in 2000 using the AutoSum button:

1. Click cell **C8** to make it the active cell.

2. Click the **AutoSum** Σ button on the Standard toolbar.

3. Press the **Enter** key to complete the formula. The result, 1148446, appears in cell C8.

Next you need to enter the formula to calculate the percentage change in sales for North America between 2001 and 2000.

Entering Formulas

Recall that a formula is an equation that performs calculations in a cell. By entering an equal sign (=) as the first entry in the cell, you are telling Excel that the numbers or symbols that follow constitute a formula, not just data. Reviewing Sally's worksheet plan, you note that you need to calculate the percentage change in sales in North America. The formula is:

Percentage change in sales for North America = (2001 sales in North America - 2000 sales in North America)/2000 sales in North America

So in looking at the worksheet, the formula in Excel would be:

=(B4-C4)/C4

If a formula contains more than one arithmetic operator, Excel performs the calculations in the standard order of precedence of operators, shown in Figure 2-8. The **order of precedence** is a set of predefined rules that Excel uses to unambiguously calculate a formula by determining which part of the formula to calculate first, which part second, and so on.

Figure 2-8 ORDER OF PRECEDENCE FOR ARITHMETIC OPERATIONS

ORDER	OPERATOR	DESCRIPTION
First	^	Exponentiation
Second	* or /	Multiplication or division
Third	+ or -	Addition or subtraction

Exponentiation is the operation with the highest precedence, followed by multiplication and division, and finally addition and subtraction. For example, because multiplication has precedence over addition, the result of the formula =3+4*5 is 23.

When a formula contains more than one operator with the same order of precedence, Excel performs the operation from left to right. Thus, in the formula =4*10/8, Excel multiplies 4 by 10 before dividing the product by 8. The result of the calculation is 5. You can add parentheses to a formula to make it easier to understand or to change the order of operations. Enclosing an expression in parentheses overrides the normal order of precedence. Excel always performs any calculations contained in parentheses first. In the formula =3+4*5, the multiplication is performed before the addition. If instead you wanted the formula to add 3+4 and then multiply the sum by 5, you would enter the formula =(3+4)*5. The result of the calculation is 35. Figure 2-9 shows examples of formulas that will help you understand the order of precedence rules.

Figure 2-9	EXAMPLES ILLUSTRATING ORDER OF PRECEDENCE RULES	
FORMULA VALUE A1=10, B1=20, C1=3	**ORDER OF PRECEDENCE RULE**	**RESULT**
=A1+B1*C1	Multiplication before addition	70
=(A1+B1)*C1	Expression inside parentheses executed before expression outside	90
=A1/B1+C1	Division before addition	3.5
=A1/(B1+C1)	Expression inside parentheses executed before expression outside	.435
=A1/B1*C1	Two operators at same precedence level, leftmost operator evaluated first	1.5
=A1/(B1*C1)	Expression inside parentheses executed before expression outside	.166667

Now enter the percentage change formula as specified in Sally's planning sheet.

To enter the formula for the percentage change in sales for North America:

1. Click cell **D4** to make it the active cell.

2. Type **=(B4-C4)/C4** and then press the **Enter** key. Excel performs the calculations and displays the value 0.1612 in cell D4. The formula is no longer visible in the cell. If you select the cell, the result of the formula appears in the cell, and the formula you entered appears in the formula bar.

Next you need to enter the percentage change formulas for the other regions, as well as the percentage change for the total company sales. You could type the formula =(B5-C5)/C5 in cell D5, the formula =(B6-C6)/C6 in cell D6, the formula =(B7-C7)/C7 in cell D7, and the formula =(B8-C8)/C8 in cell D8. However, this approach is time consuming and error prone. Instead, you can copy the formula you entered in cell C4 (percentage change in North American sales) into cells D5, D6, D7, and D8. Copying duplicates the cell's underlying formula into other cells, automatically adjusting cell references to reflect the new cell address. Copying formulas from one cell to another saves time and reduces the chances of entering incorrect formulas when building worksheets.

Copying a Formula Using the Fill Handle

You can copy formulas using menu commands, toolbar buttons, or the fill handle. The **fill handle** is a small black square located in the lower-right corner of the selected cell, as shown in Figure 2-10. In this section you will use the fill handle to copy the formulas. In other situations you can also use the fill handle for copying values and labels from one cell or a group of cells.

Figure 2-10	FILL HANDLE

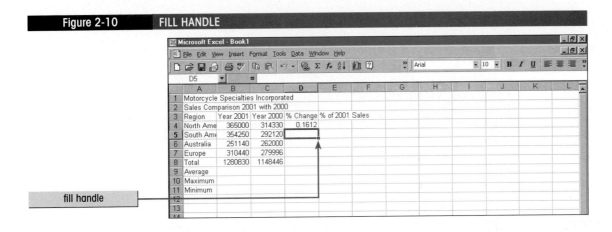

fill handle

REFERENCE **WINDOW**   **RW**

Copying Cell Contents with the Fill Handle

■ Click the cell that contains the label, value, or formula you want to copy. If you want to copy the contents of more than one cell, select the range of cells you want to copy.

■ To copy to adjacent cells, click and drag the fill handle to outline the cells where you want the copy or copies to appear, and then release the mouse button.

You want to copy the formula from cell D4 to cells D5, D6, D7, and D8.

To copy the formula from cell D4 to cells D5, D6, D7, and D8:

1. Click cell **D4** to make it the active cell.

2. Position the pointer over the fill handle (in the lower-right corner of cell D4) until the pointer changes to $+$.

3. Click and drag the pointer down the worksheet to outline cells **D5** through **D8**. See Figure 2-11.

Figure 2-11	COPYING A FORMULA

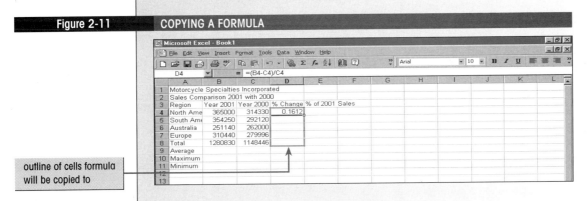

outline of cells formula will be copied to

4. Release the mouse button. Excel copies the formula from D4 to cells D5 to D8. Values now appear in cells D5 through D8.

5. Click any cell to deselect the range. See Figure 2-12.

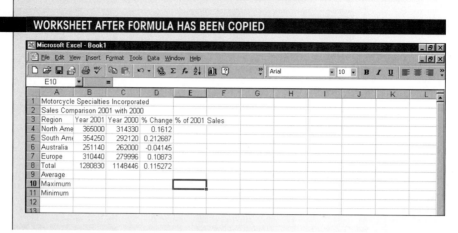

| Figure 2-12 | WORKSHEET AFTER FORMULA HAS BEEN COPIED |

Notice that Excel didn't copy the formula =(B4-C4)/C4 exactly. It automatically adjusted the cell references for each new formula location. Why did that happen?

Copying a Formula Using Relative References

When you copy a formula that contains cell references, Excel automatically adjusts the cell references for the new locations. For example, when Excel copied the formula from cell D4, =(B4-C4)/C4, it automatically changed the cell references in the formula to reflect the formula's new position in the worksheet. So in cell D5 the cell references adjust to =(B5-C5)/C5. Cell references that change when copied are called **relative cell references**.

Take a moment to look at the formulas in cells D5, D6, D7, and D8.

To examine the formulas in cells D5, D6, D7, and D8:

1. Click cell **D5**. The formula =(B5-C5)/C5 appears in the formula bar.

When Excel copied the formula from cell D4 to cell D5, the cell references changed. The formula =(B4-C4)/C4 became =(B5-C5)/C5 when Excel copied the formula down one row to row 5.

2. Examine the formulas in cells D6, D7, and D8. Notice that the cell references were adjusted for the new locations.

Copying a Formula Using an Absolute Reference

According to Sally's plan, the worksheet should display the percentage that each region contributed to the total sales in 2001. For example, if the company's total sales were $100,000 and sales in North America were $25,000, then sales in North America would be 25% of total sales. To complete this calculation for each region, you need to divide each region's sales by the total company sales, as shown in the following formulas:

Contribution by North America	=B4/B8
Contribution by South America	=B5/B8
Contribution by Australia	=B6/B8
Contribution by Europe	=B7/B8

First enter the formula to calculate the percentage North America contributed to total sales.

To calculate North America's percentage of total 2001 sales:

1. Click cell **E4** to make it the active cell.

2. Type **=B4/B8** and then press the **Enter** key to display the value .284971 in cell E4.

Cell E4 displays the correct result. Sales in North America for 2001 were 365,000, which is approximately .28 of the 1,280,830 in total sales in 2001. Next, you decide to copy the formula in cell E4 to cells E5, E6, and E7.

To copy the percentage formula in cell E4 to cells E5 through E7:

1. Click cell **E4**, and then move the pointer over the fill handle in cell E4 until it changes to $+$.

2. Click and drag the pointer to cell **E7** and release the mouse button.

3. Click any blank cell to deselect the range. The error value "#DIV/0!" appears in cells E5 through E7. See Figure 2-13.

| Figure 2-13 | ERROR VALUE IN WORKSHEET AFTER COPYING FORMULA |

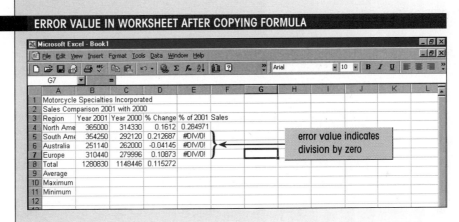

Something is wrong. Cells E5 through E7 display "#DIV/0!" a special constant, called an **error value.** Excel displays an error value constant when it cannot resolve the formula **#DIV/0!**, one of seven error value constants means that Excel was instructed to divide by zero. Take a moment to look at the formulas you copied into cells E5, E6, and E7.

To examine the formulas in cells E5 through E7:

1. Click cell **E5** and then look at the formula appearing in the formula bar, =B5/B9. The first cell reference changed from B4 in the original formula to B5 in the copied formula. That's correct because the sales data for South America is entered in cell B5. The second cell reference changed from B8 in the original formula to B9, which is not correct. The correct formula should be =B5/B8 because the total sales are in cell B8, not cell B9.

2. Look at the formulas in cells E6 and E7 and see how the cell references changed in each formula.

As you observed, the cell reference to total company sales (B8) in the original formula was changed to B9, B10, and B11 in the copied formulas. The problem with the copied formulas is that Excel adjusted *all* the cell references relative to their new location.

Absolute Versus Relative References

Sometimes when you copy a formula, you don't want Excel to change all cell references automatically to reflect their new positions in the worksheet. If you want a cell reference to point to the same location in the worksheet when you copy it, you must use an **absolute reference**. An absolute reference is a cell reference in a formula that does not change when copied to another cell.

To create an absolute reference, you insert a dollar sign ($) before the column and row of the cell reference. For example, the cell reference $B$8 is an absolute reference, whereas the cell reference B8 is a relative reference. If you copy a formula that contains the absolute reference $B$8 to another cell, the cell reference to $B$8 does not change. On the other hand, if you copy a formula containing the relative reference B8 to another cell, the reference to B8 changes. In some situations, a cell might have a **mixed reference**, such as $B8; in this case, when the formula is copied, the row number changes but the column letter does not.

To include an absolute reference in a formula, you can type a dollar sign when you type the cell reference, or you can use the F4 key to change the cell reference type while in Edit mode.

REFERENCE WINDOW	RW

Changing Absolute, Mixed, and Relative References
- Double-click the cell that contains the formula you want to edit.
- Use the arrow keys to move the insertion point to the part of the cell reference you want to change.
- Press the F4 key until the reference is correct. Press the Enter key to complete the edit.

To correct the problem in your worksheet, you need to use an absolute reference, instead of a relative reference, to indicate the location of total sales in 2001. That is, you need to change the formula from =B4/B8 to =B4/$B$8. The easiest way to make this change is in Edit mode.

To change a cell reference to an absolute reference:

1. Click cell **E4** to move to the cell that contains the formula you want to edit.

2. Double-click the mouse button to edit the formula in the cell. Notice that each cell reference in the formula in cell E4 appears in a different color and the corresponding cells referred to in the formula are outlined in the same color. This feature is called **Range Finder** and is designed to make it easier for you to check the accuracy of your formula.

3. Make sure the insertion point is to the right of the division (/) operator, anywhere in the cell reference B8.

4. Press the **F4** key to change the reference to $B$8.

   TROUBLE? If your reference shows the **mixed reference** B$8 or $B8, continue to press the F4 key until you see $B$8.

5. Press the **Enter** key to update the formula in cell E4.

Cell E4 still displays .284971, which is the formula's correct result. But remember, the problem in your original formula did not surface until you copied it to cells E5 through E7. To correct the error, you need to copy the revised formula and then check the results. Although you can again use the fill handle to copy the formula, you can also copy the formula using the Clipboard and the Copy and Paste buttons on the Standard toolbar.

Copying Cell Contents Using the Copy-and-Paste Method

You can duplicate the contents of a cell or range by making a copy of the cell or range and then pasting the copy into one or more locations in the same worksheet, another worksheet, or another workbook.

When you copy a cell or range of cells, the copied material is placed on the Clipboard. You can copy labels, numbers, dates, or formulas.

REFERENCE WINDOW **RW**

<u>Copying and Pasting a Cell or Range of Cells</u>
- Select the cell or range of cells to be copied.
- Click the Copy button on the Standard toolbar.
- Select the range into which you want to copy the formula.
- Click the Paste button on the Standard toolbar.
- Press the Enter key.

You need to copy the formula in cell E4 to the Clipboard and then paste that formula into cells E5 through E7.

To copy the revised formula from cell E4 to cells E5 through E7:

1. Click cell **E4** because it contains the revised formula that you want to copy.

2. Click the **Copy** button on the Standard toolbar. A moving dashed line surrounds cell E4, indicating that the formula has been copied and is available to be pasted into other cells.

3. Click and drag to select cells **E5** through **E7**.

4. Click the **Paste** button on the Standard toolbar. Excel adjusts the formula and pastes it into cells E5 through E7.

5. Click any cell to deselect the range and view the formulas' results. Press the **Escape** key to clear the Clipboard and remove the dashed line surrounding cell E4. See Figure 2-14.

Figure 2-14 **RESULTS OF COPYING THE FORMULA WITH AN ABSOLUTE REFERENCE**

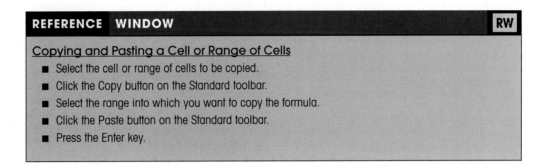

result of copied formula

Copying this formula worked. When you pasted the formula from cell E4 into the range E5:E7, Excel automatically adjusted the relative reference (B4), while using the cell reference ($B$8) for all absolute references. You have now implemented most of the design as specified in the planning analysis sheet. Now rename the worksheet to accurately describe its contents, then save the workbook on your Data Disk before entering the formulas to compute the summary statistics.

Renaming the Worksheet

Before saving the workbook, look at the sheet tab in the lower-left corner of the worksheet window: the sheet is currently named Sheet1—the name Excel automatically uses when it opens a new workbook. Now that your worksheet is taking shape, you want to give it a more descriptive name that better indicates its contents. Change the worksheet name to Sales Comparison.

To change a worksheet name:

1. Double-click the **Sheet1** sheet tab to select it.

2. Type the new name, **Sales Comparison**, over the current name, Sheet1, and then click any cell in the worksheet. The sheet tab displays the name "Sales Comparison."

Saving the New Workbook

Now you want to save the workbook. Because this is the first time you have saved this workbook, you use the Save As command and name the file MSI Sales Report.

To save the workbook as MSI Sales Report:

1. Click **File** on the menu bar, and then click **Save As** to open the Save As dialog box.

2. In the File name text box, type **MSI Sales Report** but don't press the Enter key yet. You still need to check some other settings.

3. Click the **Save in** list arrow, and then click the drive containing your Data Disk.

4. In the folder list, select the **Tutorial** folder for **Tutorial.02**, into which you want to save the workbook. Your Save As dialog box should look like the dialog box in Figure 2-15.

| Figure 2-15 | SAVING THE WORKBOOK AS MSI SALES REPORT |

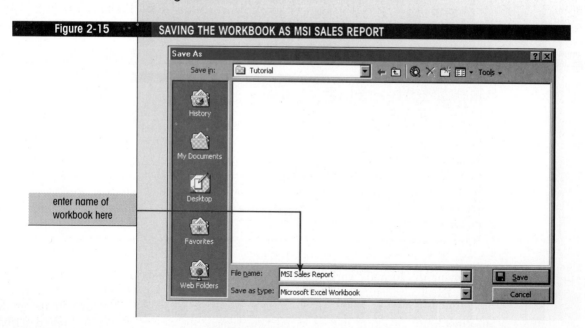

enter name of workbook here

5. Click the **Save** button to save the workbook.

TROUBLE? If you see the message "Replace Existing MSI Sales Report," Excel found a file with the same name on the current folder. Click the Yes button to replace the file on the folder with the current version.

Session 2.1 QUICK CHECK

1. List the steps to follow to create a worksheet.

2. Describe how AutoSum works.

3. In cell D3 you have the formula =B3-C3. After you copy this formula to cell D4, the formula in cell D4 would appear in the formula bar as _____.

4. The _____ is a small black square located in the lower-right corner of a selected cell.

5. In the formula =D10*C10, D10 and C10 are examples of _____ references.

6. In the formula =A8+(1+$C$1), $C$1 is an example of a(n) _____.

7. When you copy a formula using the Copy and Paste buttons on the Standard toolbar, Excel uses the _____ to temporarily store the formula.

8. Describe the steps you take to change the name of the sheet tab.

9. What is meant by order of precedence?

Now that you have planned and built the Sales Comparison worksheet by entering labels, values, and formulas, you need to complete the worksheet by entering some functions and formatting the worksheet. You will do this in Session 2.2.

SESSION 2.2

In this session you will finish the worksheet. As you do this you will learn how to enter several statistical functions, increase the column width, insert a row between the titles and column headings, move the contents of a range to another location, and apply one of the Excel predefined formats to the report. You will also spell check the worksheet, preview, and print it.

Excel Functions

According to Sally's planning analysis sheet, you still need to enter the formulas for the summary statistics. To enter these statistics you'll use three Excel functions, AVERAGE, MAX, and MIN. The many Excel functions help you enter formulas for calculations and other specialized tasks, even if you don't know the mathematical details of the calculations. As you recall, a function is a calculation tool that performs a predefined operation. You are already familiar with the SUM function, which adds the values in a range of cells. Excel provides hundreds of functions, including a function to calculate the average of a list of numbers, a function to find a number's square root, a function to calculate loan payments, and a function to calculate the number of days between two dates.

Each function has a **syntax**, which specifies the order in which you must type the parts of the function and where to put commas, parentheses, and other punctuation. The general syntax of an Excel function is:

FUNCTION NAME(*argument1,argument2,...*)

The syntax of most functions requires you to type the function name followed by one or more arguments in parentheses. The name of the function, such as SUM or AVERAGE, describes the operation the function performs. Function **arguments** specify the values the function must use in the calculation, or the cell references that Excel must include in the calculation. For example, in the function SUM(A1:A20) the function name is SUM and the argument is A1:A20, which is the range of cells you want to total.

You can use a function in a simple formula such as =SUM(A1:A20), or a more complex formula such as =SUM(A1:A20)*52. As with all formulas, you enter the formula that contains a function in the cell where you want to display the results. The easiest way to enter a function in a cell is to use the Paste Function button on the Standard toolbar, which leads you step-by-step through the process of entering a formula containing a function.

If you prefer, you can type the function directly into the cell. Although the function name is always shown in uppercase, you can type it in either uppercase or lowercase. Also, even though parentheses enclose the arguments, you need not type the closing parenthesis if the function ends the formula. Excel automatically adds the closing parenthesis when you press the Enter key to complete the formula.

Figure 2-16 shows a few of the functions available in Excel organized by category. To learn more about functions, use the Paste Function button on the Standard toolbar or use the Help system. According to Sally's planning analysis sheet, the next step is to calculate the average regional sales for 2001.

Figure 2-16		SELECTED EXCEL FUNCTIONS	
CATEGORY	**FUNCTION NAME**	**SYNTAX**	**DEFINITION**
Finance	PMT	PMT(rate,nper,pv,fv,type)	Calculates the payment for a loan based on constant payments and a constant interest rate
	FV	FV(rate,nper,pmt,pv,type)	Returns the future value of an investment based on periodic, constant payments and a constant interest rate
Math	ROUND	ROUND(number,num_digits)	Rounds a number to a specified number of digits
	RAND	RAND( )	Returns an evenly distributed random number greater than or equal to 0 and less than 1
Logical	IF	IF(logical_test,value_if_true, value_if_false)	Returns one value if a condition you specify evaluates to TRUE and another value if it evaluates to FALSE
	AND	AND(logical1,logical2, ...)	Returns TRUE if all its arguments are TRUE; returns FALSE if one or more arguments is FALSE
Lookup and Reference	VLOOKUP	VLOOKUP(lookup_value, table_array,col_index_num, range_lookup)	Searches for a value in the leftmost column of a table, and then returns a value in the same row from a column you specify in the table
	INDIRECT	INDIRECT(ref_text,a1)	Returns the reference specified by a text string–references are immediately evaluated to display their contents
Text	CONCATENATE	CONCATENATE (text1,text2,...)	Joins several text strings into one text string
	LEFT	LEFT(text,num_chars)	Returns the first (or leftmost) character or characters in a text string
Date and Time	TODAY	TODAY( )	Returns the serial number of the current date
	YEAR	YEAR(serial_number)	Returns the year corresponding to serial number–the year is given as an integer in the range 1900-9999
Statistical	COUNT	COUNT(value1,value2, ...)	Counts the number of cells that contain numbers and numbers within the list of arguments
	STDEV	STDEV(number1,number2,...)	Estimates standard deviation based on a sample

AVERAGE Function

AVERAGE is a statistical function that calculates the average, or the arithmetic mean. The syntax for the AVERAGE function is:
AVERAGE(*number1,number2,...*)

Generally, when you use the AVERAGE function, *number* is a range of cells. To calculate the average of a range of cells, Excel sums the values in the range, then divides by the number of non-blank cells in the range.

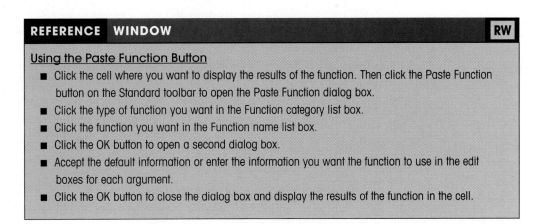

REFERENCE WINDOW   **RW**

Using the Paste Function Button
- Click the cell where you want to display the results of the function. Then click the Paste Function button on the Standard toolbar to open the Paste Function dialog box.
- Click the type of function you want in the Function category list box.
- Click the function you want in the Function name list box.
- Click the OK button to open a second dialog box.
- Accept the default information or enter the information you want the function to use in the edit boxes for each argument.
- Click the OK button to close the dialog box and display the results of the function in the cell.

Sally wants you to calculate the average sales in 2001. You'll use the Paste Function button to enter the AVERAGE function, which is one of the statistical functions.

To enter the AVERAGE function using the Paste Function button:

1. If you took a break after the last session, make sure Excel is running and the MSI Sales worksheet is open. Click cell **B9** to select the cell where you want to enter the AVERAGE function.

2. Click the **Paste Function** button [fx] on the Standard toolbar to open the Paste Function dialog box.

   TROUBLE? If the Office Assistant opens and offers help on this feature, click the No option button.

3. Click **Statistical** in the Function category list box.

4. Click **AVERAGE** in the Function name list box. See Figure 2-17. The syntax for the AVERAGE function, AVERAGE(number1,number2,...), appears beneath the Function category box.

Figure 2-17   **PASTE FUNCTION DIALOG BOX**

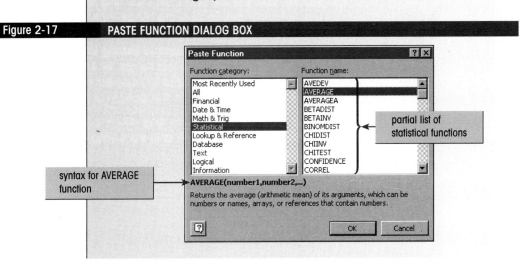

5. Click the **OK** button to open the formula palette for the Average function. The **formula palette** displays the name of the function, a text box for each argument of the function you selected, a description of the function and each argument, the current values of the arguments, the current results of the function, and the current results of the entire formula. Notice that the range B4:B8 appears in the Number1 edit box, and =AVERAGE(B4:B8) appears in the formula bar. See Figure 2-18.

Figure 2-18	AVERAGE FORMULA PALETTE

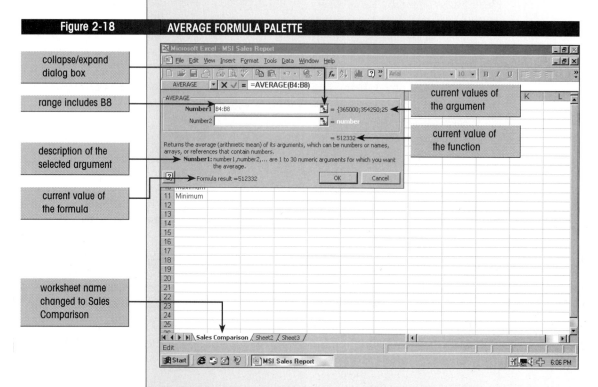

Excel has incorrectly included the total sales for 2001 (cell B8) in the range to calculate the average. The correct range is B4:B7.

6. Click the **Collapse** dialog box button to the right of the Number1 text box to collapse the dialog box to the size of one row. This makes it easier for you to identify and select the correct range.

7. Position the cell pointer over cell **B4**, and then click and drag to select the range **B4:B7**. As you drag the mouse over the range, notice that the message "4Rx1C" appears in a ScreenTip, informing you that four rows and one column have been selected, and then click the **Expand Dialog Box** button. The collapsed dialog box is restored and the correct range, B4:B7, appears in the Number1 text box. The formula =AVERAGE(B4:B7) appears in the formula bar and the formula result 320207.5 appears in the bottom of the formula palette.

8. Click the **OK** button to close the dialog box and return to the worksheet. The average, 320207.5, now appears in cell B9 and the completed function appears in the formula bar.

According to your plan, you need to enter a formula to find the largest regional sales amount in 2001. To do this, you'll use the MAX function.

MAX Function

MAX is a statistical function that finds the largest number. The syntax of the MAX function is:
MAX(*number1,number2,...*)

In the MAX function, *number* can be a constant number such as 345, a cell reference such as B6, or a range of cells such as B5:B16. You can use the MAX function to simply display the largest number or to use the largest number in a calculation. Although you can use the Paste Function to enter the MAX function, this time you'll type the MAX function directly into cell B10.

To enter the MAX function by typing directly into a cell:

1. If necessary, click cell **B10** to select it as the cell into which you want to type the formula that uses the MAX function.

2. Type **=MAX(B4:B7)** and then press the **Enter** key. Cell B10 displays 365000, the largest regional sales amount in 2001.

Next you need to find the smallest regional sales amount in 2001. For that, you'll use the MIN function.

MIN Function

MIN is a statistical function that finds the smallest number. The syntax of the MIN function is:
MIN(*number1,number2,...*)

You can use the MIN function to display the smallest number or to use the smallest number in a calculation.

You'll enter the MIN function directly into cell B11 using the pointing method.

Building Formulas by Pointing

Excel provides several ways to enter cell references into a formula. One is to type the cell references directly, as you have done so far in all the formulas you've entered. Another way to put a cell reference in a formula is to point to the cell reference you want to include while creating the formula. To use the **pointing method** to enter the formula, you click the cell or range of cells whose cell references you want to include in the formula. You may prefer to use this method to enter formulas because it minimizes typing errors.

Now use the pointing method to enter the formula to calculate the minimum sales.

To enter the MIN function using the pointing method:

1. If necessary, click cell **B11** to move to the cell where you want to enter the formula that uses the MIN function.

2. Type **=MIN(** to begin the formula.

3. Position the cell pointer in cell **B4**, and then click and drag to select cells **B4** through **B7**. As you drag the mouse over the range, notice that the message "4Rx1C" appears in a ScreenTip, informing you that four rows and one column have been selected. See Figure 2-19.

Figure 2-19   **WORKSHEET IN PROCESS OF ENTERING FORMULA USING POINTING METHOD**

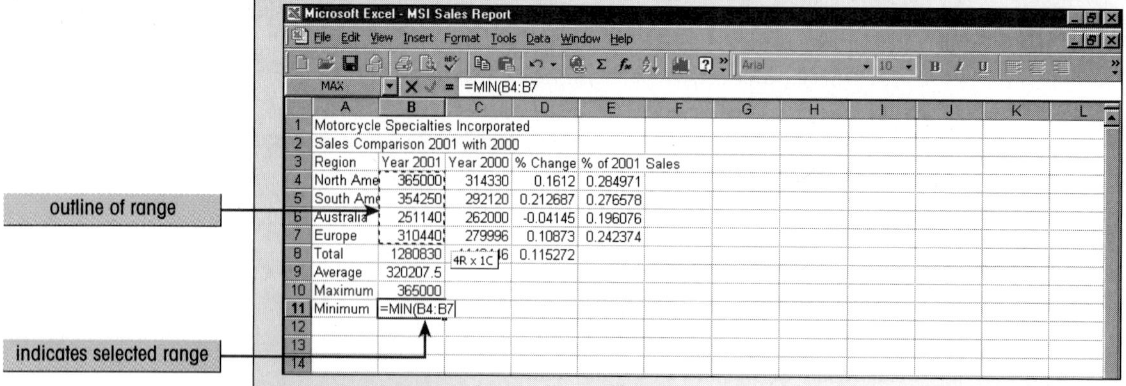

outline of range

indicates selected range

4. Release the mouse button, and then press the **Enter** key. Cell B11 displays 251140, the smallest regional sales amount for 2001.

Now that the worksheet labels, values, formulas, and functions have been entered, Sally reviews the worksheet.

Testing the Worksheet

Before trusting a worksheet and its results, you should test it to make sure you entered the correct formulas. You want the worksheet to produce accurate results.

Beginners often expect their Excel worksheets to work correctly the first time. Sometimes they do work correctly the first time, but even well-planned and well-designed worksheets can contain errors. It's best to assume that a worksheet has errors and test it to make sure it is correct. While there are no rules for testing a worksheet, here are some approaches:

- Entering **test values**, numbers that generate a known result, to determine whether your worksheet formulas are accurate. For example, try entering a 1 into each cell. After you enter the test values, you compare the results in your worksheet with the known results. If the results on your worksheet don't match the known results, you probably made an error.

- Entering **extreme values**, such as very large or very small numbers, and observing their effect on cells with formulas.

- Working out the numbers ahead of time with pencil, paper, and calculator, and comparing these results with the output from the computer.

Sally used the third approach to test her worksheet. She had calculated her results using a calculator (Figure 2-2) and then compared them with the results on the screen (Figure 2-19). The numbers agree, so she feels confident that the worksheet she created contains accurate results.

Spell Checking the Worksheet

You can use the Excel spell check feature to help identify and correct spelling and typing errors. Excel compares the words in your worksheet to the words in its dictionary. If Excel finds a word in your worksheet not in its dictionary, it shows you the word and some suggested corrections, and you decide whether to correct it or leave it as is.

REFERENCE WINDOW   **RW**

Checking the Spelling in a Worksheet
- Click cell A1 to begin the spell check from the top of the worksheet.
- Click the Spelling button on the Standard toolbar.
- Change the spelling or ignore the spell check's suggestion for each identified word.
- Click the OK button when the spell check is complete.

You have tested your numbers and formulas for accuracy. Now you can check the spelling of all text entries in the worksheet.

To check the spelling in a worksheet:

1. Click cell **A1** to begin spell checking in the first cell of the worksheet.

2. Click the **Spelling** button ⬜ on the Standard toolbar to check the spelling of the text in the worksheet. A message box indicates that Excel has finished spell checking the entire worksheet. No errors were found.

   TROUBLE? If the spell check does find a spelling error in your worksheet, use the Spelling dialog box options to correct the spelling mistake and continue checking the worksheet.

Improving the Worksheet Layout

Although the numbers are correct, Sally wants to present a more polished-looking worksheet. She feels that there are a number of simple changes you can make to the worksheet that will improve its layout and make the data more readable. Specifically, she asks you to increase the width of column A so that the entire region names are visible, insert a blank row between the titles and column headings, move the summary statistics down three rows from their current location, and apply one of the predefined Excel formats to the worksheet.

Changing Column Width

Changing the column width is one way to improve the appearance of the worksheet, making it easier to read and interpret data. In Sally's worksheet, you need to increase the width of column A so that all of the labels for North America and South America appear in their cells.

Excel provides several methods for changing column width. For example, you can click a column heading or click and drag the pointer to select a series of column headings and then use the Format menu. You can also use the dividing line between column headings in the column header row. When you move the pointer over the dividing line between two column headings, the pointer changes to ↔. You can then use the pointer to drag the dividing line to a new location. You can also double-click the dividing line to make the column as wide as the longest text label or number in the column.

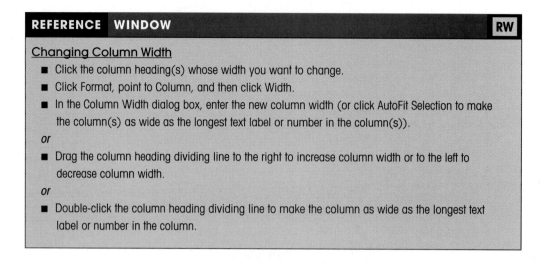

REFERENCE WINDOW   RW

Changing Column Width
- Click the column heading(s) whose width you want to change.
- Click Format, point to Column, and then click Width.
- In the Column Width dialog box, enter the new column width (or click AutoFit Selection to make the column(s) as wide as the longest text label or number in the column(s)).

or

- Drag the column heading dividing line to the right to increase column width or to the left to decrease column width.

or

- Double-click the column heading dividing line to make the column as wide as the longest text label or number in the column.

Sally has asked you to change the width of column A so that the complete region name is visible.

To change the width of column A:

1. Position the pointer ✛ on the A in the column heading area.

2. Move the pointer to the right edge of the column heading dividing columns A and B. Notice that the pointer changes to the resize arrow ↔.

3. Click and drag the resize arrow to the right, increasing the column width 12 characters or more, as indicated in the ScreenTip that pops up on the screen.

4. Release the mouse button. See Figure 2-20.

Figure 2-20   WORKSHEET AFTER WIDTH OF COLUMN A INCREASED

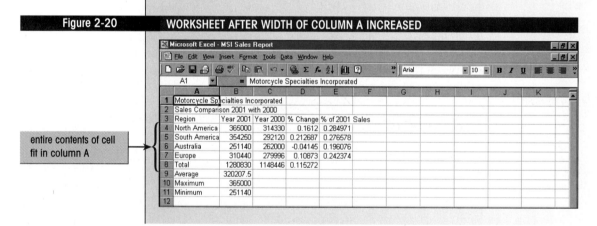

entire contents of cell fit in column A

Next you need to insert a row between the title and the column heading.

Inserting a Row into a Worksheet

At times you may need to add one or more rows or columns to a worksheet to make room for new data or to make the worksheet easier to read. The process of inserting columns and rows is similar; you select the number of columns or rows you want to insert and then use the Insert command to insert them. When you insert rows or columns, Excel repositions other rows and columns in the worksheet and automatically adjusts cell references in formulas to reflect the new location of values used in calculations.

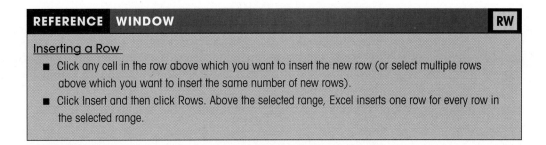

REFERENCE WINDOW **RW**

Inserting a Row
- Click any cell in the row above which you want to insert the new row (or select multiple rows above which you want to insert the same number of new rows).
- Click Insert and then click Rows. Above the selected range, Excel inserts one row for every row in the selected range.

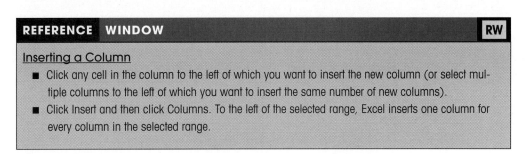

REFERENCE WINDOW **RW**

Inserting a Column
- Click any cell in the column to the left of which you want to insert the new column (or select multiple columns to the left of which you want to insert the same number of new columns).
- Click Insert and then click Columns. To the left of the selected range, Excel inserts one column for every column in the selected range.

Sally wants one blank row between the titles and column headings in her worksheet.

To insert a row into a worksheet:

1. Click cell **A2**.

2. Click **Insert** on the menu bar, and then click **Rows**. Excel inserts a blank row above the original row 2. All other rows shift down one row. Click any cell. See Figure 2-21.

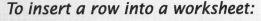

| Figure 2-21 | WORKSHEET AFTER ONE ROW INSERTED ABOVE ORIGINAL ROW 2 |

use this button
to reverse action

row inserted in
wrong position

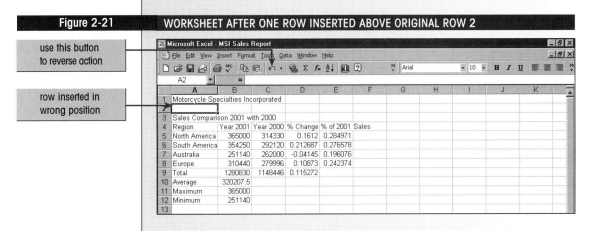

The blank row isn't really where you wanted it. You inserted a row between the two lines of the title instead of between the title and the column heading. To correct this error you can either delete the row or use the Undo button. If you need to delete a row or column, select the row(s) or column(s) you want to delete, then click Delete on the Edit menu, or press the Delete key on your keyboard. You use the Undo button because it is a feature you find valuable in many situations.

Using the Undo Button

The Excel Undo button lets you cancel recent actions one at a time. Click the Undo button to reverse the last command or delete the last entry you typed. To reverse more than one action, click the arrow next to the Undo button and click the action you want to undo from the drop-down list.

Now use the Undo button to reverse the row insertion.

To reverse the row insertion:

1. Click the **Undo** button [icon] on the Standard toolbar to restore the worksheet to its status before the row was inserted.

Now you can insert the blank row in the correct place—between the second line of the worksheet title and the column heads.

To insert a row into a worksheet:

1. Click cell **A3** because you want to insert one row above row 3. If you wanted to insert several rows, you would select as many rows as you wanted to insert immediately below where you want the new rows inserted before using the Insert command.

2. Click **Insert** on the menu bar, and then click **Rows**. Excel inserts a blank row above the original row 3. All other rows shift down one row.

Adding a row changed the location of the data in the worksheet. For example, the percentage change in North American sales, originally in cell D4, is now in cell D5. Did Excel adjust the formulas to compensate for the new row? Check cell D5 and any other cells you want to view to verify that the cell references were adjusted.

To examine the formula in cell D5 and other cells:

1. Click cell **D5**. The formula =(B5-C5)/C5 appears in the formula bar. You originally entered the formula =(B4-C4)/C4 in cell D4 to calculate percentage change in North America. Excel automatically adjusted the cell reference to reflect the new location of the data.

2. Inspect other cells below row 3 to verify that their cell references were automatically adjusted when the new row was inserted.

Sally has also suggested moving the summary statistics down three rows from their present location to make the report easier to read. So you will need to move the range of cells containing the average, minimum, and maximum sales to a different location in the worksheet.

Moving a Range Using the Mouse

To place the summary statistics three rows below the other data in the report, you could use the Insert command to insert three blank rows between the total and average sales. Alternatively, you could use the mouse to move the summary statistics to a new location. Because you already know how to insert a row, try using the mouse to move the summary statistics to a new location. This technique is called drag and drop. You simply select the cell range you want to move and use the pointer ⍃ to drag the cells' contents to the desired location.

REFERENCE WINDOW   **RW**

Moving a Range Using the Mouse

- Select the cell or range of cells you want to move.
- Place the mouse pointer over any edge of the selected range until the pointer changes to an arrow.
- Click and drag the outline of the range to the new worksheet location.
- Release the mouse button.

Sally has asked you to move the range A10 through B12 to the new destination area A13 through B15.

To move a range of cells using the drag-and-drop technique:

1. Select the range of cells **A10:B12,** which contains the sales summary statistics you want to move.

2. Place the mouse pointer over any edge of the selected range until the pointer changes to an arrow ⍃. See Figure 2-22.

Figure 2-22   **RANGE TO BE MOVED**

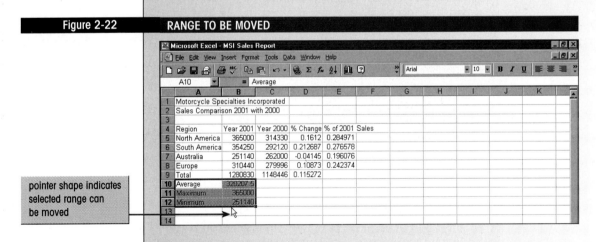

pointer shape indicates
selected range can
be moved

3. Click the mouse button and then hold the button down as you move (drag) the outline of the three rows down to range A13:B15. Notice how Excel displays a gray outline and a box with a range address that shows the destination of the cells.

4. Release the mouse button. Excel moves the selected cells to the designated location, A13:B15.

5. Click any cell to deselect the range. See Figure 2-23.

Figure 2-23 | **WORKSHEET AFTER RANGE MOVED**

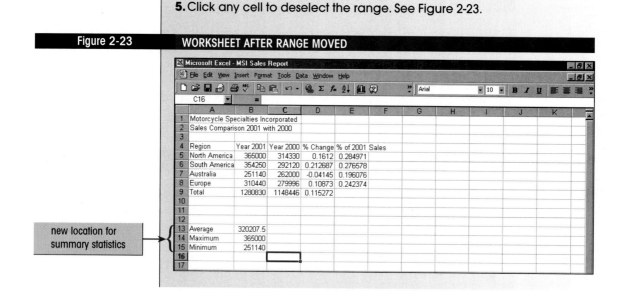

new location for
summary statistics

Next Sally wants you to use the Excel AutoFormat feature to improve the worksheet's appearance by emphasizing the titles and aligning numbers in cells.

Using AutoFormat

The AutoFormat feature lets you change the appearance of your worksheet by selecting from a collection of predefined worksheet formats. Each worksheet format in the AutoFormat collection gives your worksheet a more professional appearance by applying attractive fonts, borders, colors, and shading to a range of data. AutoFormat also adjusts column widths, row heights, and the alignment of text in cells to improve the appearance of the worksheet.

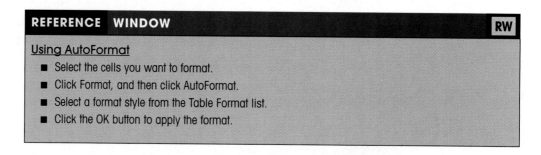

REFERENCE   WINDOW   RW

Using AutoFormat
- Select the cells you want to format.
- Click Format, and then click AutoFormat.
- Select a format style from the Table Format list.
- Click the OK button to apply the format.

Now you'll use AutoFormat's Simple format to improve the worksheet's appearance.

To apply AutoFormat's Simple format:

1. Select cells **A1:E9** as the range you want to format using AutoFormat.

2. Click **Format** on the menu bar, and then click **AutoFormat**. The AutoFormat dialog box opens. See Figure 2-24.

| Figure 2-24 | AUTOFORMAT DIALOG BOX |

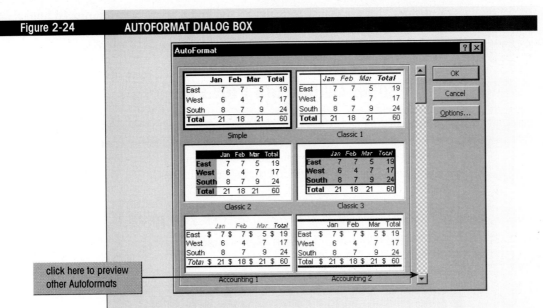

click here to preview
other Autoformats

3. The dialog box displays a preview of how each format will appear when
   applied to a worksheet. Notice the dark border around the Simple format indicating it is the selected format.

4. Click the **OK** button to apply the Simple format.

5. Click any cell to deselect the range. Figure 2-25 shows the newly formatted
   worksheet.

| Figure 2-25 | WORKSHEET AFTER USING THE SIMPLE AUTOFORMAT |

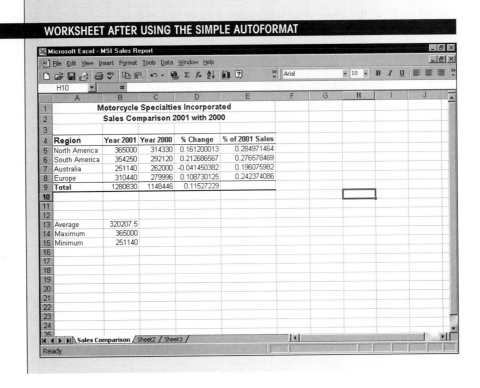

You show the worksheet to Sally. She's impressed with the improved appearance and decides to hand it out to the regional sales managers at their next meeting. She asks you to print it so she can make copies.

Previewing the Worksheet Using Print Preview

Before you print a worksheet, you can use the Excel Print Preview window to see how it will look when printed. The Print Preview window shows you margins, page breaks, headers, and footers that are not always visible on the screen. If the preview isn't what you want, you can close the Print Preview window and change the worksheet before printing it.

To preview the worksheet before you print it:

1. Click the Print Preview button 🔍 to display the worksheet in the Print Preview window. See Figure 2-26.

   TROUBLE? If you do not see the Print Preview button on the Standard toolbar, click More Buttons ⏷ to display the Print Preview button.

| Figure 2-26 | PRINT PREVIEW OF SALES COMPARISON WORKSHEET |

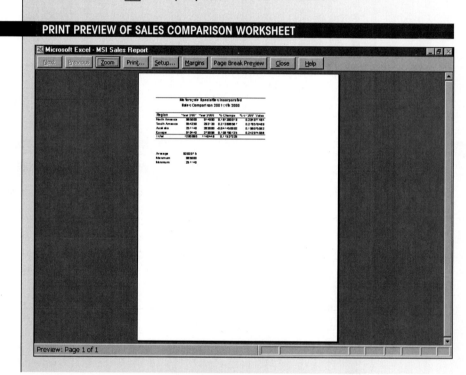

When Excel displays a full page in the Print Preview window, you might have difficulty seeing the text of the worksheet because it is so small. Don't worry if the preview isn't completely readable. One purpose of the Print Preview window is to see the overall layout of the worksheet and how it will fit on the printed page. If you want a better view of the text, you can use the Zoom button.

To display an enlarged section of the Print Preview window:

1. Click the **Zoom** button to display an enlarged section of the Print Preview.

2. Click the **Zoom** button again to return to the full-page view.

Notice that the Print Preview window contains several other buttons. Figure 2-27 describes each of these buttons.

Figure 2-27	DESCRIPTION OF PRINT PREVIEW BUTTONS
CLICKING THIS BUTTON	**RESULTS IN**
Next	Moving forward one page
Previous	Moving backward one page
Zoom	Magnifying the Print Preview screen to zoom in on any portion of the page; click again to return to full-page preview
Print	Printing the document
Setup	Displaying the Page Setup dialog box
Margins	Changing the width of margins, columns in the worksheet and the position of headers and footers
Page Break Preview	Showing where page breaks occur in the worksheet and which area of the worksheet will be printed; you can adjust where data will print by inserting or moving page breaks
Close	Closing the Print Preview window
Help	Activating Help

Looking at the worksheet in Print Preview, you observe that it is not centered on the page. By default, Excel prints a worksheet at the upper left of the page's print area. You can specify that the worksheet be centered vertically, horizontally, or both.

Centering the Printout

Worksheet printouts generally look more professional centered on the printed page. You decide that Sally would want you to center the sales comparison worksheet both horizontally and vertically on the printed page.

To center the printout:

1. In Print Preview, click the **Setup** button to open the Page Setup dialog box.

2. Click the **Margins** tab. See Figure 2-28. Notice that the preview box displays a worksheet positioned at the upper-left edge of the page.

| Figure 2-28 | MARGINS TAB OF PAGE SETUP DIALOG BOX |

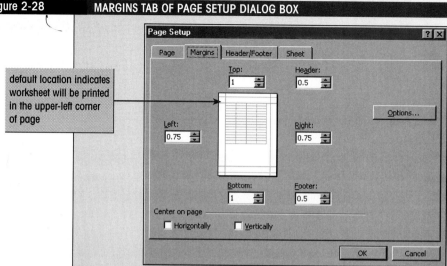

default location indicates worksheet will be printed in the upper-left corner of page

3. Click the **Horizontally** check box in the Center on page section to place a check in it.

4. Click the **Vertically** check box to place a check in it.

Notice that the sample window shows that the worksheet is now centered vertically and horizontally on the page.

5. Click the **OK** button to return to the Print Preview window. Notice that the output in the Print Preview window is centered vertically and horizontally.

TROUBLE? If you see only the worksheet name, click the Zoom button to view the entire page.

Adding Headers and Footers

Headers and footers can provide useful documentation on your printed worksheet, such as the name of the person who created the worksheet, the date it was printed, and its filename. The **header** is text printed in the top margin of every worksheet page. A **footer** is text printed in the bottom margin of every page. Headers and footers are not displayed in the worksheet window. To see them, you must preview or print the worksheet.

Excel uses formatting codes in headers and footers to represent the items you want to print. Formatting codes produce dates, times, and filenames that you might want a header or footer to include. Using formatting codes instead of typing the date, time, filename and so on provides flexibility. For example, if you use a formatting code for date, the current date appears on the printout whenever the worksheet is printed. You can type these codes, or you can click a formatting code button to insert the code. Figure 2-29 shows the formatting codes and the buttons for inserting them.

| Figure 2-29 | HEADER AND FOOTER FORMATTING BUTTONS | | |

BUTTON	BUTTON NAME	FORMATTING CODE	ACTION
A	Font	none	Sets font, text style, and font size
	Page number	&[Page]	Inserts page number
	Total pages	&[Pages]	Inserts total number of pages
	Date	&[Date]	Inserts current date
	Time	&[Time]	Inserts current time
	Filename	&[File]	Inserts filename
	Sheet name	&[Tab]	Inserts name of active worksheet

Sally asks you to add a custom header that includes the filename and today's date. She also wants you to add a custom footer that displays the preparer's name.

To add a header and a footer to your worksheet:

1. In the Print Preview window, click the **Setup** button to open the Page Setup dialog box, and then click the **Header/Footer** tab.

2. Click the **Custom Header** button to open the Header dialog box.

3. With the insertion point in the Left section box, click the **Filename** button 🖹. The code &(File) appears in the Left section box.

   TROUBLE? If you clicked the wrong code, double-click the code, press the Delete key, then repeat Steps 2 and 3.

4. Click the **Right section** box to move the insertion point to the Right section box.

5. Click the **Date** button 📅. The code &(Date) appears in the Right section box. See Figure 2-30.

| Figure 2-30 | INSERTING FORMATTING CODES INTO THE HEADER DIALOG BOX |

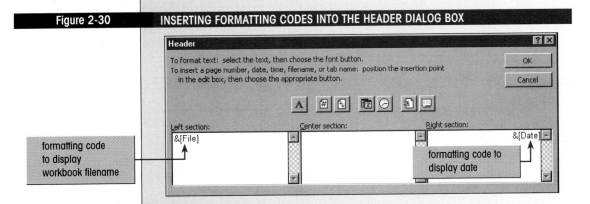

    formatting code to display workbook filename

    formatting code to display date

TROUBLE? If you clicked the wrong code, double-click the code, press the Delete key, and then repeat Step 5.

6. Click the **OK** button to complete the header and return to the Page Setup dialog box. Notice that the header shows the filename on the left and the date on the right.

7. Click the **Custom Footer** button to open the Footer dialog box.

8. Click the **Center section** box to move the insertion point to the Center section box.

9. Type **Prepared by (*enter your name here*)**.

10. Click the **OK** button to complete the footer and return to the Page Setup dialog box. Notice that the footer shows your name in the bottom, center of the page.

11. Click the **OK** button to return to the Print Preview window. The new header and footer appear in the Print Preview window.

12. Click the **Close** button to exit the Print Preview window and return to the worksheet.

You'll use the Print button on the Standard toolbar to print one copy of the worksheet with the current settings. First, save the worksheet before printing it.

To save your page setup settings with the worksheet and print the worksheet:

1. Click the **Save** button 🖫 on the Standard toolbar.

2. Click the **Print** button 🖨 on the Standard toolbar. See Figure 2-31.

TROUBLE? If you see a message that indicates that you have a printer problem, click the Cancel button to cancel printing. Check your printer to make sure it is turned on and is online; also make sure it has paper. Then go back and try Step 2 again. If you have no printer available, click the Cancel button.

Figure 2-31	PRINTED WORKSHEET

Motorcycle Specialties Incorporated
Sales Comparison 2001 with 2000

Region	Year 2001	Year 2000	% Change	% of 2001 Sales
North America	365000	314330	0.161200013	0.284971464
South America	354250	292120	0.212686567	0.276578469
Australia	251140	262000	-0.041450382	0.196075982
Europe	310440	279996	0.108730125	0.242374086
Total	1280830	1148446	0.11527229	

Average	320207.5	
Maximum	365000	
Minimum	251140	

Sally reviews the printed worksheet and is satisfied with its appearance. Now she asks for a second printout without the average, minimum, and maximum statistics.

Setting the Print Area

By default, Excel prints the entire worksheet. There are situations in which you are interested in printing a portion of the worksheet. To do this, you first select the area you want to print, and then use the Set Print Area command to define the print area.

To print a portion of the worksheet:

1. Select the range **A1:E9**.

2. Click **File**, point to Print Area, and then click **Set Print Area**.

3. Click the **Print Preview** button. Notice the average, minimum and maximum values are not included in the print preview window.

4. Click **Close** to return to the worksheet.

5. Click any cell outside the highlighted range. Notice the range A1: E9 is surrounded with a dashed line indicating the current print area for the worksheet.

If you want to print the entire worksheet once a print area has been set, you need to remove the current print area. Select File, point to Print Area, and click the Clear Print Area to remove the print area. Now the entire worksheet will print.

Documenting the Workbook

Documenting the workbook provides valuable information to those using the workbook. Documentation includes external documentation as well as notes and instructions within the workbook. This information could be as basic as who created the worksheet and the date it was created, or it could be more detailed, including formulas, summaries, and layout information.

Depending on the use of the workbook, the required amount of documentation varies. Sally's planning analysis sheet and sketch for the sales comparison worksheet are one form of external documentation. This information can be useful to someone who would need to modify the worksheet in any way because it states the goals, required input, output, and the calculations used.

One source of internal documentation would be a worksheet placed as the first worksheet in the workbook, such as the Documentation worksheet in Tutorial 1 to determine the best location for the new Inwood golf course. In more complex workbooks, this sheet may also include an index of all worksheets in the workbook, instructions on how to use the worksheets, where to enter data, how to save the workbook, and how to print reports. This documentation method is useful because the information is contained directly in the workbook and can easily be viewed upon opening the workbook, or printed if necessary. Another source of internal documentation is the **Property** dialog box. This dialog box enables you to electronically capture information such as the name of the workbook's creator, the creation date, the number of revisions, and other information related to the workbook.

If you prefer, you can include documentation on each sheet of the workbook. One way is to attach notes to cells by using the Comments command to explain complex formulas, list assumptions, and enter reminders.

The worksheet itself can be used as documentation. Once a worksheet is completed, it is a good practice to print and file a hardcopy of your work as documentation. This hardcopy file should include a printout of each worksheet displaying the values and another printout of the worksheet displaying the cell formulas.

Sally asks you to include a note in the worksheet that will remind her that the sales in Europe do not include an acquisition that was approved in December. You suggest inserting a cell comment.

Adding **Cell Comments**

Cell comments can help users remember assumptions, explain complex formulas, or place reminders related to the contents of a specific cell.

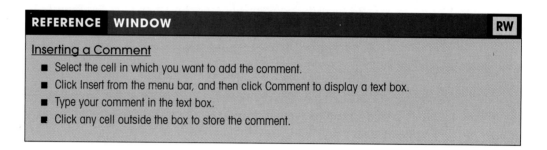

REFERENCE   WINDOW   **RW**

Inserting a Comment

- Select the cell in which you want to add the comment.
- Click Insert from the menu bar, and then click Comment to display a text box.
- Type your comment in the text box.
- Click any cell outside the box to store the comment.

Use the cell comment to insert the note for Sally.

To add a comment to a cell:

1. Click cell **B8**.

2. Click **Insert** and then click **Comment** to display a text box.

   TROUBLE? If the Comment item does not appear on the Insert menu, click [⊗] to view additional items on the Insert menu.

   Now enter your comment in the text box.

3. Type **Does not include sales from company acquired in December**. See Figure 2-32.

Figure 2-32	**INSERTING A CELL COMMENT**

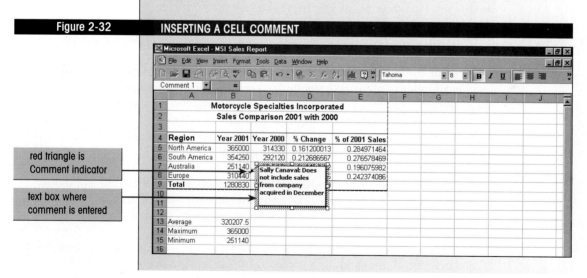

red triangle is Comment indicator

text box where comment is entered

4. Click any cell outside the text box. The comment disappears. Notice, the **Comment indicator**, a tiny red triangle, appears in the upper-right corner of the cell indicating the cell contains a comment.

Now view the comment.

TROUBLE? If the comment remains on the screen, click View, then click Comments.

5. Move the mouse pointer over cell **B8**. The Comment appears, preceded by the name of the user who made the comment.

6. Move the mouse pointer to another cell. The comment disappears.

7. Save the workbook.

Once a comment is inserted, you can edit or delete the comment by right-clicking the cell and selecting Edit Comment or Delete Comment from the shortcut menu.

Now Sally asks for a printout of the worksheet formulas for her file.

Displaying and Printing Worksheet Formulas

You can document the formulas you entered in a worksheet by displaying and printing them. When you display formulas, Excel shows the formulas you entered in each cell instead of showing the results of the calculations. You want a printout of the formulas in your worksheet for documentation.

To display worksheet formulas:

1. Click **Tools** on the menu bar, and then click **Options** to open the Options dialog box.

2. Click the **View** tab, and then click the **Formulas** check box in the Window options section to select it.

3. Click the **OK** button to return to the worksheet. The width of each column nearly doubles to accommodate the underlying formulas. See Figure 2-33.

| Figure 2-33 | DISPLAYING FORMULAS IN A WORKSHEET |

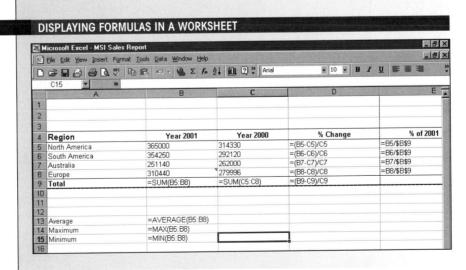

> You may find the keyboard shortcut, Ctrl + ` (` is found next to the 1 in the upper-left area of the keyboard) easier to use when displaying formulas. Press the shortcut key once to display formulas and again to display results.

Now print the worksheet displaying the formulas. Before printing the formulas, you need to change the appropriate settings in the Page Setup dialog box to show the gridlines and the row/column headings, center the worksheet on the page, and fit the printout on a single page.

To adjust the print setups to display formulas:

1. Click **File** on the menu bar, and then click **Page Setup** to open the Page Setup dialog box.

2. Click the **Sheet** tab to view the sheet options, and then click the **Row and Column Headings** check box in the Print section to print the row numbers and column letters along with the worksheet results.

3. Click the **Gridlines** check box to select that option.

4. Click the **Page** tab and then click the **Landscape** option button. This option prints the worksheet with the paper positioned so it is wider than it is tall.

5. Click the **Fit to** option button in the Scaling section of the Page tab. This option reduces the worksheet when you print it, so it fits on the specific number of pages in the Fit to check box. The default is 1.

6. Click the **Print Preview** button to open the Print Preview window.

7. Click the **Print** button. See Figure 2-34. Notice that your printout does not include the formulas for average, minimum and maximum because the print area is still set for the range A1:E9.

Figure 2-34	PRINTOUT OF WORKSHEET FORMULAS

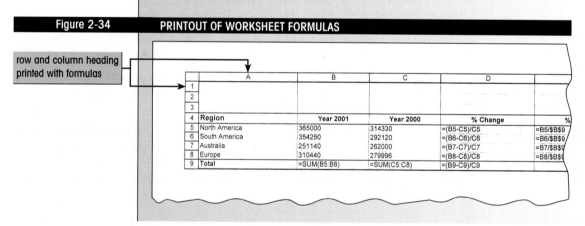

row and column heading printed with formulas

	A	B	C	D	
1					
2					
3					
4	Region	Year 2001	Year 2000	% Change	%
5	North America	365000	314330	=(B5-C5)/C5	=B5/$B$9
6	South America	354250	292120	=(B6-C6)/C6	=B6/$B$9
7	Australia	251140	262000	=(B7-C7)/C7	=B7/$B$9
8	Europe	310440	279996	=(B8-C8)/C8	=B8/$B$9
9	Total	=SUM(B5:B8)	=SUM(C5:C8)	=(B9-C9)/C9	

After printing the formulas, return the worksheet so it displays the worksheet values.

To display the worksheet values:

1. Press **Ctrl + `** to display the worksheet values.

2. Close the workbook without saving it, and then exit Excel.

Session 2.2 QUICK CHECK

1. What is meant by syntax?

2. In the function MAX(A1:A8), identify the function name. Identify the argument(s).

3. Describe how you use the pointing method to create a formula that includes the SUM function.

4. Describe how to insert a row or a column.

5. To reverse your most recent action, which button should you click?

   a.

   b.

   c.

6. To move a range of cells, you must _____ the range first.

7. _____ is a command that lets you change your worksheet's appearance by selecting a collection of predefined worksheet formats.

8. A _____ is text that is printed in the top margin of every worksheet page.

9. A _____ is a tiny red triangle in the upper-right corner of a cell that indicates the cell contains a _____.

10. To display formulas instead of values in your worksheet, what command should you choose?

11. If your worksheet has too many columns to fit on one printed page, you should try _____ orientation.

You have planned, built, formatted, and documented Sally's sales comparison worksheet. It is ready for her to present to the regional sales managers at their next meeting.

REVIEW ASSIGNMENTS

After Sally meets with the regional sales managers for MSI, she decides it would be a good idea to provide the managers with their own copy of the sales comparison worksheet, so they can update the report with next year's sales data and also modify it to use for their own sales tracking purposes. Before passing it on to them, she wants to provide more documentation and add some additional information that the managers thought would be useful to them. Complete the following for Sally:

1. Start Windows and Excel, if necessary. Insert your Data Disk into the appropriate disk drive. Make sure the Excel and Book1 windows are maximized.

2. Open the workbook **MSI 1** in the Review folder for Tutorial 2 on your Data Disk.

3. Save your workbook as **MSI Sales Report 2** in the Review folder for Tutorial 2 on your Data Disk.

4. Make Sheet2 the active sheet. Use Sheet2 to include information about the workbook. Insert the information in Figure 2-35 into Sheet2. Increase the width of column A as necessary.

Figure 2-35

CELL	TEXT ENTRY
A1	Motorcycle Specialties Incorporated
A3	Created by:
A4	Date Created:
A6	Purpose:
B3	enter your name
B4	enter today's date
B6	Sales report comparing sales by region 2001 with 2000

5. Change the name of the worksheet from **Sheet2** to **Documentation** and print the Documentation sheet.

Explore 6. Move the Documentation sheet so it is the first sheet in the workbook.

7. Make Sales Comparison the active sheet.

8. Insert a row between Australia and Europe. Add the following data (Africa, 125000, 100000) in columns A, B, and C. Copy the formulas for % Change and % of 2001 Sales into the row containing the data for Africa.

9. Open the Office Assistant and then enter the search phrase "Insert a column" to obtain instructions on inserting a new column into a worksheet. Insert a new column between columns C and D.

10. In cell D4, enter the heading "Change".

11. In cell D5, enter the formula to calculate the change in sales for North America from 2000 to 2001. (*Hint*: Check that the figure in cell D5 is 50670.)

12. Copy the formula in D5 to the other regions and total (D6 through D10) using the fill handle.

13. Calculate summary statistics for the year 2000. In cell C14 display the average sales, in cell C15 display the maximum, and in cell C16 display the minimum.

14. Save the workbook.

15. Print the sales comparison worksheet.

16. a. Insert the following comment into cell F4: "Divide 2001 sales in each region by total sales in 2001".
    b. Use the Office Assistant to learn how to print comments to a cell. List the steps.

17. a. Insert a new sheet into the workbook using the Worksheet command from the Insert menu. Activate the **Sales Comparison** sheet and select the range A1:E10. Copy the selected range to the Clipboard. Activate Sheet1 and paste the selected range to the corresponding cells in Sheet1. Apply a different AutoFormat to this range. Print Sheet1. *Note:* If the Office Clipboard toolbar appears, you can use the Office Assistant to learn "About collecting and pasting multiple items" in the Office Clipboard.
    b. Use the Delete Sheet command from the Edit menu to delete Sheet1.
    c. Save the workbook.

CASE PROBLEMS

Case 1. Annual Stockholders' Meeting at MJ Inc.   Jeanne Phelp, chief financial officer (CFO) of MJ Incorporated is responsible for preparing the annual financial reports and mailing them to stockholders before the annual stockholder's meeting. She has completed some of the work for the annual meeting and is now in the process of finishing a report comparing the changes in net income between the current year and last year. Now you can help her complete this report.

1. Use columns A through D to enter the title, labels, and constants from Figure 2-36 into a worksheet.

Figure 2-36   **MJ INCORPORATED INCOME STATEMENT**

	2001	2000	PERCENTAGE CHANGE
Net Sales	1818500	1750500	
Cost of Goods Sold	1005500	996000	
Gross Profit			
Selling and Administrative expenses	506000	479000	
Income from Operations			
Interest expense	18000	19000	
Income before taxes			
Income tax expense	86700	77000	
Net Income			
Outstanding shares	20000	20000	
Earnings Per Share			

2. Complete the income statement for 2001 and 2000 by entering the following formulas for each year:

   - Gross profit = Net sales – Cost of goods sold
   - Income from operations = Gross profit – Selling and administrative expenses
   - Income before taxes = Income from operations – Interest expense
   - Net income = Income before taxes – Income tax expense

3. Compute the percentage change between the two years for each item in the income statement.

4. Compute earnings per share (net income / outstanding shares).

5. In cell B4 add the cell comment "Unaudited results".

6. Select an AutoFormat to improve the appearance of your worksheet.

7. Prepare a Documentation sheet, and then place it as the first sheet in the workbook.

8. Save the workbook as **MJ Income** in the Cases folder for Tutorial 2 on your Data Disk. *Note:* The workbook should open so the user can see the contents of the Documentation sheet. (*Hint:* Make the Documentation sheet the active sheet before you save the workbook.)

9. Add your name and date in the custom footer, then print the worksheet, centered horizontally and vertically.

10. Print the Documentation sheet.

11. Save the worksheet, and then print the formulas for the worksheet. Include row and column headings in the output. Do not save the workbook after printing the formulas.

Case 2. Compiling Data on the U.S. Airline Industry   The editor of *Aviation Week and Space Technology* has asked you to research the current status of the U.S. airline industry. You collect information on the revenue-miles and passenger-miles for each major U.S. airline (Figure 2-37).

Figure 2-37	REVENUE-MILES AND PASSENGER MILES FOR MAJOR U.S. AIRLINES	
AIRLINE	**REVENUE-MILES (IN 1000S OF MILES)**	**PASSENGER-MILES (IN 1000S OF MILES)**
American	26000	2210000
Continental	9300	620500
Delta	21500	1860000
Northwest	20800	1900500
US Airways	9850	1540000
United	35175	3675000

You want to calculate the following summary information to use in the article:

■ total revenue-miles for the U.S. airline industry
■ total passenger-miles for the U.S. airline industry
■ each airline's share of the total revenue-miles
■ each airline's share of the total passenger-miles
■ average revenue-miles for U.S. airlines
■ average passenger-miles for U.S. airlines

In order to provide the editor with your researched information, complete these steps:

1. Open a new workbook and then enter the title, column and row labels, and data from Figure 2-37.

2. Enter the formulas to compute the total and average revenue-miles and passenger-miles. Use the SUM and AVERAGE functions where appropriate. Remember to include row labels to describe each statistic.

3. Add a column to display each airline's share of the total revenue-miles. Remember to include a column heading. You decide the appropriate location for this data.

4. Add a column to display each airline's share of the total passenger-miles. Remember to include a column heading. You decide the appropriate location for this data.

5. In a cell two rows after the row of data you entered, insert a line reading : "Compiled by: *XXXX*", where *XXXX* is your name.

6. Rename the worksheet tab Mileage Data.

7. Save the worksheet as **Airline** in the Cases folder for Tutorial 2.

8. Print the worksheet. Make sure you center the report, do not include gridlines, and place the date in the upper-right corner of the header.

9. Select an AutoFormat to improve the appearance of your output.

10. Save your workbook.

11. Print the worksheet, centered on the page.

12. Save the worksheet and then print the formulas for the worksheet. Include row and column headings in the printout.

Case 3. *Fresh Air Sales Incentive Program*   Carl Stambaugh is assistant sales manager at Fresh Air Inc., a manufacturer of outdoors and expedition clothing. Fresh Air sales representatives contact retail chains and individual retail outlets to sell the Fresh Air line.

This year, to stimulate sales, Carl has decided to run a sales incentive program for sales representatives. Each sales representative has been assigned a sales goal 12% higher than his or her total sales last year. All sales representatives who reach this new goal will be awarded an all-expenses-paid trip for two to Cozumel, Mexico.

Carl wants to track the results of the sales incentive program with an Excel worksheet. He has asked you to complete the worksheet by adding the formulas to compute:

■ actual sales in 2001 for each sales representative

■ sales goal in 2001 for each sales representative

■ percentage of goal reached for each sales representative

He also wants a printout before he presents the worksheet at the next sales meeting. Complete these steps:

1. Open the workbook **Fresh** in the Cases folder for Tutorial 2 on your Data Disk. Maximize the worksheet window and then save the workbook as **Fresh Air Sales Incentives** in the Cases folder for Tutorial 2.

2. Complete the worksheet by adding the following formulas:
   a. 2001 actual for each employee = Sum of actual sales for each quarter
   b. Goal 2001 for each employee = 2000 Sales X (1 + Goal % increase)
   c. % goal reached for each employee = 2001 actual / 2001 goal

   (*Hint:* Use the Copy command. Review relative versus absolute references.)

3. At the bottom of the worksheet (three rows after the last sales rep), add the average, maximum, and minimum statistics for columns C through I.

4. Make formatting changes using an Autoformat to improve the appearance of the worksheet. Begin the formatting in row 6.

5. In cell C4, insert the cell comment "entered sales goal values between 10 and 15 percent".

6. Save the workbook.

7. Print the worksheet. Make sure you center the worksheet horizontally, add an appropriate header, and place your name, course, and date in the footer. Print the worksheet so it fits on one page.

8. Add a Documentation sheet. Save the workbook and then print the Documentation worksheet.

9. Change the sales goal to 14 percent. Print the worksheet.

Explore

10. As you scroll down the worksheet, the column headings no longer appear on the screen, making it difficult to know what each column represents. Use the Office Assistant to look up "Keep column labels visible." Implement this feature in your worksheet. Save the workbook. Explain the steps you take to keep the columns visible.

11. Print the formulas in columns H, I, and J. The printout should include row and column headings. Use the Set Print Area command so you only print the formulas in these three columns. Do not save the workbook after you complete this step.

Case 4. Stock Portfolio for Juan Cortez   Your close friend, Juan Cortez, works as an accountant at a local manufacturing company. While in college, with a double major in accounting and finance, Juan dabbled in the stock market and expressed an interest in becoming a financial planner and running his own firm. To that end, he has continued his professional studies in the evenings with the aim of becoming a certified financial planner. He has already begun to provide financial planning services to a few clients. Because of his hectic schedule as a full-time accountant, part-time student, and part-time financial planner, Juan finds it difficult to keep up with the data-processing needs for his clients. You have offered to assist him.

Juan asks you to set up a worksheet to keep track of a stock portfolio for one of his clients.

Open a new workbook and do the following:

1. Figure 2-38 shows the data you will enter into the workbook. For each stock, you will enter the name, number of shares purchased, and purchase price. Periodically, you will also enter the current price of each stock so Juan can review the changes with his clients.

Figure 2-38

STOCK	NO. OF SHARES	PURCHASE PRICE	COST	CURRENT PRICE	CURRENT VALUE	GAINS/LOSSES
Excite	100	67.30		55.50		
Yahoo	250	121		90.625		
Netscape	50	24.50		26.375		
Microsoft	100	89.875		105.375		
Intel	50	69		83		

2. In addition to entering the data, you need to make the following calculations:

   a. Cost = No. of shares * Purchase price
   b. Current value = No. of shares * Current price
   c. Gains/Losses = Current value minus cost
   d. Totals for cost, Current value, and Gains/Losses

Enter the formulas to calculate the cost, current value, gains/losses, and totals.

3. In the cell where you enter the label for Current Price, insert the cell comment "As of 9/1/2001".

4. Apply an AutoFormat that improves the appearance of the worksheet.

5. Add a Documentation sheet to the workbook.

6. Save the workbook as **Portfolio** in the Cases folder for Tutorial 2.

7. Print the worksheet. Make sure you center the worksheet horizontally and add an appropriate header and footer.

8. Print the Documentation sheet.

9. Clear the prices in the Current Price column of the worksheet.

10. Enter the following prices:

Excite	57.250
Yahoo	86.625
Netscape	30.75
Microsoft	102.375
Intel	84.375

Print the worksheet.

11. Print the formulas for the worksheet. Make sure you include row and column headings in the printed output.

12. From the financial section of your newspaper, look up the current price of each stock (all these stocks are listed on the NASDAQ Stock Exchange). Enter these prices in the worksheet. Print the worksheet.

INTERNET ASSIGNMENTS

The purpose of the Internet Assignments is to challenge you to find information on the Internet that you can use to create effective documents. The actual assignments are updated and maintained on the Course Technology Web site. Log on to the Internet and use your Web browser and go to the Student Online Companion to accompany this text at **www.course.com/NewPerspectives/office2000**. Click the Excel link, and then click the link for Tutorial 2.

QUICK | CHECK ANSWERS

Session 2.1

1. Determine the purpose of the worksheet, enter the data and formulas, test the worksheet; correct errors, improve the appearance, document the worksheet, save and print.

2. Select the cell where you want the sum to appear. Click the AutoSum button. Excel suggests a formula that includes the SUM function. To accept the formula press the Enter key.

3. =B4-C4

4. fill handle

5. Cell references; if you were to copy the formula to other cells, these cells are relative references.

6. absolute reference

7. Windows clipboard

8. Double-click the sheet tab, then type the new name, and then press the Enter key or click any cell in the worksheet to accept the entry.

9. Order of precedence is a set of predefined rules that Excel uses to unambiguously calculate a formula by determining which part of the formula to calculate first, which part second, and so on.

Session 2.2

1. Syntax specifies the set of rules that determine the order and punctuation of formulas and functions in Excel.

2. MAX is the function name; A1:A8 is the argument.

3. Assuming you are entering a formula with a function, first select the cell where you want to place a formula, type =, the function name and a left parenthesis, and then click and drag over the range of cells to be used in the formula. Press the Enter key.

4. Click any cell in the row above which you want to insert a row. Click Insert, then click Rows.

5. c

6. select

7. AutoFormat

8. header

9. comment indicator, comment

10. Click Tools, click Options, and then in the View tab, click the Formula check box.

11. landscape

OBJECTIVES

·In this tutorial you will:

- Format data using the Number, Currency, Accounting, and Percentage formats

- Align cell contents

- Center text across columns

- Change fonts, font style, and font size

- Clear formatting from cells

- Delete cells from a worksheet

- Use borders and color for emphasis

- Add text box and graphics to a worksheet using the Drawing toolbar

- Remove gridlines from the worksheet

- Print in landscape orientation

- Hide and unhide rows and columns

DEVELOPING A PROFESSIONAL-LOOKING WORKSHEET

Producing a Projected Sales Report for the Pronto Salsa Company

Pronto Salsa Company

Anne Castelar owns the Pronto Salsa Company, a successful business located in the heart of Tex-Mex country. She is working on a plan to add a new product, de Chili Guero Four-Alarm Red Hot, to Pronto's gourmet salsa line.

Anne wants to take out a bank loan to purchase additional food-processing equipment to handle the requirements of the increased salsa production. She has an appointment with her loan officer at 2:00 p.m. today. To prepare for the meeting, Anne creates a worksheet to show the projected sales of the new salsa and the expected effect on profits. Although the numbers and formulas are in place on the worksheet, Anne has no time to format the worksheet to create the greatest impact. She planned to do that now, but an unexpected problem with today's produce shipment requires her to leave the office for a few hours. Anne asks you to complete the worksheet. She shows you a printout of the unformatted worksheet and explains that she wants the finished worksheet to look very professional—like those you see in business magazines. She also asks you to make sure that the worksheet emphasizes the profits expected from sales of the new salsa.

SESSION 3.1

In this session you will learn how to make your worksheets easier to understand through various formatting techniques. You will format values using Currency, Number, and Percentage formats. You will also change font styles and font sizes, and change the alignment of data within cells and across columns. As you perform all these tasks, you'll find the Format Painter button an extremely useful tool.

Opening the Workbook

After Anne leaves, you develop the worksheet plan in Figure 3-1 and the worksheet format plan in Figure 3-2.

Figure 3-1	PLANNING ANALYSIS WORKSHEET

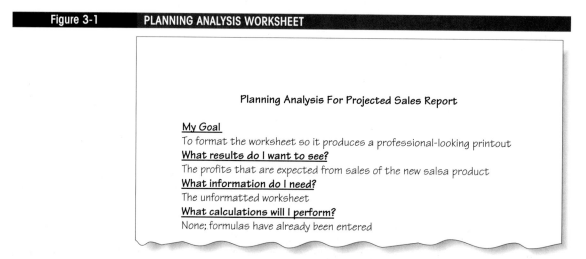

Planning Analysis For Projected Sales Report

My Goal
To format the worksheet so it produces a professional-looking printout
What results do I want to see?
The profits that are expected from sales of the new salsa product
What information do I need?
The unformatted worksheet
What calculations will I perform?
None; formulas have already been entered

Figure 3-2	FORMAT PLAN

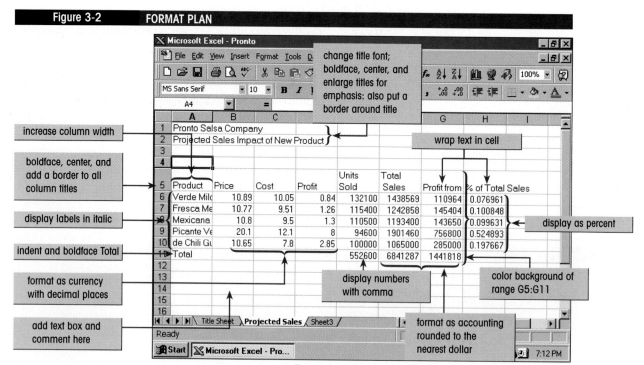

Anne has already entered all the formulas, numbers, and labels. Your main task is to format this information so it is easy to read and understand, and appears professional. This can be accomplished on two levels—by formatting the detailed data in the worksheet and by enhancing the appearance of the worksheet as a whole.

On the data level, you decide that the numbers should be formatted according to their use. For example, the product prices need to appear as dollar values, the column and row labels need to fit within their cells, and the labels need to stand out more. To enhance the worksheet as a whole, you need to structure it so that related information is visually grouped together using lines and borders. Anne also wants certain areas of the worksheet containing key information to stand out, color may be a useful tool for this.

With all that needs to be done before Anne's 2:00 p.m. meeting, you decide that the best place to begin is with formatting the data within the worksheet. Once that is done, you will work to improve the worksheet's overall organization and appearance.

Now that the planning is done, you are ready to start Excel and open the workbook of unformatted data that Anne created.

To start Excel and organize your desktop:

1. Start Excel as usual.

2. Make sure your Data Disk is in the appropriate disk drive.

3. Make sure the Microsoft Excel and Book1 windows are maximized.

Now you need to open Anne's file and begin formatting the worksheet. Anne stored the workbook as Pronto, but before you begin to change the workbook, save it using the filename Pronto Salsa Company. This way, the original workbook, Pronto, remains unchanged in case you want to work through this tutorial again.

To open the Pronto workbook and save the workbook as Pronto Salsa Company:

1. Click the **Open** button 📂 on the Standard toolbar to open the Open dialog box.

2. Open the Pronto workbook in the Tutorial folder for Tutorial 3 on your Data Disk.

3. Click **File** on the menu bar, and then click **Save As** to open the Save As dialog box.

4. In the File name text box, change the filename to **Pronto Salsa Company**.

5. Click the **Save** button 🖫 to save the workbook under the new filename. The new filename, Pronto Salsa Company, appears in the title bar.

   TROUBLE? If you see the message "Replace existing file?", click the Yes button to replace the old version of Pronto Salsa Company with your new version.

6. Click the **Projected Sales** sheet tab. See Figure 3-3.

| Figure 3-3 | PRONTO SALSA COMPANY WORKSHEET |

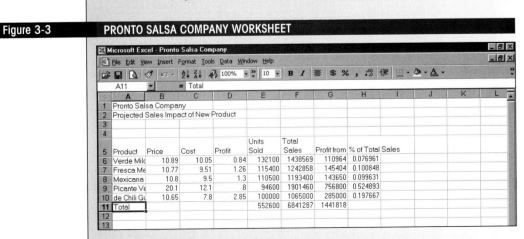

Studying the worksheet, you notice that the numbers are difficult to read. You decide to improve the appearance of the numbers in worksheet cells first.

Formatting Worksheet Data

Formatting is the process of changing the appearance of the data in worksheet cells. Formatting can make your worksheets easier to understand, and draw attention to important points.

In the previous tutorial you used AutoFormat to improve the appearance of your worksheet. AutoFormat applies a predefined format to a selected range in a worksheet. AutoFormat is easy to use, but its predefined format might not suit every application. If you decide to customize a worksheet's format, you can use the extensive Excel formatting options. When you select your own formats, you can format an individual cell or a range of cells.

Formatting changes only the appearance of the worksheet; it does not change the text or numbers stored in the cells. For example, if you format the number .123653 using a Percentage format that displays only one decimal place, the number appears in the worksheet as 12.4%; however, the original number, .123653, remains stored in the cell. When you enter data into cells, Excel applies an automatic format, referred to as the General format. The **General format** aligns numbers at the right side of the cell, uses a minus sign for negative values, and displays numbers without trailing zeros to the right of the decimal point. You can change the General format by using AutoFormat, the Format menu, the Shortcut menu, or toolbar buttons.

There are many ways to access the Excel formatting options. The Format menu provides access to all formatting commands.

The Shortcut menu provides quick access to the Format dialog box. To display the Shortcut menu, make sure the pointer is positioned within the range you have selected to format, and then click the right mouse button.

The Formatting toolbar contains formatting buttons, including the style and alignment buttons, and the Font Style and Font Size boxes, as shown in Figure 3-4.

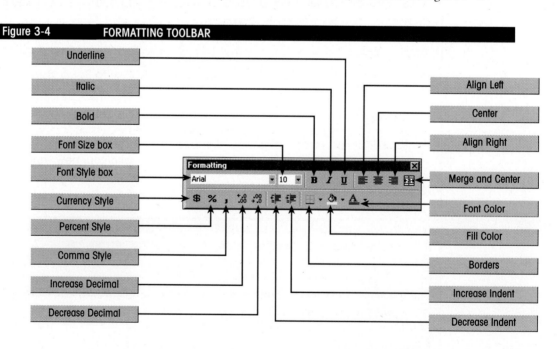

Figure 3-4   FORMATTING TOOLBAR

Most experienced Excel users develop a preference for which menu or buttons they use to access the Excel formatting options; however, most beginners find it easy to remember that all formatting options are available from the Format menu.

Looking at Anne's worksheet, you decide to change the appearance of the numbers first.

Changing the Appearance of Numbers

When the data in the worksheet appears as numbers, you want each number to appear in a style appropriate for what it is representing. The Excel default General format is often not the most appropriate style. For example, dollar values may require the dollar symbol ($) and thousand separators, and these can be applied to numerical data simply by changing the data's format. You can also use formatting to standardize the number of decimal places appearing in a cell. Excel has a variety of predefined number formats. Figure 3-5 describes some of the most commonly used formats.

Figure 3-5	COMMONLY USED NUMBER FORMATS
CATEGORY	**DISPLAY OPTION**
General	Excel default Number format; displays numbers without dollar signs, commas, or trailing decimal places
Number	Sets decimal places, negative number display, and comma separator
Currency	Sets decimal places and negative number display, and inserts dollar signs and comma separators
Accounting	Specialized monetary value format used to align dollar signs, decimal places, and comma separators
Date	Sets date or date and time display
Percentage	Inserts percent sign to the right of a number with a set number of decimal places

REFERENCE WINDOW **RW**

Formatting Numbers
- Select the cells in which you want the new format applied.
- Click Format, click Cells, and then click the Numbers tab in the Format Cells dialog box.
- Select a format category from the Category list box.
- Select the desired options for the selected format.
- Click the OK button.

To change the number formatting, you select the cell or range of cells to be reformatted, and then use the Format Cells command or the Formatting toolbar buttons to apply a different format.

Currency and Accounting Formats

In reviewing Anne's unformatted worksheet, you recognize that there are several columns of data that represent currency. You decide to apply the Currency format to the Price, Cost, and Profit columns.

You have several options when formatting values as currency. You need to decide the number of decimal places you want visible; whether or not you want to see the dollar sign; and how you want negative numbers to look. Keep in mind that if you want the currency symbols and decimal places to line up within a column, you should choose the Accounting format rather than the Currency format.

In the Pronto Salsa Company worksheet, you want to apply the Currency format to the values in columns B, C, and D. The numbers will be formatted to include a dollar sign with two decimal places. You also decide to put parentheses around negative numbers in the worksheet.

To format columns B, C, and D using the Currency format:

1. Select the range **B6:D10**.

2. Click **Format** on the menu bar, and then click **Cells** to open the Format Cells dialog box.

3. If necessary, click the **Number** tab. See Figure 3-6.

| Figure 3-6 | NUMBER TAB OF FORMAT CELLS DIALOG BOX |

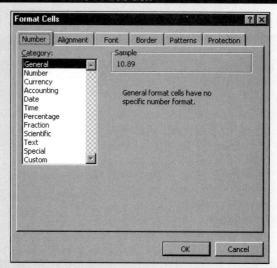

4. Click **Currency** in the Category list box. The Number tab changes to display the Currency formatting options, as shown in Figure 3-7. Notice that a sample of the selected format appears near the top of the dialog box. As you make further selections, the sample automatically changes to reflect your choices.

| Figure 3-7 | SELECTING A CURRENCY FORMAT |

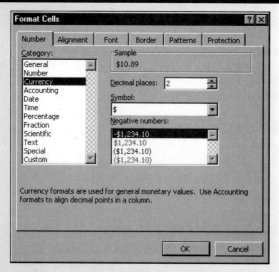

Notice that 2 decimal places is the default setting. A dollar sign ($) appears in the Symbol list box, indicating that the dollar sign will appear. If you are using a different currency, click the down arrow in the Symbol list box to select the currency symbol you want to use. Given the current options selected, you only need to select a format for negative numbers.

5. Click the third option **($1,234.10)** in the Negative numbers list box.

6. Click the **OK** button to format the selected range.

7. Click any cell to deselect the range and view the new formatting. See Figure 3-8.

| Figure 3-8 | **CURRENCY FORMATS IN COLUMNS B, C, AND D** |

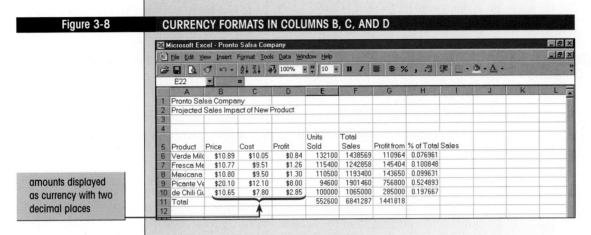

amounts displayed
as currency with two
decimal places

When your worksheet has large dollar amounts, you might want to use a Currency or Accounting format that does not display any decimal places. To do this you use the Decrease Decimal button on the Formatting toolbar, or change the decimal places setting in the Format Cells dialog box. Currency values appearing with no decimal places are rounded to the nearest dollar: $15,612.56 becomes $15,613; $16,507.49 becomes $16,507; and so on.

You decide to format the Total Sales column as using the Accounting style format rounded to the nearest dollar. The Accounting style format lines up the currency symbol and decimal points in a column.

To format cells F6 through F11 using the Accounting style format rounded to the nearest dollar:

1. Select the range **F6:F11**.

2. Click **Format** on the menu bar, and then click **Cells** to open the Format Cells dialog box.

3. If necessary, click the **Number** tab.

4. Click **Accounting** in the Category list box.

5. Click the **Decimal places** spin box down arrow twice to change the setting to 0 decimal places. Notice that the sample format changes to reflect the new settings.

6. Click the **OK** button to apply the format. Notice that Excel automatically increased the column width to accommodate the formatted numbers.

7. Click any cell to deselect the range.

After formatting the Total Sales figures in column F, you realize you should have used the same format for the numbers in column G. To save time, you simply copy the formatting from column F to column G.

The Format Painter Button

The Format Painter button on the Standard toolbar lets you copy formats quickly from one cell or range to another. You simply click a cell containing the formats you want to copy, click the Format Painter button, and then use the click-and-drag technique to select the range to which you want to apply the copied formats.

To copy the format from cell F6:

1. Click cell **F6** because it contains the format you want to copy.

2. Click the **Format Painter** button 🖌 on the Standard toolbar. As you move the pointer over the worksheet cells, notice that the pointer turns to ⬇🖌.

   TROUBLE? If you do not see the Format Painter button on the Standard toolbar, click More Buttons 🔽 to display the Format Painter button.

3. Position ⬇🖌 over cell G6, and then click and drag to select cells **G6:G11**. When you release the mouse button, you notice that cells G6:G11 contain number symbols (######) instead of values. This is because the formatting change has caused the data to exceed the width of the cell.

4. Click any cell to deselect the range and view the formatted Profit from Sales column. See Figure 3-9.

Figure 3-9 **WORKSHEET AFTER FORMAT PAINTER USED TO COPY FORMATS**

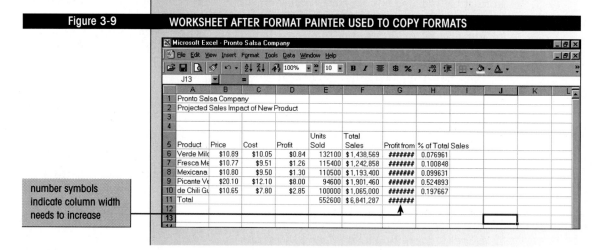

number symbols indicate column width needs to increase

As you review the changes on the screen, you notice that cells G6:G11 contain number symbols (######) instead of values. This is because the formatting change has caused the data to exceed the width of the cell.

Number Symbol (###) Replacement

If a number is too long to fit within a cell's boundaries, Excel displays a series of number symbols (###) in the cell. The number symbols indicate that the number of digits in the value exceeds the cell's width. The number or formula is still stored in the cell, but the current cell width is not large enough to display the value. To display the value, you just need to increase the column width. One way you can do this is to use the Shortcut menu.

To replace the number symbols by increasing the column width:

1. Position the mouse pointer over the column heading for column G, and then right-click to display the Shortcut menu.

2. Click **Column Width** to open the Column Width dialog box.

3. Type **11** in the Column Width box.

4. Click the **OK** button to view the total sales.

5. Click any cell to view the formatted data. See Figure 3-10.

Figure 3-10	WORKSHEET AFTER COLUMN WIDTH INCREASED TO DISPLAY FORMATTED NUMBERS

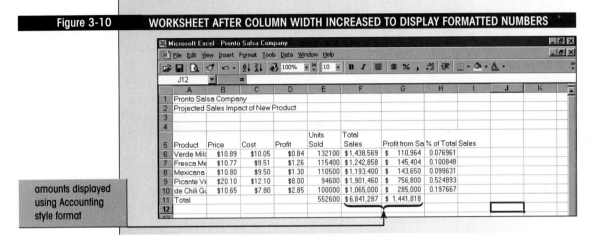

amounts displayed using Accounting style format

Now the cells containing price, cost, profit, total sales, and profit from sales are formatted using the currency and accounting styles. Next you want to apply formats to the numbers in columns E and H so they are easier to read.

Number Formats

Like Currency formats, the Excel Number formats offer many options. You can select Number formats to specify

■ the number of decimal places that are visible

■ whether to display a comma to delimit thousands, millions, and billions

■ whether to display negative numbers with a minus sign, parentheses, or red numerals

To access all Excel Number formats, you can use the Number tab in the Format Cells dialog box. You can also use the Comma Style button, the Increase Decimal button, and the Decrease Decimal button on the Formatting toolbar to select some Number formats.

Looking at your planning sheet and sketch, you can see that the numbers in column E need to be made easier to read by changing the format to include commas.

To format the contents in column E with a comma and no decimal places:

1. Select the range **E6:E11**.

2. Click the **Comma Style** button 🔲 on the Formatting toolbar to apply the Comma Style. The default for the Comma Style is to display numbers with two places to the right of the decimal. Click the **Decrease Decimal** button 🔲 on the Formatting toolbar to decrease the number of decimal places to zero.

TROUBLE? If you do not see the Comma Style button on the Standard toolbar, click More Buttons to display the Comma Style button.

3. Click any cell to deselect the range and view the formatted Units Sold column. See Figure 3-11.

Figure 3-11   **CELLS FORMATTED WITH NUMBER FORMAT**

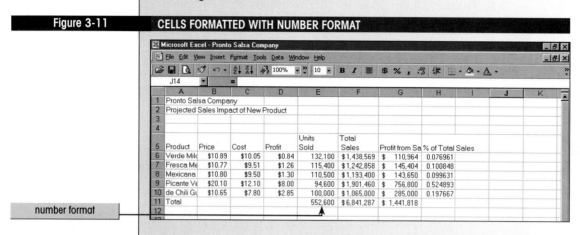

number format

Looking at the numbers in column H, you realize that they are difficult to interpret and decide that you do not need to display so many decimal places. These numbers would be much more readable as percentages; what are your options for displaying percentages?

Percentage Format

When formatting values as percentages, you need to select how many decimal places you want visible. The Percentage format with no decimal places displays the number 0.18037 as 18%. The Percentage format with two decimal places displays the same number as 18.04%. If you want to use the Percentage format with two decimal places, you select this option using the Number tab in the Format Cells dialog box. You can also use the Percent Style button on the Formatting toolbar, and then click the Increase Decimal button twice to add two decimal places.

Your format plan (see Figure 3-2) specifies a Percentage format with no decimal places for the values in column H. You could use the Number tab to choose this format, but it's faster to use the Percent Style button on the Formatting toolbar.

To format the values in column H as percentages with no decimal places:

1. Select the range **H6:H10**.

2. Click the **Percent Style** button % on the Formatting toolbar.

3. Click any cell to deselect the range and view the Percent Style. See Figure 3-12.

Figure 3-12   **PERCENTAGE OF TOTAL SALES FORMATTED WITH PERCENT STYLE**

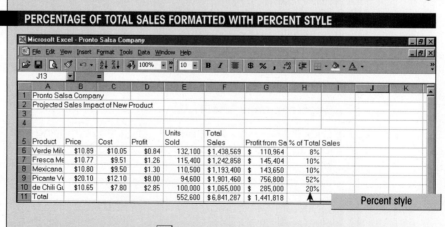

Percent style

4. Click the **Save** button 💾 on the Standard toolbar to save your work.

You review the worksheet. You have now formatted all the numbers in the worksheet appropriately. The next step in formatting Anne's worksheet is to improve the alignment of the data in the cells.

Aligning Cell Contents

The **alignment** of data in a cell is the position of the data relative to the right and left edges of the cell. Cell contents can be aligned on the left or right side of the cell, or centered in the cell. When you enter numbers and formulas, Excel automatically aligns them on the cell's right side. Excel automatically aligns text entries on the cell's left side. The default Excel alignment does not always create the most readable worksheet. As a general rule, you should center column titles, format columns of numbers so that the decimal places are in line, and leave columns of text aligned on the left. You can change the alignment of cell data using the four alignment tools on the Formatting toolbar, or you can access additional alignment options by selecting the Alignment tab in the Format Cells dialog box.

To center the column titles within a cell:

1. Select the range **A5:H5**.

2. Click the **Center** button on the Formatting toolbar to center the cell contents.

3. Click any cell to deselect the range and view the centered titles. See Figure 3-13.

| Figure 3-13 | WORKSHEET WITH CENTERED COLUMN TITLES |

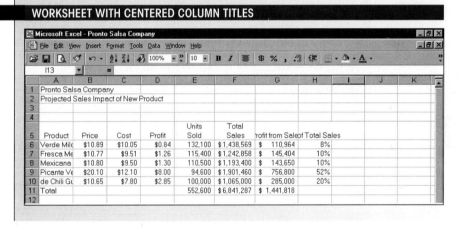

Notice that the column titles in columns G and H are not fully visible. Although you could widen the column widths of these two columns to display the entire text, the Excel Wrap Text option enables you to display a label within a cell's existing width.

Wrapping Text in a Cell

As you know, if you enter a label that's too wide for the active cell, Excel extends the label past the cell border and into the adjacent cells—provided those cells are empty. If you select the Wrap Text option, Excel will display your label entirely within the active cell. To accommodate the label, the height of the row in which the cell is located is increased, and the text is "wrapped" onto the additional lines.

Now wrap the column titles in columns G and H.

To wrap text within a cell:

1. Select the range **G5:H5**.

2. Click **Format** on the menu bar, and then click **Cells** to open the Format Cells dialog box.

3. Click the **Alignment** tab. See Figure 3-14.

| Figure 3-14 | ALIGNMENT TAB OF FORMAT CELLS DIALOG BOX |

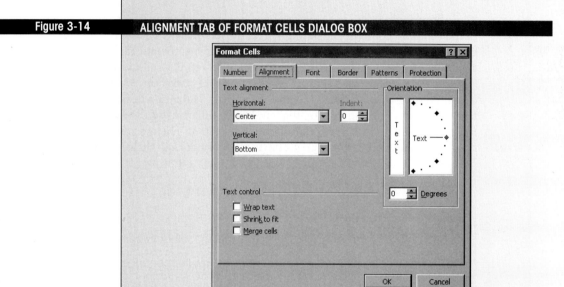

4. Click the **Wrap text** check box in the Text control area to select that option.

5. Click the **OK** button to apply the text wrapping.

6. Click any cell to deselect the range and view the entire text displayed in the cell. See Figure 3-15.

| Figure 3-15 | WRAPPING TEXT IN A CELL |

wrapped text

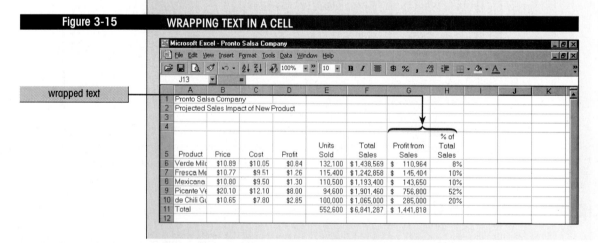

Now you are ready to center the main worksheet titles.

Centering Text Across Cells

Sometimes you might want to center the contents from one cell across more than one column. This is particularly useful for centering a title at the top of a worksheet. Now you use the Center Across Selection option in the Alignment tab from the Format Cells dialog box to center the worksheet titles in cells A1 and A2 across columns A through H.

To center the worksheet titles across columns A through H:

1. Select the range **A1:H2**.

2. Click **Format**, click **Cells**, and then, if necessary, click the **Alignment** tab in the Format Cells dialog box.

3. Click the arrow next to the **Horizontal** text alignment list box to display the horizontal text alignment options.

4. Click the **Center Across Selection** option to center the title lines across columns A through H.

5. Click the **OK** button.

6. Click any cell to deselect the range. See Figure 3-16.

| Figure 3-16 | WORKSHEET WITH TITLES CENTERED ACROSS SEVERAL COLUMNS |

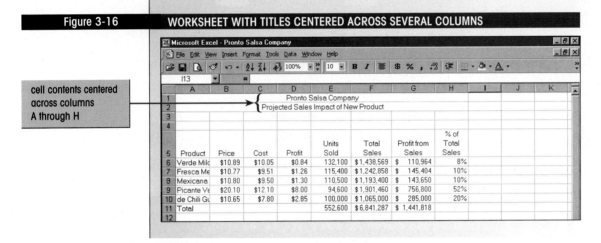

cell contents centered across columns A through H

Indenting Text Within a Cell

When you type text in a cell it is left-aligned. You can indent text from the left edge by using the Increase Indent button on the Formatting toolbar or the Index spinner button in the Alignment tab of the Format Cells dialog box. You decide to indent the word "Total" to provide a visual cue of the change from detail to summary information.

To indent text within a cell:

1. Click cell **A11** to make it the active cell.

2. Click the **Increase Indent** button ▥ on the Formatting toolbar to indent the word "Total" within the cell.

3. Click the **Save** button 🖫 on the Standard toolbar to save the worksheet.

You check your plan and confirm that you selected formats for all worksheet cells containing data and that the data within the cells is aligned properly. The formatting of the worksheet contents is almost complete. Your next task is to improve the appearance of the labels by changing the font style of the title and the column headings.

You decide to use the Bold button on the Formatting toolbar to change some titles in the worksheet to boldface.

Changing **the Font, Font Style, and Font Size**

A font is a set of letters, numbers, punctuation marks, and symbols with a specific size and design. Figure 3-17 shows some examples. A font can have one or more of the following font styles: regular, italic, bold, and bold italic.

Figure 3-17	SELECTED FONTS			
FONT	**REGULAR STYLE**	**ITALIC STYLE**	**BOLD STYLE**	**BOLD ITALIC STYLE**
Times	AaBbCc	*AaBbCc*	**AaBbCc**	***AaBbCc***
Courier	AaBbCc	*AaBbCc*	**AaBbCc**	***AaBbCc***
Garamond	AaBbCc	*AaBbCc*	**AaBbCc**	***AaBbCc***
Helvetica Condensed	AaBbCc	*AaBbCc*	**AaBbCc**	***AaBbCc***

Most fonts are available in many sizes, and you can also select font effects, such as strikeout, underline, and color. The Formatting toolbar provides tools for changing font style by applying boldface, italics, underline, and increasing or decreasing font size. To access and preview other font effects, you can open the Format Cells dialog box from the Format menu.

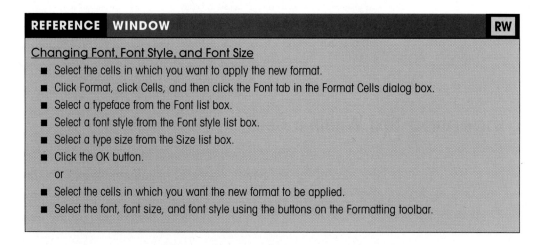

REFERENCE WINDOW   **RW**

Changing Font, Font Style, and Font Size
- Select the cells in which you want to apply the new format.
- Click Format, click Cells, and then click the Font tab in the Format Cells dialog box.
- Select a typeface from the Font list box.
- Select a font style from the Font style list box.
- Select a type size from the Size list box.
- Click the OK button.

   or
- Select the cells in which you want the new format to be applied.
- Select the font, font size, and font style using the buttons on the Formatting toolbar.

You begin by formatting the word "Total" in cell A11 in boldface letters.

To apply the boldface font style:

1. If necessary, click cell **A11**.

2. Click the **Bold** button **B** on the Formatting toolbar to set the font style to bold-face. Notice that when a style like bold is applied to a cell's content, the toolbar button appears depressed to indicate that the style is applied to the active cell.

You also want to display the column titles in boldface. To do this, first select the range you want to format, and then click the Bold button to apply the format.

To display the column titles in boldface:

1. Select the range **A5:H5**.

2. Click the **Bold** button **B** on the Formatting toolbar to apply the boldface font style.

3. Click any cell to deselect the range.

Next you want to change the font and size of the worksheet titles for emphasis. You use the Font dialog box (instead of the toolbar) so you can preview your changes. Remember, although the worksheet titles appear to be in columns A through F, they are just spilling over from column A. To format the titles, you need to select only cells A1 and A2—the cells where the titles were originally entered.

To change the font and font size of the worksheet titles:

1. Select the range **A1:A2**. Although the title is centered within the range A1:H2, the values are stored in cells A1 and A2.

2. Click **Format** on the menu bar, and then click **Cells** to open the Format Cells dialog box.

3. Click the **Font** tab. See Figure 3-18.

Figure 3-18	FONT TAB IN FORMAT CELLS DIALOG BOX

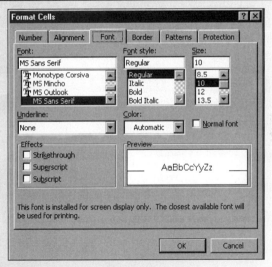

4. Use the Font box scroll bar to find the Times New Roman font. Click the **Times New Roman** font to select it.

5. Click **Bold** in the Font style list box.

6. Click **14** in the Size list box. A sample of the font appears in the Preview box.

7. Click the **OK** button to apply the new font, font style, and font size to the worksheet titles.

8. Click any cell to deselect the titles. See Figure 3-19.

Figure 3-19   **TITLES AFTER NEW FONT, FONT STYLE, AND FONT SIZE APPLIED**

reformatted title

text indented

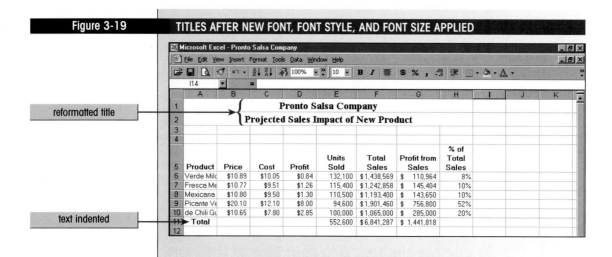

9. Click the **Save** button 🖫 on the Standard toolbar to save the worksheet.

Next you decide to display the products names in italics.

To italicize the row labels:

1. Select the range **A6:A10**.

2. Click the **Italic** button 🖊 on the Formatting toolbar to apply the italic font style.

3. Click any cell to deselect the range and view the formatting you have done so far. See Figure 3-20.

Figure 3-20   **BOLD AND ITALIC FORMATS APPLIED**

italic

bold

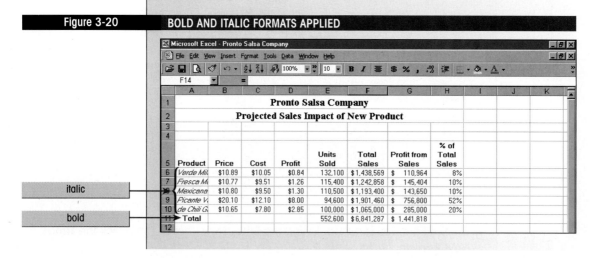

You hope Anne will approve of the Times New Roman font—it looks like the font on the Pronto salsa jar labels and would like to use it to create a style that can be applied to other worksheets.

Using **Styles**

A **style** is a saved collection of formatting, such as font, font size, pattern, and alignment that you combine, name and save as a group. A style can include from one to six attributes—Number, font, Alignment, Border, Pattern, and Protection. Once you have saved a style, you can apply it to a cell or range to achieve consistency in formatting. Excel has six predefined styles—Comma, Comma[0], Currency, currency[0], Normal, and Percent. By default, every cell in a worksheet is automatically formatted with the Normal style, which you use whenever you start typing in a new worksheet.

You can create a style in two ways: by using an example of the cell that has the formats you want associated with the style; or manually, by choosing formats from the Style dialog box and selecting the format you want associated with the style.

Although you won't create a style in this tutorial, you can follow the steps in the reference window if you want to create a style.

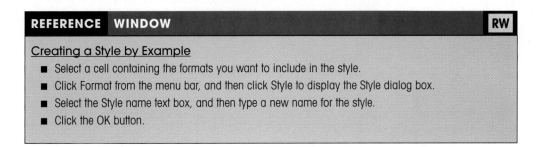

REFERENCE   WINDOW   **RW**

Creating a Style by Example
- Select a cell containing the formats you want to include in the style.
- Click Format from the menu bar, and then click Style to display the Style dialog box.
- Select the Style name text box, and then type a new name for the style.
- Click the OK button.

Clearing **Formats from Cells**

Anne reviews the worksheet and decides the italics format applied to the product names is not necessary. She asks you to remove the formatting from cells A6:A10. Although you could use Undo to remove the last step, you'll use the Edit, Clear command which erases formatting while leaving the cell's content intact. This command can be issued at any time to clear formatting from a cell.

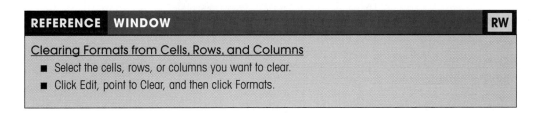

REFERENCE   WINDOW   **RW**

Clearing Formats from Cells, Rows, and Columns
- Select the cells, rows, or columns you want to clear.
- Click Edit, point to Clear, and then click Formats.

To clear the formatting of a cell:

1. Select cells A6:A10, the cells whose format you want to clear.

2. Click **Edit**, point to **Clear** and then click **Formats** to return the cell to its default (General) format. Notice the contents of the cells have not been erased.

3. Click any cell to deselect and view the product names in Regular style.

Deleting Cells from a Worksheet

Anne again reviews the worksheet and decides to remove the Cost data, range C5:C11, from the worksheet. You will use the Delete command from the Edit menu to remove these cells from the worksheet. When you delete one or more cells from a worksheet, you remove the space occupied by these cells and must specify if you want the cells beneath the deleted cells to shift up or the cells to the right of the deleted cells to shift to the left.

REFERENCE WINDOW **RW**

Deleting Cells, Rows, or Columns

- Select the cells, rows, or columns you want to delete.
- Click Edit, then click Delete to open the Delete dialog box.
- Select the direction in which you want the remaining cells to move:

  Select Shift cells left to move cells to the right of deleted cells to the left.

  Select Shift cells up to move cells below the deleted cell up to fill space previously occupied by deleted cells.

  If you want to delete the entire row or column:

  Select Entire Row to delete each row containing a selected cell.

  Select Entire column to delete each column containing a selected cell.

- Click OK.

To delete cells from the worksheet

1. Select the range **C5:C11**, the cells to be deleted from the worksheet.

2. Click **Edit**, click **Delete** to open the Delete dialog box .See Figure 3-21.

Figure 3-21 **DELETE DIALOG BOX**

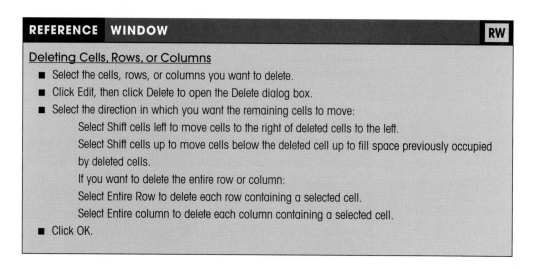

3. If necessary, click the **Shift cells left** option button.

4. Click OK. Notice all the cells from D5:H6 shift left one column.

5. Click any cell to observe that the Cost data no longer appears in the worksheet. See Figure 3-22. Save the worksheet.

Figure 3-22	WORKSHEET AFTER COST CELLS DELETED

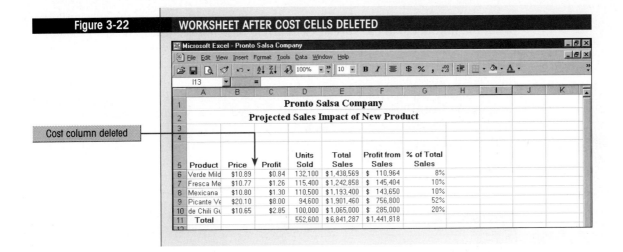

Cost column deleted

Session 3.1 QUICK CHECK

1. List three ways you can access formatting commands, options, and tools.

2. If the number .05765 is in a cell, what will Excel display if you:

   a. format the number using the Percentage format with one decimal place?

   b. format the number using the Currency format with 2 decimal places and the dollar sign?

3. The _____ copies formats quickly from one cell or range to another.

4. A series of ####### in a cell indicates _____.

5. Explain two ways to completely display a label that currently is not entirely displayed.

6. Explain why Excel might display 3,045.39 in a cell, but 3045.38672 in the formula bar.

7. What are the general rules you should follow for aligning column headings, numbers, and text labels?

8. List the options available on the Formatting toolbar for aligning data.

Now that you have finished formatting the data in the worksheet, you need to enhance the worksheet's appearance and readability as a whole. You will do this in Session 3.2 by applying borders, colors, and a text box.

SESSION 3.2

In this session you will learn how to enhance a worksheet's overall appearance by adding borders and color. You will use the Drawing toolbar to add a text box and graphic to the worksheet and use landscape orientation to print the worksheet.

Adding and Removing Borders

A worksheet is often divided into zones that visually group related information. Lines, called **borders**, can help to distinguish different zones of the worksheet and add visual interest.

You can create lines and borders using either the Borders button on the Formatting toolbar or the Border tab in the Format Cells dialog box. You can place a border around a single cell or a group of cells using the Outline option. To create a horizontal line, you place a border at the top or bottom of a cell. To create a vertical line, you place a border on the right or left side of a cell.

The Border tab lets you choose from numerous border styles, including different line thicknesses, double lines, dashed lines, and colored lines. With the Borders button, your choice of border styles is more limited.

To remove a border from a cell or group of cells, you can use the Border tab in the Format Cells dialog box. To remove all borders from a selected range of cells, select the None button in the Presets area.

REFERENCE WINDOW   **RW**

Adding a Border
- Select the cell to which you want to add the border.
- Click Format, click Cells, and then click the Border tab.
- Click the line style you want to apply.
- Click the appropriate button to indicate the border placement you want.
- Click the OK button.

    or

- Select the cell to which you want to add the border.
- Click the Borders button list arrow on the Formatting toolbar, and then click the type of border you want.

You decide that a thick line under all column titles will separate them from the data in the columns. To do this, you use the Borders button on the Formatting toolbar.

To underline column titles:

1. If you took a break after the last session, make sure Excel is running and the Projected Sales worksheet of the Pronto Salsa Company workbook is open.

2. Select the range **A5:G5**.

3. Click the **Borders** button ⊞ list arrow on the Formatting toolbar. The Borders palette appears. See Figure 3-23.

Figure 3-23   BORDERS PALETTE

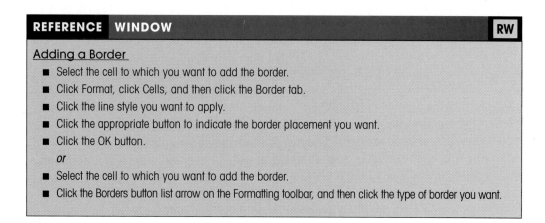
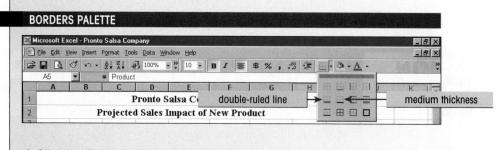

4. Click the **Thick Bottom Border** button (second button in the second row).

5. Click any cell to deselect the column titles and view the border.

You also want a line to separate the data from the totals in row 11, and a double-ruled line below the totals for added emphasis. This time you use the Border tab in the Format Cells dialog box to apply borders to cells.

To add a line separating the data and the totals and a double-ruled line below the totals:

1. Select the range **A11:G11**.

2. Click **Format** on the menu bar, click **Cells**, and then click the **Border** tab in the Format Cells dialog box. See Figure 3-24

Figure 3-24	BORDER TAB IN FORMAT CELLS DIALOG BOX

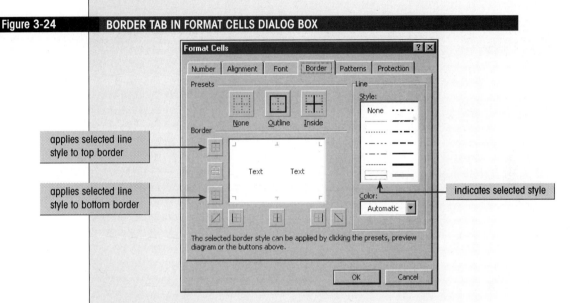

applies selected line style to top border

applies selected line style to bottom border

indicates selected style

3. Click the **medium thick line** in the Line Style box (third from the bottom in the second column).

4. Click the **top border** button. A thick line appears at the top of the Border preview window.

5. Click the **double-ruled line** in the Line Style box.

6. Click the **bottom border** button. A double-ruled line appears at the bottom of the Border preview window.

7. Click the **OK** button to apply the borders.

8. Click any cell to deselect the range and view the borders. See Figure 3-25.

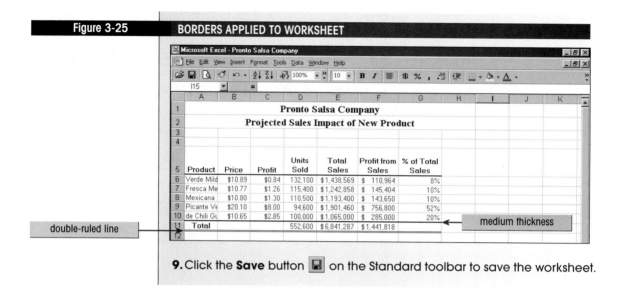

Figure 3-25   BORDERS APPLIED TO WORKSHEET

double-ruled line

medium thickness

9. Click the **Save** button 🖫 on the Standard toolbar to save the worksheet.

In addition to borders, you want to add color to emphasize the Profit from Sales column.

Using Color for Emphasis

Patterns and colors provide visual interest, emphasize worksheet zones, or indicate data-entry areas. The way you intend to use the worksheet should guide your use of patterns or colors. If you print the worksheet in color and distribute a hard copy of it, or if you plan to use a color projection device to display your worksheet on screen, you can take advantage of the Excel color formatting options. If you do not have a color printer, you can use patterns because it is difficult to predict how colors you see on your screen will translate into gray shades on your printout.

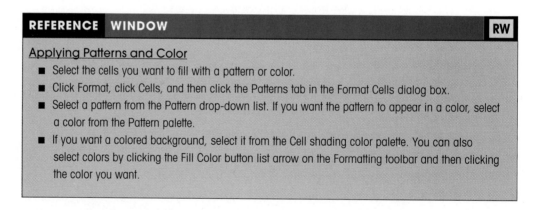

REFERENCE WINDOW   **RW**

Applying Patterns and Color
- Select the cells you want to fill with a pattern or color.
- Click Format, click Cells, and then click the Patterns tab in the Format Cells dialog box.
- Select a pattern from the Pattern drop-down list. If you want the pattern to appear in a color, select a color from the Pattern palette.
- If you want a colored background, select it from the Cell shading color palette. You can also select colors by clicking the Fill Color button list arrow on the Formatting toolbar and then clicking the color you want.

You want your worksheet to look good when you print it in black and white on the office laser printer, but you also want it to look good on the screen when you show it to Anne. You decide that a yellow background will enable the Profit from Sales column to stand out and looks fairly good both on the screen and the printout. You apply this format using the Patterns tab in the Format Cells dialog box.

To apply a color to the Profit from Sales column:

1. Select the range **F5:F11**.

2. Click **Format** on the menu bar, click **Cells**, and then click the **Patterns** tab in the Format Cells dialog box. See Figure 3-26. A color palette appears.

Figure 3-26	COLOR PALETTE IN PATTERNS TAB OF FORMAT CELLS DIALOG BOX

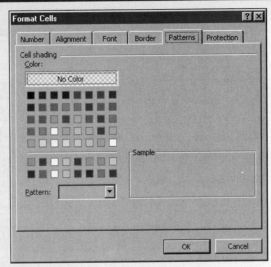

3. Click the **yellow square** in the fourth row (third square from the left) of the Cell shading Color palette.

4. Click the **OK** button to apply the color.

5. Click any cell to deselect the range and view the color in the Profit from Sales column. See Figure 3-27.

Figure 3-27	WORKSHEET AFTER APPLYING COLOR TO A COLUMN

Product	Price	Profit	Units Sold	Total Sales	Profit from Sales	% of Total Sales
Verde Mild	$10.89	$0.84	132,100	$1,438,569	$ 110,964	8%
Fresca Me	$10.77	$1.26	115,400	$1,242,858	$ 145,404	10%
Mexicana	$10.80	$1.30	110,500	$1,193,400	$ 143,650	10%
Picante Ve	$20.10	$8.00	94,600	$1,901,460	$ 756,800	52%
de Chili Gu	$10.65	$2.85	100,000	$1,065,000	$ 285,000	20%
Total			552,600	$6,841,287	$1,441,818	

Pronto Salsa Company

Projected Sales Impact of New Product

yellow background

You can also use buttons on the Formatting toolbar to change the color for the cell background (Fill Color button) and text in a cell (Text Color button).

Now that you have finished formatting labels and values, you can change the width of column A to best display the information in that column. To do this, you use Excel's Automatic Adjustment feature to change the width of a column to fit the widest entry in a cell.

To change the column width to fit the contents of a column:

1. Position the pointer over the column boundary between column A and column B. The pointer changes to **↔**.

2. Double-click the boundary. The column width automatically adjusts to accommodate the widest entry in column A. See Figure 3-28.

Figure 3-28   **RESULTS OF CHANGING COLUMN WIDTH**

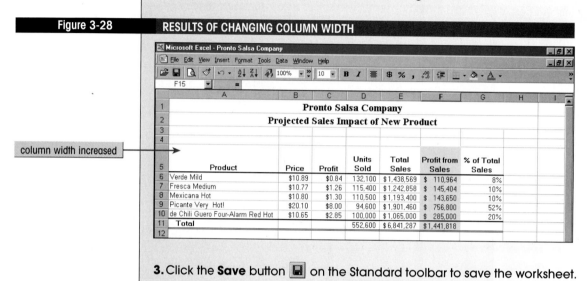

column width increased

3. Click the **Save** button 🖫 on the Standard toolbar to save the worksheet.

Using the Drawing Toolbar for Emphasis

The Excel Text Box feature lets you display notes, comments, and headings in a worksheet. A **text box** is like an electronic Post-it note that appears on top of the worksheet cells.

To add a text box you use the Text Box button, which is located on the Drawing toolbar, and type the note in the text box.

Activating the Drawing Toolbar

Excel provides many toolbars. You have been using two: the Standard toolbar and the Formatting toolbar. Some of the other toolbars include the Chart toolbar, the Drawing toolbar, and the Visual Basic toolbar. To activate a toolbar, it's usually easiest to use the toolbar Shortcut menu, but to activate the Drawing toolbar, you can simply click the Drawing button on the Standard toolbar. When you finish using a toolbar, you can easily remove it from the worksheet.

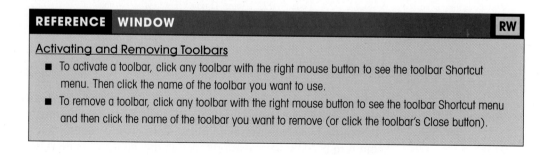

REFERENCE WINDOW   **RW**

Activating and Removing Toolbars
- To activate a toolbar, click any toolbar with the right mouse button to see the toolbar Shortcut menu. Then click the name of the toolbar you want to use.
- To remove a toolbar, click any toolbar with the right mouse button to see the toolbar Shortcut menu and then click the name of the toolbar you want to remove (or click the toolbar's Close button).

You need the Drawing toolbar to accomplish your next formatting task. (If your Drawing toolbar is already active, skip the following step.)

To display the Drawing toolbar:

1. Click the **Drawing** button 🖉 on the Standard toolbar.

The toolbar might appear in any location in the worksheet window; this is called a **floating** toolbar. You don't want the toolbar obstructing your view of the worksheet, so drag it to the bottom of the worksheet window to **anchor** it there. (If your toolbar is already anchored at the bottom of the worksheet window, or at the top, skip the next set of steps.)

To anchor the Drawing toolbar to the bottom of the worksheet window:

1. Position the pointer on the title bar of the Drawing toolbar.

2. Click and drag the toolbar to the bottom of the screen.

3. Release the mouse button to attach the Drawing toolbar to the bottom of the worksheet window. See Figure 3-29.

| Figure 3-29 | DRAWING TOOLBAR ATTACHED TO BOTTOM OF WINDOW |

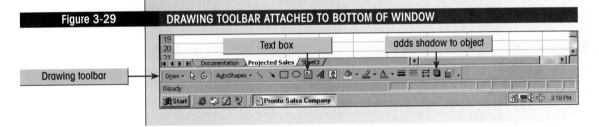

Now that the Drawing toolbar is where you want it, you proceed with your plan to add a comment to the worksheet.

Adding a Text Box

A **text box** is a drawing tool that contains text. It sits on top of the cells in a worksheet and is useful for drawing attention to important points in a worksheet or chart. With Excel you can use a variety of drawing tools, such as boxes, lines, circles, arrows, and text boxes to add graphic objects to your worksheet. To move, modify, or delete a graphic object, you first select it by moving the pointer over the object, then click it. Small square handles indicate that the object is selected. Use these handles to adjust the object's size, change its location, or delete it.

REFERENCE WINDOW RW

Adding a Text Box

- Click the Text Box button on the Drawing toolbar.
- Position the pointer where you want the text box to appear in the worksheet.
- Click and drag to outline the size and shape of the text box.
- Type the text for the text box.
- Click outside the text box.

You want to draw attention to the low price and high profit margin of the new salsa product. To do this, you plan to add a text box to the bottom of the worksheet that contains a note about expected profits.

To add a text box:

1. Click the **Text Box** button on the Drawing toolbar. As you move the pointer inside the worksheet area, the pointer changes to ↓. Position the crosshair of the pointer at the top of cell **A13** to mark the upper-left corner of the text box.

2. Click and drag + to cell **C18**, and then release the mouse button to mark the lower-right corner of the text box. See Figure 3-30.

   You are ready to type the text into the text box.

Figure 3-30 ADDING A TEXT BOX

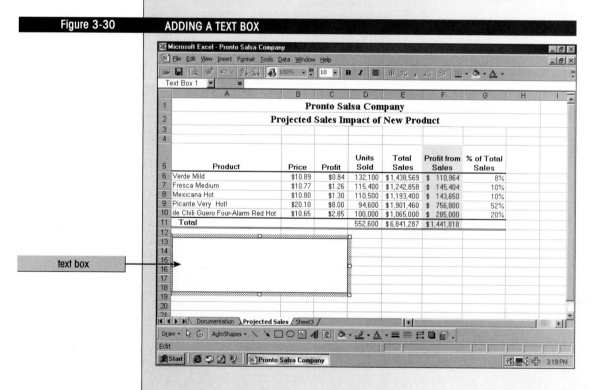

text box

3. Make sure the insertion point is in the text box and then type **Notice the high profit margin of the de Chili Guero Four-Alarm Red Hot. It has the second highest profit per unit.**

You want to use a different font style to emphasize the name of the new salsa product in the text box.

To italicize the name of the new salsa product:

1. Position $\bigl[$ in the text box just before the word "de Chili."

2. Click and drag $\bigl[$ to the end of the word "Hot," and then release the mouse button.

   TROUBLE? If the size of your text box differs slightly from the one in the figure, the lines of text might break differently. So don't worry if the text in your text box is not arranged exactly like the text in the figure.

3. Click the **Italic** button $\boxed{I}$ on the Formatting toolbar.

4. Click any cell to deselect the product name, which now appears italicized.

You decide to change the text box size so that there is no empty space at the bottom.

To change the text box size:

1. Click the **text box** to select it and display the patterned border with handles.

2. Position the pointer on the center handle at the bottom of the text box. The pointer changes to $\updownarrow$.

3. Click and drag $\updownarrow$ up to shorten the box, and then release the mouse button.

You want to change the text box a bit more by adding a drop shadow to it.

To add a shadow to the text box:

1. Make sure the text box is still selected. (Look for the patterned border and handles.)

2. Click the **Shadow** button $\boxed{\square}$ on the Drawing toolbar to display the gallery of Shadow options. See Figure 3-31.

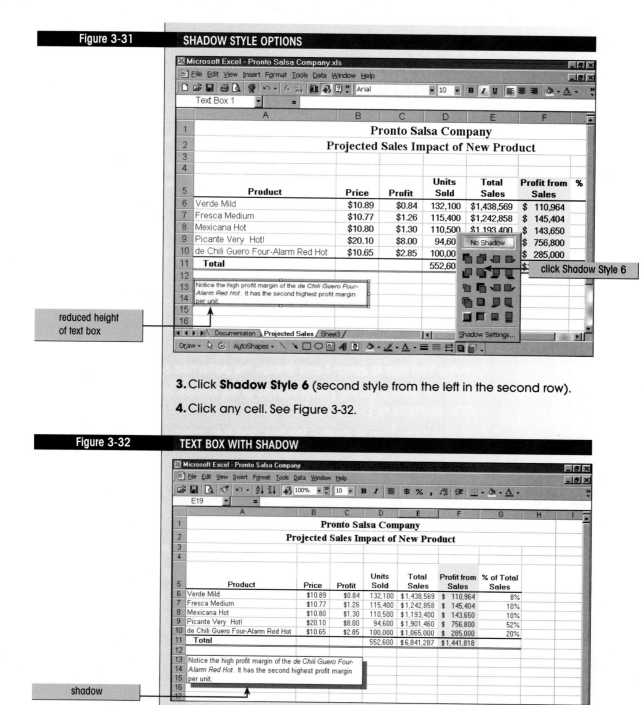

| Figure 3-31 | SHADOW STYLE OPTIONS |

3. Click **Shadow Style 6** (second style from the left in the second row).

4. Click any cell. See Figure 3-32.

| Figure 3-32 | TEXT BOX WITH SHADOW |

Adding an Arrow

You decide to add an arrow pointing from the text box to the row with information on the new salsa.

To add an arrow:

1. Click the **Arrow** button 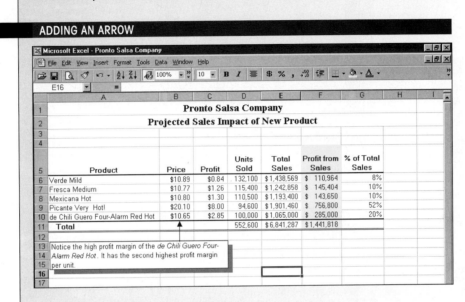 on the Drawing toolbar. As you move the mouse pointer inside the worksheet, the pointer changes to ─┼─.

2. Position ─┼─ on the top edge of the text box in cell **B12**. To ensure a straight line, press and hold the **Shift** key as you drag to cell **B10**, and then release the mouse button.

3. Click any cell to deselect the arrow. See Figure 3-33.

| Figure 3-33 | ADDING AN ARROW |

Pronto Salsa Company
Projected Sales Impact of New Product

Product	Price	Profit	Units Sold	Total Sales	Profit from Sales	% of Total Sales
Verde Mild	$10.89	$0.84	132,100	$1,438,569	$ 110,964	8%
Fresca Medium	$10.77	$1.26	115,400	$1,242,858	$ 145,404	10%
Mexicana Hot	$10.80	$1.30	110,500	$1,193,400	$ 143,650	10%
Picante Very Hot!	$20.10	$8.00	94,600	$1,901,460	$ 756,800	52%
de Chili Guero Four-Alarm Red Hot	$10.65	$2.85	100,000	$1,065,000	$ 285,000	20%
Total			552,600	$6,841,287	$1,441,818	

Notice the high profit margin of the *de Chili Guero Four-Alarm Red Hot*. It has the second highest profit margin per unit.

You want the arrow to point to cell C10 instead of B10, so you need to reposition it.

Like a text box, an arrow is an Excel object. To modify the arrow object, you must select it. When you do so, two small square handles appear on it. You can reposition either end of the arrow by dragging one of the handles.

To reposition the arrow:

1. Move the pointer over the arrow object until the pointer changes to ⇖.

2. Click the **arrow**. Handles appear at each end of the arrow.

3. Move the pointer to the top handle on the arrowhead until the pointer changes to ↗.

4. Click and drag ─┼─ to cell **C10**, and then release the mouse button.

5. Click any cell to deselect the arrow object. See Figure 3-34.

Figure 3-34   MOVING AN ARROW

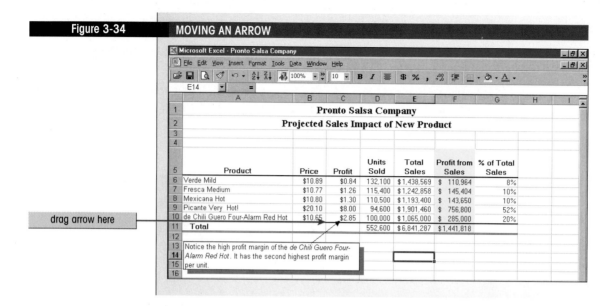

drag arrow here

Now that the text box is finished, you can remove the Drawing toolbar from the worksheet.

To remove the Drawing toolbar:

1. Click the **Drawing** button 🖉 on the Standard toolbar. The Drawing toolbar is removed from the window, and the Drawing button no longer appears depressed (selected).

2. Press **Ctrl + Home** to make cell A1 the active cell.

3. Click the **Save** button 🖫 on the Standard toolbar to save your work.

You have now made all the formatting changes and enhancements to Anne's worksheet. She has just returned to the office, and you show her the completed worksheet. She is very pleased with how professional the worksheet looks, but she thinks of one more way to improve the appearance of the worksheet. She asks you to remove the gridlines from the worksheet display.

Controlling the Display of Gridlines

Although normally the boundaries of each cell are outlined in black, Anne has decided the worksheet will have more of a professional appearance if you remove the gridlines. To remove the gridline display, you deselect the Gridlines option in the View tab of the Options dialog box.

To remove the display of gridlines in the worksheet:

1. Click **Tools** on the menu bar, click **Options**, and if necessary, then click the **View** tab in the Options dialog box.

2. Click the **Gridlines** check box in the Window option to remove the check and deselect the option.

3. Click the **OK** button to display the worksheet without gridlines. See Figure 3-35.

| Figure 3-35 | **WORKSHEET WITHOUT GRIDLINES** |

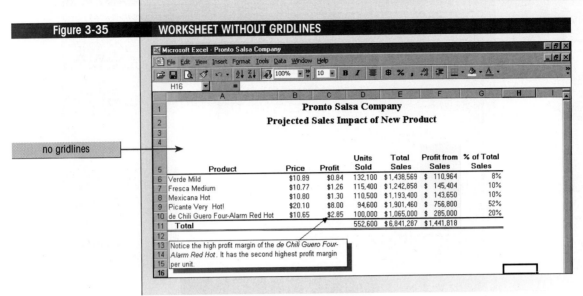

no gridlines

Now you are ready to print the worksheet.

Printing the Worksheet

Before you print a worksheet, you can use the Excel Print Preview window to see how it will look when printed. Recall that the Print Preview window shows you margins, page breaks, headers, and footers that are not always visible on the screen.

To preview the worksheet before you print it:

1. Click the **Print Preview** button ⬚ on the Standard toolbar to display the first worksheet page in the Print Preview window. See Figure 3-36.

Figure 3-36

active Next button
indicates more pages

indicates number
of pages

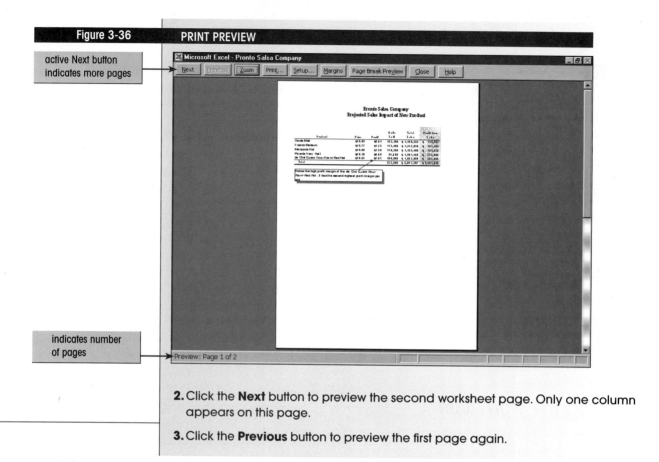

2. Click the **Next** button to preview the second worksheet page. Only one column appears on this page.

3. Click the **Previous** button to preview the first page again.

Looking at the Print Preview, you see that the worksheet is too wide to fit on a single page. You realize that if you print the worksheet horizontally (lengthwise), it will fit on a single sheet of paper.

Portrait and Landscape Orientations

Excel provides two print orientations, **portrait** and **landscape**. Portrait orientation prints the worksheet with the paper positioned so it is taller than it is wide. Landscape orientation prints the worksheet with the paper positioned so it is wider than it is tall. Because some worksheets are wider than they are tall, landscape orientation is very useful.

You can specify print orientation using the Page Setup command on the File menu or using the Setup button in the Print Preview window. Use the landscape orientation for the Projected Sales worksheet.

To change the print orientation to landscape:

1. In the Print Preview window, click the **Setup** button to open the Page Setup dialog box. If necessary, click the **Page** tab.

2. Click the **Landscape** option button in the Orientation section to select this option.

3. Click the **OK** button to return to the Print Preview window. See Figure 3-37. Notice the landscape orientation; that is, the page is wider than it is tall. The worksheet will now print on one page.

| Figure 3-37 | LANDSCAPE ORIENTATION |

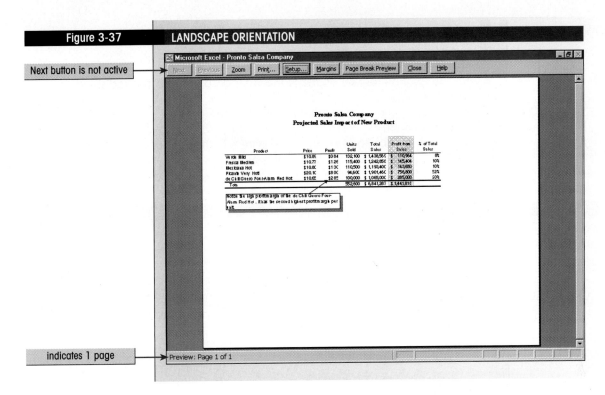

Next button is not active

indicates 1 page

Before printing the worksheet, center the output on the page, and use the header/footer tab to document the printed worksheet.

To center the printed output:

1. Click the **Setup** button to open the Page Setup dialog box. Click the **Margins** tab.

2. Click the **Center on page Horizontally** check box to place a check in it and select that option.

Next modify the printed footer by adding your name in the center section.

To insert a custom footer for the worksheet:

1. Click the **Header/Footer** tab, and then click the **Custom footer** to open the Footer dialog box.

2. In the **Center section** box, type **Prepared by (enter your name here)**.

3. Click the **OK** button to complete the footer and return to the Page Setup dialog box.

4. Click the **OK** button to return to the Print Preview window.

5. Click the **Close** button to return to the worksheet.

The worksheet is ready to print, but you should always save your work before printing.

To save your Page Setup settings and print the worksheet:

1. Click the **Save** button 🖫 on the Standard toolbar.

2. Click the **Print** button 🖨 on the Standard toolbar to print the worksheet. See Figure 3-38.

    TROUBLE? If you see a message that indicates that you have a printer problem, click the Cancel button to cancel the printout. Check your printer to make sure it is turned on and is online; also make sure it has paper. Then go back and try Step 2 again. If you have no printer available, click the Cancel button.

| Figure 3-38 | PRINTED WORKSHEET |

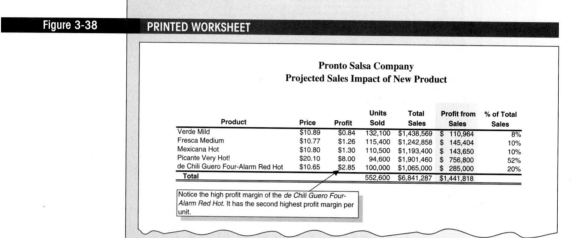

Pronto Salsa Company
Projected Sales Impact of New Product

Product	Price	Profit	Units Sold	Total Sales	Profit from Sales	% of Total Sales
Verde Mild	$10.89	$0.84	132,100	$1,438,569	$ 110,964	8%
Fresca Medium	$10.77	$1.26	115,400	$1,242,858	$ 145,404	10%
Mexicana Hot	$10.80	$1.30	110,500	$1,193,400	$ 143,650	10%
Picante Very Hot!	$20.10	$8.00	94,600	$1,901,460	$ 756,800	52%
de Chili Guero Four-Alarm Red Hot	$10.65	$2.85	100,000	$1,065,000	$ 285,000	20%
Total			552,600	$6,841,287	$1,441,818	

Notice the high profit margin of the *de Chili Guero Four-Alarm Red Hot*. It has the second highest profit margin per unit.

TROUBLE? If the title for the last two columns didn't print completely, you need to increase the row height for row 5. Select row 5, drag the border below row 5 until the row height is 42.75 or greater (check the reference area of the formula bar), and then click the Print button.

Hiding and Unhiding Rows and Columns

Anne asks for one more printout, this one omitting the Units Sold column. The printout will include the product name, price, profit, total sales, profit from sales and % of total sales.

Hiding rows and columns is useful if you don't want to display certain information when the worksheet is open, or don't want to print certain information in the worksheet.

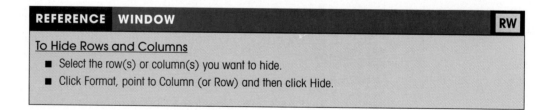

REFERENCE WINDOW   RW

To Hide Rows and Columns
- Select the row(s) or column(s) you want to hide.
- Click Format, point to Column (or Row) and then click Hide.

To hide the Units Sold column:

1. Click the column header in column D. Notice the entire column is selected.

2. Click **Format**, point to **Column** and then click **Hide**.

3. Click any cell to observe that column D is hidden. See Figure 3-39.

Figure 3-39	WORKSHEET WITH COLUMN HIDDEN

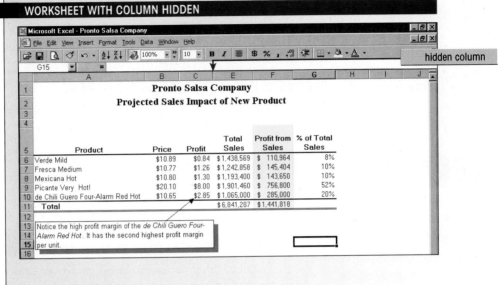

4. Print the report.

Before saving the workbook, unhide the hidden column.

To unhide the hidden column:

1. Position the pointer over the column header in column C.

2. Click and drag the pointer to the column header in column E. Notice that columns C and E are highlighted.

3. Click **Format**, point to **Column**, and then click **Unhide**. Column D is no longer hidden.

4. Click any cell to view column D.

   Now that you are done formatting the worksheet, close the workbook and exit Excel.

5. Save, then Close the workbook and exit Excel.

You have completed formatting the Projected Sales worksheet and are ready to give it to Anne to check over before she presents it at her meeting with the bank loan officer.

Session 3.2 QUICK CHECK

1. List two ways you can place a double-ruled line at the bottom of a range of cells.

2. Describe how to activate the Drawing toolbar.

3. To move, modify, or delete an object, you must _____ it first.

4. A _____ is a block of text that is placed in the worksheet.

5. _____ orientation prints the worksheet with the paper positioned so it is taller than it is wide, and _____ orientation prints so the paper is positioned wider than it is tall.

6. An arrow is an example of a _____ .

7. What steps are needed to remove the gridlines from the worksheet display?

REVIEW ASSIGNMENTS

After you show Anne the Projected Sales worksheet, the two of you discuss alternative ways to improve the worksheet's appearance. You decide to make some of these changes and give Anne the choice between two formatted worksheets. Do the following:

1. Start Windows and Excel, if necessary. Insert your Data Disk into the appropriate disk drive. Make sure the Excel and Book1 windows are maximized. Open the workbook **Pronto2** in the Review folder for Tutorial 3, and then save it as **Pronto3**.

2. Right-align the column heading in the Projected Sales worksheet.

3. Make the contents of cells A10:G10 bold to emphasize the new product. Make any necessary column-width adjustments.

4. Apply a yellow color to the range A1:G2.

5. Right-align the label in cell A11.

Explore 6. Draw borders around the data in A1:G10 so it appears in a grid.

7. Replace the name currently in the footer with your name so that it appears on the printout of the worksheet. Make sure the footer also prints the date and filename. Place the sheet name in the center section of the custom header.

8. Make sure the Page Setup menu settings are set for centered horizontally and vertically.

9. Preview the printout to make sure it fits on one page. Save and print the worksheet.

Explore 10. Fill the text box with the color yellow so that it appears as a "yellow sticky note." (*Hint:* select the text box by clicking on one of the selection handles. Use the Fill Color button on the Drawing toolbar.)

11. Change the color of the two-line title to blue (the text, not the background color).

12. In Step 4 you applied the color yellow to the cells A1 through G2. Remove the yellow color so that the background is the same as the rest of your worksheet.

13. If you've completed Steps 10, 11, or 12, save the worksheet as **Pronto4**.

Explore

14. a. Study the worksheet shown in Figure 3-40. Then open the Office Assistant and inquire about rotating data and merging cells.

Figure 3-40

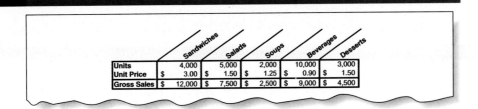

	Sandwiches	Salads	Soups	Beverages	Desserts
Units	4,000	5,000	2,000	10,000	3,000
Unit Price	$ 3.00	$ 1.50	$ 1.25	$ 0.90	$ 1.50
Gross Sales	$ 12,000	$ 7,500	$ 2,500	$ 9,000	$ 4,500

   b. Open the workbook **Explore3** in the Tutorial 3 Review folder and then save it as **Explore3 Solution** in the same folder.
   c. Use the Rotate Text formatting feature to change the worksheet so it is similar to Figure 3-40. Make any other changes to make the worksheet as similar as possible to the one shown in Figure 3-40.
   d. Save and then print the worksheet.

CASE PROBLEMS

Case 1. Jenson Sports Wear Quarterly Sales   Carol Roberts is the national sales manager for Jenson Sports Wear, a company that sells sportswear to major department stores. She has been using an Excel worksheet to track the results of her staff's sales incentive program. She has asked you to format the worksheet so it looks professional. She also wants a print-out before she presents the worksheet at the next sales meeting. Complete these steps to format and print the worksheet:

1. Start Windows and Excel, if necessary. Insert your Data Disk into the appropriate disk drive. Make sure the Excel and Book1 windows are maximized. Open the workbook **Running** in the Cases folder for Tutorial 3 on your Data Disk. Maximize the worksheet window and then save the workbook as **Running2**.

2. Complete the worksheet by doing the following:
   a. Calculating totals for each product
   b. Calculating quarterly subtotals for the Shoes and Shirts departments
   c. Calculating totals for each quarter and an overall total

3. Modify the worksheet so it is formatted as shown in Figure 3-41.

4. Use the Page Setup dialog box to center the output both horizontally and vertically.

5. Add the filename, your name, and the date in the custom footer and delete both the formatting code &[File] from the Center section of the header.

6. Save the workbook.

7. Preview the worksheet and adjust the page setup as necessary for the printed results you want.

8. Print the worksheet. Your printout should fit on one page.

Explore

9. Place the note "Leading product" in a text box. Remove the border from the text box. (*Hint*: Use the Format Textbox dialog box—Colors and Lines Tab.) Draw an oval object around the text box. (*Hint*: Use the Oval tool on the Drawing toolbar and right-click to determine which command sends the oval object to the back.) Draw an arrow from the edge of the oval to the number in the worksheet representing the leading product. Save and print the worksheet. Your printout should fit on one page.

Figure 3-41

Sports Wear Inc. Quarterly Sales by Product					
Shoes	**Qtr 1**	**Qtr 2**	**Qtr 3**	**Qtr 4**	**Total**
Running	2,250	2,550	2,650	2,800	10,250
Tennis	2,800	1,500	2,300	2,450	9,050
Basketball	1,250	1,400	1,550	1,550	5,750
Subtotal	$ 6,300	$ 5,450	$ 6,500	$ 6,800	$ 25,050
Shirts	**Qtr 1**	**Qtr 2**	**Qtr 3**	**Qtr 4**	**Total**
Tee	1,000	1,150	1,250	1,150	4,550
Polo	2,100	2,200	2,300	2,400	9,000
Sweat	250	250	275	300	1,075
Subtotal	$ 3,350	$ 3,600	$ 3,825	$ 3,850	$ 14,625
Grand Total	$ 9,650	$ 9,050	$ 10,325	$ 10,650	$ 39,675

Case 2. State Recycling Campaign   Fred Birnbaum is working as an intern in the state's Waste Disposal Department. They have a pilot project on recycling for three counties (Seacoast, Metro, and Pioneer Valley). You have been asked to complete the worksheet, summarizing the results of the pilot program and formatting it for presentation to their board of directors.

1. Start Windows and Excel, if necessary. Insert your Data Disk into the appropriate disk drive. Make sure the Excel and Book1 windows are maximized. Open the workbook **Recycle** in the Cases folder for Tutorial 3 on your Data Disk, and then save it as **Recycle2**.

2. Add two columns to calculate yearly totals for tons and a dollar value for each material in each county.

3. Insert three rows at the top of the worksheet to include:
State Recycling Project
Material Reclamation 1999
<blank row>

4. Format the worksheet until you feel confident that the board of directors will be impressed with the appearance of the report.

5. Rename the worksheet **Recycle Data**.

6. Save the worksheet.

7. Print the worksheet centered horizontally and vertically on the page using landscape orientation. Include your name in the custom footer.

8. Remove the gridlines from the display. Use the Border tab of the Format Cells dialog box to place the recycle data in a grid. Save the workbook as **Recycle3**.

Explore

9. Change the magnification of the sheet so you can view the recycle data on the screen without having to scroll. (*Hint*: Use the Zoom control on the Standard toolbar.)

Case 3. State Government Expenditures   Ken Dry, an assistant to the governor, has started an Excel worksheet summarizing current and proposed expenditures for all the state agencies. Ken has been called away on an emergency and asked you to complete the worksheet. He left the following note:

The column headings and agency and division names have been entered in the worksheet. Column A includes Divisions, which appear as the rows with no expenditure data in columns B and C. Agencies are those rows that include expenditure data in columns B and C. For example, the first division is General Government and the first agency within this division is Administration; the next division is Human Services and its first agency is Children and Families, and so on. See Figure 3-42.

You need to modify the worksheet by:

Figure 3-42

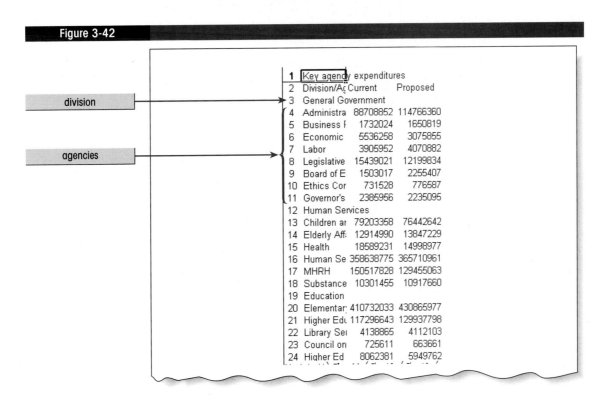

■ Calculating overall government totals (for all agencies) for both current and proposed expenditures

■ Calculating totals for each division. Remember that the agencies in a division follow in the rows below the division name (if necessary, you can insert rows to provide room for totals).

■ Add the following calculations in columns D, E, and F:

   a. percentage change between current and proposed (next year's) expenditures (column D)

   b. for proposed expenditures-percentage of agency's expenditures in a division to total expenditures in that division; for example, Administration is 81.4% of the General Government division expenditures and Children and Families is 12.4% of Health and Services (column E)

   c. for proposed expenditures-percentage of agency's expenditures to total government expenditures; for example, Administration is 7.5% of overall government expenditures, while Business Regulation is .1% of overall government expenditures (column F)

Do the following:

1. Open the workbook **StateGov.xls** in the Cases folder for Tutorial 3, and then save it as **State Government**.

2. Use the note left by Ken to complete the worksheet.

3. Your output will be handed out at a press conference, so you need to improve the appearance of the worksheet so it will look more professional.

4. Assign a descriptive sheet name to Sheet1.

5. Print your report on one page. Include your name, class, and date in the print footer and the sheet name as part of the print header.

6. Include a Documentation sheet in your workbook. In this sheet, include the title of the project, your name, date completed, and brief purpose. Print this sheet.

7. Save the workbook.

8. Print the formulas that underlie the worksheet. Save the worksheet before you display the formulas in the worksheet. Print the formulas on one page and include row and column headings as part of the printout.

Case 4. Ortiz Marine Services   Vince DiOrio is an information systems major at a local college. He works three days a week at a nearby marina, Ortiz Marine Services, to help pay for his tuition. Vince works in the business office, and his responsibilities range from making coffee to keeping the company's books.

Recently, Jim Ortiz, the owner of the marina, asked Vince if he could help computerize the payroll for their employees. He explained that the employees work a different number of hours each week for different rates of pay. Jim does the payroll manually now and finds it time-consuming. Moreover, whenever he makes an error, he is embarrassed and annoyed at having to take the additional time to correct it. Jim was hoping Vince could help him.

Vince immediately agrees to help. He tells Jim that he knows how to use Excel and that he can build a worksheet that will save him time and reduce errors. Jim and Vince meet. They review the present payroll process and discuss the desired outcomes of the payroll spreadsheet. Figure 3-43 is a sketch of the output Jim wants to get.

Figure 3-43

Ortiz Marine Service Payroll
Week Ending

Employee	Hours	Pay Rate	Gross Pay	Federal Withholding	State Withholding	Total Deductions	Net Pay
Bramble	16	6					
Juarez	25	6.25					
Smith	30	8					
DiOrio	25	7.75					
Smiken	10	5.90					
Cortez	30	7					
Fulton	20	6					
Total							

Do the following:

1. Create the worksheet sketched in Figure 3-43.

2. Use the following formulas in your workbook to calculate total hours, gross pay, federal withholding, state withholding, total deductions and net pay for the company:

   a. Gross pay is hours times pay rate.
   b. Federal withholding is 15% of gross pay.
   c. State withholding is 4% of gross pay.
   d. Total deductions is the sum of federal and state withholding.
   e. Net pay is the difference between gross pay and total deductions.

3. Apply the formatting techniques learned in this tutorial to create a professional-looking workbook.

4. Assign a descriptive sheet name.

5. Create a Documentation sheet.

6. Save the workbook as **Payroll** in the Cases folder for Tutorial 3.

7. Print the worksheet, including appropriate headers and footers.

8. Remove the hours for the seven employees.

9. Enter the following hours: 18 for Bramble, 25 for Juarez, 35 for Smith, and 20 for DiOrio, 15 for Smiken, 35 for Cortez, and 22 for Fulton.

10. Print the new worksheet.

11. Print the formulas on one page. Include row and column headers in the printed output.

INTERNET ASSIGNMENTS

The purpose of the Internet Assignments is to challenge you to find information on the Internet that you can use to create effective spreadsheets. The actual assignments are updated and maintained on the Course Technology Web site. Log on to the Internet and use your Web browser to go to the Student Online Companion to accompany this text at **www.course.com/NewPerspectives/Office2000**. Click the Excel link, and then click the link for Tutorial 3.

QUICK | CHECK ANSWERS

Session 3.1

1. click Format, click Cells; right-click mouse in cell you want to format; use buttons on the Formatting toolbar
2. **a.** 5.8%   **b.** $0.06
3. Format Painter button
4. The column width of a cell is not wide enough to display the numbers, and you need to increase the column width.
5. Position the mouse pointer over the column header, right-click the mouse and click Column Width. Enter the new column width in the Column Width dialog box. Position the mouse pointer over the right edge of the column you want to modify, and then click and drag to increase the column width.
6. The data in the cell is formatted with the Comma style using two decimal places.
7. center column headings, right-align numbers, and left-align text
8. Left align button, Center button, Right align button, and Merge and Center button

Session 3.2

1. use the Borders tab on the Format Cells dialog box, or the Borders button on the Formatting toolbar
2. click the Drawing button on the Standard toolbar
3. select
4. text box
5. Portrait; landscape
6. drawing object
7. click Tools, click Options, click View tab, and then remove the check from the Gridlines check box

OBJECTIVES

In this tutorial you will:

- Identify the elements of an Excel chart

- Learn which type of chart will represent your data most effectively

- Create an embedded chart

- Move and resize a chart

- Edit a chart

- Change the appearance of a chart

- Place a chart in a chart sheet

- Select nonadjacent ranges

- Work with three-dimensional chart types

- Add a picture to a chart

CREATING CHARTS

Charting Sales Information for Cast Iron Concepts

CASE

Cast Iron Concepts

Andrea Puest, the regional sales manager of Cast Iron Concepts (CIC), a distributor of cast iron stoves, is required to present information concerning sales of the company's products within her territory. Andrea sells in the New England region, which currently includes Massachusetts, Maine, and Vermont. She sells four major models—Star Windsor, Box Windsor, West Windsor, and Circle Windsor. The Circle Windsor is CIC's latest entry in the cast iron stove market. Due to production problems, it was only available for sale the last four months of the year.

Andrea will make a presentation before the director of sales for CIC and the other regional managers next week when the entire group meets at corporate headquarters. Andrea gives you the basic data on sales in her territory for the past year. She must report on both total regional sales and total state sales for each model in her territory. She knows that this kind of information is often understood best when it is presented in graphical form. So she thinks she would like to show this information in a column chart as well as in a pie chart. You help her prepare for her presentation by creating the charts she needs.

SESSION 4.1

In this session you will learn about the variety of Excel chart types and how to identify the elements of a chart. You will learn how to create a column chart and a number of techniques for improving your chart, including moving and resizing it, adding and editing chart text, enhancing a chart title by adding a border, and using color for emphasis.

Excel Charts

Andrea's sales data is saved in a workbook named Concepts. You generate the charts from the data in this workbook.

To start Excel, open the Concepts workbook, and rename it:

1. Start Excel as usual.

2. Open the Concepts workbook in the Tutorial folder for Tutorial 4 on your Data Disk.

   The Documentation sheet appears as the first sheet in the workbook.

3. Type your name and the current date in the appropriate cells in the Documentation sheet.

4. Save the workbook as **Cast Iron Concepts**. After you do so, the new filename appears in the title bar.

5. Click the **Sales Data** tab to move to that sheet. See Figure 4-1.

| Figure 4-1 | SALES DATA WORKSHEET IN CAST IRON CONCEPTS WORKBOOK |

The worksheet shows the annual sales in dollars for each Windsor stove model by state. The total sales during the year for each model are in column E, and the total sales for each state appear in row 7.

It is easy to visually represent this kind of worksheet data. You might think of these graphical representations as "graphs;" however, in Excel they are referred to as **charts**. Figure 4-2 shows the 14 chart types that you can use to represent worksheet data in Excel.

Each chart type has two or more subtypes that provide various alternative chart formats for the selected chart type. For example, the column chart type has seven subtypes, as shown in Figure 4-3.

Figure 4-2	EXCEL CHART TYPES	
ICON	**CHART TYPE**	**PURPOSE**
	Area	Shows magnitude of change over a period of time
	Column	Shows comparisons between the data represented by each column
	Bar	Shows comparisons between the data represented by each bar
	Line	Shows trends or changes over time
	Pie	Shows the proportion of parts to a whole
	XY (Scatter)	Shows the pattern or relationship between sets of (x,y) data points
	Radar	Shows change in data relative to a center point
	Surface	Shows the interrelationships between large amounts of data
	Bubble	A special type of XY (Scatter) that shows the pattern or relationship between sets of data points; compares three sets of data
	Stock	Compares high, low, open, and close prices of a stock
	Cylinder	Shows comparisons between the data represented by each cylinder
	Cone	Shows comparisons between the data represented by each cone
	Pyramid	Shows comparisons between the data represented by each pyramid
	Doughnut	Shows the proportion of parts to a whole

Figure 4-3	CHART SUBTYPES FOR COLUMN CHART TYPE

CHART SUBTYPE ICON	**DESCRIPTION**
	Clustered column
	Stacked column
	100% stacked column
	Clustered column with 3-D visual effect
	Stacked column with 3-D visual effect
	100% stacked column with 3-D visual effect
	3-D column

Figure 4-4 shows the elements of a typical Excel chart. Understanding the Excel chart terminology is particularly important so you can successfully construct and edit charts.

Figure 4-4   **EXCEL CHART ELEMENTS**

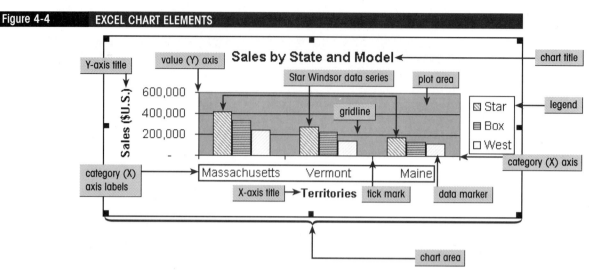

The entire chart and all its elements are contained in the **chart area**. The **plot area** is the rectangular area defined by the axes, with the Y-axis forming the left side and the X-axis forming the base; in Figure 4-4 the plot area is in gray. The **axis** is a line that borders one side of the plot area, providing a frame for measurement or comparison in a chart. Data values are plotted along the **value** or **Y-axis**, which is typically vertical. Categories are plotted along the **category** or **X-axis**, which is usually horizontal. Each axis in a chart can have a title that identifies the scale or categories of the chart data; in Figure 4-4 the **X-axis title** is "Territories" and the **Y-axis** title is "Sales ($U.S.)." The chart title identifies the chart.

A **tick mark label** identifies the categories, values, or series in the chart. **Tick marks** are small lines that intersect an axis, like divisions on a ruler, and represent the scale used for measuring values in the chart. Excel automatically generates this scale based on the values selected for the chart. **Gridlines** extend the tick marks on a chart axis to make it easier to see the values associated with the data markers. The **category names** or **category labels**, usually appearing on the X-axis, correspond to the labels you use for the worksheet data.

A **data point** is a single value originating from a worksheet cell. A **data marker** is a graphic representing a data point in a chart; depending on the type of chart, a data marker can be a bar, column, area, slice, or other symbol. For example, sales of the Star Windsor stove in Massachusetts (value 418,679 in cell B3 of the worksheet on your screen) is a data point. Each column in the chart in Figure 4-4 that shows the sales of Windsor stoves is a data marker. A **data series** is a group of related data points, such as the Star Windsor sales shown as red column markers in the chart.

When you have more than one data series, your chart will contain more than one set of data markers. For example, Figure 4-4 has three data series, one for each type of Windsor stove. When you show more than one data series in a chart, it is a good idea to use a **legend** to identify which data marker represents each data series.

Placement of Charts

Charts can be placed in the same worksheet as the data; this type of chart is called an **embedded chart** and enables you to place the chart next to the data so it can easily be reviewed and printed on one page. You can also place a chart in a separate sheet, called a **chart sheet**, which contains only one chart and doesn't have rows and columns. In this tutorial you create both an embedded chart and a chart that resides in a separate chart sheet.

Planning a Chart

Before you begin creating a chart you should plan it. Planning a chart includes the following steps:

- identifying the data points to be plotted, as well as the labels representing each data series and categories for the X-axis
- choosing an appropriate chart type
- sketching the chart, including data markers, axes, titles, labels, and legend
- deciding on the location of the chart within the workbook

Remember, Andrea wants to compare sales for each model in each state in which she sells. She thinks that a column chart is the best way to provide her audience with an accurate comparison of sales of Windsor stoves in her New England territory. She also needs to show sales of each stove model as a percentage of total sales. A pie chart is most effective when showing the size of each part as a percentage of a whole, so she will create a pie chart to use in her presentation as well.

Andrea sketched the column chart and pie chart shown in Figure 4-5.

Figure 4-5   **SKETCH OF COLUMN AND PIE CHARTS**

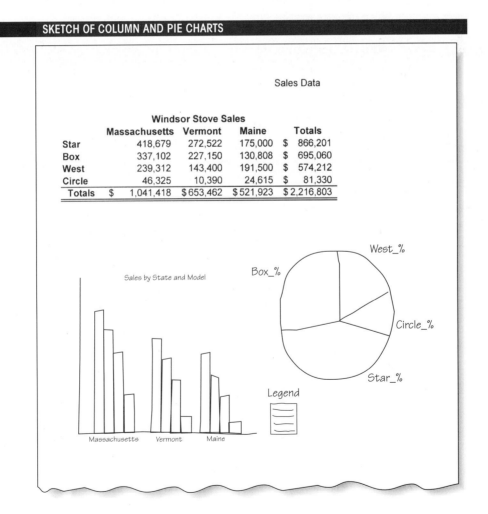

Sales Data

Windsor Stove Sales

	Massachusetts	Vermont	Maine	Totals
Star	418,679	272,522	175,000	$ 866,201
Box	337,102	227,150	130,808	$ 695,060
West	239,312	143,400	191,500	$ 574,212
Circle	46,325	10,390	24,615	$ 81,330
Totals	$ 1,041,418	$ 653,462	$ 521,923	$ 2,216,803

The sketches show roughly how Andrea wants the charts to look. It is difficult to envision exactly how a chart will look until you know how the data series looks when plotted; therefore, you don't need to incorporate every detail in the chart sketch. As you construct the charts, you can take advantage of Excel previewing capabilities to try different formatting options until your charts look just the way you want.

Create the column chart first. In looking at the sketch for this chart, note that Andrea wants to group the data by states; that is, the four models are shown for each of the three states. The names of the states in cells B2:D2 of the worksheet will be used as category labels. The names of each stove model, in cells A3:A6, will represent the legend text. The data series for the chart are in rows B3:D3, B4:D4, B5:D5, and B6:D6.

Creating a Column Chart

After studying Andrea's sketch for the column chart, you are ready to create it using the Sales Data worksheet. When you create a chart, you first select the cells that contain the data you want to appear in the chart and then you click the Chart Wizard button on the Standard toolbar. The Chart Wizard consists of four dialog boxes that guide you through the steps required to create a chart. Figure 4-6 identifies the tasks you perform in each of the Chart Wizard dialog boxes.

Figure 4-6	TASKS PERFORMED IN EACH STEP OF THE CHART WIZARD
DIALOG BOX	**TASKS PERFORMED**
Chart Type	Select the type of chart you want to create—lists the chart types available in Excel; for each chart type, presents you with several chart subtypes from which you can choose
Chart Source Data	Specify the worksheet cells that contain the data and labels that will appear in the chart
Chart Options	Change the look of the chart by changing options that affect the titles, axes, gridlines, legends, data labels, and data tables
Chart Location	Specify where to place the chart: embedded in a worksheet along with the worksheet data, or in a separate sheet called a chart sheet

You know that Andrea intends to create a handout of the worksheet and chart, so you want to embed the column chart in the same worksheet as the sales data, making it easier for her to create a one-page handout.

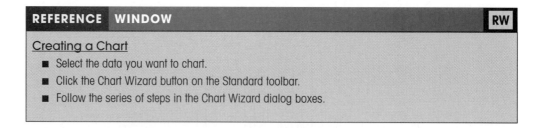

REFERENCE WINDOW   RW

Creating a Chart
- Select the data you want to chart.
- Click the Chart Wizard button on the Standard toolbar.
- Follow the series of steps in the Chart Wizard dialog boxes.

Before activating the Chart Wizard, you need to select the cells containing the data the chart will depict. If you want the column and row labels to appear in the chart, include the cells that contain them in your selection as well. For this chart, select the range A2 through D6, which includes the sales of each Windsor stove model in the three states as well as names of the stove models and states.

To create the column chart using the Chart Wizard:

1. Select cells **A2:D6**, making sure no cells are highlighted in column E or row 7. Notice the totals are not included in the range. To include the totals along with the data points that make up totals in the same chart would make the comparison more difficult and might result in a misinterpretation of the data.

   Now that you have selected the chart range, you use the Chart Wizard to create the column chart.

2. Click the **Chart Wizard** button 📊 on the Standard toolbar to open the Chart Wizard - Step 1 of 4 - Chart Type dialog box. See Figure 4-7.

   TROUBLE? If the Office Assistant appears on your screen, click the button next to the message "No, don't provide help now" to close the Office Assistant.

   This first dialog box asks you to select the type of chart you want to create. The Chart type list box lists each of the 14 chart types available in Excel. The default chart type is the Column chart type. To the right of the Chart type list box is a gallery of chart subtypes for the selected chart. Select the chart type you want to create.

Figure 4-7	CHART WIZARD STEP 1 OF 4 - CHART TYPE DIALOG BOX

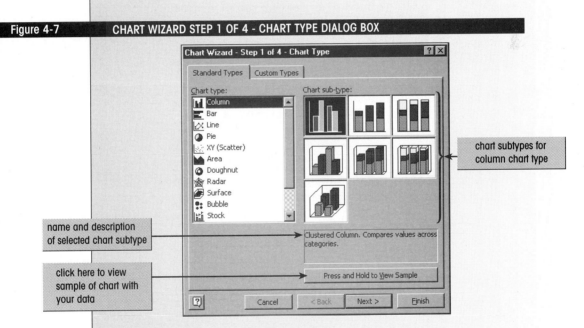

You want to create a column chart.

3. If necessary, click the **Column** chart type (the default) to select it. Seven Column chart subtypes, preformatted chart designs for the column chart, appear. The Clustered Column chart subtype is the default subtype for the Column chart type. Click and hold the **Press and Hold to View Sample** button to see a preview of the Clustered Column chart subtype.

   To view any other Column chart subtype, select another subtype option and click the **Press and Hold to View Sample** button. If you select a different chart type, you will see a different set of subcharts.

   You decide to use the Clustered Column chart type, the default selection.

4. Click the **Next** button to open the Chart Wizard - Step 2 of 4 - Chart Source Data dialog box. See Figure 4-8. In this step you confirm or specify the worksheet cells that contain the data and labels to appear in the chart.

Figure 4-8	CHART WIZARD - STEP 2 OF 4 - CHART SOURCE DATA DIALOG BOX

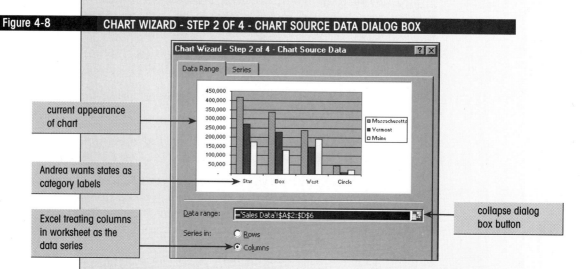

current appearance of chart

Andrea wants states as category labels

Excel treating columns in worksheet as the data series

collapse dialog box button

5. Make sure the Data range text box shows "='Sales Data'!$A$2:$D$6." This dialog box provides a preview of your chart.

TROUBLE? If the range shown on your screen is not ='Sales Data'!$A$2:$D$6, type the necessary corrections in the Data range text box, or click the Collapse dialog box button to the right of the Data range text box and select the correct range in the worksheet.

In Step 2 of the Chart Wizard, you can also modify how the data series is organized—by rows or by columns—using the **Series in** option. In Figure 4-8, the chart uses the columns in the worksheet as the data series. To see how the chart would look if the rows in the worksheet were used as the data series, you can modify the settings in this dialog box.

Does the sample chart shown on your screen and in Figure 4-8 look like the sketch Andrea prepared (Figure 4-5)? Not exactly. The problem is that the Chart Wizard assumes that if the range to plot has more rows than columns (which is true in this case), then the data in the columns (states) becomes the data series. Andrea wants the stove models (rows) as the data series, so you need to make this change in the dialog box.

To change the data series and continue the steps in the Chart Wizard:

1. Click the **Rows** option button in the Series in area of the dialog box. The sample chart now shows the stove models as the data series and the states as category labels. See Figure 4-9.

Figure 4-9   **ROWS AS DATA SERIES**

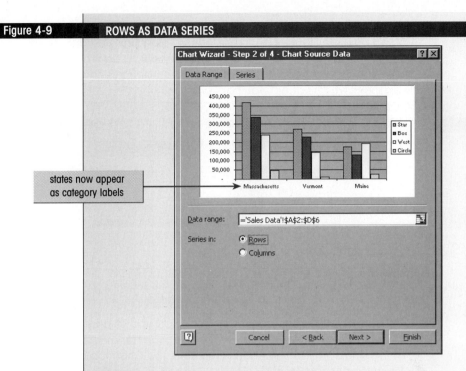

states now appear
as category labels

2. Click the **Next** button to open the Chart Wizard - Step 3 of 4 - Chart Options dialog box. See Figure 4-10. A preview area displays the current appearance of the chart. This tabbed dialog box enables you to change various chart options, such as titles, axes, gridlines, legends, data labels, and data tables. As you change these settings, check the preview chart in this dialog box to make sure you get the look you want.

Now add a title for the chart.

Figure 4-10   **CHART WIZARD - STEP 3 OF 4 - CHART OPTIONS DIALOG BOX**

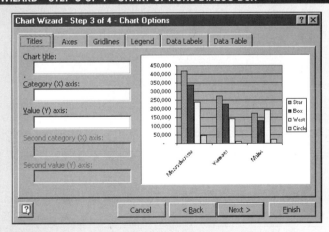

3. If necessary click the **Titles** tab, click the **Chart title** text box, and then type **Sales by State** for the chart title. Notice that the title appears in the preview area.

4. Click the **Next** button to display the Chart Wizard - Step 4 of 4 - Chart Location dialog box. See Figure 4-11. In this fourth dialog box, you decide where to place the chart. You can place a chart in a worksheet as an embedded chart, or place it in its own chart sheet. You want to embed this chart in the Sales Data worksheet, which is the default option.

| Figure 4-11 | CHART WIZARD - STEP 4 OF 4 - CHART LOCATION DIALOG BOX |

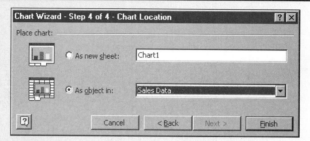

You have finished the steps in the Chart Wizard.

5. Click the **Finish** button to complete the chart and display it in the Sales Data worksheet. See Figure 4-12. Notice the selection handles around the chart; these handles indicate that the chart is selected. The Chart toolbar automatically appears when the chart is selected. Figure 4-13 describes each button on the chart toolbar. Also, notice that the data and labels for the chart are outlined in blue, green, and purple in the worksheet. This enables you to quickly see which cells make up the chart.

TROUBLE? If you don't see the Chart toolbar, click View on the menu bar, click Toolbars, and then click the Chart check box to select that option.

| Figure 4-12 | COMPLETED COLUMN CHART |

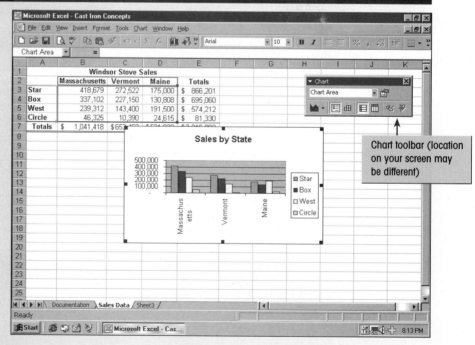

Chart toolbar (location on your screen may be different)

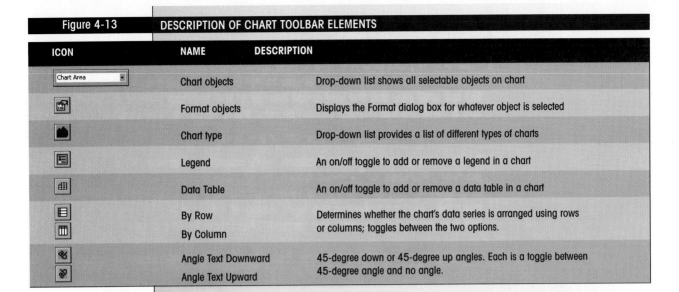

Figure 4-13	**DESCRIPTION OF CHART TOOLBAR ELEMENTS**	
ICON	**NAME**	**DESCRIPTION**
Chart Area ▾	Chart objects	Drop-down list shows all selectable objects on chart
🖼	Format objects	Displays the Format dialog box for whatever object is selected
⬛	Chart type	Drop-down list provides a list of different types of charts
📋	Legend	An on/off toggle to add or remove a legend in a chart
⊞	Data Table	An on/off toggle to add or remove a data table in a chart
📊	By Row	Determines whether the chart's data series is arranged using rows
📊	By Column	or columns; toggles between the two options.
🔽	Angle Text Downward	45-degree down or 45-degree up angles. Each is a toggle between
🔼	Angle Text Upward	45-degree angle and no angle.

6. Click anywhere outside the chart to deselect it. Notice that the selection handles no longer surround the chart, indicating that the chart is no longer selected, and the Chart toolbar is no longer visible. The Chart toolbar only appears when the chart is selected.

After reviewing the column chart, you think that the area outlined for the chart is too small to highlight the comparison between models. You also note that you need to move the chart so that it does not cover the worksheet data.

Moving and Resizing a Chart

When you use the Chart Wizard to create an embedded chart, Excel displays the chart in the worksheet. The size of the chart may not be large enough to accentuate relationships between data points or display the labels correctly. Because a chart is an object, you can move, resize, or copy it like any object in the Windows environment. However, before you can move, resize, or copy a chart, you must select, or **activate** it. You select a chart by clicking anywhere within the chart area. Small black squares, called **selection handles** or **sizing handles**, appear on the boundaries of the chart, indicating that it is selected. You will also notice that some of the items on the menu bar change to enable you to modify the chart instead of the worksheet.

You decide to move and resize the chart before showing it to Andrea.

To change the size and position of the chart:

1. Click anywhere within the white area of the chart border to select the chart. Selection handles appear on the chart border.

TROUBLE? If the Name box does not display the name "Chart Area," click the Chart Objects list box arrow on the Chart toolbar to display the list of chart objects. Select Chart Area.

TROUBLE? If the Chart toolbar is in the way, click and drag it to the bottom of the window to anchor it there.

2. Position the pointer anywhere on the chart border. Click and hold down the mouse button (the pointer changes to ✛) as you drag the chart down and to the left until you see the upper-left corner of the dashed outline in column A of row 8. Release the mouse button to view the chart in its new position.

   Now increase the height and width of the chart.

3. Position the pointer on the bottom, right selection handle. When the pointer changes to ↖, hold down the mouse button (note the pointer now changes to +) and drag the selection handle downward to the right until the chart outline reaches the right edge of column H and row 23. Release the mouse button to view the resized chart. See Figure 4-14.

Figure 4-14	CHART AFTER BEING MOVED AND RESIZED

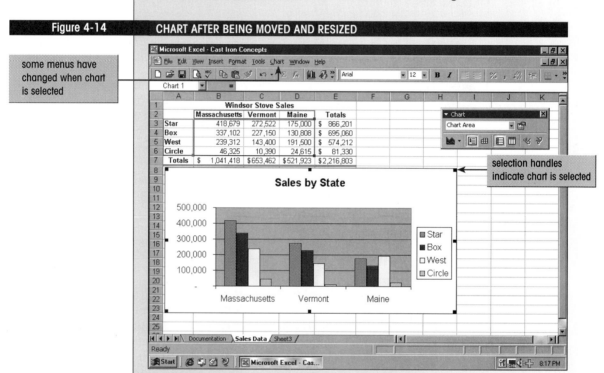

some menus have changed when chart is selected

selection handles indicate chart is selected

4. Click anywhere outside the chart border to deselect the chart. Notice that some of the menus on the menu bar change because the chart is no longer active.

The chart is repositioned and resized. You show Andrea the chart embedded in her Sales Data worksheet. As she reviews the chart, Andrea notices an error in the value entered for West Windsor stoves sold in Maine.

Updating a Chart

Every chart you create is linked to the worksheet data. As a result, if you change the data in a worksheet, Excel automatically updates the chart to reflect the new values. Andrea noticed that sales of West Windsor in Maine were entered incorrectly. She accidentally entered sales as 191,500, when the correct entry should have been 119,500. Correct this data entry error and observe how it changes the column chart.

To change the worksheet data and observe changes to the column chart:

1. Observe the height of the data marker for the West model in Maine (yellow data marker) in the column chart.

2. Click cell **D5**, type **119500**, and then press the **Enter** key. See Figure 4-15. The total West sales (cell E5) and total sales for Maine (cell D7) automatically change. In addition, Excel automatically updates the chart to reflect the new source value. Now the data marker for the West Windsor sales in Maine is shorter.

| Figure 4-15 | MODIFIED COLUMN CHART AFTER CHART'S SOURCE DATA CHANGED |

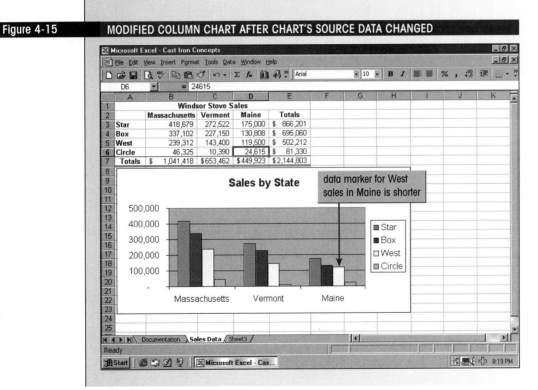

Now that the data for the West stove sales in Maine is corrected, you review the chart with Andrea for ways you can improve the presentation of the chart data.

Modifying **an Excel Chart**

You can make many modifications to a chart, including changing the type of chart, the text, the labels, the gridlines, and the titles. To make these modifications, you need to activate the chart. Selecting, or activating, a chart, as mentioned earlier, allows you to move and resize it. It also gives you access to the Chart commands on the menu bar and displays the Chart toolbar to use as you alter the chart.

After reviewing the column chart, Andrea believes that the Circle Windsor will distract the audience from the three products that were actually available during the entire period. Recall that the Circle Windsor was only on the market for four months and even then there were production problems. She wants to compare sales only for the three models sold during the entire year.

Revising the Chart Data Series

After you create a chart, you might discover that you specified the wrong data range, or you might decide that your chart should display a different data series. Whatever your reason, you do not need to start over in order to revise the chart's data series.

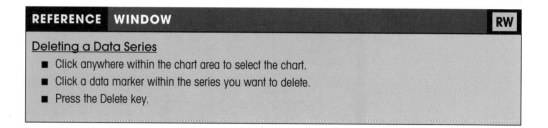

REFERENCE WINDOW **RW**

Deleting a Data Series
- Click anywhere within the chart area to select the chart.
- Click a data marker within the series you want to delete.
- Press the Delete key.

Andrea asks you to remove the data series representing the Circle Windsor model from the column chart.

To delete the Circle Windsor data series from the column chart:

1. Click anywhere within the chart border to select the chart.

2. Click any data marker representing the Circle data series (any light blue data marker). Selection handles appear on each column of the Circle Windsor data series and a ScreenTip appears identifying the selected chart item. See Figure 4-16.

Figure 4-16   **CHART WITH CIRCLE DATA SERIES SELECTED**

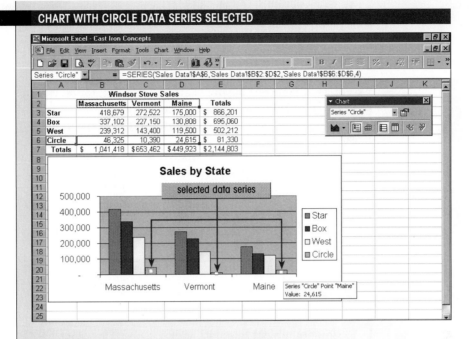

3. Press the **Delete** key. See Figure 4-17. Notice that the Circle Windsor data series disappears from the chart.

Figure 4-17   **COLUMN CHART AFTER DATA SERIES REMOVED**

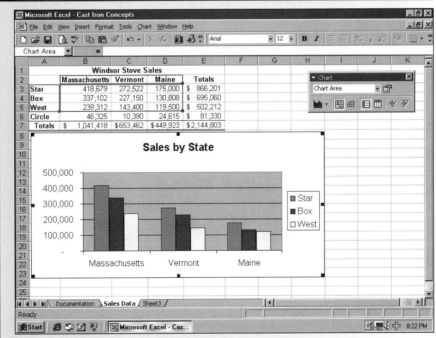

TROUBLE? If you deleted the wrong data series, click the Undo 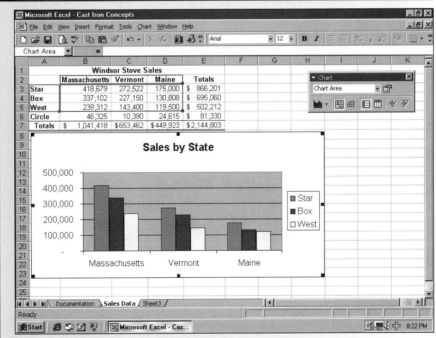 button and then repeat Steps 2 and 3.

Andrea reviews her sketch and notices that the chart title is incomplete; the intended title was "Sales by State and Model." She asks you to make this change to the chart.

Editing Chart Text

Excel classifies the text in your charts in three categories: label text, attached text, and unattached text. **Label text** includes the category names, the tick mark labels, the X-axis labels, and the legend. Label text often derives from the cells in the worksheet; you usually specify it using the Chart Wizard.

Attached text includes the chart title, X-axis title, and Y-axis title. Although attached text appears in a predefined position, you can edit it, and move it using the click-and-drag technique.

Unattached text includes text boxes or comments that you type in the chart after it is created. You can position unattached text anywhere in the chart. To add unattached text to a chart, you use the Text Box tool on the Drawing toolbar.

As noted earlier, you need to change the chart title to "Sales by State and Model." To do this you must select the chart, select the chart title, and then add "and Model" to the title.

To revise the chart title:

1. If the chart is not selected, click the **chart** to select it.

2. Click the **Chart Title** object to select it. Notice that the object name Chart Title appears in the Name box and as a ScreenTip; also, selection handles surround the Chart Title object.

3. Position the pointer in the Chart Title text box at the end of the title, and then click to remove the selection handles from the Chart Title object. The pointer changes to an insertion point I.

   TROUBLE? If the insertion point is not at the end of the title, press the End key to move it to the end.

4. Press the **spacebar**, type **and Model**, and then click anywhere within the chart border to complete the change in the title and deselect it.

Checking Andrea's sketch, you notice that the Y-axis title was not included. To help clarify what the data values in the chart represent, you decide to add "Sales ($U.S.)" as a Y-axis title. You use the Chart Option command on the Chart menu to add this title.

To add the Y-axis title:

1. Make sure that the chart is still selected.

2. Click **Chart** on the menu bar, and then click **Chart Options** to open the Chart Options dialog box. If necessary, click the **Titles** tab.

3. Click the **Value (Y) axis** text box, and then type **Sales ($U.S.)**.

4. Click the **OK** button to close the Chart Options dialog box.

5. Click anywhere within the chart border to deselect the Y-axis title. See Figure 4-18.

Figure 4-18	CHART AFTER TITLE MODIFIED AND VALUE AXIS LABEL INSERTED

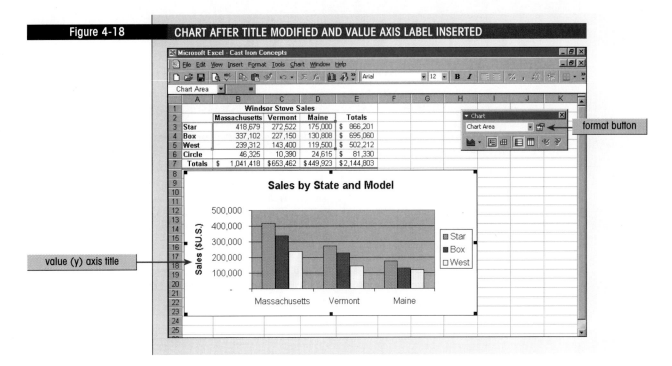

Now that the titles accurately describe the chart data, Andrea asks you to add data labels to show the exact values of the Star Windsor data series—CIC's leading model.

Adding Data Labels

A data label provides additional information about a data marker. Depending on the type of chart, data labels can show values, names of data series (or categories), or percentages. You can apply a label to a single data point, an entire data series, or all data markers in a chart.

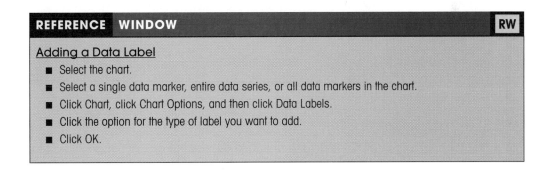

REFERENCE WINDOW   RW

Adding a Data Label
- Select the chart.
- Select a single data marker, entire data series, or all data markers in the chart.
- Click Chart, click Chart Options, and then click Data Labels.
- Click the option for the type of label you want to add.
- Click OK.

In this case, Andrea wants to add data labels to the Star model data series.

To apply data labels to a data series:

1. If the column chart is not selected, click anywhere within the chart border to select it.

2. Click any **Star Windsor** data marker (blue data marker) within the chart. Selection handles appear on all columns in the Star Windsor data series.

   To format any chart element, you can use the Format button on the Chart toolbar. The Format button's ScreenTip name and function change depending on what chart element is selected for formatting. The list box that appears to the left of the Format button on the toolbar also displays the name of the currently selected chart element. In this case, the Star Windsor data series marker is selected, so the Format button on the Chart toolbar appears as the Format Data Series button, and when selected, opens the Format Data Series dialog box.

3. Click the **Format Data Series** button 📠 on the Chart toolbar to open the Format Data Series dialog box, and then click the **Data Labels** tab if necessary. See Figure 4-19.

| Figure 4-19 | DATA LABELS TAB IN FORMAT DATA SERIES DIALOG BOX |

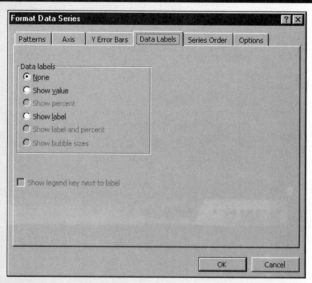

4. Click the **Show value** option button.

5. Click the **OK** button to display the column chart with data labels.

6. Click anywhere within the chart border to deselect the Star Windsor data series. See Figure 4-20.

Figure 4-20	CHART WITH DATA LABELS

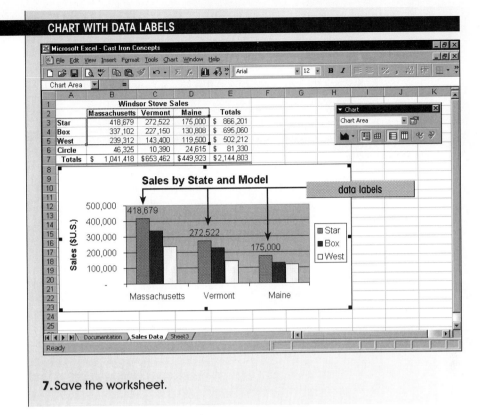

7. Save the worksheet.

Andrea is pleased with the changes in the chart. Now she wants to add visual interest to the chart, making it look more polished.

Enhancing the Appearance of the Chart

There are many ways to give charts a more professional look. The use of different font styles, types, and sizes can make chart labels and titles stand out. Using colors, borders, and patterns can also make a chart more interesting to view.

Andrea thinks that a border and some color could accentuate the title of the chart.

Emphasizing the Title with Border and Color

The chart title is an object that you can select and format using the menu options or the toolbar buttons. Now make the changes to the chart title.

To display the title with border and color:

1. Click the **Chart Title** to select it and display selection handles. Now that the chart title is selected, notice that the Format button [icon] on the Chart toolbar becomes the Format Chart Title button, and the Chart Objects list box displays "Chart Title."

2. Click the **Format Chart Title** button [icon] on the Chart toolbar to open the Format Chart Title dialog box, and then, if necessary, click the **Patterns** tab.

3. Click the **Weight** list arrow in the Border section to display a list of border weights.

4. Click the **second line** in the list.

5. Click the **gray** square in the Color palette (fourth row, last column) in the Area section.

6. Click the **OK** button to apply the format changes to the chart title, and then click anywhere within the chart area to deselect the title.

Andrea thinks that the chart looks better with its title emphasized. Now she wants you to work on making the data markers more distinctive. They certainly stand out on her computer's color monitor, but she is concerned that this will not be the case when she prints the chart on the office's black and white printer.

Changing Colors and Patterns

Patterns add visual interest to a chart and they can be useful when your printer has no color capability. Although your charts appear in color on a color monitor, if your printer does not have color capability, Excel translates colors to gray shades when printing. It's difficult to distinguish some colors, particularly darker ones, from one another when Excel translates them to gray shades and then prints them. To solve this potential problem, you can make your charts more readable by selecting a different pattern for each data marker.

To apply a different pattern to each data series you use the Patterns dialog box.

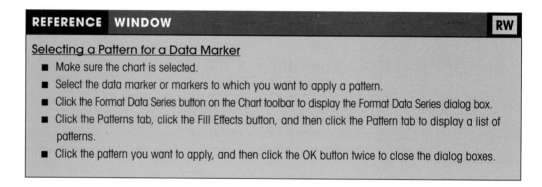

REFERENCE WINDOW   **RW**

Selecting a Pattern for a Data Marker
- Make sure the chart is selected.
- Select the data marker or markers to which you want to apply a pattern.
- Click the Format Data Series button on the Chart toolbar to display the Format Data Series dialog box.
- Click the Patterns tab, click the Fill Effects button, and then click the Pattern tab to display a list of patterns.
- Click the pattern you want to apply, and then click the OK button twice to close the dialog boxes.

You want to apply a different pattern to each data series.

To apply a pattern to a data series:

1. Make sure the chart is selected.

2. Click any **data marker** for the Star data series (blue data marker) to display selection handles for all three data markers for that data series.

3. Click the **Format Data Series** button 🖾 on the Chart toolbar to open the Format Data Series dialog box.

4. If necessary, click the **Patterns** tab, click the **Fill Effects** button to open the Fill Effects dialog box, and then click the **Pattern** tab to display the Pattern palette. See Figure 4-21.

Figure 4-21 **PATTERN OPTIONS IN FILL EFFECTS DIALOG BOX**

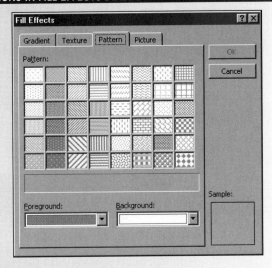

5. Click the **dark downward diagonal** pattern (third row, third column) to select it. Notice that the pattern you selected appears in the Sample box for you to preview.

6. Click the **OK** button to close the Fill Effects dialog box, and then click the **OK** button to close the Format Data Series dialog box and apply the pattern to the Star data series in the chart.

7. Repeat Steps 2 through 6 to select a **narrow horizontal** pattern (fourth row, fourth column) for the Box data series, and again to select a **dark upward diagonal** pattern (fourth row, third column) for the West data series. After you select patterns for the data series, your chart should look like Figure 4-22.

Figure 4-22   **PATTERN COLUMN CHART DATA MARKERS**

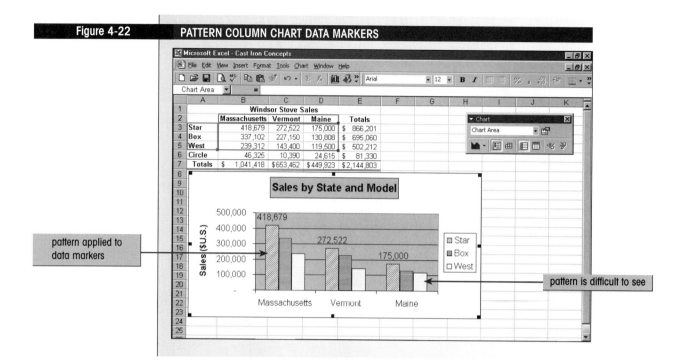

You notice that the West markers appear to have no pattern applied because the pattern is very difficult to see when applied against the yellow color. You decide to change the color of the West markers to a darker color—green, so the pattern will be more visible.

Instead of changing the color using the Chart toolbar or the Chart menu on the menu bar, you'll use Excel's shortcut menu. Many elements within a chart have a shortcut menu providing context-sensitive commands. To use the shortcut menu, right-click on the chart element and choose a command.

To change the color of data markers:

1. Position the mouse pointer over any West data marker and right-click the mouse button. A shortcut menu appears.

2. Click **Format Data Series** to open the Format Data Series dialog box.

3. If necessary, click the **Patterns** tab, click the **Fill Effects** button, and then click the **Pattern** tab in the Fill Effects dialog box to display the patterns palette.

4. In the Pattern tab, click the **Background** list arrow to display a color palette. Click the **green** square in the third row, third column, and then click the **OK** button to close the Fill Effects dialog box and return to the Format Data Series dialog box.

5. Click the **OK** button to close the Format Data Series dialog box, and then click anywhere outside the chart border to deselect the chart.

You show the chart to Andrea, and she decides that it is ready to be printed and duplicated for distribution at the meeting.

Previewing and Printing the Chart

Before you print you should preview the worksheet to see how it will appear on the printed page. Remember that Andrea wants the embedded chart and the worksheet data to print on one page that she can use as a handout at the meeting.

To save and print an embedded chart:

1. Click the **Save** button 🖫 on the Standard toolbar to save the workbook.

2. Click the **Print Preview** button 🔍 on the Standard toolbar to display the Print Preview window.

3. Add your name in the custom footer.

4. Click the **Print** button to open the Print dialog box, and then click the **OK** button. See Figure 4-23.

Figure 4-23   **PRINTOUT OF WORKSHEET WITH EMBEDDED COLUMN CHART**

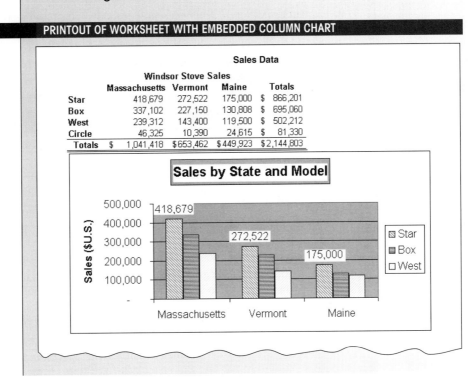

You have finished creating the column chart showing stove sales by state and model for Andrea. Next, you need to create the pie chart showing percentage of total stove sales by model. You will do this in Session 4.2.

Session 4.1 QUICK CHECK

1. A column chart is used to show _____.

2. Explain the difference between a data point and a data marker.

3. What is the purpose of a legend?

4. Describe the action you're likely to take before beginning Step 1 of the Chart Wizard.

5. When you click an embedded chart, it is _____.

6. How do you move an embedded chart to a new location using the mouse?

7. What happens when you change a value in a worksheet that is the source of data for a chart?

8. Explain how to revise a chart's data series.

9. Explain the difference between an embedded chart and a chart.

SESSION 4.2

In this session you will create a pie chart. You will also learn how to select nonadjacent ranges, how to change a two-dimensional pie chart to a three-dimensional pie chart, and how to "explode" a slice from a pie chart. You will also learn how to use chart sheets and how to add a border to a chart.

Creating a Chart in a Chart Sheet

Now Andrea wants to show the contribution of each Windsor model to the total stove sales. Recall from the planning sketch she did (Figure 4-5) that she wants to use a pie chart to show this relationship.

A pie chart shows the relationship, or proportions, of parts to a whole. The size of each slice is determined by the value of that data point in relation to the total of all values. A pie chart contains only one data series. When you create a pie chart, you generally specify two ranges. Excel uses the first range for the category labels and the second range for the data series. Excel automatically calculates the percentage for each slice, draws the slice to reflect the percentage of the whole, and gives you the option of displaying the percentage as a label in the completed chart.

Andrea's sketch (see Figure 4-5) shows estimates of each stove's contribution and how she wants the pie chart to look. The pie chart will have four slices, one for each stove model. She wants each slice labeled with the stove model's name and its percentage of total sales. Because she doesn't know the exact percentages until Excel calculates and displays them in the chart, she put "__%" on her sketch to show where she wants the percentages to appear.

Creating a Pie Chart

You begin creating a pie chart by selecting the data to be represented from the worksheet. You refer to your worksheet and note in the sketch that the data labels for the pie slices are in cells A3 through A6 and the data points representing the pie slices are in cells E3 through E6. You must select these two ranges to tell the Chart Wizard the data that you want to chart, but you realize that these ranges are not located next to each other in the worksheet. You know how to select a series of adjacent cells; now you need to learn how to select two separate ranges at once.

Selecting Nonadjacent Ranges

A nonadjacent range is a group of individual cells or ranges that are not next to each other. Selecting nonadjacent ranges is particularly useful when you construct charts because the cells that contain the data series and those that contain the data labels are often not side by side in the worksheet. When you select nonadjacent ranges, the selected cells in each range are highlighted. You can then format the cells, clear them, or use them to construct a chart.

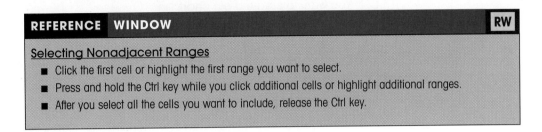

REFERENCE WINDOW   **RW**

Selecting Nonadjacent Ranges
- Click the first cell or highlight the first range you want to select.
- Press and hold the Ctrl key while you click additional cells or highlight additional ranges.
- After you select all the cells you want to include, release the Ctrl key.

Now select the nonadjacent ranges to be used to create the pie chart.

To select range A3:A6 and range E3:E6 in the Sales Data sheet:

1. If you took a break after the last session, make sure that Excel is running, the Cast Iron Concepts workbook is open, and the Sales Data worksheet is open.

2. Click anywhere outside the chart border to make sure the chart is not activated. Press **Ctrl + Home** to make cell A1 the active cell.

3. Select cells **A3** through **A6**, and then release the mouse button.

4. Press and hold the **Ctrl** key while you select cells **E3** through **E6,** and then release the mouse and the Ctrl key. The two nonadjacent ranges are now selected: A3:A6 and E3:E6. See Figure 4-24.

   TROUBLE? If you didn't select the cells you want on your first try, click any cell to remove the highlighting, then go back to Step 2 and try again.

Figure 4-24   **SELECTING NONADJACENT CELL RANGES**

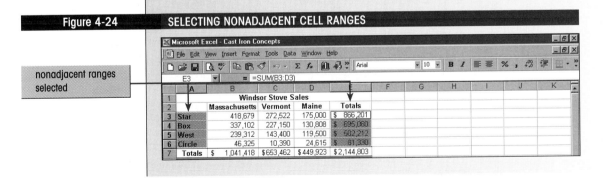

nonadjacent ranges selected

This time you'll place your new chart in a chart sheet, a special sheet that contains only one chart. It does not have the rows and columns of a regular worksheet. If you have many charts to create, you may want to place each chart in a separate chart sheet to avoid cluttering the worksheet. This approach also makes it easier to locate a particular chart because you can change the name on the chart sheet tab.

To create a pie chart in a chart sheet:

1. Click the **Chart Wizard** button 📊 on the Standard toolbar to open the Chart Wizard - Step 1 of 4 - Chart Type dialog box.

   TROUBLE? If the Office Assistant appears on your screen, click the button next to the message "No, don't provide help now" to close the Office Assistant.

   You want to create a pie chart.

2. Click the **Pie** chart type to select it. Six Pie chart subtypes appear. The Two-dimensional Pie chart subtype is the default subtype for the Pie chart type. Click the **Press and hold to view sample** button to display a preview of the Pie chart type.

   You decide to use the default chart subtype.

3. Click the **Next** button to open the Chart Wizard - Step 2 of 4 - Chart Source Data dialog box. Make sure the Data range text box displays "='SalesData'!$A$3:$A$6, 'Sales Data'!$E$3:$E$6." This dialog box also displays a preview of your chart.

   TROUBLE? If the range shown on your screen is not "='Sales Data'!$A$3:$A$6, 'Sales Data'!$E$3:$E$6," type the necessary corrections in the Data range text box, or click the Collapse Dialog button located to the right of the Data range text box, and then select the correct range in the worksheet.

4. Click the **Next** button to open the Chart Wizard - Step 3 of 4 - Chart Options dialog box.

   Add a title for the chart.

5. If necessary, click the **Titles** tab, click the **Chart title** text box, and then type **Sales by Model** for the chart title. Notice that the title appears in the preview area.

6. Click the **Data Labels** tab, and then click the **Show label and percent** option button to place the label and percentage next to each slice.

   Now remove the legend because it is no longer needed.

7. Click the **Legend** tab, and then click the **Show legend** check box to remove the check and deselect that option.

8. Click the **Next** button to open the Chart Wizard - Step 4 of 4 - Chart Location dialog box. Recall that in the fourth dialog box you decide where to place the chart. You can place a chart in a worksheet or in its own chart sheet. You want to place this chart in a chart sheet.

9. Click the **As new sheet** option button to place the chart in the Chart1 chart sheet.

   You have finished the steps in the Chart Wizard.

10. Click the **Finish** button to complete the chart. The new chart, along with the Chart toolbar, appears in the chart sheet named Chart1. The chart sheet is inserted into the workbook before the worksheet on which it is based. See Figure 4-25.

Figure 4-25	PIE CHART IN A CHART SHEET

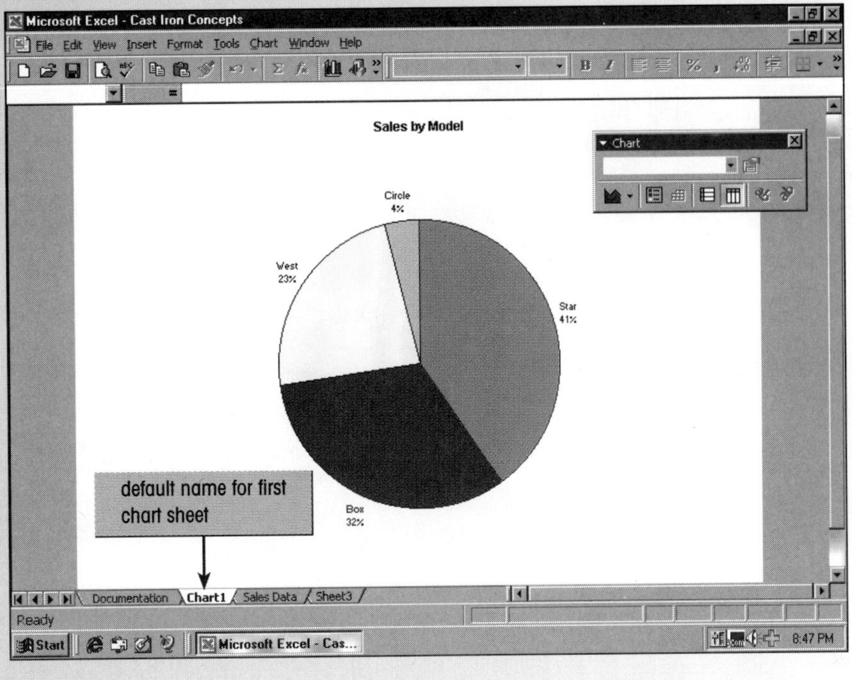

After reviewing the pie chart, Andrea asks you to change the current pie chart to a three-dimensional design to give the chart a more professional look.

Changing the Chart Type from Two-Dimensional to Three-Dimensional

As you recall, Excel provides 14 different chart types that you can choose from as you create a chart. You can also access these chart types after the chart is created and change from one type to another. To change the chart type, you can use the Chart Type command on the Chart menu or the Chart Type button on the Chart toolbar. You use the Chart toolbar to change this two-dimensional pie chart to a three-dimensional pie chart.

To change the pie chart to a three-dimensional pie chart:

1. Make sure the chart area is selected, and then click the **Chart Type** 📊▾ arrow on the Chart toolbar to display a palette of chart types. See Figure 4-26.

    TROUBLE? If the Chart toolbar does not appear on the screen, click View on the menu bar, point to Toolbars, and then click the Chart check box to display the Chart toolbar.

Figure 4-26	PALETTE OF CHART TYPES

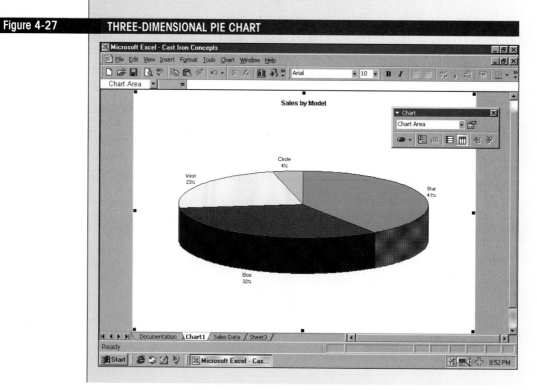

2. Click the **3-D Pie Chart** sample in the fifth row of the second column. The chart reappears as a three-dimensional pie chart. Notice that the Chart Type icon now reflects the new chart type. See Figure 4-27.

Figure 4-27	THREE-DIMENSIONAL PIE CHART

In her presentation, Andrea plans to emphasize the importance of the Star model because it is her best-selling model in the New England territory. She decides to "explode" the Star slice.

Exploding a Slice of a Pie Chart

When you create a pie chart, you may want to focus attention on a particular slice in the chart. You can present the data so a viewer can easily focus attention on one component, for example, which product sold the most. One method of emphasizing a particular slice over others is separating or "exploding" the slice from the rest of the pie. The *cut* slice is more distinct because it is not connected to the other slices. A pie chart with one or more slices separated from the whole is referred to as an exploded pie chart.

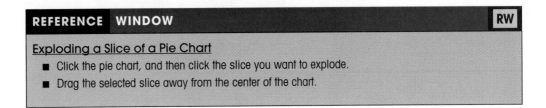

REFERENCE WINDOW   **RW**

Exploding a Slice of a Pie Chart
- Click the pie chart, and then click the slice you want to explode.
- Drag the selected slice away from the center of the chart.

Andrea asks you to explode the slice that represents sales for the Star model.

To explode the slice that represents the Star model sales:

1. Click anywhere in the pie chart to select it. One selection handle appears on each pie slice and the Name box indicates that Series 1 is the selected chart object.

2. Now that you have selected the entire pie, you can select one part of it, the Star slice. Position the pointer over the slice that represents Star model sales. As you move the pointer over this slice, the ScreenTip "Series 1 Point: "Star" Value: $866,201 (41%)" appears. Click to select the slice. Selection handles now appear on only this slice.

3. With the pointer on the selected slice, click and hold down the mouse button while dragging the slice to the right, away from the center of the pie chart. As you drag the slice, an outline of the slice marks your progress.

4. Release the mouse button to leave the slice in the new position. See Figure 4-28.

Figure 4-28   PIE CHART WITH EXPLODED SLICE

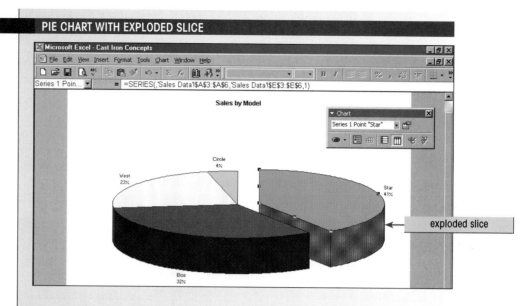

5. Click any white chart area of the pie chart to deselect the exploded slice.

The Star model now is exploded in the pie chart, but Andrea still isn't satisfied. You suggest moving the slice to the front of the pie.

Rotating a Three-Dimensional Chart

When working with a three-dimensional chart, you can modify the view of your chart to change its perspective, elevation, or rotation. You can change the elevation to look down on the chart or up from the bottom. You can also rotate the chart to adjust the placement of objects on the chart. Now rotate the chart so that the Star slice appears at the front of the chart.

To change the three-dimensional view of the chart:

1. Click **Chart** on the menu bar, and then click **3-D View** to open the 3-D View dialog box. See Figure 4-29.

Figure 4-29   3-D VIEW DIALOG BOX

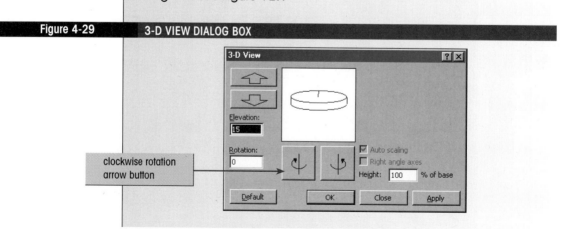

2. Click the **clockwise rotation arrow** button until the Rotation box shows **90**; as you do this, notice that the pie chart sketch in the dialog box rotates to show the new position.

3. Click the **OK** button to apply the changes.

4. Click anywhere in the white area of the chart. See Figure 4-30.

Figure 4-30	THREE-DIMENSIONAL PIE CHART AFTER VIEW ROTATED TO DISPLAY CUT SLICE

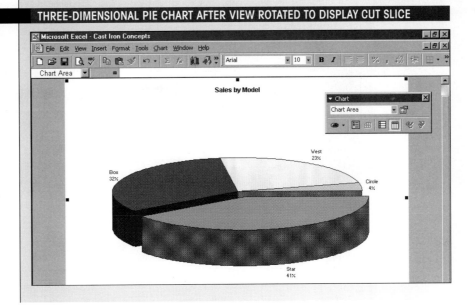

After looking over the chart, you decide to increase the size of the chart labels so that they are easier to read.

Formatting **Chart Labels**

You can change the font type, size, style, and the color of text in a chart using the Formatting toolbar buttons.

You look at the chart and decide that it will look better if you increase the size of the data labels from 10 to 14 points and apply a bold style to them.

To change the font size and style of the chart labels:

1. Click any one of the four data labels to select all the data labels. Selection handles appear around all four labels, and the Name box displays "Series 1 Data Labels."

2. Click the **Font Size** list arrow on the Formatting toolbar, and then click **14**.

3. Click the **Bold** button on the Formatting toolbar.

Now increase the font size of the title to 20 points.

To change the font size of the chart title:

1. Click the **chart title** to select it. Selection handles appear around the title.

2. Click the **Font Size** list arrow on the Formatting toolbar, and then click **20**.

3. Click any white area of the pie chart to deselect the title. See Figure 4-31.

Figure 4-31   THREE-DIMENSIONAL PIE CHART AFTER FONT SIZE OF DATA LABELS AND TITLE INCREASED

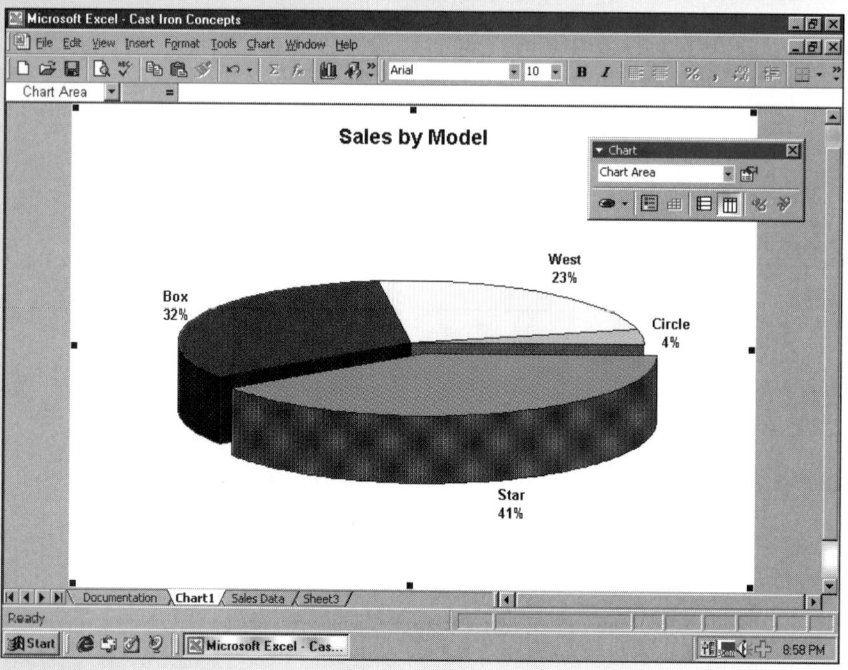

The pie chart looks good but Andrea has one last request. She asks you to apply a blue texture to the chart background.

Applying a Texture Fill Effect to the Chart Background

You can apply texture or gradient fill effects to chart walls, floors, bars, columns, and chart and plot background areas. These fill effects provide a professional look. You want to change the white chart area of the pie chart to a blue texture.

To apply a texture fill effect to the chart background:

1. Make sure the chart area is selected. If it is not, click the white area around the pie chart.

2. Click the **Format Chart Area** button on the Chart toolbar to open the Format Chart Area dialog box.

3. If necessary, click the **Patterns** tab, click the **Fill Effects** button to open the Fill Effects dialog box, and then click the **Texture** tab. See Figure 4-32.

Figure 4-32 | **TEXTURE OPTIONS IN FILL EFFECTS DIALOG BOX**

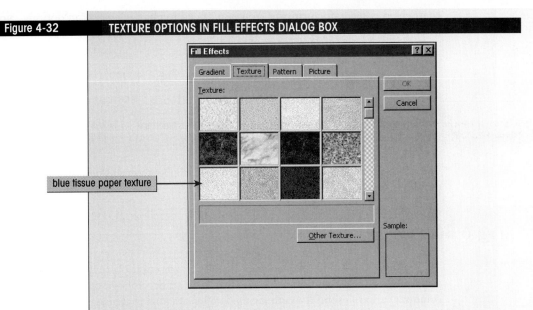

blue tissue paper texture

4. Click the **Blue tissue paper** texture box (third row, first column).

5. Click the **OK** button twice to apply the texture to the chart area. See Figure 4-33.

Figure 4-33 | **COMPLETED THREE-DIMENSIONAL PIE CHART**

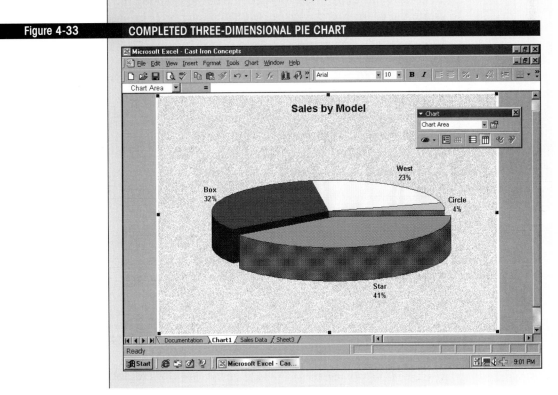

The chart is now complete. You decide to print it and show it to Andrea.

Printing the Chart from the Chart Sheet

When you create a chart in a separate sheet, you can print that sheet separately. If necessary, you can make page setup decisions for the chart sheet alone. In this case, the chart in the chart sheet is ready for printing. You don't need to change any setup options. Now that the three-dimensional pie chart is complete, save the workbook and print a copy of the chart.

To save the workbook and print the chart:

1. Click the **Save** button 🖫 on the Standard toolbar to save the workbook.
2. Click the **Print** button 🖨 on the Standard toolbar to print the chart.

Andrea is pleased with the printed chart and believes it will help her when she makes her presentation next week.

Creating a Bar Chart

Andrea decides to spend some time during her presentation reviewing sales of all stoves in each state in her territory. She recalls from one of her college classes that both the bar and column chart are useful for comparing data by categories. The bar chart may have an advantage if you have long labels, because the category labels in bar charts are easier to read. Andrea asks you to prepare a bar chart comparing sales of all stoves by state.

To prepare this chart, you first select the cells containing the categories and data needed to create the chart. For this chart, select the range B2 through D2 for the category axis (states) and B7 through D7 for the data series (total sales in each state).

To select range B2:D2 and range B7:D7 in the Sales Data sheet:

1. Click the **Sales Data** tab to activate the Sales Data worksheet, and then press **Ctrl + Home** to make cell A1 the active cell.
2. Select cells **B2:D2**, and then release the mouse button.
3. Press and hold the **Ctrl** key while you select cells **B7:D7**, and then release the mouse and the Ctrl key. The two nonadjacent ranges are now selected: B2:D2 and B7:D7.

   TROUBLE? If you didn't select the cells you want on your first try, click any cell to remove the highlighting, and then go back to Step 2 and try again.

Place the bar chart in a separate chart sheet so that Andrea can easily locate it.

To create a bar chart in a chart sheet:

1. Click the **Chart Wizard** button 🛍 on the Standard toolbar to open the Chart Wizard - Step 1 of 4 - Chart Type dialog box.

   You want to create a bar chart.

2. Click the **Bar** chart type to select it. Six Bar chart subtypes appear. The Clustered Bar chart is the default subtype for the Bar chart. Click the **Press and Hold to View Sample** button to display a preview of the Clustered Bar chart subtype.

   You decide to use the Clustered Bar chart type.

3. Click the **Next** button to open the Chart Wizard - Step 2 of 4 - Chart Source Data dialog box. Make sure the Data range box displays "='Sales Data'!$B$2:$D$2, 'Sales Data'!$B$7:$D$7." This dialog box also displays a preview of your chart.

   TROUBLE? If the range shown on your screen is not "='Sales data'!$B$2:$D$2, 'Sales Data'!$B$7:$D$7," type the necessary corrections in the Data range text box, or click the Collapse Dialog button, and then select the correct range in the worksheet.

4. Click the **Next** button to open the Chart Wizard - Step 3 of 4 - Chart Options dialog box.

   Add a title for the chart.

5. If necessary, click the **Titles** tab, and click the **Chart title** text box. Type **Sales by State** for the chart title. Notice that the title appears in the preview area. Click the **Category (X) axis** box, and type **Territories**. Click the **Value (Y) axis** box, and then type **Sales ($U.S.)**.

   There is only one data series, so remove the legend.

6. Click the **Legend** tab and then click the **Show legend** check box to remove the check and deselect that option.

7. Click the **Next** button to open the Chart Wizard - Step 4 of 4 - Chart Location dialog box. You want this chart to be placed in a chart sheet.

8. Click the **As new sheet option** button to place this chart in a chart sheet, and then type **Bar Chart** in the As new sheet text box to rename the chart sheet.

   You have finished the steps in the Chart Wizard.

9. Click the **Finish** button to complete the chart. The new chart, along with the Chart toolbar, appears in the chart sheet named Bar Chart. The chart sheet is inserted into the workbook before the worksheet on which it is based. See Figure 4-34.

| Figure 4-34 | BAR CHART IN A CHART SHEET |

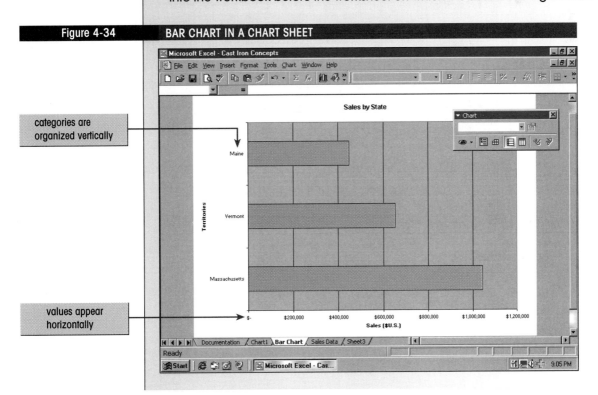

categories are organized vertically

values appear horizontally

Andrea reviews the bar chart and believes it will focus the audience's attention on sales in each state.

Using Pictures in a Bar Chart

When making a presentation, an interesting way to enhance a bar or column chart is to replace the data markers with graphic images, thereby creating a picture chart. Any graphic image that can be copied to the Clipboard can serve as the basis for a picture chart. Andrea wants you to use a picture of the Windsor stove from CIC's latest catalog as the data marker in your bar chart.

REFERENCE WINDOW | **RW**

Using a Picture in a Bar or Column Chart
- Create a bar or column chart using the Chart Wizard.
- Select all the bars or columns you want to replace with the picture.
- Click Insert, point to Picture, and then click From File to display the Insert Picture dialog box.
- Select the image file you want to use.
- Click Insert.

The graphic image of the Windsor stove is located in the Tutorial folder for Tutorial 4 on your Data Disk. The file is named Stove. To replace the plain bars with the graphic image, you need to select one bar or column of the chart and use the Picture command on the Insert menu.

To insert the picture into the bar chart:

1. Click any bar in the chart so that all three data markers are selected.

2. Click **Insert** on the menu bar, point to Picture, and then click **From File** to open the Insert Picture dialog box.

3. Make sure the Tutorial folder for Tutorial 4 is shown in the Look In list box, and then click **Stove**.

4. Click the **Insert** button to insert the picture into the chart. The three bars are each filled by the picture of the stove. See Figure 4-35. Notice that each picture is "stretched" to fit the bar it fills.

   TROUBLE? If a dialog box appears asking for the Import Graphic feature, please consult your instructor or technical support person.

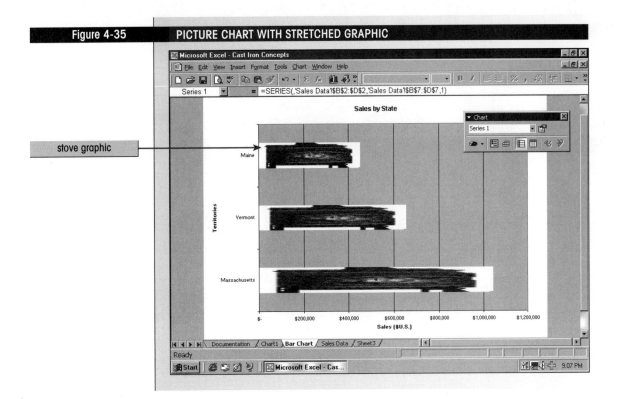

Figure 4-35   PICTURE CHART WITH STRETCHED GRAPHIC

stove graphic

When you insert a picture into a bar or column chart, Excel automatically stretches the picture to fill the space formerly occupied by the marker. Some pictures stretch well, but others become distorted, and detract from, rather than add to, the chart's impact.

Stretching and Stacking Pictures

As an alternative to stretching a picture, you can stack the picture so that it appears repeatedly in the bar, reaching the height of the original bar in the chart. You'll stack the Windsor stove picture in your chart to improve its appearance.

The value axis has tick mark labels at $200,000; $400,000; $600,000; and so on. To match the axis labels, you'll stack one stove each 200,000 units.

To stack the picture:

1. If the handles have disappeared from the bars, click any bar in the chart to select all the bars.

2. Click **the Format Data Series** button 📄 on the Chart toolbar to open the Format Data Series dialog box, and if necessary, click the **Patterns** tab.

3. Click the **Fill Effects** button to open the Fill Effects dialog box, and then click the **Picture** tab if necessary.

4. Click the **Stack and scale to** option button. Accept the Units/Picture value in the format section.

5. Click the **OK** button to close the Fill Effects dialog box, and then click the **OK** button to close the Format Data Series dialog box and return to the chart sheet where the data markers now contain stacked stoves.

6. Click the white area of the chart to deselect the data markers. See Figure 4-36.

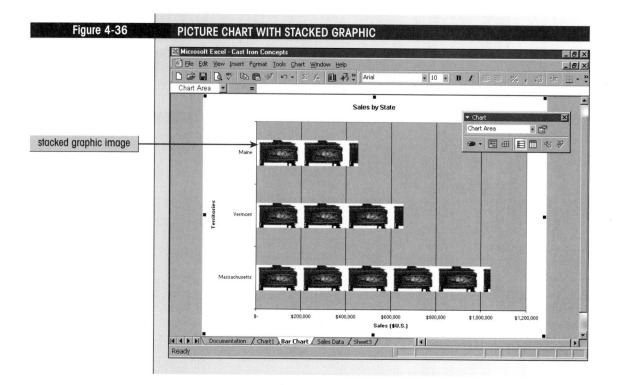

Figure 4-36   PICTURE CHART WITH STACKED GRAPHIC

Andrea likes the picture chart but is not sure how her audience will react to it. She asks you to save the workbook with the picture chart included and will let you know whether to print the picture chart or return to the bar chart. If Andrea asks you to return to the original bars for the data markers, you will select the data series, click Edit, click Clear, and then click Formats.

Now save the workbook.

To save the workbook:

1. Click the **Documentation** tab to make it the active worksheet.

2. Click the **Save** button 🖫 on the Standard toolbar.

3. Close the workbook and exit Excel.

You have finished creating the column chart, pie chart, and bar chart that Andrea needs.

Session 4.2 QUICK CHECK

1. What type of chart shows the proportion of parts to a whole?

2. Define the following terms in relation to a pie chart:
   a. data point   **b.** data marker   **c.** data series

3. When creating charts, why is it important to know how to select nonadjacent ranges?

4. Explain how to select cells A1, C5, and D10 at the same time.

5. When you change a two-dimensional pie chart to a three-dimensional pie chart, you change the _____.

6. Explain how to explode a slice from a pie chart.

7. Explain how to rotate a three-dimensional pie chart.

REVIEW ASSIGNMENTS

Andrea comes to work the next morning and asks you to create one more chart for her presentation. Do the following:

1. Start Windows and Excel, if necessary. Insert your Data Disk into the disk drive. Make sure that the Excel and Book1 windows are maximized. Open the file **Concept2** in the Review folder for Tutorial 4.

2. Save the file under the new name **Cast Iron Concepts 2** in the Review folder.

3. Type your name and the current date in the Documentation sheet.

4. In the Sales Data sheet, select the range that contains the models (A3:D6).

5. Use the Chart Wizard to create a stacked column chart with three-dimensional visual effect.

6. Move the legend to the bottom and add "Total Stove Sales" as the chart title.

7. Place the completed chart in a chart sheet. Rename the chart sheet "Stacked Column".

Explore ▷ 8. Put a box around the chart's title, using a thick line for a border. Add a drop shadow.

9. Save the workbook. Print the chart. Include your name, the filename, and the date in the footer.

Explore ▷ 10. Select the Walls chart element and apply a one-color gradient fill effect. Select an appropriate color. Also apply a one-color gradient fill effect to the floor chart element. (*Hint:* Move the pointer over the different chart elements to identify the floor and wall elements.)

Explore ▷ 11. Select the value axis and change its scale so that the major unit is 150000. (*Hint*: Format the value axis, Scale tab.)

12. Annotate the column chart with the note "Star model our best seller!" by adding a text box and arrow using the tools on the Drawing toolbar.

13. Save the workbook, and then print the stacked bar chart.

14. Open the workbook **ElectronicFilings** and save it as **Filing Solution**.
    a. Prepare an embedded line chart. Add the title "Electronic Filings at the IRS" and the value axis label "Number filed". Remove the legend.
    b. Move and resize the chart until you are satisfied with its appearance.
    c. Change the line weight to the thickest option.
    d. Add a square yellow data marker at each data point.
    e. Save and print the worksheet with the chart.

CASE PROBLEMS

Case 1. Illustrating Production Data at TekStar Electronics   You are an executive assistant at TekStar Electronics, a manufacturer of consumer electronics. You are compiling the yearly manufacturing reports and have collected production totals for each of TekStar's four manufacturing plants. The workbook TekStar contains these totals. You need to create a three-dimensional pie chart showing the relative percentage of CD players each plant produced.

1. Open the workbook **Tekstar** in the Cases folder for Tutorial 4 and add information to the Documentation sheet to create a summary of the workbook. Save the workbook as **TekStar Electronics** in the Cases folder for Tutorial 4.

2. Activate the Units Sold sheet. Use the Chart Wizard to create a three-dimensional pie chart in a chart sheet that shows the percentage of CD players produced at each plant location. Use the Pie with three-dimensional visual effect subtype.

3. Enter "Production of CD Players" as the chart title. Show "Label" and "Percent" as the data labels. Remove the legend.

4. Pull out the slice representing the Chicago plant's CD player production.

5. Increase the font size of the title and data labels so that they are easier to read.

6. Name the chart sheet "3D Pie Chart".

7. Preview and print the chart sheet. Save your work.

8. Create an embedded chart comparing sales of all the products by city. Select the appropriate range and then use the Chart Wizard to create a clustered bar chart. Use the products as the data series and the cities as the X-axis (category) labels. Enter "Production by Product and Plant Location" as the title.

9. Move the bar chart under the table, and then enhance the chart in any way you think appropriate.

10. Preview and print the embedded bar chart, and then save your work.

11. Create a clustered column chart with three-dimensional visual effect comparing the production of VCRs by city. Remove the legend, and then place the chart in a chart sheet named "VCRs".
   a. Add a data table (a grid in a chart that contains the numeric data used to create the chart) to the chart. (*Hint*: Use the Office Assistant to find out how to add a data table to a chart.)
   b. Save the workbook, and then print the chart.

Case 2. Dow Jones Charting   You work for a stock analyst who plans to publish a weekly newsletter. One component of the newsletter will be a 15-week chart tracking the Dow Jones average. Create the chart to be used for the newsletter.

1. Open the workbook **DowJones** in the Cases folder for Tutorial 4. Save the workbook as **Dow Jones Chart** in the Cases folder for Tutorial 4.

2. Use the Chart Wizard to create an embedded line chart (Line subtype) in the Dow Jones worksheet. Specify "Dow Jones Average" as the chart title and "Index" as the title for the Y-axis. Do not add a legend or X-axis title.

3. Place the chart to the right of the present worksheet data and resize it until you are satisfied.

4. Edit the chart as follows:
   a. Change the line marker to a thick line.
   b. Apply a texture fill effect to the chart area. You decide the texture.
   c. Change the color of the plot area. You decide the color.

   Explore
   d. Angle the text upward for the dates on the category axis. (*Hint*: Select the category axis and review the buttons on the chart toolbar.)
   e. Change the scale of the Y-axis so the minimum value is 7000.

5. Add your name to a custom footer, and then print the data and the chart.

6. Add the text box with the note "Market roars back to new high" and then insert an arrow pointing from the text box to anywhere between 11/27/98 and 12/11/98.

7. Save your workbook. Print only the chart.

8. The Dow Jones average for the week ending 12/18/98 was 8600.
   a. Insert this data in the row before the 12/11/98 entry.

   Explore
   b. Modify the chart by plotting the 15-week period beginning 9/11/98 and ending 12/18/98. (*Hint*: Modify the source data range.)

   Explore
   c. Change the location of the chart to a chart sheet. (*Hint*: Check out the Location command on the Chart menu.)
   d. Save the workbook as **Dow Jones 2**, preview your work, and then print the chart.

Case 3. California Chronicle   You work as an intern for Gerry Sindle, business economist, of the *California Chronicle*. The paper plans to publish an economic profile of regions in the state, and you are assisting.

1. Open the workbook **California** in the Cases folder for Tutorial 4. Save the workbook as **California Economic Data**. Create three charts, each in its own chart sheet.

2. Create a pie chart that compares the population of the five geographic areas in the study. Title the chart and enhance it as you think appropriate. Rename the chart sheet to reflect the chart it contains.

3. Create a column chart that compares the number of establishments in retail and services by the five geographic areas. Place the type of establishment on the category axis; each geographic area is a data series. Title the chart and enhance it as you think appropriate. Rename the chart sheet to reflect the chart it contains.

4. Create a bar chart comparing Retail sales and Service receipts by geographic area (categorize by geographic area; the data series is sales and receipts). Title the chart and enhance it as you think appropriate. Rename the chart sheet to reflect the chart it contains.

5. Add a documentation sheet that includes your name, date created, purpose, and a brief description of each sheet in the workbook.

6. Save the workbook.

7. Print the entire workbook (documentation, data worksheet, and the three chart sheets).

Case 4. Association of Realtors   Each year the Association of Realtors collects data on the number of homes sold and the median prices of those sales. Figure 4-37 shows data compiled by the Association since 1987. To better inform the community about occurrences in the home sales market over a ten-year period, the Association wants to release information to the press. Because charts show the data in a more understandable format, the Association has hired you as a part-time analyst to create charts.

Figure 4-37

	Houses Sold	Median Price
1988	4344	$118,500
1989	4294	$127,500
1990	4224	$129,900
1991	3728	$126,000
1992	3477	$123,000
1993	4352	$117,000
1994	4784	$115,300
1995	5081	$115,000
1996	4567	$115,000
1997	5115	$117,000
1998	5199	$117,500

1. Prepare a worksheet using the data from Figure 4-37. (*Hint*: Enter the year as text by typing an apostrophe (') in front of the year.)

2. Create an embedded chart showing the trend in house sales between 1988 and 1998. Title the chart and enhance it as you think appropriate.

3. Create an embedded chart showing the trend in median prices for houses between 1988 and 1998. Title the chart and enhance it as you think appropriate. Print the worksheet including the embedded charts.

Explore

4. Create a chart showing the trend in house sales and median price between 1988 and 1998 (one chart). Place this chart in a chart sheet. Title the chart and enhance it as you think appropriate. (*Hint*: Look up Secondary Value Axis in Help.)

5. The Association of Realtors touted the home sales figures as "shattering all records." Do you agree? Modify the chart in Step 4 by inserting annotated comments supporting or disagreeing with the Association. Print the chart.

6. Save the workbook as **RealtorCharts** in the Cases folder for Tutorial 4.

INTERNET ASSIGNMENTS

The purpose of the Internet Assignments is to challenge you to find information on the Internet that you can use to create effective spreadsheets. The actual assignments are updated and maintained on the Course Technology Web site. Log on to the Internet and use your Web browser to go to the Student Online Companion to accompany this text at **www.course.com/NewPerspectives/office2000**. Click the Excel link, and then click the link for Tutorial 4.

QUICK CHECK ANSWERS

Session 4.1

1. comparison among items or changes in data over a period of time
2. A data point is a value in the worksheet, whereas the data marker is the symbol (pie slice, column, bar, and so on) that represents the data point in a chart.
3. identifies the pattern or colors assigned to the data series in a chart
4. select the range of cells to be used as the source of data for the chart
5. selected; also referred to as activated
6. select the chart, move the pointer over the chart area until the pointer changes to an arrow, and then click and drag to another location on the worksheet
7. The data marker that represents that data point will change to reflect the new value.
8. Select the appropriate chart, click Chart menu, and then Source Data. Click the Collapse dialog box button, select values to be included in the chart, press the Enter key, and then click the OK button.
9. An embedded chart is a chart object placed in a worksheet and saved with the worksheet when the workbook is saved; a chart sheet is a sheet in a workbook that contains only a chart.

Session 4.2

1. pie chart
2. **a.** a value that originates from a worksheet cell
   b. a slice in a pie chart that represents a single point
   c. a group of related data points plotted in a pie chart that originate from rows or columns in a worksheet
3. often, the data you want to plot is not in adjacent cells
4. select cell A1, press and hold Ctrl key, and then select cells C5 and D10
5. chart type
6. select the slice you want to "explode," and then click and drag the slice away from the center
7. select the pie chart you want to rotate, click Chart on the Menu bar, click 3-D View to open the 3-D View dialog box, and then click one of the rotate buttons to rotate the chart

New Perspectives on

MICROSOFT®
EXCEL 2000

Read **This Before You Begin**

To the Student

Data Disks

To complete the Level II tutorials, Review Assignments, and Case Problems in this book, you need four Data Disks. Your instructor will either provide you with Data Disks or ask you to make your own.

If you are making your own Data Disks, you will need five blank, formatted high-density disks. You will need to copy a set of folders from a file server, standalone computer, or the Web onto your disks. Your instructor will tell you which computer, drive letter, and folders contain the files you need. You could also download the files by going to **www.course.com**, clicking Data Disk Files, and following the instructions on the screen.

The following shows you which folders go on each of your disks, so that you will have enough disk space to complete all of the Tutorials, Review Assignments, and Case Problems:

Data Disk 1

Write this on the disk label:
Data Disk 1: Level II Tutorial 5

Put these folders on the disk:
Tutorial.05

Data Disk 2

Write this on the disk label:
Data Disk 2: Level II Tutorial 6

Put these folders on the disk:
Tutorial.06

Data Disk 3

Write this on the disk label:
Data Disk 3: Level II Tutorial 7

Put these folders on the disk:
Tutorial.07

Data Disk 4

Write this on the disk label:
Data Disk 4: Level II Tutorial 8

Put these folders on the disk:
Tutorial.08

Data Disk 5

Write this on the disk label:
Data Disk 5: Level II Appendix 1

Put these folders on the disk:
Appendix.01

When you begin each tutorial, be sure you are using the correct Data Disk. See the inside front or inside back cover of this book for more information on Data Disk files, or ask your instructor or technical support person for assistance.

Using Your Own Computer

If you are going to work through this book using your own computer, you need:

- ■ **Computer System** Microsoft Excel 2000 and Windows 95 or higher must be installed on your computer. This book assumes a complete installation of Excel 2000.

- ■ **Data Disks** You will not be able to complete the tutorials or exercises in this book using your own computer until you have Data Disks.

Visit Our World Wide Web Site

Additional materials designed especially for you are available on the World Wide Web.
Go to **http://www.course.com**.

To the Instructor

The Data files are available on the Instructor's Resource Kit for this title. Follow the instructions in the Help file on the CD-ROM to install the programs to your network or standalone computer. For information on creating Data Disks, see "To the Student" section above.

WORKING WITH EXCEL LISTS

Managing Faculty Data at North State University

CASE

North State University

Janice Long is the dean of the College of Business Administration at North State University (NSU). The College of Business Administration has three academic departments: management, marketing, and accounting. Each faculty member holds an academic rank, such as professor or associate professor. Most faculty members are hired as instructors or assistant professors, and then after a period of time, might be promoted to associate professor and then to full professor. Faculty salaries usually reflect the faculty member's rank and length of service in the department.

The dean frequently asks you to locate and summarize information about the College of Business Administration faculty. This week, she has several important budget and staffing meetings to attend in which she will need to produce detailed and specific information regarding her faculty. She asks for your help to compile the necessary data. She has provided an Excel worksheet that contains the name, academic rank, department, hire date, salary, and sex of each faculty member in the College of Business Administration (CBA). She asks you to use the worksheet to create several reports that will organize the information to produce the specific output she requires for each meeting.

SESSION 5.1

You already know how to use Excel to perform calculations using numeric data or values you enter into worksheet cells. In this session you will learn how to use Excel to manage lists of data. You will learn how to increase the amount of a worksheet that appears on the screen at one time and how to find and replace values in a large worksheet. You will discover how easy it is to sort the information in a worksheet, to add and delete data, and to search for specific information.

Introduction to Lists

One of the more common uses of a worksheet is to manage lists of data, such as client lists, phone lists, and transaction lists. Excel provides you with the tools to manage such tasks. Using Excel, you can store and update data, sort data, search for and retrieve data, summarize and compare data, and create reports.

In Excel a **list** is a collection of similar data stored in a structured manner, in rows and columns. Figure 5-1 shows a portion of the College of Business Administration faculty list. Within an Excel list, each column represents a **field** that describes some attribute or characteristic of an object, person, place, or thing. In this situation, a faculty member's last name, the department in which the faculty member works, and the faculty member's annual salary are all examples of fields. When related fields are grouped together in a row, they form a **record**, a collection of fields that describes a person, place, or thing. For example, the data for each faculty member—first name, last name, department, rank, year hired, sex, and salary—represents a record. A collection of related records makes up an Excel list.

Figure 5-1	PORTION OF FACULTY LIST

If you have worked with spreadsheets before, you may associate the term *database* with what Excel now calls a list. Since the introduction of Excel Version 5, Microsoft refers to database tables in Excel worksheets as lists. The term **database** refers to files created using database management software, such as dBASE, Access, and Paradox. In this tutorial we focus on Excel lists.

Planning **and Creating a List**

Before you create a list, you will want to do some planning. As you spend time thinking about how you will use the list, consider the types of reports, queries, and searches you may need. This process should help you determine the kind of information to include for each record and the contents of each field. As with most projects, the planning you do will help you avoid redesigning the list later.

To create the faculty list, the dean first determined her information requirements. As a way of documenting the information requirements of the faculty list, she developed a **data definition table** that describes the fields she plans to maintain for each faculty member at the College of Business Administration. Figure 5-2 shows the data definition table the dean developed to define her data requirements. She used this as a guide in creating the faculty list.

Figure 5-2	DATA DEFINITION TABLE FOR FACULTY LIST	

FIELD NAME	DESCRIPTION
LASTNAME	Faculty member's last name
FIRSTNAME	Faculty member's first name
DEPARTMENT	Name of department (accounting, finance, and management)
RANK	Faculty rank (instructor, assistant, associate, and full)
YEARHIRED	Year in which faculty member was hired
SEX	Female (F) or male (M)
SALARY	Annual salary

Once you determine the design of your list, you can create the list in a worksheet. You can use a blank worksheet or one that already contains data.

When creating a list in Excel, use the following guidelines:

- The top row of the list should contain a **field name**, a unique label describing the contents of the data in the rows below it. This row of field names is sometimes referred to as the **field header row**.

- Field names can contain up to 255 characters. Usually a short name is easier to understand and remember. Short field names also enable you to display more fields on the screen at one time.

- You should boldface the field names, change the font, or use a different color to make it easier for Excel to distinguish between the data in the list and the field names.

- Each column should contain the same kind of information for each row in the list.

The list should be separated from any other information in the same worksheet by at least one blank row and one blank column because Excel automatically determines the range of the list by identifying blank rows and columns. For the same reason, you should avoid blank rows and columns within the list.

Now open the workbook the dean created to help you maintain the data on faculty at NSU's College of Business Administration.

To open the Faculty workbook:

1. Start Excel. Make sure your Data Disk is in the appropriate drive, and then open the workbook **Faculty** in the Tutorial folder for Tutorial .05 on your Data Disk, and immediately save it as **CBA Faculty**.

2. Switch to the **Faculty Data** worksheet to display the faculty list. See Figure 5-3. The dean's worksheet contains the list of faculty at the College of Business Administration. Currently there are 41 faculty. Each faculty record is stored as a separate row (rows 3 through 43). There are seven fields for each faculty record (columns A through G). Notice that the field names are boldfaced to make it easier for Excel to distinguish the field names from the data in the list.

Figure 5-3	FACULTY LIST

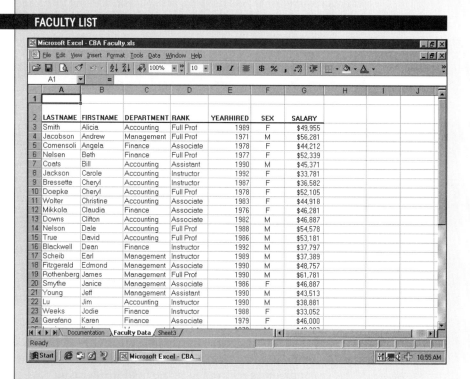

To become familiar with the data, you decide to scroll the faculty list.

3. Click the **vertical scroll bar down arrow** to scroll to the bottom of the list (row 43). As you scroll, notice that the column headings are no longer visible.

4. After viewing the last record in the faculty list, press **Ctrl + Home** to return to cell A1.

You want to keep the column headings on the screen as you scroll the faculty list because not being able to see the column headings makes it difficult to know what the data in each column represents.

Freezing **Rows and Columns**

You can freeze rows and columns so they will not scroll off the screen as you move around the worksheet. This lets you keep headings on the screen as you work with the data in a large worksheet.

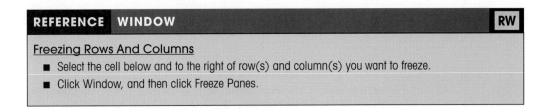

Freezing Rows And Columns

- Select the cell below and to the right of row(s) and column(s) you want to freeze.
- Click Window, and then click Freeze Panes.

You decide to freeze the row with the column headings and the LASTNAME column so that they remain on the screen as you scroll the list.

To freeze rows and columns:

1. Click cell **B3** to make it the active cell.

2. Click **Window** on the menu bar, and then click **Freeze Panes** to freeze the rows above row 3 and the columns to the left of column B. Excel displays dark horizontal and vertical lines to indicate which rows and columns are frozen.

   Now scroll the list.

3. Click the **vertical scroll bar down arrow** to scroll down to the bottom of the list (row 43). As you scroll, notice that the column headings remain visible. See Figure 5-4.

Figure 5-4	FACULTY LIST WITH COLUMN LABELS VISIBLE AS YOU SCROLL

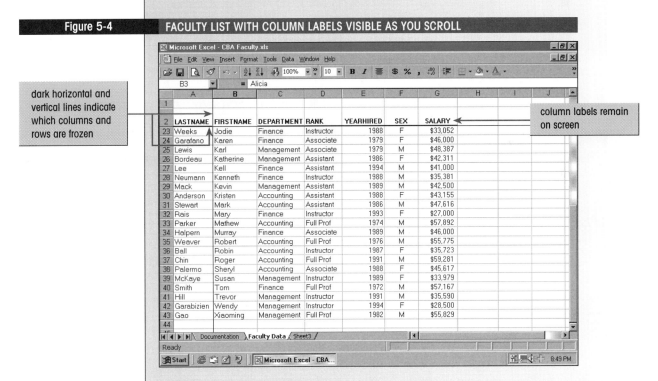

4. Click the **horizontal scroll bar right arrow**. As you scroll to the right, notice that column A, LASTNAME, remains visible.

5. Press **Ctrl + Home** to return to cell B3. Notice that Ctrl + Home no longer returns you to cell A1—instead it returns you to the cell directly below and to the right of the frozen row and column.

To unfreeze the rows and columns, select Unfreeze Panes from the Window menu, but for now, keep the frozen settings.

Changing the Zoom Setting of a Worksheet

Normally, a worksheet appears at 100% magnification. The Zoom command on the View menu (or the Zoom box on the Standard toolbar) enables you to reduce the Zoom percentage so you can see more of the worksheet on a screen (zooming out) or magnify a portion of the worksheet by increasing the Zoom percentage (zooming in) so you can make it easier to read the worksheet.

You want to see how the Zoom command will effect the display of the faculty list.

To change the zoom setting of the Faculty worksheet:

1. Click **View**, click **Zoom** to open the Zoom dialog box. See Figure 5-5.

Figure 5-5	ZOOM DIALOG BOX

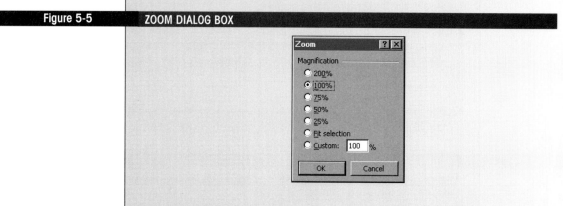

2. Click the **50%** option button.

3. Click **OK**. See Figure 5-6. Notice that you can see all the rows in the faculty list.

Figure 5-6	ZOOM OUT TO SEE MORE OF WORKSHEET

Zoom box

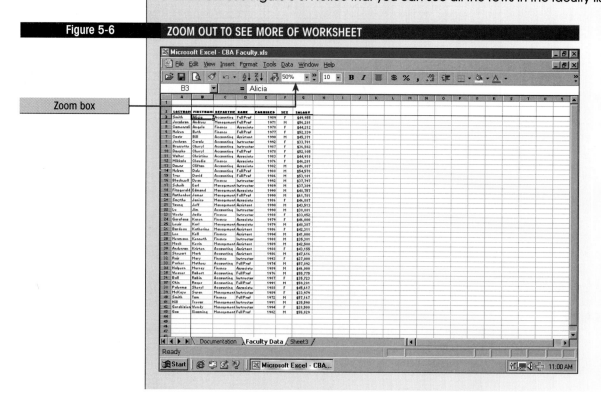

The values are small and too hard to read, so you decide to return to the normal zoom setting—100%. Although you can use the Zoom command to make this change, you'll use the Zoom box on the Standard toolbar instead.

> **To return the zoom setting to 100% size using the Zoom box:**
>
> 1. Click the **Zoom** control drop-down list arrow on the standard toolbar to display a list of magnifications.
>
> 2. Click **100%**. Notice the worksheet returns to normal view.

As you review the worksheet with the dean, the dean observes the value "Full Prof" in the Rank column of the Faculty list. She asks you to change the code to "Full" instead of "Full Prof" before any reports are prepared.

Using **Find and Replace**

To find every occurrence of a character string or value in a large worksheet, you can use the Find and Replace commands. The Find command locates a value or character string, and the Replace command overwrites values or character strings.

Now, change every faculty rank containing "Full Prof" to "Full".

> **To replace the value Full Prof with Full in the Rank column:**
>
> 1. Select the cells **D3:D43**, the rank column.
>
> 2. Click **Edit**, then click **Replace** to open the Replace dialog box. See Figure 5-7.

Figure 5-7	REPLACE DIALOG BOX

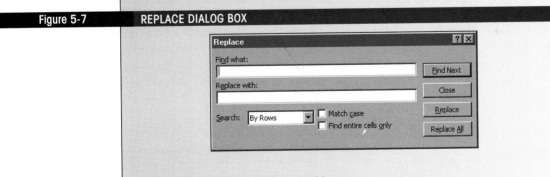

> 3. Type **Full Prof** in the Find what box.
>
> 4. Type **Full** in the Replace with box.
>
> 5. Click the **Find entire cells only** check box to specify that the text in the Find what box must match the entire cell contents.
>
> 6. Click the **Replace All** button to replace all matches. See Figure 5-8. Notice the "Full Prof" entries have all changed to "Full".

Figure 5-8   **FACULTY LIST AFTER THE RANK CODE FOR FULL PROFESSORS CHANGED**

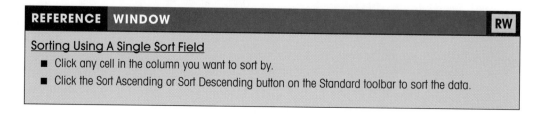

	LASTNAME	FIRSTNAME	DEPARTMENT	RANK	YEARHIRED	SEX	SALARY
3	Smith	Alicia	Accounting	Full	1989	F	$49,955
4	Jacobson	Andrew	Management	Full	1971	M	$56,281
5	Comensoli	Angela	Finance	Associate	1978	F	$44,212
6	Nelsen	Beth	Finance	Full	1977	F	$52,339
7	Coats	Bill	Accounting	Assistant	1990	M	$45,371
8	Jackson	Carole	Accounting	Instructor	1992	F	$33,781
9	Bressette	Cheryl	Accounting	Instructor	1987	F	$36,582
10	Doepke	Cheryl	Accounting	Full	1978	F	$52,105
11	Wolter	Christine	Accounting	Associate	1983	F	$44,918
12	Mikkola	Claudia	Finance	Associate	1976	F	$46,281
13	Downs	Clifton	Accounting	Associate	1982	M	$46,887
14	Nelson	Dale	Accounting	Full	1988	M	$54,578
15	True	David	Accounting	Full	1986	M	$53,181

7. Press **Ctrl + Home**.

Sorting Data

In preparation for her meetings this week, the dean wants a list of faculty members sorted by last name so she can have quick access to faculty data when not near a computer. She asks you to prepare a list of all faculty, alphabetized by last name.

When you initially enter records into a list, each new record is placed at the bottom of the list. To rearrange records in a list, you sort based on the data in one or more of the fields (columns). The fields you use to order your data are called **sort fields** or **sort keys**.

For example, to sort the faculty list alphabetically by last name, you order the data using the values in the LASTNAME field. LASTNAME becomes the sort field. Because LASTNAME is the first sort field, and in this case the only sort field, it is the **primary sort field**.

Before you complete the sort, you will need to decide whether you want to put the list in ascending or descending order. **Ascending order** arranges labels alphabetically from A to Z and numbers from smallest to largest. **Descending order** arranges labels in reverse alphabetical order from Z to A and numbers from largest to smallest. In both ascending and descending order, any blank fields are placed at the bottom of the list. For the quick reference list of faculty, the dean wants to sort the list by last name in ascending order.

Sorting a List Using One Sort Field

To sort data in an Excel worksheet, you can use the Sort Ascending and Sort Descending buttons on the Standard toolbar, or you can use the Sort command on the Data menu. The easiest way to sort data when there is only one sort key is to use the Sort Ascending or Sort Descending buttons. If you are sorting using more than one sort key, you should use the Sort command to specify the columns on which you want to sort.

REFERENCE WINDOW   **RW**

Sorting Using A Single Sort Field
- Click any cell in the column you want to sort by.
- Click the Sort Ascending or Sort Descending button on the Standard toolbar to sort the data.

Produce the dean's alphabetized list by sorting the faculty list using LASTNAME as the sort field.

To sort a list using a single sort field:

1. Click any cell in the LASTNAME column. Notice that you do not select the entire faculty list, range A2:G43. Excel automatically determines the range of the faculty list when you click any cell inside the list.

2. Click the **Sort Ascending button** 🔼 on the Standard toolbar. The data is sorted in ascending order by last name. See Figure 5-9.

   TROUBLE? If you selected the wrong column before sorting the list, and your data is sorted in the wrong order, you can undo it. To undo a sort, click the Undo button 🔙 on the Standard toolbar.

Figure 5-9	FACULTY LIST SORTED BY LAST NAME

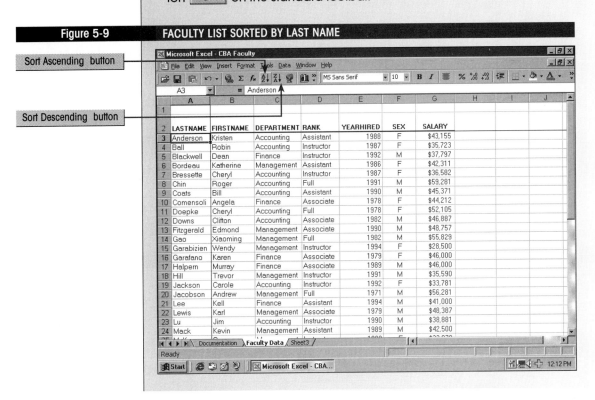

Sort Ascending button

Sort Descending button

When sorting, do not highlight the entire sort key column. If you do, Excel will only sort the values in the selected column rather than sort the entire record.

The dean also requests a list of faculty sorted alphabetically by department, and within each department, by last name.

Sorting a List Using More than One Sort Field

Sometimes sorting by one sort field results in ties. A **tie** occurs when more than one record has the same value for a field. For example, if you sort the faculty list on the DEPARTMENT field, all employees with the same department name would be grouped together. To break a tie you can sort the list on multiple fields. For example, you can sort the faculty list by department, and then by last name within each department. In this case, you specify the DEPARTMENT field as the primary sort field and the LASTNAME field as the **secondary sort field**.

REFERENCE WINDOW   **RW**

Sorting A List Using More Than One Sort Field
- Click any cell in the list.
- Click Data on the menu bar, and then click Sort to open the Sort dialog box.
- Click the Sort By list arrow to display a list of column headings. Select the column you want to use as the primary sort field. Click the appropriate option button to specify sort order.
- Click the first Then By list box and use the list arrow to select the desired column heading for the secondary sort field. Click the appropriate option button to specify sort order.
- If you want to sort out a third column, click the second Then By list box and select the desired column heading. Click the appropriate option button to specify sort order.
- Click the OK button to sort the list.

The dean asked you to sort by department and then alphabetically by last name within each department. To prepare this second list, you will need to sort the data using two columns: DEPARTMENT will be the primary sort field and LASTNAME will be the secondary sort field. When you have more than one sort key, you should use the Sort command on the Data menu to specify the columns you want to sort.

To sort the records by department and within department by last name:

1. Click any cell in the list.

2. Click **Data** on the menu bar, and then click **Sort** to open the Sort dialog box. See Figure 5-10.

Figure 5-10   SORT DIALOG BOX

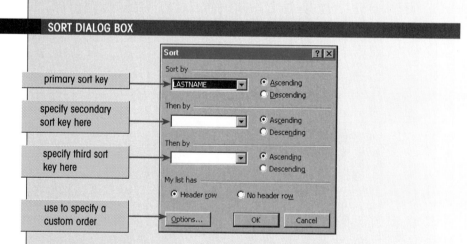

3. Click the **Sort By** list arrow to display the list of column headings, and then click **DEPARTMENT**.

4. If necessary, click the **Ascending** option button to specify that you want to sort the DEPARTMENT field in ascending order.

   Now specify the secondary sort field.

5. Click the first **Then By** list arrow to display the list of column headings, and then click **LASTNAME**.

6. Make sure the Ascending option button is selected.

7. Click the **OK** button. See Figure 5-11.

| Figure 5-11 | FACULTY LIST SORTED BY DEPARTMENT AND WITHIN DEPARTMENT BY LAST NAME |

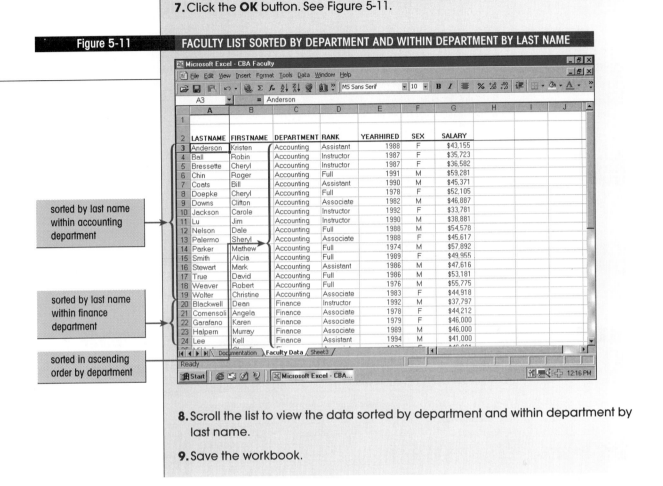

8. Scroll the list to view the data sorted by department and within department by last name.

9. Save the workbook.

Now the dean has a list of faculty members sorted by department and then by last name. This will make finding information about faculty members much easier.

Maintaining a List Using a Data Form

The dean has several changes regarding the faculty status that need to be reflected in the faculty list. First, the accounting department has hired an instructor, Mary Hutch, to teach the introductory accounting courses. Her record needs to be added to the faculty list. Second, Kevin Mack just received official confirmation on his promotion to associate professor. Kevin's record must be updated to reflect his change in rank and new salary of $45,000. Finally, Wendy Garabizien retired at the end of the term; her record needs to be deleted from the faculty list. The dean asks you to update the faculty list to reflect these changes.

One of the easiest ways to maintain a list in Excel is to use a data form. A **data form** is a dialog box in which you can add, find, edit, and delete records in a list. A data form displays one record at a time, as opposed to the table of rows and columns you see in the worksheet. Although you can use the worksheet to make changes directly to the list, using the data form can help prevent mistakes that can occur if you accidentally enter data in the wrong column or row.

REFERENCE WINDOW RW

<u>Adding A Record Using A Data Form</u>
- Click any cell in the list.
- Click Data, and then click Form to display a data form.
- Click the New button to display a blank form.
- Type the values for the new record, pressing the Tab key to move from field to field.
- Press the Enter key to add the record.
- When finished adding records, click the Close button.

Begin updating the faculty list by adding Mary Hutch's data, using the data form.

To add a new record using the data form:

1. Click any cell in the list.

2. Click **Data** on the menu bar, and then click **Form** to display the Faculty Data data form. The first record in the list appears. See Figure 5-12. Notice that Excel uses the worksheet name, "Faculty Data", as the title of the data form.

Figure 5-12   FACULTY DATA DATA FORM

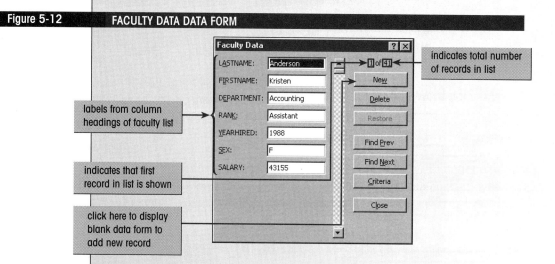

The names that appear on the left side of the data form are taken from the header row of the faculty list.

In the upper-right corner of the form, there is information on how many records are in the list and which row is currently selected.

Now add the new record.

3. Click the **New** button to display a blank data form. Notice that the label "New Record" appears in the upper-right corner of the data form. Enter the values for the record in the text boxes next to each field name.

4. Type **Hutch** in the LASTNAME text box, and then press the Tab key to move to the FIRSTNAME text box.

> **TROUBLE?** If you pressed the Enter key instead of the Tab key, a blank data form appears. Click the Find Prev button to return to the previous record, the record you were entering, and continue entering the data.
>
> **5.** Type **Mary** in the FIRSTNAME text box, and then press the **Tab** key to move to the DEPARTMENT text box.
>
> **6.** Type **Accounting** in the DEPARTMENT text box, and then press the Tab key to move to the RANK text box. Continue entering the remaining data. Remember to press the Tab key after you complete each entry.
>
> RANK: **Instructor**   YEARHIRED: **2001**   SEX: **F**   SALARY: **28000**
>
> **7.** Press the **Enter** key to add the record to the bottom of the list.
>
> The data form is blank again, ready for you to add a new record. But since you don't have any new records to add now, return to the worksheet.
>
> **8.** Click the **Close** button to close the data form and return to the worksheet.
>
> Confirm that the new record has been added to the faculty list. It should appear at the bottom of the list.
>
> **9.** Press **Ctrl + Home** to return to cell B3.
>
> **10.** Press **End + (Down Arrow)** to move to the last record in the list, in cell B44. Verify that the last record contains the data for Mary Hutch.
>
> **11.** Press **Ctrl + Home** to return to cell B3.

Now you can make the other updates to the faculty list. You still need to complete two tasks: change Kevin Mack's rank and salary, and delete Wendy Garabizien's record. Although you can manually scroll through the list to find a specific record, with larger lists of data this method is slow and prone to error. The quicker and more accurate way to find a record is to use the data form's search capabilities. You will use this method to make Kevin Mack's changes and delete Wendy Garabizien's record.

Using the Data Form to Search for Records

You can use the data form to search for a specific record or group of records. When you initiate a search, you specify the search criteria, or instructions for the search. Excel starts from the current record and moves through the list, searching for any records that match the search criteria. If Excel finds more than one record that matches the search criteria, it displays the first record that matches the criteria. You can use the Find Next button in the data form to display the next record that matches the search criteria.

You need to find Kevin Mack's record to change his salary. Use the data form to find this record.

> *To search for a record in a list using the data form:*
>
> **1.** Make sure the active cell is inside the faculty list.
>
> **2.** Click **Data** on the menu bar, and then click **Form** to display the Faculty Data data form.

3. Click the **Criteria** button to display a blank data form. The label "Criteria" in the upper-right corner of the data form indicates that the form is ready to accept search criteria.

   Enter the search criterion in the appropriate field.

4. Click the **LASTNAME** text box, and then type **Mack**.

   If necessary, you can enter multiple criteria. If you enter multiple criteria, all criteria must be met for Excel to find a match.

5. Click the **Find Next** button to display the next record in the list that meets the specified criterion—LASTNAME equal to Mack. See Figure 5-13.

Figure 5-13	DATA FORM AFTER FINDING KEVIN MACK'S RECORD

Kevin Mack is the record you're looking for. However, if more than one employee were named Mack and this was not the record you were interested in, you could click the Find Next button again and the next record meeting the search criterion would appear.

If no records meet the search criterion, no message appears. Instead, the data form simply displays the current record.

Now update his record.

6. Double-click the **RANK** text box, and then type **Associate**.

7. Double-click the **Salary** text box, and then type **45000**.

8. Click the **Close** button to return to the faculty list. The rank and salary for Kevin Mack have been updated.

9. Scroll the list to verify that Kevin Mack's salary is now $45,000, and then press **Ctrl + Home** to return to cell B3.

Now complete the final update to the list, deleting Wendy Garabizien's record.

Using the Data Form to Delete a Record

To delete Wendy Garabizien's record, you will again use a search criterion to find the record. If you enter the full name as the search criterion, the spelling must be absolutely correct; otherwise there will be no match and Wendy Garabizien's record won't be found.

As an alternative, the data form allows you to use wildcard characters when you enter search criteria. A **wildcard character** is a symbol that stands for one or more characters. Excel recognizes two wildcards: the question mark (?) and the asterisk (*).

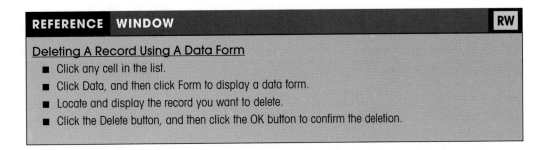

REFERENCE WINDOW   **RW**

Deleting A Record Using A Data Form
- Click any cell in the list.
- Click Data, and then click Form to display a data form.
- Locate and display the record you want to delete.
- Click the Delete button, and then click the OK button to confirm the deletion.

You use the asterisk (*) wildcard to represent any group of characters. For example, if you use "Gar*" as the search criterion for LASTNAME, Excel will find all the records with a last name that begins with Gar, no matter what letters follow. You use the question mark (?) to substitute for a single character. For example, if you enter "Richm?n" as the search criterion, and you might find Richman, Richmen, or Richmon.

To avoid entering Wendy Garabizien's name incorrectly, use the asterisk wildcard character to help find her record.

To search for a record using a wildcard character:

1. Click any cell in the list, click **Data** on the menu bar, and then click **Form** to display the Faculty Data data form.

2. Click the **Criteria** button to begin entering the search criterion.

   Specify the new search criterion.

3. Click the **LASTNAME** text box, and then type **Gar***. See Figure 5-14.

| Figure 5-14 | SEARCHING FOR FACULTY MEMBERS USING WILDCARD CHARACTER |

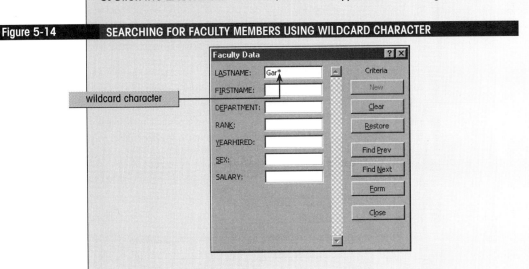

4. Click the **Find Next** button to display the first record in the list that contains the letters Gar as first three letters of the last name. Karen Garafano is not the record you want to delete.

TROUBLE? If you did not retrieve Karen Garafano's record, click the Close button, click Data on the menu bar, and then click Form before repeating Steps 1 through 4.

5. Click the **Find Next** button to display the next record that contains the letters Gar at the beginning of the name. Wendy Garabizien is the record you're looking for.

6. Click the **Delete** button. A message box appears warning you that the displayed record will be permanently deleted from the list.

7. Click the **OK** button to confirm the record deletion. Wendy Garabizien's record has been deleted from the list, and the next record in the list appears in the data form.

8. Click the **Close** button to close the data form and return to the worksheet.

Session 5.1 QUICK | CHECK

1. A row within a data list is often called a _____.

2. A column within a data list is often called a _____.

3. In Excel, a _____ is a collection of similar data stored in a structured manner.

4. Explain how to order a student list so that all students in the same major appear together in alphabetical order by the student's last name.

5. A _____ sort key is a field used to arrange records in a list.

6. If you sort the faculty list from the most recent start date to the earliest start date, you have sorted the faculty in _____ order.

7. The _____ button in the Data Form is used to add a record to a list.

8. You have a list of 250 employees. Explain how to find Jin Shinu's record using the data form.

You have now provided the dean with a current list of all faculty members, sorted alphabetically by department. Now she requires specific information on only some of the faculty at different levels on her staff. She could work with the complete list to find this information, but a customized list limited to just the information she requires would be more useful to her. You can help the dean by filtering the faculty list to show just the information she requires. You will do this in Session 5.2.

SESSION 5.2

In this session you will learn to filter a list to display only specific information using AutoFilters, and you will learn how to customize filters to meet more complex criteria. You will use conditional formatting to highlight data in the list. You will also expand the list to include a new field using natural language formulas, and insert subtotals to display summary information in the list. Finally, you will use Page Break Preview to insert custom page breaks for printing the list.

Filtering a List Using AutoFilters

Now that the dean has the full list of faculty organized for easy reference, she is ready to use the list to prepare the reports she needs for her upcoming meetings. The first scheduled meeting is with the other deans at NSU—their task is to form a university-wide accreditation committee comprising faculty representatives from each of the individual colleges and departments at the university. The dean needs to select a faculty member from the College of Business Administration to serve on the committee. She wants to select a senior faculty member and asks you for a list of full professors.

To get a list of faculty members who are full professors, you could scan the entire faculty list. However, locating the data you need within large lists can be difficult and time-consuming. Sorting can help you group the data; however, you're still working with the entire list. You could use a data form, but if you use a data form to find records that meet specified criteria, you will only display one record at a time. A better solution is to have Excel find the specific records you want, displaying only these records in the worksheet. This process of "hiding" certain records and viewing the ones you want is called **filtering** your data. All records that do not meet your criteria are temporarily hidden from view.

REFERENCE WINDOW	RW

Filtering A List With AutoFilter
- Click any cell in the list.
- Click Data, point to Filter, and then click AutoFilter to insert list arrows next to each column label in your list.
- Click the list arrow in the column that contains the data you want to filter.
- Click the criteria you want to filter.

The Excel AutoFilter feature allows you to filter your data so you view only the records you want. You will use this feature to create a list of full professors in the College of Business Administration.

To filter a list using the AutoFilter command:

1. If you took a break after the last session, make sure Excel is running, the CBA Faculty workbook is open, and the Faculty Data worksheet is active. Make sure the active cell is within the faculty list.

2. Click **Data** on the menu bar, point to **Filter**, and then click **AutoFilter**. List arrows appear next to each column label in the list. To see a list of filtering criteria for a specific column, click the list arrow next to the column heading.

3. Click the **RANK column** list arrow in cell D2 to display a list of criteria you can use to filter the data. See Figure 5-15. In addition to the unique values—Assistant, Associate, Full, and Instructor in the RANK column, three other choices appear that apply to every column. Figure 5-16 describes these three options.

Figure 5-15 **FILTERING OPTIONS FOR RANK FIELD**

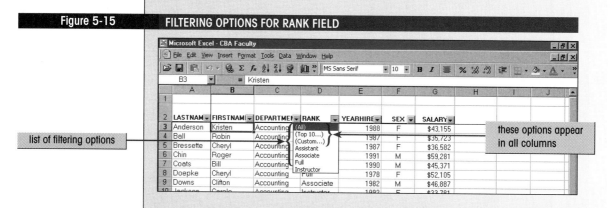

Figure 5-16 **DEFAULT FILTERING OPTIONS**

OPTION	DESCRIPTION
All	Displays all items in the column and removes filtering for the column
Top 10	Displays the top or bottom *n* items in the list
Custom	Specifies more complex criteria

Now select your criterion for filtering the data.

4. Click **Full** to display only full professors. See Figure 5-17. In the status bar, Excel displays the number of records found out of the total records in the list. Review the list to verify that only records with a value equal to Full in the RANK column are visible. Excel hides all rows (records) that do not have the value Full in this column.

| Figure 5-17 | FACULTY LIST DISPLAYING ONLY FULL PROFESSORS |

blue arrow indicator column used to filter list

gaps in row numbers show records have been filtered

indicates number of records found out of all records in list

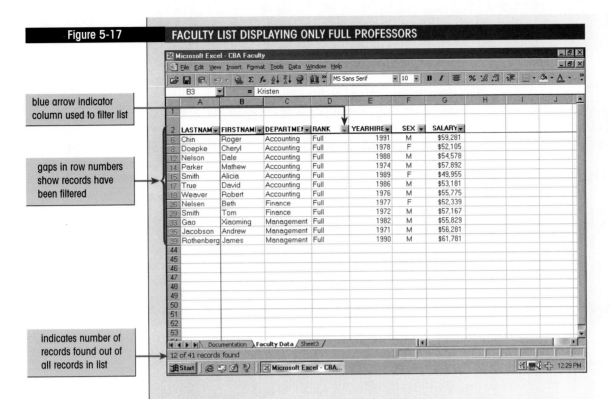

Notice the gaps in the row numbers in the worksheet, and the blue color of the row numbers of the filtered records. In addition the color of the list arrow next to the RANK column changes to blue to let you know that this column has been used to filter the list. The dean will find this useful in making her recommendation for faculty to serve on the accreditation committee.

If you need to, you can further restrict the records that appear in the filtered list by selecting entries from another drop-down list. For instance, if the dean wanted to select from a pool of female faculty with a rank of full professor, you could simply click the SEX column and then click F.

To filter by more than one criterion:

1. Click the **SEX** column list arrow in cell F2, and then click **F** to display the female full professors. See Figure 5-18.

| Figure 5-18 | FACULTY LIST SHOWING FEMALE FULL PROFESSORS |

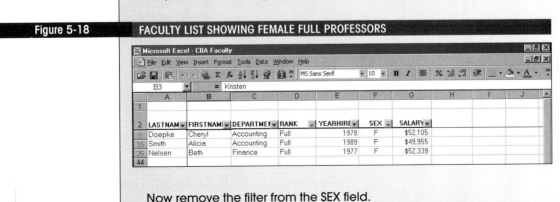

Now remove the filter from the SEX field.

2. Click the **SEX** column list arrow, and then click **All** to remove the filter from this field. Notice all full professors, males and females, are now listed.

Now that you have provided the dean with the list of full professors, restore the list so all the records can be viewed again.

To restore all the data to the list:

1. Click **Data** on the menu bar, point to **Filter**, and then click **Show All**. All the records appear in the worksheet, but all the list arrows remain next to the column headings. Therefore, you can continue to customize the list by filtering it to show certain data.

Now that the list again shows all the faculty records, the dean has a more complex task, which requires you to provide specific information based on customized criteria.

Using Custom AutoFilters to Specify More Complex Criteria

Although you can often find the information you need by selecting a single item from a list of values in the filter list, there are times when you need to specify a custom set of criteria to find certain records. **Custom AutoFilters** allow you to specify relationships other than "equal to" to filter records. For instance, the dean will be meeting with the university's budget director, Bin Chi, later this week to review the College of Business Administration's budget needs for the next fiscal cycle. She received a memo today from the budget office asking for a list of faculty who earn over $50,000 a year and were hired during the 1980s. The dean asks you to print this information. You can develop a custom set of criteria using the Custom option in the AutoFilter list to retrieve these records for the dean.

To use a custom AutoFilter to filter a list:

1. Click the **YEARHIRED** list arrow, and then click **Custom** to open the Custom AutoFilter dialog box. See Figure 5-19.

Figure 5-19	CUSTOM AUTOFILTER DIALOG BOX

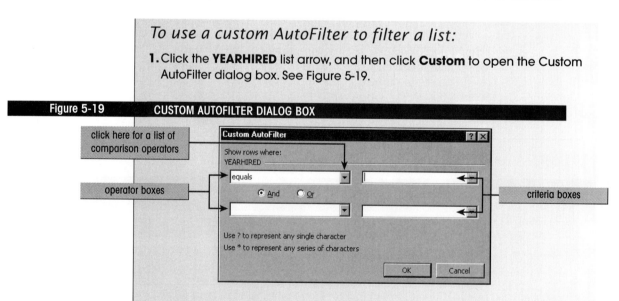

click here for a list of comparison operators

operator boxes

criteria boxes

The operator list box, the first list box in the Show rows where section of the dialog box, lets you specify a comparison operator by selecting an item from a list.

The criteria list box, the list box to the right of the operator list box, lets you specify the field value by typing a value or selecting an item from a list.

The And and Or option buttons are used if you want to display rows that meet two conditions for the field. You select And to display rows that meet both criteria. You select Or to display rows that meet either criterion.

2. Click the first operator list arrow, and then click **is greater than or equal to**.

3. Click the first criteria list box, and then type **1980** in the list box.

4. If necessary, click the **And** option button.

5. Click the second operator list arrow, and then click **is less than**.

6. Click the second criteria list box, and then type **1990**. See Figure 5-20.

Figure 5-20	CUSTOM AUTOFILTER DIALOG BOX SHOWING CUSTOM CRITERIA

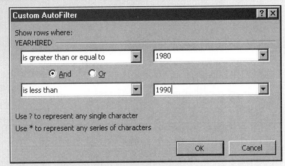

7. Click the **OK** button to display the filtered list consisting of all faculty hired between 1980 and 1989. Notice the status bar indicates 19 of 41 records found.

You have only some of the information the dean requires, however, because she also needs to know all the faculty hired during the 1980s who earn more than $50,000. So you need to further restrict the filtered list to those faculty earning more than $50,000.

8. Click the **SALARY** list arrow, and then click **Custom** to open the Custom AutoFilter dialog box.

9. Click the first operator list arrow, click **is greater than** from the list of operators, click the **first criteria** list box, and then type **50000**.

10. Click the **OK** button to view the filtered list showing faculty hired between 1980 and 1989 and who earn more than $50,000. See Figure 5-21.

Figure 5-21	FILTERED LIST OF FACULTY HIRED 1980 – 1989 EARNING MORE THAN $50,000

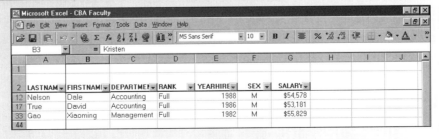

You show the list to the dean. She asks you to sort the list in descending order by salary.

To sort the filtered list, and then restore all the records to the list:

1. Click any field in the SALARY column.

2. Click the **Sort Descending** button ![Z↓] on the Standard toolbar to sort the filtered list in descending order by salary.

   You can now remove all the filters to return to the original complete faculty list.

3. Click **Data** on the menu bar, point to **Filter**, and then click **AutoFilter** to remove all the filters. All the records are listed and the list arrows no longer appear in the column headings.

   The dean wants to be able to quickly identify faculty earning more than $50,000 and asks you to apply the new Excel conditional formatting feature to the SALARY field.

Using Conditional Formatting

Excel lets you apply **conditional formatting**—formatting that appears in a cell only when data in the cell meets conditions that you specify or are the result of a formula. Using this feature, it's easy to spot critical highs or lows in a report. For example, cells representing large amounts of overtime, or sales not meeting projections can be formatted in bold font style or with a red background. You can specify up to three conditions that apply to the value of a cell or the formula that produces the value in that cell. For each condition, you specify the formatting (font, font style, font color, border, etc.) that will be applied to the cell if the condition is true.

REFERENCE WINDOW   RW

Apply Conditional Formats To Cells

■ Select the cells you want to format.

■ Click Format on the menu bar, then click Conditional Formatting to open the Conditional Formatting dialog box.

■ Specify the condition on which to apply formatting.

■ Click the Format button to open the Format Cells dialog box.

■ Select the font style, font color, underlining, borders, shading, or patterns you want to apply, then click the OK button to return to the Conditional Formatting dialog box.

■ Click the OK button to apply conditional formats to cells.

To help the dean quickly identify faculty earning more than $50,000, you decide to apply conditional formatting to any cell in the SALARY field containing a value exceeding $50,000, so that the background color of these cells is green.

Now apply the conditional formatting to the SALARY field.

To apply conditional formatting to the SALARY field:

1. Select the range **G3:G43**.

2. Click **Format** on the menu bar, and then click **Conditional Formatting** to open the Conditional Formatting dialog box. See Figure 5-22. First, specify the condition that will be applied to the salary range.

   TROUBLE? If the Office Assistant appears, select the option "No, don't provide help now."

Figure 5-22	CONDITIONAL FORMATTING DIALOG BOX

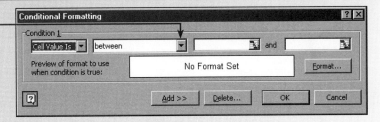

click here to see list of comparison operators

3. Because the contents of the cells in the SALARY field are values, as opposed to formulas or text, make sure Cell Value Is appears in the Condition 1 list box.

   Next, choose the comparison operator to compare with the cell value.

4. Click the list arrow in the second list box to display a list of comparison operators, and then click **greater than**. Notice the number of boxes in the dialog box changes to reflect the comparison operator you selected.

   Now enter the value.

5. Click the third list box for Condition 1, and type **50000**. The condition has been defined. If you needed to, you could specify two additional conditions by clicking the **Add>>** button in the Conditional Formatting dialog box.

   Now define the formatting to be applied to the cell or range if the condition is true.

6. Click the **Format** button in the Conditional Formatting dialog box to open the Format Cells dialog box.

7. Click the **Patterns** tab, and then click the color **green** from the Cell Shading palette (fourth row, fourth column).

8. Click the **OK** button to return to the Conditional Formatting dialog box. Notice that green shading appears in the Preview box.

9. Click the **OK** button to apply the conditional formatting to the selected cells.

   If you had additional conditions to specify, three can be entered, click the **Add>>** button and return to Step 3. To remove a conditional format, click the Delete button and select the condition to delete.

10. Click any cell to deselect the range. See Figure 5-23. Notice that the background color of several cells in the range is now green.

Figure 5-23	FACULTY LIST AFTER CONDITIONAL FORMATTING APPLIED

	LASTNAME	FIRSTNAME	DEPARTMENT	RANK	YEARHIRED	SEX	SALARY
3	Anderson	Kristen	Accounting	Assistant	1988	F	$43,155
4	Ball	Robin	Accounting	Instructor	1987	F	$35,723
5	Bressette	Cheryl	Accounting	Instructor	1987	F	$36,582
6	Chin	Roger	Accounting	Full	1991	M	$59,281
7	Coats	Bill	Accounting	Assistant	1990	M	$45,371
8	Doepke	Cheryl	Accounting	Full	1978	F	$52,105
9	Downs	Clifton	Accounting	Associate	1982	M	$46,887
10	Jackson	Carole	Accounting	Instructor	1992	F	$33,781
11	Lu	Jim	Accounting	Instructor	1990	M	$38,881
12	Gao	Xiaoming	Management	Full	1982	M	$55,829
13	Palermo	Sheryl	Accounting	Associate	1988	F	$45,617
14	Parker	Mathew	Accounting	Full	1974	M	$57,892
15	Smith	Alicia	Accounting	Full	1989	F	$49,955
16	Stewart	Mark	Accounting	Assistant	1986	M	$47,616
17	Nelson	Dale	Accounting	Full	1988	M	$54,578
18	Weaver	Robert	Accounting	Full	1976	M	$55,775
19	Wolter	Christine	Accounting	Associate	1983	F	$44,918
20	Blackwell	Dean	Finance	Instructor	1992	M	$37,797

these cells contain values that exceed $50,000

Note that if the value of the cell changes and no longer meets the specified condition(s), Excel temporarily suppresses the formats associated with that cell. However, the conditional formats remain applied to the cells until you remove them, even when none of the conditions are met and the specified cell formats do not appear.

The dean has a request for information she needs for her meeting with the budget director, and she meets with you to discuss how the faculty list can be used in this task.

Using Worksheet Labels in Formulas

Bin, the budget director, is getting ready to start the next budget cycle. He asks each college dean to provide him with a list of faculty and their proposed salary for next year. Currently, the plan is to increase each faculty member's salary by 3% to keep pace with inflation. The report requested by Bin should list each faculty member by department and should include a departmental subtotal for the PROPOSED SALARY field.

You will need to add a new field to the faculty list—PROPOSED SALARY. This is a calculated field equal to each faculty member's current salary times 1.03.

Although you can use cell references to build this formula, Excel 2000 has a feature that enables you to refer to related data within worksheet formulas by using labels at the top of each column and to the left of each row. For example, in Figure 5-24 you have two labels, Sales and Expenses, which identify the values in cells B1 and B2. These labels can be used to build the formula to compute net income. Instead of entering the formula =B1-B2, the formula =Sales - Expenses uses row labels to calculate net income.

Excel doesn't automatically recognize column and row labels used in formulas. First you must turn this feature on.

To turn the Accept Labels in Formula feature on:

1. Click **Tools**, then click **Options** to display the Options dialog box.

2. Click the **Calculation** tab.

3. In the worksheet options section, click the **Accept Labels in Formula** check box to turn this feature on.

4. Click **OK**.

| Figure 5-24 | EXAMPLE OF A FORMULA USING WORKSHEET LABELS |

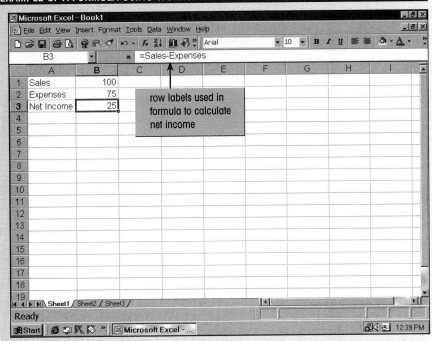

Now, add the PROPOSED SALARY field to the faculty list using the worksheet label to create the formula.

To enter and format the column heading for proposed salary:

1. Click cell **H2**, and then type **PROPOSED SALARY**.

2. Click cell **G2**, click the **Format Painter** button  on the Standard toolbar, and then click cell **H2** to copy the format in cell G2 to cell H2.

3. Click **Format** on the menu bar, and then click **Cells** to open the Format Cells dialog box.

4. Click the **Alignment** tab, click the **Wrap Text** check box, and then click the **OK** button to apply text wrapping to cell H2.

Now enter the formula to calculate the proposed salary.

To use a worksheet label to create a formula:

1. In cell H3, type **=salary*1.03**, and then press the **Enter** key. "Salary" in the formula is the column heading. Excel uses the corresponding cell in the SALARY column (G3) to multiply times 1.03.

TROUBLE? If the #NAME? error value appears in the cell, you need to turn the Accept Labels in Formula feature on and then reenter the formula. Return to the steps labeled "To turn the Accept Labels in Formula feature on."

Apply the format used in the SALARY field to the PROPOSED SALARY field.

2. Click cell G3, click the **Format Painter** button and then click cell H3 to copy the formatting.

3. Copy the formula in cell H3 to the range H4:H43. Scroll to the top of the list.

4. Click any cell to deselect the range. See Figure 5-25.

| Figure 5-25 | FACULTY LIST WITH NEW FIELD |

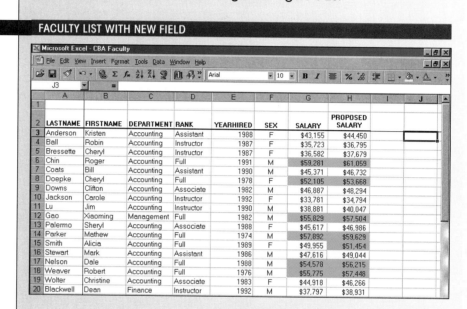

Now that the PROPOSED SALARY field has been added to the list, you can prepare the information for the dean. Remember, this report will list the faculty by department, followed by totals for each department.

Inserting Subtotals into a List

Excel can summarize data in a list by inserting subtotals. The Subtotals command offers many kinds of summary information, including counts, sums, averages, minimums, and maximums. The Subtotals command automatically inserts a subtotal line into the list for each group of data. A grand total line is also added to the bottom of the list. Because Excel inserts subtotals whenever the value in a specified field changes, you need to sort the list so records with the same value in a specified field are grouped together before you can use the subtotals command.

Calculating Subtotals In A List

- Sort the list by the column for which you want a subtotal.
- Click a cell in the list.
- Click Data, and then click Subtotals to open the Subtotal dialog box.
- In the At each change in list box, select the column containing the group you want to subtotal.
- In the Use function list box, select the function you want to use to summarize the data.
- In the Add subtotal to list box, select the column containing the values you want to summarize.
- Click the OK button.

To supply Bin with the information he requested, you will develop a list of faculty, sorted by department, with subtotals calculated for the PROPOSED SALARY field. Each subtotal will be inserted after each departmental grouping.

To calculate subtotals by department:

1. If the list is not sorted by department, click any cell in the DEPARTMENT column, and then click the **Sort Ascending** button 2↓ on the Standard toolbar. The list is sorted by department.

   Now calculate the subtotals in the list.

2. Click **Data** on the menu bar, and then click **Subtotals** to open the Subtotal dialog box. See Figure 5-26.

Figure 5-26	SUBTOTAL DIALOG BOX

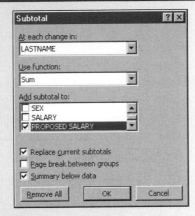

3. Click the **At each change in** list arrow, and then click **DEPARTMENT** to select the column containing the field for which you want subtotals.

4. If necessary, click the **Use function** list arrow, and then click **Sum** to select the function you want to use to summarize the data.

   You want departmental subtotals for the PROPOSED SALARY field.

5. In the Add subtotal to list box, scroll the list and, if necessary, remove any check marks in the category check boxes, and then click the **PROPOSED SALARY** check box, the column containing the field you want to summarize.

6. Make sure the Replace current subtotals and the Summary below data check boxes are checked so that the subtotals appear below the related data.

7. Click the **OK** button to insert subtotals into the list. Subtotals are added to the PROPOSED SALARY column, showing the total salaries for each department.

8. Scroll through the list to be sure you can see all the subtotals and the grand total at the bottom. If necessary, increase the column width so you can view the subtotal values. See Figure 5-27. Notice the Outline buttons to the left of the worksheet, which show the levels of detail possible while the Subtotals command is active.

Figure 5-27	FACULTY LIST WITH SUBTOTALS

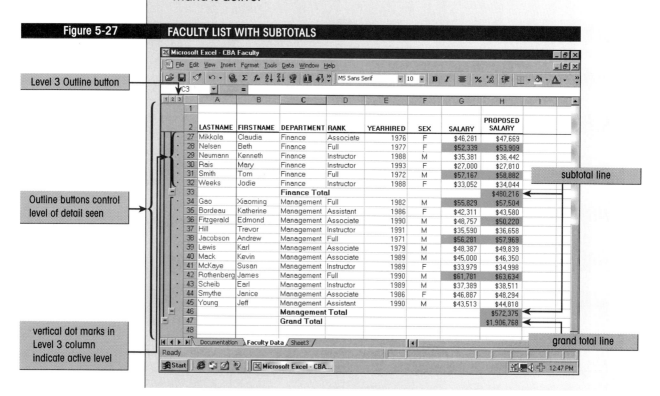

The subtotals are useful for the dean to see, but she asks if there is a way to isolate the different subtotal sections so that she can focus on them individually.

Using the Subtotals Outline View

In addition to displaying subtotals, the Subtotals command "outlines" your worksheet so you can control the level of detail that is displayed. The three Outline buttons at the top of the outline area in Figure 5-27 allow you to show or hide different levels of detail in your worksheet. By default, the highest level is active, in this case Level 3. Level 3 displays the most detail—the individual faculty records, the subtotals, and the grand total. If you click the Level 2 Outline button, only the subtotals and the grand total appear but not the individual records. If you click the Level 1 Outline button, only the grand total appears. Now, use the Outline buttons to prepare a report that includes only subtotals and the grand total.

To use the Outline buttons to hide the detail:

1. Press **Ctrl + Home** to make cell B3 the active cell.

2. Click the **Level 2** Outline button. See Figure 5-28. Notice that the worksheet hides the individual faculty records and shows only the subtotals for each department and the grand total.

Figure 5-28	SUBTOTALS AFTER LEVEL 2 OUTLINE BUTTON SELECTED

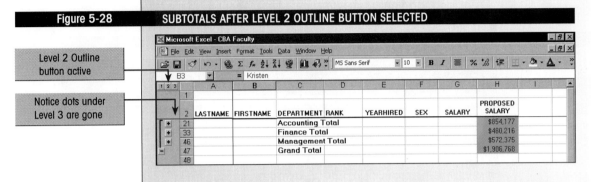

Level 2 Outline button active

Notice dots under Level 3 are gone

	LASTNAME	FIRSTNAME	DEPARTMENT	RANK	YEARHIRED	SEX	SALARY	PROPOSED SALARY	
21			Accounting Total					$854,177	
33			Finance Total					$480,216	
46			Management Total					$572,375	
47			Grand Total					$1,906,768	
48									

3. Include your name in a custom footer and then print the worksheet.

4. Click the **Level 3** Outline button to show all the records again.

Now that you have prepared the list with subtotals, you can remove the subtotals from the list.

To remove the subtotals from the list:

1. Click any cell in the list, click **Data** on the menu bar, and then click **Subtotals** to open the Subtotal dialog box.

2. Click the **Remove All** button to remove the subtotals from the list.

3. If necessary, click **Ctrl + Home** to return to the top of the list.

4. Save the worksheet.

The dean is very pleased with the way you have manipulated the faculty list to provide her with the data she needs. She now needs printouts she can hand out to the various department heads.

Printing the List Using Page Breaks

When you printed the faculty list, it printed on one page. The dean has asked that the data for each department be printed on a separate page so copies can be shared with each department head as well as the budget director. You can use the Page Break Preview button from the Print Preview window to view where Excel breaks pages in your worksheet and to change either a horizontal or a vertical page break. Alternatively, you can also activate Page Break Preview by clicking View from the menu bar and then clicking Page Break Preview.

To insert a page break to start a new page:

1. Click the **Print Preview** button 🔍 on the Standard toolbar to display the faculty list. Notice that only one page is needed to print the list.

2. Click the **Page Break Preview** button to view a version of the worksheet that shows the entire print area with page breaks and page numbers superimposed on it. Excel is now in Page Break Preview view. See Figure 5-29.

TROUBLE? If the Message, "Welcome to Page Break View. You can adjust where the page breaks are by clicking and dragging them with your mouse" appears, click the check box, and then click the OK button, so the message does not appear again.

Figure 5-29	PAGE BREAK PREVIEW VIEW

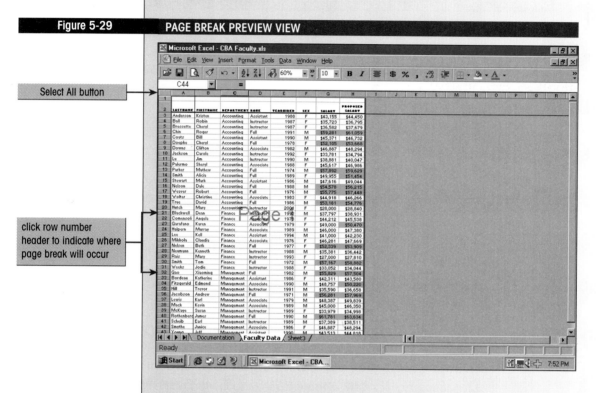

Page Break Preview is different from Print Preview in that you can make some modifications to the worksheet in this mode.

3. Click the **row number header** to the left of column A at row 21, the row where you want to start a new page.

4. Click **Insert** on the menu bar, and then click **Page Break**.

5. Repeat Steps 3 and 4 to insert a page break at row 32. Notice that after you insert the page break, a thick blue line appears to indicate where the break is located.

6. Click the **Print** button 🖨 on the Standard toolbar to print the faculty list on separate pages for each department.

Printing Row and Column Titles on Every Page

As you review the printouts, you notice the column headings only appear on the first page. By default, the row and column titles just print on the first page. If you want to repeat the row and column titles printed on every page, use the Rows to Repeat At Top and Column To Repeat at Left text boxes on the Sheet tab of the Page Setup dialog box to specify the rows and columns you want to repeat. Although you won't step through this task in the tutorial, you can try it in the Review Assignments by following the steps in the reference window below.

<u>Printing Row And Column Titles On Every Page</u>
- Click File, then click Page Setup to open the Page Setup dialog box.
- Click the Sheet tab.
- In the Print titles section, click the Collapse dialog box button of the Rows to repeat at top or Columns to repeat at left text boxes, and then select the row or column titles to repeat on each page.
- Click the Collapse dialog box button again to restore the Page Setup dialog box.
- Click OK.

Removing Page Breaks

Because you will not need these page breaks for future printouts of the faculty list, remove them now.

To remove page breaks from the worksheet:

1. Click the **Select All** button located at the intersection of the row and column headings of your worksheet (if necessary, refer to Figure 5-29), click **Insert** on the menu bar, and then click **Reset All Page Breaks**.

   Now return to normal view.

2. Click **View** on the menu bar, and then click **Normal**. The worksheet returns to normal view.

3. Click any cell, and save the workbook.

Session 5.2 QUICK CHECK

1. If you have a list of 300 students in the College of Business Administration and wanted to print only finance majors, you would use the _____ commands from the menu.

2. Explain how you can display a list of marketing majors with a GPA of 3.0 or greater from a list of 300 students.

3. _____ enables formatting to appear only when the data in a cell meets a condition you specify.

4. If you had a worksheet with the column headings Shares and Cost Per Share, and entered the formula =*Shares * Cost Per Share* to compute Total Cost, you used _____ in the formula.

5. Explain the relationship between the Sort and Subtotals commands.

6. Once subtotals are visible, you can use the _____ button to control the level of detail displayed.

7. If you have a list of students sorted by major and you wanted to print the students in each major on a separate page, you would use the _____.

You have supplied the dean with the information she needs for her meeting with the budget director to review financial plans for the next fiscal cycle. Now the dean needs to generate some information for a meeting with the affirmative action task force. You will work with the CBA faculty list in the next session to gather the information she needs for that meeting.

SESSION 5.3

In this session you will learn to summarize data from an Excel list in different formats using the PivotTable and PivotChart Wizard.

Creating and Using Pivot Tables to Summarize a List

An Excel list can contain a wealth of information, but because of the large amounts of detailed data, it is often difficult to form a clear, overall view of the information. You can use a pivot table to help organize the information. A **pivot table** is an interactive table that enables you to group and summarize an Excel list into a concise, tabular format for easier reporting and analysis. A pivot table summarizes data in different categories using functions such as COUNT, SUM, AVERAGE, MAX, and MIN.

All pivot tables have similar elements. These include **column fields**, **row fields**, and **page fields**. Typically, the values in category fields, such as department, rank, year hired, and sex, appear in pivot tables as rows, columns, or pages. In creating a pivot table, you also specify which fields you want to summarize. Salaries, sales, and costs are examples of fields that you usually summarize. In pivot table terminology, these are known as **data fields**.

One advantage of pivot tables is that you can easily rearrange, hide, and display different categories in the pivot table to provide alternative views of the data. This ability to "pivot" your table—for example, change column headings to row positions and vice versa—gives the pivot table its name and makes it a powerful analytical tool.

The dean now wants some tabulated information for an affirmative action report. She first reviewed the data within the faculty list to try to get a feel for whether men and women in comparable positions are making comparable salaries. She became overwhelmed and asked you to set up a pivot table.

You consider the information that the dean wants and create a pivot table plan (Figure 5-30) and a pivot table sketch (Figure 5-31). Your plan and sketch will help you work with the PivotTable and PivotChart Wizard to produce the pivot table you want.

Figure 5-30	PIVOT TABLE PLAN FOR CALCULATING AVERAGE SALARIES

Pivot Table Plan

My Goal:
Create a table that compares female and male average salary for each academic rank

What results do I want to see?
Average female salary for each rank
Average male salary for each rank
Overall average female salary
Overall average male salary
The average salary at each rank for males and females combined

What information do I need?
The table rows will show the data for each rank
The table columns will show the data for each sex
The table will summarize salary data

What calculation method will I use?
The salary data will be averaged for each rank and sex

Figure 5-31	SKETCH OF TABLE TO COMPARE AVERAGE SALARIES

Average Salaries by Rank for Females and Males

Rank	Females	Males	Totals
Instructor	xx	xx	xx
Assistant	xx	xx	xx
Associate	xx	xx	xx
Full	xx	xx	xx
Totals	xx	xx	xx

Now you are ready to create a pivot table summarizing average faculty salaries of men and women by rank.

Creating a Pivot Table

To create the pivot table for the dean, you use the Excel PivotTable and PivotChart Wizard to guide you through a three-step process. Although the PivotTable and PivotChart Wizard will prompt you for the information necessary to create the table, the preliminary plan and sketch you created will be helpful in achieving the layout the dean wants.

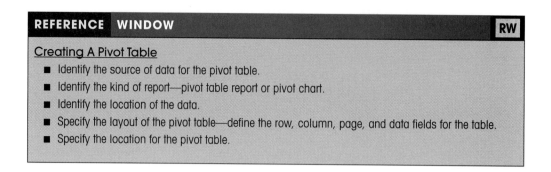

Creating A Pivot Table
- Identify the source of data for the pivot table.
- Identify the kind of report—pivot table report or pivot chart.
- Identify the location of the data.
- Specify the layout of the pivot table—define the row, column, page, and data fields for the table.
- Specify the location for the pivot table.

Most often when creating a pivot table, you begin with a list stored in a worksheet. In this case, you will use the faculty list in the Faculty Data worksheet to create the pivot table.

To create a pivot table:

1. If you took a break after the last session, make sure the CBA Faculty workbook is open and the Faculty Data worksheet is active. Click any cell in the list, click **Data** on the menu bar, and then click **PivotTable and PivotChart Report** to open the PivotTable and PivotChart Wizard - Step 1 of 3 dialog box. See Figure 5-32. In this dialog box, you specify the source of the data that is to be used to create the pivot table. You can select from an Excel list; an external data source, such as a dBase or Access file; multiple consolidation ranges; or another pivot table. To develop the average salaries pivot table, you use the Excel list in the Faculty Data worksheet. In this step you also specify the kind of report to create: a pivot table only or a pivot chart along with a pivot table.

   TROUBLE? If the Office Assistant appears, select the option "No, don't provide help now."

Figure 5-32	PIVOTTABLE AND PIVOTCHART WIZARD - STEP 1 OF 3 DIALOG BOX

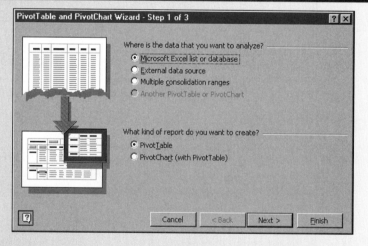

2. Make sure the Microsoft Excel list or database option is selected as the source of data and the PivotTable option is selected as the kind of report. Then, click the **Next** button to open the PivotTable and PivotChart Wizard - Step 2 of 3 dialog box. See Figure 5-33.

Figure 5-33 | PIVOTTABLE AND PIVOTCHART WIZARD - STEP 2 OF 3 DIALOG BOX

range of faculty list →

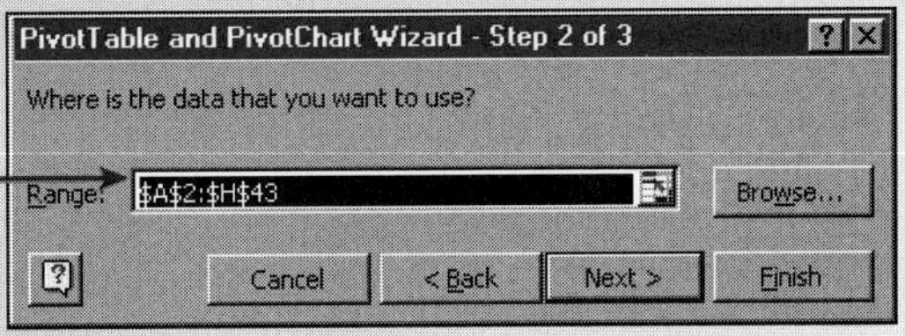

At this point, you need to identify the location of the data you are going to summarize in the pivot table.

Because the active cell is located within the range of the Excel list, the Wizard automatically selects the range of the faculty list, 'Faculty Data'!$A$2:$H$43, as the source of data for the pivot table.

TROUBLE? If the Range box in the PivotTable and PivotChart Wizard - Step 2 of 3 displays "Database" instead of $A$2:$H$43 as the source of the data, click the Next button to go to Step 3 of the PivotTable and PivotChart Wizard. If an error message appears when you click the Next button, click OK, click the Collapse Dialog box button and select the range A2:H43, then click the Collapse Dialog box button again, and then continue to Step 3.

3. Click the **Next** button to open the PivotTable and PivotChart Wizard - Step 3 of 3 dialog box. See Figure 5-34.

In this step you decide where to place the pivot table—either in a new worksheet or in an existing worksheet. You also have the opportunity to complete the layout of the pivot table within the Wizard by selecting the Layout button, otherwise you can complete the pivot table directly on the worksheet.

You will place the pivot table in a new worksheet and complete the pivot table directly in the worksheet.

Figure 5-34 | PIVOTTABLE AND PIVOTCHART WIZARD - STEP 3 OF 3 DIALOG BOX

4. Make sure the **New worksheet** option button is selected, and then click the **Finish** button to create the pivot table report framework. See Figure 5-35. A new worksheet, Sheet1, appears to the left of the Faculty Data sheet. This sheet contains a PivotTable report framework, a diagram containing blue outlined drop areas, which will assist you in completing the pivot table. Additionally, the PivotTable toolbar appears. Figure 5-36 describes the tools available on this toolbar.

TROUBLE? If you don't see the field buttons on the toolbar, make sure the toolbar is undocked, click within the PivotTable diagram and make sure the Display Fields button on the toolbar is pressed in.

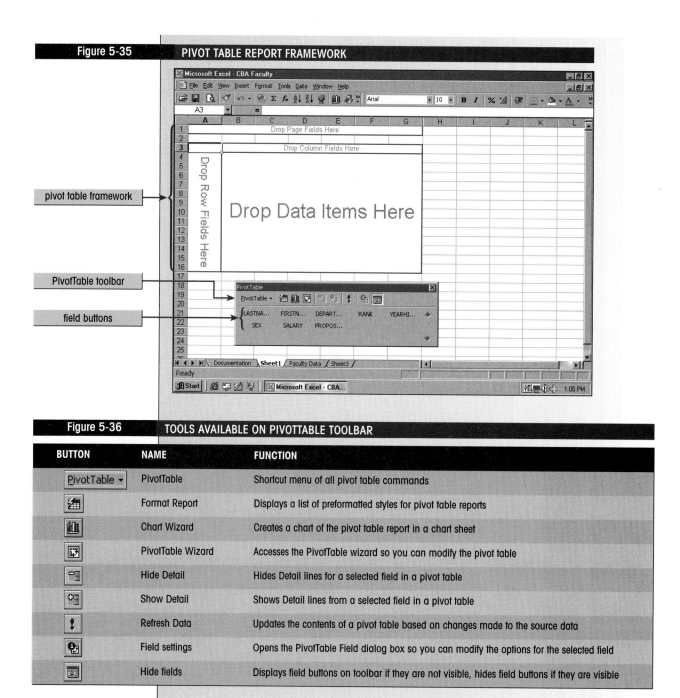

Figure 5-35   PIVOT TABLE REPORT FRAMEWORK

pivot table framework

PivotTable toolbar

field buttons

Figure 5-36   TOOLS AVAILABLE ON PIVOTTABLE TOOLBAR

BUTTON	NAME	FUNCTION
PivotTable ▾	PivotTable	Shortcut menu of all pivot table commands
	Format Report	Displays a list of preformatted styles for pivot table reports
	Chart Wizard	Creates a chart of the pivot table report in a chart sheet
	PivotTable Wizard	Accesses the PivotTable wizard so you can modify the pivot table
	Hide Detail	Hides Detail lines for a selected field in a pivot table
	Show Detail	Shows Detail lines from a selected field in a pivot table
	Refresh Data	Updates the contents of a pivot table based on changes made to the source data
	Field settings	Opens the PivotTable Field dialog box so you can modify the options for the selected field
	Hide fields	Displays field buttons on toolbar if they are not visible, hides field buttons if they are visible

Now you are ready to layout the pivot table directly on the worksheet.

Laying Out the Pivot Table Directly on the Worksheet

In the PivotTable report framework, you specify which fields will appear as column, row, and page headings in the pivot table and which fields contain the data you want to summarize. In this step the fields are represented by a set of field buttons found on the PivotTable toolbar. You create the layout by dragging the field buttons from the toolbar to any of the four areas of the pivot table diagram: Drop Rows Fields Here, Drop Column Fields Here, Drop Page Fields Here, or Drop Data Items Here.

REFERENCE WINDOW   **RW**

Laying Out the Pivot Table on the Worksheet
- Click and drag the fields you want to appear in rows to the area of the pivot table diagram labeled Drop Row Fields Here.
- Click and drag the fields you want to appear in columns to the area of the pivot table diagram labeled Drop Column Fields Here.
- Click and drag the fields you want to appear in pages to the area of the pivot table diagram labeled Drop Page Fields Here.
- Click and drag the fields that contain the data you want to summarize to the area of the pivot table diagram labeled Drop Data Items Here.

In the pivot table you are creating, you will compute average salaries for males and females for each rank and sex. The values in the RANK field will appear as row labels, the values in the SEX field will appear as column headings, and the SALARY field will be the data that is summarized.

Now layout the pivot table in the worksheet.

To layout a pivot table on the worksheet:

1. From the group of field buttons on the toolbar, click and drag the **RANK** field button to the area on the PivotTable diagram labeled Drop Row Fields Here. When you release the mouse button, the RANK button appears in the pivot table report framework. See Figure 5-37. When the pivot table is complete the report will contain a row label for each unique value in the RANK field.

| Figure 5-37 | PIVOTTABLE DIAGRAM WITH RANK FIELD ADDED |

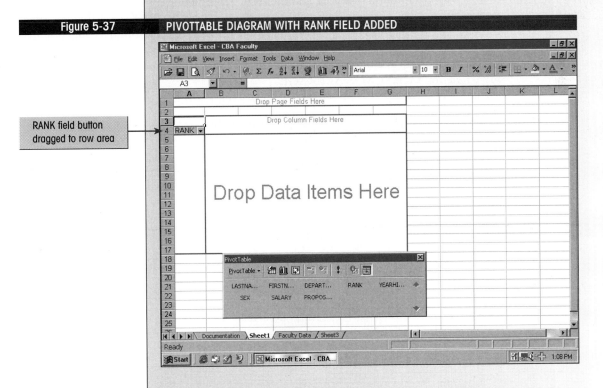

RANK field button dragged to row area

TROUBLE? If you moved the wrong field into the pivot table diagram, you can remove it by dragging it anywhere outside the diagram or clicking the Undo button.

2. Click and drag the **SEX** field button from the PivotTable toolbar to the area of the diagram labeled Drop Column Fields Here. When you release the mouse button, the SEX button appears in the report framework. When the pivot table is complete, the report will contain a column label for each unique value in the SEX field.

3. Click and drag the **SALARY** field button from the PivotTable toolbar to the area of the diagram labeled Drop Data Items Here. When you release the mouse button, the pivot table appears. See Figure 5-38. The Sum of Salary button on the report indicates the type of summary; the report contains total salaries for men and women for each rank.

| Figure 5-38 | PIVOT TABLE COMPARING TOTAL SALARIES FOR MALES AND FEMALES BY RANK |

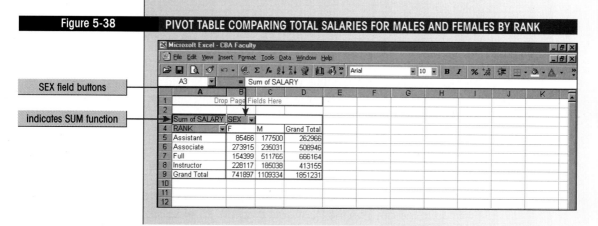

SEX field buttons

indicates SUM function

By default, Excel uses the SUM function for calculations involving numeric values placed in the Drop Data Items Here area, and the COUNT function for nonnumeric values. If you want to use a different summary function, such as AVERAGE, MAX, or MIN, you can click the Field Settings button in the PivotTable toolbar and select the summary function from a list of available functions in the PivotTable Field Settings box.

The dean wants to compare average salary by rank and sex. You need to change the summary function from SUM to AVERAGE.

To change the pivot table to compute average salaries by sex and rank:

1. Make sure a value inside the pivot table is selected, then click the **Field Settings** button 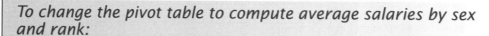 on the PivotTable toolbar to open the PivotTable Field dialog box. See Figure 5-39.

| Figure 5-39 | PIVOTTABLE FIELD SETTINGS DIALOG BOX |

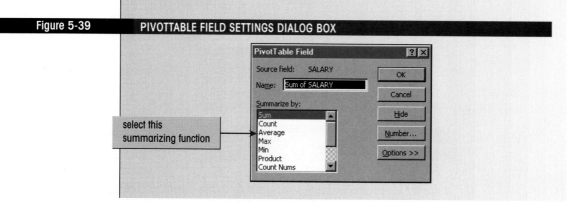

select this
summarizing function

2. Click **Average** in the Summarize by list box, and then click the **OK** button to return to the pivot table report. See Figure 5-40. Notice that the summary button indicates Average of SALARY and the data in the pivot table represents average salaries by rank and sex.

| Figure 5-40 | PIVOT TABLE SHOWING AVERAGE SALARIES FOR MALES AND FEMALES BY RANK |

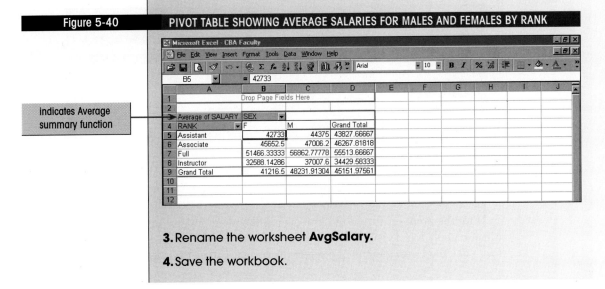

indicates Average summary function

3. Rename the worksheet **AvgSalary.**

4. Save the workbook.

The pivot table in Figure 5-40 shows the average salaries paid to male and female faculty members in each rank. Although the data in a pivot table may look like data in any other worksheet, you cannot directly enter or change data in the DATA area of the pivot table, because the pivot table is linked to the source data. Any changes that affect the pivot table must first be made to the Excel list. Later in the tutorial, you will update a faculty member's salary and learn how to reflect that change in the pivot table.

Changing the Layout of a Pivot Table

Although you cannot change the values inside the pivot table, there are many ways you can change the layout, formatting, and computational options of a pivot table. For example, once the pivot table is created, you have numerous ways of rearranging, adding, and removing fields.

Formatting Numbers in the Pivot Table

As the dean runs off to a meeting, she mentions to you that the numbers in the pivot table are difficult to read. You can apply number formats to the cells in the pivot table just as you would format any cell in a worksheet. You will format the average salary using the Currency style.

To specify the currency style format for pivot table values:

1. Select the range **B5:D9**.

2. Click the **Currency Style** button 🛇 on the Formatting toolbar. Click the **Decrease Decimal** button 🛇 on the Formatting toolbar twice to reduce the number of decimal places to zero. If necessary, increase the column width so the formatted average salary values can fit in the cell.

3. Click any cell to deselect the range and view the newly formatted pivot table. See Figure 5-41.

Figure 5-41   **PIVOT TABLE AFTER FORMATTING**

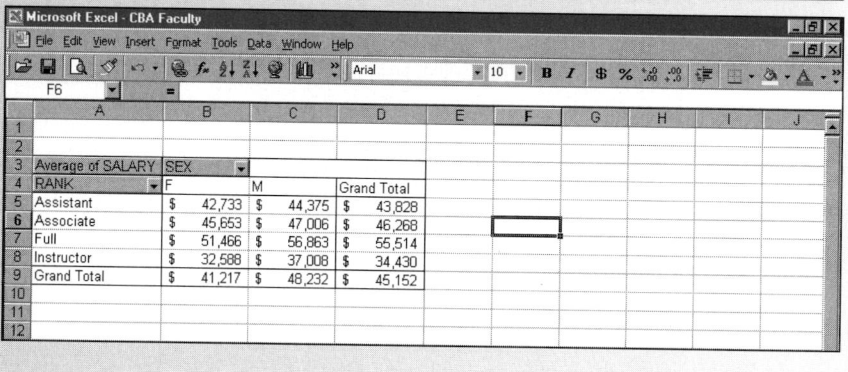

With the numbers formatted, the data in the pivot table is much easier to interpret. You can also apply Excel's AutoFormats to format a pivot table. Select the range you want to format, click the Format menu and select the format you want to apply.

Repositioning a Field in the Pivot Table

Recall that the benefit of a pivot table is that it summarizes large amounts of data into a readable format. Once you have created the table, you can also choose to view the same data from different angles. At the top of the pivot table's ROW and COLUMN areas are field buttons that enable you to change, or pivot, the view of the data by dragging these buttons to different locations in the pivot table.

The dean reviews the tabular format of the pivot table you have created and decides it might be more useful if it displayed males and females as row classifications under rank. Reposition the column headings for the SEX field as row labels.

To move a column field to a row field in the pivot table:

1. Click and drag the **SEX** field button below the RANK field button. See Figure 5-42. Notice that when you place the mouse over the SEX field button, your mouse pointer changes to ⊕. As you click and drag below the RANK field button, the mouse pointer changes to ▧.

Figure 5-42   **REPOSITIONING SEX FIELD BUTTON IN PIVOT TABLE**

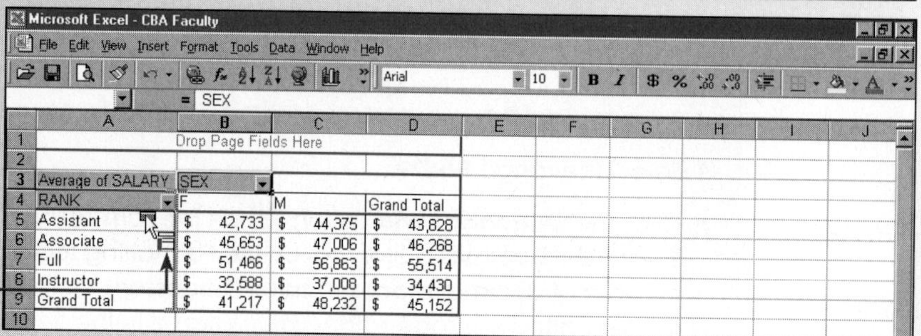

indicates field button
is being moved

2. Release the mouse button. See Figure 5-43. The pivot table is reordered so that the SEX field is treated as a row field instead of a column field.

TROUBLE? If the SEX field appears to the left of the RANK field, click the Undo button ⟲ ▾ on the Standard toolbar to undo the last step and then repeat Step 1. When you drag the SEX field button, just drag the button into the blank area under the RANK button. If you drag the button much farther to the left, you will change the order of the fields.

Figure 5-43	REARRANGED PIVOT TABLE

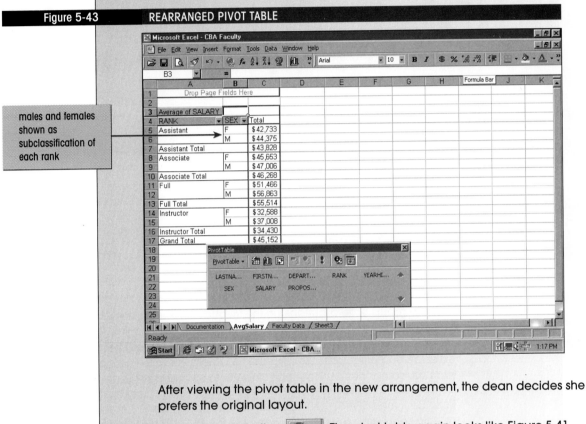

males and females shown as subclassification of each rank

After viewing the pivot table in the new arrangement, the dean decides she prefers the original layout.

3. Click the Undo button ⟲ ▾. The pivot table again looks like Figure 5-41.

Sorting Items Within the Pivot Table

After reviewing the pivot table, the dean asks you to rearrange it so that it displays the rank with the highest average salary first. To complete this task, you can sort the data in the pivot table.

To sort a pivot table:

1. Click cell **D5** to place the cell pointer in the cell that contains the field you want to sort.

2. Click the **Sort Descending** button ⤵ on the Standard toolbar. See Figure 5-44. The full professor rank is now the first rank in the pivot table.

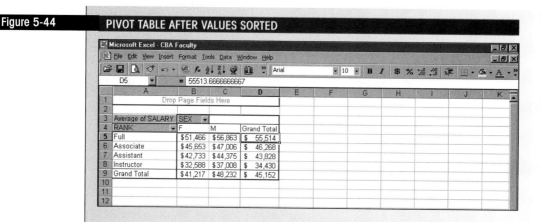

Figure 5-44   PIVOT TABLE AFTER VALUES SORTED

Adding a Field to a Pivot Table

You can expand a pivot table by adding columns, rows, page fields, and data fields; this creates a more informative table. For example, the dean believes that a more accurate comparison of average salaries would include the DEPARTMENT field. Adding this field to the pivot table enables you to calculate average salaries based on an additional breakdown—one that categorizes faculty in each rank into departmental classifications as well as by sex. The dean thinks the additional information will be useful in her discussion with the affirmative action task force, and she asks you to add it to the pivot table.

To add a field to the pivot table:

1. From the group of field buttons on the PivotTable toolbar, click and drag the **DEPARTMENT** field button immediately below the arrow of the RANK field button, and release the mouse button. Excel adds the DEPARTMENT field button and redisplays the pivot table. See Figure 5-45. The pivot table now displays department subcategories (accounting, finance, and management) for each rank.

   TROUBLE? If the DEPARTMENT field button appears to the left of the RANK field button, click and drag the RANK button over the DEPARTMENT button and release the mouse button.

   TROUBLE? If the PivotTable toolbar is in the way, drag it to a different location on your screen.

Figure 5-45	PIVOT TABLE AFTER DEPARTMENT FIELD ADDED

DEPARTMENT field
button added to
pivot table

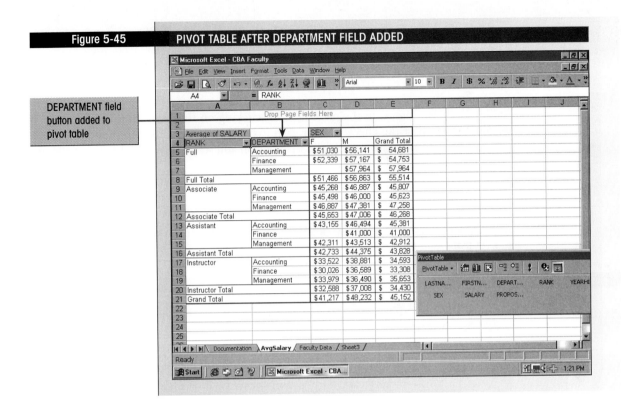

Removing a Field from the Pivot Table

If you decide you want to remove a field from the pivot table, just drag the field button outside the pivot table. The dean reviews the pivot table showing the data arranged by rank, department, and sex. While she thinks this is important information, she feels the additional breakdown is not needed to show the difference in average salaries between men and women. She asks you to remove the DEPARTMENT field from the pivot table.

To remove a field from the pivot table:

1. Click and drag the **DEPARTMENT** field button outside the pivot table range. When the field button is outside the pivot table, it changes to ⍴x. See Figure 5-46.

Figure 5-46	DEPARTMENT FIELD BUTTON OUTSIDE PIVOT TABLE RANGE

removing this
field button

indicates that the field
button will be removed
from pivot table

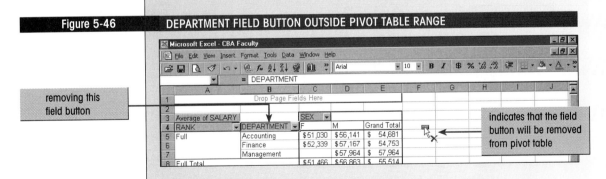

2. Release the mouse button. The DEPARTMENT field is removed from the pivot table. Removing a field from the pivot table has no effect on the underlying list; the DEPARTMENT field is still in the faculty list.

The Dean wants to focus the analysis on the faculty ranks eligible for tenure—assistant, associate and full professors. She asks you to remove the instructors from the report.

Hiding Field Items on a Pivot Table

You can hide field items in the pivot table by clicking on the arrow at the right of the field button and clearing the check box for each item you want to hide. To show hidden items, you click the arrow to the right of the field button and select the check box for the item you want to show. Now hide the Instructor item.

To hide the Instructor item from the pivot table:

1. Click the **arrow** to the right of the RANK field button to display a list of each item in the RANK field. See Figure 5-47.

Figure 5-47	LIST OF FIELD ITEMS FOR RANK FIELD

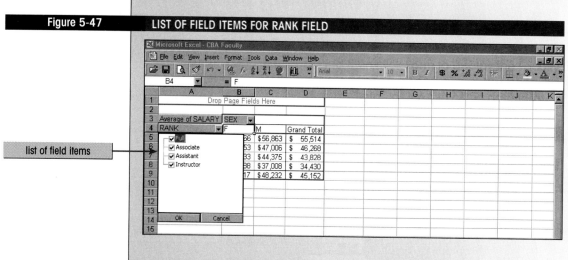

list of field items

2. Click the **check box** next to Instructor to clear the check.

3. Click **OK** to display the pivot table with the Instructor row hidden. See Figure 5-48.

Figure 5-48	PIVOT TABLE WITH INSTRUCTOR ITEM HIDDEN

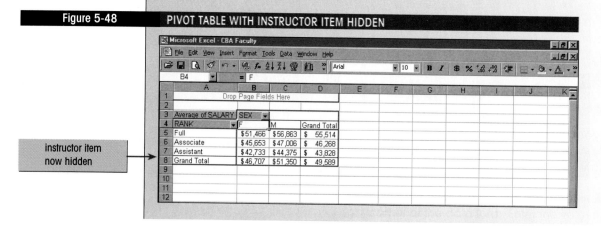

instructor item now hidden

Now, the report contains the faculty ranks the dean wants to review. Before making copies of the pivot table for her meeting, the dean asks you to include Karen Garafano's $3,000 salary increase into the pivot table report.

Refreshing a Pivot Table

Recall that you cannot directly change the data in the pivot table; in order to change the data in the pivot table, you must first make the changes to the original Excel list; you can then update the pivot table. To update a pivot table so it reflects the current state of the faculty list, you update, or "refresh," the pivot table using the Refresh command.

You receive a memo from the dean informing you that Karen Garafano, a faculty member in the finance department, will receive an additional $3,000 in salary because her merit increase was approved. Her new salary is $49,000. Update her record in the faculty list and see how this affects the pivot table. (Make a note at this point that the average salary for female associate professors is $45,653.) Observe whether there is any change in the pivot table after you update Karen Garafano's salary in the Excel list.

To update Karen Garafano's salary:

1. Activate the **Faculty Data** worksheet, and then click any cell in the list.

2. Click **Data** on the menu bar, and then click **Form** to open the Faculty Data data form dialog box.

3. Click the **Criteria** button to display a blank data form.

   Enter the search criterion in the appropriate field.

4. If necessary, click the **LASTNAME** text box, and then type **Garafano**.

5. Click the **Find Next** button to display the next record in the list that meets the specified criterion—LASTNAME equal to Garafano.

6. Change Karen Garafanos' salary to **$49,000**.

7. Click the **Close** button. The salary for Karen Garafano has been updated in the Faculty list.

   Now return to the pivot table to observe whether there is any change in the average salary for female associate professors.

8. Switch to the **AvgSalary** worksheet. Notice that the average salary for female associate professors remains at $45,653.

Because the pivot table is not automatically updated when data in the source list is updated, the pivot table must be "refreshed."

To refresh a pivot table:

1. Select any cell inside the pivot table.

2. Click the **Refresh Data** button ⚡ on the PivotTable toolbar to update the pivot table. See Figure 5-49. The new average salary for female associate professors is $46,153.

Figure 5-49	PIVOT TABLE AFTER BEING REFRESHED

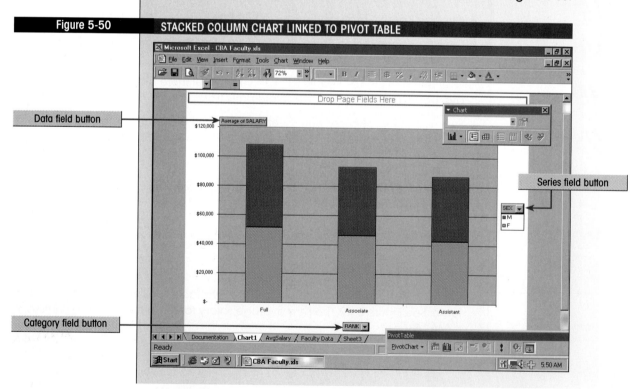

this average has changed

Making a Chart from a Pivot Table

The dean thinks a chart can more effectively convey the summary information of the pivot table. She asks you to create a Clustered column chart. Creating a pivot chart linked directly to a pivot table takes a single mouse click.

To link a chart to a pivot table:

1. Click the **Chart Wizard** on the PivotTable toolbar. A Stacked column chart and Chart toolbar appear in a new chart sheet, Chart1. See Figure 5-50.

Figure 5-50	STACKED COLUMN CHART LINKED TO PIVOT TABLE

Data field button

Series field button

Category field button

Convert the chart to a Clustered column chart.

2. Click 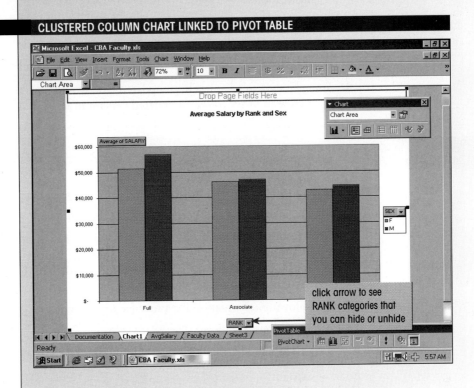. The Chart Wizard-Step 1 of 4-Chart Type dialog box opens.

3. Click the **Clustered column** chart sub-type (first sub-type option).

4. Click **Next** to open the Chart Wizard-Step 3 of 4-Chart Options dialog box.

5. Click the **Chart title** box and type **Average Salary by Rank and Sex**.

6. Click **Finish** to display the Clustered column chart. See Figure 5-51.

Figure 5-51 **CLUSTERED COLUMN CHART LINKED TO PIVOT TABLE**

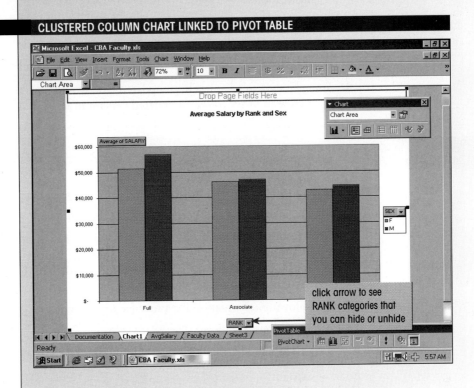

7. Click the **Documentation** sheet tab and save the workbook.

8. Preview and print the pivot table and pivot chart.

9. Close the workbook and exit Excel.

The dean is pleased with the appearance of the pivot table and chart. Both the table and chart show that the average salary paid to females is lower in every rank than the average salary paid to males.

You have modified and added data to an Excel list. You have also filtered the data in the list in numerous ways to highlight certain budget information that the dean of the College of Business Administration needs for her meeting with the university's budget director. Finally, you have created a pivot table and pivot chart from the list to further organize the information into specialized reports that the dean can use in her upcoming meetings with the affirmative action task force.

Session 5.3 QUICK CHECK

1. Assume that you have a list of students; the list includes codes for males and females and a field identifying the student major. Which tool, AutoFilter or pivot table, would you use in each of the following situations:

   a. You want a list of all females majoring in history.
   b. You want a count of the number of males and females in each major at your institution.

2. Fields such as region, state, country, and zip code are most likely to appear as _____ in a pivot table.

3. What is the default calculation method for numeric data in a pivot table?

4. After the data in a list has been updated, you would have to _____ the pivot table in order to see an updated version of it.

REVIEW ASSIGNMENTS

The dean has asked for more information about the College of Business Administration faculty.

To provide the answers she asks you to complete the following:

1. If necessary, start Excel and make sure your Data Disk is in the appropriate disk drive. Open the workbook **Faculty2** in the Review folder in Tutorial.05 on your Data Disk, and save it as **CBA Faculty 2**. Type your name and date in the Documentation sheet, then move to the Faculty Data sheet.

2. Add the following information for a new faculty member.

   Last name = Gerety
   First name = Estelle
   Department = Management
   Rank = Assistant
   Year hired = 2001
   Sex = F
   Salary = 42500

3. Use the data form to determine how many faculty members hold the rank of full professor. Explain the steps you followed to get your answer.

4. Sort the faculty list by sex, within sex by rank, and within rank by salary. Arrange the salaries in descending order. Include your name in the custom footer, then print the sorted list so that males and females print on separate pages.

5. Use the Subtotals command to count how many males and how many females are on the faculty. Print the faculty list with the subtotals.

6. Use the AutoFilter command to display a list of all females in the accounting department. Sort by last name. Print the filtered list.

7. Further refine the list from Question 6 so you list all female accounting faculty hired after 1990. Print the list.

8. Use the AVERAGE function to determine the average faculty salary. Based on this information, print a list of all faculty earning above the average salary.

9. Use conditional formatting to boldface the YEARHIRED field for faculty hired before 1980. Print the faculty list.

10. Use the Subtotals command to compute the average salary paid by department.

11. Based on Question 10, use the appropriate Outline button to display only the subtotals and the grand total. Print the result.

12. Create a pivot table to show the maximum salary by rank and sex. Place your pivot table in a blank worksheet. Format your pivot table to produce an attractive printout. Add an appropriate title. Rename the pivot table sheet using an appropriate name. Include your name in the custom footer, then print the pivot table.

Explore   13. Modify the pivot table in Question 12 to also display the minimum salary by rank and sex. (*Hint*: Use the Office Assistant to learn about "Using more than one summary function for a PivotTable data field.") Print the modified pivot table.

Explore   14. Use AutoFilters to produce and then print the faculty with the top five salaries in descending order. (*Hint*: Check out the Top 10 option in the list of available AutoFilters.)

Explore   15. Print a list of faculty sorted by department and within department by last name. Include only the last name, department, year hired, and gender in the output. (*Hint*: Use the Office Assistant to learn to "hide a column".) After printing the report, unhide the columns.

Explore   16. When you used the Page Break command in the tutorial to print each department's faculty on a separate page, you may have noticed that the column headings appeared only on the first page. Use the Print Area and Print Title sections of the Page Setup dialog box (Sheet tab), along with the Page Break command, to print the column headings on each page.

17. In column H, create a new calculated field using a worksheet label to create a formula reflecting an alternative Proposed Salary of a 4 1/2% increase.

18. Save and close the workbook.

CASE PROBLEMS

Case 1. Inventory at OfficeMart Business Supplies   You are an assistant buyer at OfficeMart Business Supplies, a retail business supply store. Your boss, Ellen Kerrigan, created an Excel workbook with product and pricing information for inventory items purchased from each primary vendor. Ellen is preparing her monthly order for EB Wholesale Office Supplies, one of OfficeMart's suppliers. She wants you to print a list of all back-ordered EB Wholesale products to include in the order. She also wants a list of all discontinued items so you can remove them from the catalog. Do the following:

1. If necessary, start Excel and make sure your Data Disk is in the appropriate disk drive. Open the workbook **Office** in the Cases folder for Tutorial.05 on your Data Disk and save it as **Office Supplies**.

2. Freeze the panes so the column headings and the Part number row labels remain on the screen as you scroll the office supplies list.

3. Print the items in each status category on a separate page.

4. Display only the records for back-ordered items (Status = B). Sort the back-ordered items by part description. Print the records for back-ordered items.

5. Apply conditional formatting to all discontinued products (Status = D) so that the status code appears in red for each discontinued product.

6. Add a new field to the list. Name the field "Retail Value" and format it appropriately. For each inventory item, calculate the value at retail (quantity on hand multiplied by retail) using a worksheet label to create the formula. Format the numbers in the new field. Print the list so it prints on one page.

7. Use the Subtotals command to compute the total retail value of the inventory by status category (B, D, and S). Print the list with subtotals.

8. Prepare the same list with subtotals as in Question 7, but exclude all records whose retail value is zero.

9. Prepare a pivot table to summarize the retail value of inventory by status category. For each status category, include a count of the number of different items (this is not the sum of the quantity on hand), the total retail value, and the average retail value. (*Hint:* This pivot table uses one variable to summarize data concerning the retail value of the inventory.) Place the pivot table in a new sheet. Assign a descriptive name to the sheet. Print the pivot table.

10. Display only the discontinued items (Status = D). Copy these records to a blank worksheet. Rename the worksheet **Discontinued**. Print the list of discontinued items.

11. Save and close the workbook.

Case 2. Sales Analysis at Medical Technology, Inc.   Medical Technology, Inc. distributes supplies to hospitals, medical laboratories, and pharmacies. Records of all customer and accounts receivable data are available to department managers on the company's mainframe computer. Tom Benson, the manager of credit and collections, noticed that the outstanding balances of several customers in Rhode Island and Massachusetts appeared to be higher than the average customer balances. He thinks the average customer balance is approximately $4,000. He wants to study these accounts in more detail in order to create a plan to bring them closer to the average balance.

Tom was able to download the necessary data from the company's mainframe, and he set up an Excel list. Do the following:

1. If necessary, start Excel and make sure your Data Disk is in the appropriate disk drive. Open the workbook **Medical** in the Cases folder for Tutorial.05, and then save it as **Med Tech**.

2. Sort the list by state (ascending) and within state by Type customer (ascending) and within type by year-to-date (YTD) sales (descending). Remember to insert your name in a custom footer before printing the sorted list.

3. Insert subtotals (SUM) on Balanced Owed by type of customer. Print the list with only subtotals and the grand total included. After printing, remove the subtotals.

4. Use conditional formatting to display all customers with YTD sales above $55,000 in blue text, and apply boldface.

5. Display all customers with a balance owed above $25,000 from Rhode Island. Sort the list in descending order by balance owed. How many customers are in this list? Which customer owes the most? Print the list.

6. Print a list of customers that have the word "lab" anywhere in the customer name. Explain how you got your results.

7. Prepare and format a pivot table summarizing total YTD sales by sales rep. Include your name in a custom footer and then print it. Name the pivot table sheet Sales Rep.

Explore   8. Use the Format Report button on the PivotTable toolbar to select an autoformat for the pivot table you prepared in Question 7. Sort total YTD sales in descending order. Print the modified pivot table.

9. There appears to be a problem in the collection of money (balance) owed for one state and one type of customer. Identify the state and customer type that has the highest average outstanding balance. Print a report that supports your observation.

10. Save and close the workbook.

Case 3. Revenue at the Tea House   Arnold Tealover, sales manager for Tea House Distributors, is getting ready for a semiannual meeting at the company headquarters, at which plans to present summary data on his product line. The data he has accumulated consists of revenues by product, by month, and by region for the last six months. Help him summarize and analyze the data. Do the following:

1. If necessary, start Excel and make sure your Data Disk is in the appropriate drive. Open the workbook **Teahouse** in the Cases folder for Tutorial.05 on your Data Disk, and save it as **Teahouse Revenue**.

2. Improve the formatting of the revenue field.

3. Freeze the column headings so they remain on the screen as you scroll the worksheet.

4. Revenue for Duke Gray Tea for June in the West region was $53,420. Use the data form to enter "Duke Gray Tea", "June", "West", "53420".

5. Sort the tea list by product and within product by month. Insert subtotals by product and also by month for each product. Remember to include your name in a custom footer, then print the information for each product on a separate page.

6. Use conditional formatting to display revenue below $25,000.

7. Use the Subtotals command to display total sales by product. Print the list with subtotals.

8. Use the Outline buttons to display only the subtotals and grand total. Print this information.

Explore   9. Sort the data by month and within month by region. The months should appear in January through December sequence. (*Hint*: Click the Options button in the sort dialog box to customize your sort options.) Print the list.

10. Determine which product was the company's best seller during May or June in the West region. Print the list that supports your answer.

11. You want to determine which month had the highest sales and which region had the lowest sales. Prepare one pivot table to provide you with information to use for the answer to both questions. Use a text box to place the answer in the sheet with the pivot table. Name the sheet with the pivot table MaxMin. Print the pivot table.

Explore   12. Summarize each product's revenue using a pivot table. Use the Chart Wizard button on the PivotTable toolbar to create a column chart of total revenue by product. Improve the appearance of the chart. Print the pivot table and pie chart. Assign descriptive names to all new sheets.

13. Sort the list by region. Print the data for each region on a separate page. Use Page Break Preview to drag the automatic page breaks to the appropriate locations. (*Hint*: You may also need to insert additional page breaks manually.)

Explore   14. Sort the data by region. The region should appear in the following sequence: North, South, East, West. Print the list. (*Hint*: Use online Help to search on customizing, sort order.)

15. Save and close the workbook.

Case 4. NBA Player Salaries   Sharon Durfee is a summer intern at the National Basketball Association (NBA) headquarters in New York City. Every day the NBA office receives requests for information from sportswriters, TV and radio announcers, team owners, and agents. Sharon's assignment is to set up a database of player salaries to help the NBA staff provide accurate information quickly.

1. If necessary, start Excel and make sure your Data Disk is in the appropriate drive. Open the workbook **NBA** in the Cases folder for Tutorial.05 on your Data Disk, and save it as **NBA Salaries**.

2. Freeze the column headings and first and last name row labels.

3. Use the data form to find Antoine Walker's record. Change the salary to "$2,000,000."

4. Sort the data by team and within team by position and within position by salary (highest to lowest salary). Remember to include your name in a custom footer, then print the list.

5. Apply conditional formatting so the salary field of players earning below $500,000 appear with a red background and players earning more than $5,000,000 but less than $10,000,000 appear with a blue background.

6. Print all players earning less than $1,000,000, sorted by team.

7. Prepare a pivot table report to summarize the average salaries by team and by position. Rename the sheet tab with a more descriptive name. Print the pivot table report.

8. Save the workbook.

Explore   9. Prepare a pivot chart showing the total salaries by team. Print the chart.

Explore   10. Modify the pivot table created in Step 7 so TeamID is presented as a Page field instead of a Row field. Print the sheet.

QUICK | CHECK ANSWERS

Session 5.1

1. record

2. field

3. list

4. Sort by major and within major by last name

5. primary; alternative answer might be sort field or sort key

6. descending

7. new

8. Assuming you have the fields FirstName and LastName as part of the employee list, you would click the Criteria button in the Data Form dialog box. In the FirstName field text box type "Jin"; in the LastName field text box type "Shinu". Click the Find Next button to display the record in the data form.

Session 5.2

1. Data, AutoFilter

2. Use the AutoFilter feature. Click the Major field filter arrow and then click Marketing. For the GPA field, click Custom from the list of filtering options, enter the comparison operator > and the constant 3.0 to form the condition GPA greater than 3.0.

3. Conditional formatting

4. natural language

5. In order for Excel to calculate subtotals correctly, you must first sort the data because the subtotals are inserted whenever the value in the specified field changes

6. Outline

7. Page Break Preview view

Session 5.3

1. a. AutoFilter   b. Pivot table

2. row, columns, or pages

3. Sums the field or SUM

4. refresh

OBJECTIVES

In this tutorial you will:

- Learn about Object Linking and Embedding (OLE)

- Paste a graphic object into an Excel worksheet

- Embed a WordArt object in Excel

- Link an Excel worksheet to a Word document

- Update linked documents

- Embed an Excel chart into a Word document

- Complete a mail merge using an Excel list and a Word document

- View, preview and print a mail-merged document

- Create hyperlinks to connect files

- Convert worksheet data to HTML format

INTEGRATING
EXCEL WITH OTHER WINDOWS PROGRAMS AND THE WORLD WIDE WEB

Creating Integrated Documents for Basket Weavers

CASE

Basket Weavers

Nearly fifteen years ago, Karen Sanicola began selling gift baskets for all occasions. At the urging of her customers, she opened a small shop in her garage. Today, Karen's business, Basket Weavers, has grown to include three shops, located in Brooklyn, New York; Montvale, New Jersey; and the newest one in Greenwich, Connecticut.

The customer base has grown from townspeople and neighbors to include companies throughout the Northeast. This year, Basket Weavers has received the much-prized recognition as the largest corporate gift house in the Northeast, an award established by the Northeast Premiums Association (NPA).

Karen wants to display a flyer at the checkout counter at each store announcing the new baskets for the year. In addition to inserting the company logo, she can use WordArt, a shared program that comes with all Microsoft Office 2000 programs, to dress up the new products flyer. Karen also has drafted the body of a letter to her customers, highlighting the company's recent award from NPA, and previewing five new gift baskets that will be available this holiday season. To present this information in an easy-to-understand format, she plans to include a table listing the five new gift baskets. In addition, she wants the letter to include a chart that NPA has supplied depicting the company's status as the top company in the region. She will then merge an Excel list containing her customer addresses to the list.

Lastly, Karen wants her customers who use the Internet and the World Wide Web to have access to the new gift basket information online. She will create a Web page showing this information.

You'll complete the flyer, the letter, and the Web page for Karen using the integration features of Excel, which allow you to easily incorporate information from documents created in other programs.

SESSION 6.1

In this session you will learn about the different methods of integrating information between Windows programs to create compound documents. You will paste a logo into an Excel worksheet, create a WordArt object, link an Excel workbook to a Word document, and embed an Excel chart into a Word document.

Methods of Integration

Like Karen, you may occasionally need to copy data between two or more programs to produce the type of document you require. This type of document is referred to as a **compound document**—a document made up of parts created in more than one program. For example, you may want to incorporate data from a worksheet, a graphic design, or a chart, and insert it into a word-processed report.

Excel is part of a suite of programs called Microsoft Office 2000. In addition to Excel, the Office programs consist of Word, a word-processing program; Access, a database program; PowerPoint, a program used for creating presentations; and Outlook, a personal information manager. Microsoft Office also contains some shared programs, such as WordArt, that allow you to customize your documents even further. All of these programs can share information, which saves time and ensures consistency.

There are essentially three ways to copy data between Windows programs: you can use pasting, linking, or embedding. Regardless of the method used, a copy of the data appears in the compound document. Figure 6-1 provides a description of each of these methods, and examples of when each method would be appropriate.

Figure 6-1	COMPARISON OF METHODS OF INTEGRATING INFORMATION	
METHOD OF SHARING	**DESCRIPTION**	**USE WHEN**
Copying and Pasting	Places a copy of the information in a document	You will be exchanging the data between the two documents only once, and it doesn't matter if the data changes.
Linking	Displays an object in the destination document but doesn't store it there—only the location of the source document is stored in the destination document	You want to use the same data in more than one document, and you need to ensure that the data will be current and identical in each document. Any changes you make to the source document will be reflected in the destination document(s).
Embedding	Displays and stores an object in the destination document	You want the source data to become a permanent part of the destination document, or the source data will no longer be available to the destination document. Any changes you make to either the destination document or the source document will not affect the other.

Pasting Data

You can **paste** an object, such as a range of cells or a chart, from one program to another using copy-and-paste operations. This creates a static copy of the data. For example, you can paste a range of cells from an Excel worksheet into a Word document and use it as part of your Word document.

Once you paste an object from one program into another, that data is now part of the new document. The pasted data has no connection to the source document and can only be altered in that new document's program. For example, if you paste a range of cells from

Excel into a Word document, you can only edit or change that data using the Word commands and features. The pasted data becomes a table of text and numbers, just as if you had entered it directly from the keyboard. There is no connection to the Excel worksheet. Once you have pasted the range of cells, you need to repeat the copy-and-paste operation if you want any subsequent changes in the worksheet to appear in the Word document. Pasting is used when you need to perform a one-time exchange of information between programs.

Object Linking and Embedding

There are situations when copying and pasting information into a document is not the best solution. Excel supports a technology called **Object Linking and Embedding** (OLE, pronounced "oh-lay"). This technology enables you to copy and paste objects—a graphic file, a worksheet range, a chart, or a sound file—in such a way that the data is associated with its source. For example, using OLE you can insert a worksheet or chart into a Word document as either a linked object or an embedded object.

OLE involves the exchange of information between two programs, called the **source** or **server program** and the **destination** or **client program**. The source is the program in which the data was created. The destination is the program that receives the data. For example, if you insert an Excel pivot table into a Word document, Excel is the source program and Word is the destination program.

Using OLE, you can share data (objects) between programs by creating a **link** between files. Linking files lets information created in one file be displayed in another file. When an object is linked, the data is stored in the original source file. For example, you can link a chart from a worksheet to a Word document. Although the chart appears in the Word document, it actually exists as a separate file. The destination document simply displays the object. In effect, the destination document stores a **reference** or link (location and name of the source file) to the object in the source file. Thus, only one copy of the original, or source, object exists. If you make changes to the original object, changes also appear in the destination document. With only one version of the object, every document containing a link to the source object uses the same copy of the object.

Embedding lets you store data from multiple programs—for example, a worksheet, chart, graphic image or sound file—directly in the destination document. The information is totally contained in one file. The copied object, which is embedded, exists as a separate object within the destination document. To make changes to the embedded object, you edit the embedded object directly from within the destination document. The embedded object has no link to the original source document, which means that changes to the embedded object do not alter the original object. This also means that the changes you make to the original source data do not appear in the document that contains the embedded object.

The main differences between linked and embedded objects are where the data is stored and how it is updated after you place it in the destination document. Figure 6-2 illustrates the differences between linking and embedding.

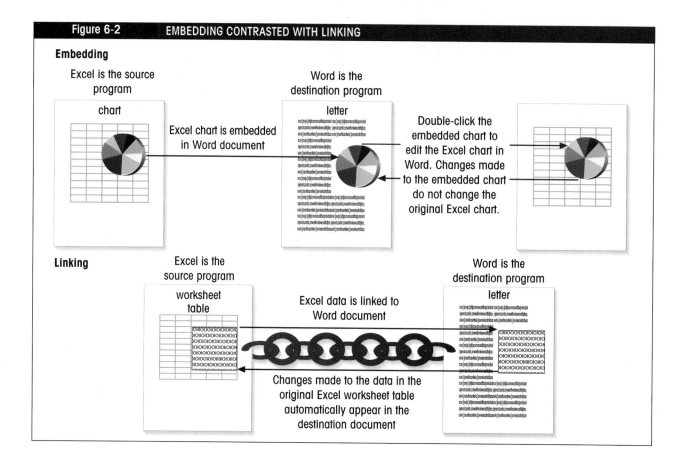

Figure 6-2   EMBEDDING CONTRASTED WITH LINKING

Planning the Integration

Recall that Karen has two documents she wants to create: a flyer and a customer letter. The flyer will describe the five new baskets being offered. The table of new baskets and their prices is contained in an Excel file, Baskets. To create the flyer, Karen needs to paste the company logo at the top, which she can do using Excel's Insert command, as this will be a one-time exchange of data. Then she will use WordArt to insert a visually pleasing title above the new baskets table.

In the case of the customer letter, Karen has already created the body of the letter in Word. However, the Excel new baskets table will be linked to the Word document because the prices of some of the baskets might change, and both customer letter and product worksheet will need to show the latest prices. The NPA pie chart depicting Basket Weavers as the leading area seller needs to be integrated into the customer letter as well. Karen knows the data in the chart will not change, but she might need to modify the chart's size and appearance once it is integrated into the letter. To do this, Karen will want to use the Excel commands for modifying a chart; therefore she decides to embed the chart. Figure 6-3 shows Karen's plan for integrating these pieces to create the flyer and the customer letter.

Figure 6-3	KAREN'S INTEGRATION PLANS FOR THE FLYER AND CUSTOMER LETTER

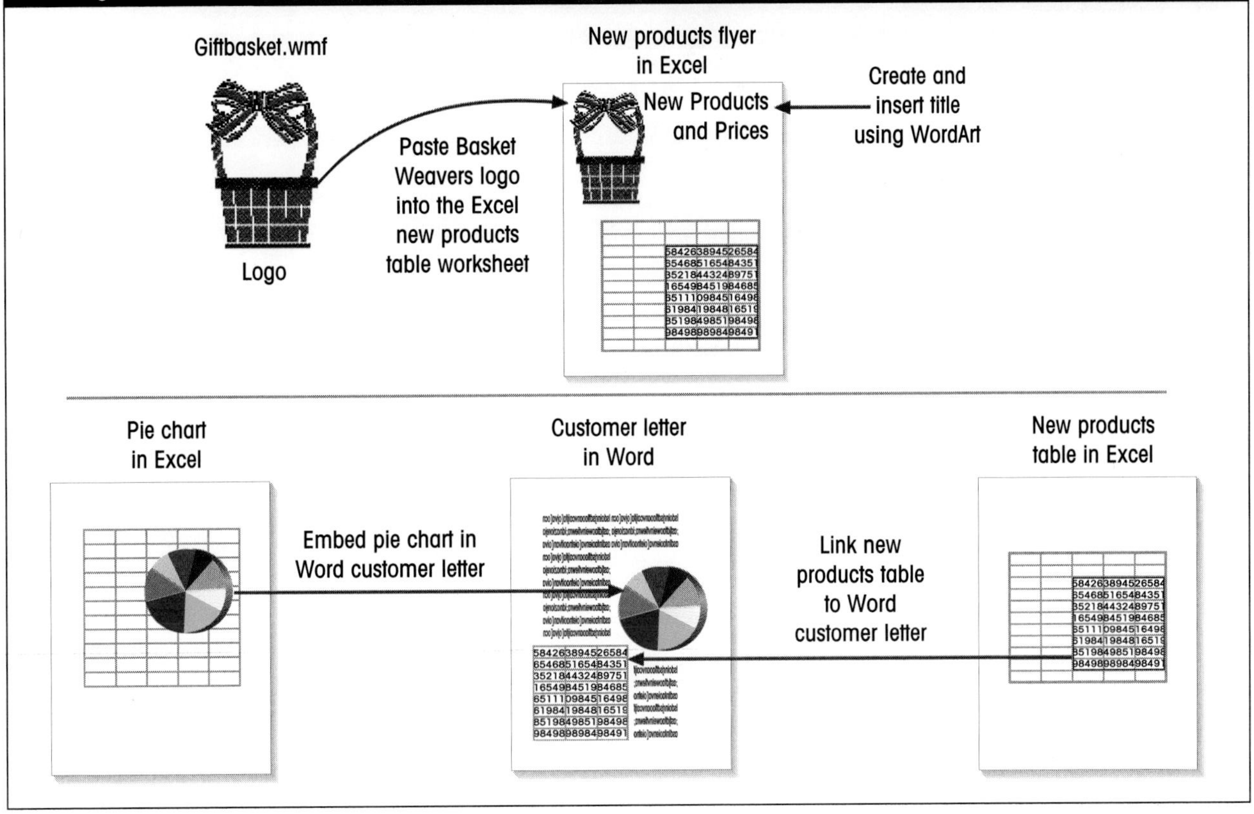

Creating the New Products Flyer

Karen wants to complete the flyer first. To create this document, she needs to insert the Basket Weavers logo, a graphic file, into the Excel worksheet, which contains the table of new baskets. She also needs to create and then insert a WordArt image in the Excel worksheet.

To open the Baskets workbook:

1. Start Excel as usual. Make sure your Data Disk is in the appropriate disk drive.

2. Open the Excel workbook named **Baskets** in the Tutorial folder for Tutorial.06 on your Data Disk. Use the Save As command to save the file as **New Baskets**.

3. Activate the **New Products** sheet. See Figure 6-4.

| Figure 6-4 | NEW PRODUCTS WORKSHEET |

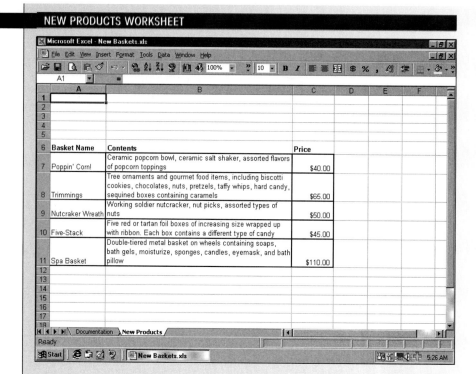

You are now ready to insert the Basket Weavers logo at the top of the new products table.

To insert the company logo into the worksheet:

1. Make sure cell A1 is selected.

2. Click **Insert** on the menu bar, point to **Picture**, and then click **From File** to open the Insert Picture dialog box.

3. Make sure the Look in list box displays the Tutorial folder for Tutorial.06, click **GiftBasket** in the list of available files, and then click the **Insert** button to paste the company logo into the worksheet.

4. Move the pointer over the lower-right selection handle until the pointer shape changes to ⬉.

5. Click and drag up and to the left to the bottom of cell A5. Release the mouse button. See Figure 6-5. Notice that the Picture toolbar appears on the screen while the graphic object is selected. The Picture toolbar contains tools you can use to change the characteristics of a graphic image. For example, you can crop the image, or adjust its brightness.

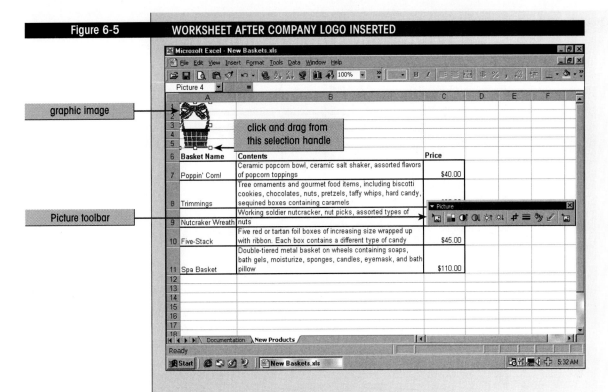

| Figure 6-5 | WORKSHEET AFTER COMPANY LOGO INSERTED |

graphic image

click and drag from this selection handle

Picture toolbar

Copy the graphic image to the right side of the table.

6. Right-click the graphic image to display the shortcut menu. Click **Copy**.

7. Click cell **C1**. Click **Edit**, then click **Paste** to display a copy of the company logo in column C.

8. Click outside the logo to deselect it. The Picture toolbar closes when the logo is no longer selected.

Karen still needs to add a title to the new baskets table.

Inserting WordArt into an Excel Worksheet

When Karen reviews her work so far, she knows that her table shows the basic data but it does nothing to attract her customers' attention. To add some pizzazz, she would like you to use WordArt, a shared application available to all Office programs. WordArt enables you to add special graphic effects to your documents. You can bend, rotate, and stretch the text, and insert the graphic object into other documents, such as an Excel worksheet.

To prepare Karen's flyer, you will start WordArt while in Excel, create the graphic object, and then return to Excel to insert the object into the Excel worksheet.

To create a WordArt graphic object:

1. If necessary, click the **Drawing** button 🖉 on the Standard toolbar to display the Drawing toolbar. You can access the WordArt program from the Drawing toolbar.

2. Click the **Insert WordArt** button 🖪 on the Drawing toolbar to display a gallery of WordArt special effects styles. See Figure 6-6.

Figure 6-6	WORDART STYLES

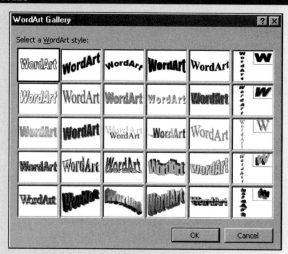

3. Click the WordArt style in the third row, fifth column, and then click the **OK** button to open the Edit WordArt Text dialog box. See Figure 6-7. In this dialog box, you specify the text you want to appear in the WordArt style you selected. If you want, you can also change the font, font size, and font style in the dialog box. For now, just type the text you want as the title of the worksheet. You will adjust the font size and style as necessary after you see how it appears in the worksheet.

Figure 6-7	EDIT WORDART TEXT DIALOG BOX

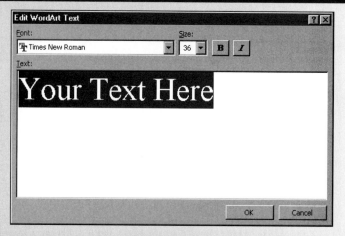

4. Type **New Products from Basket Weavers** and then click the **OK** button to place the WordArt graphic on your worksheet. See Figure 6-8. Notice that the WordArt toolbar appears on the screen while the WordArt object is selected. Figure 6-9 describes each button on the WordArt toolbar.

TROUBLE? If the WordArt toolbar does not appear on your screen, click View on the menu bar, point to Toolbars, and then click WordArt to place a check next to this option and display the WordArt toolbar on your screen.

Figure 6-8	**WORDART GRAPHIC IN WORKSHEET**

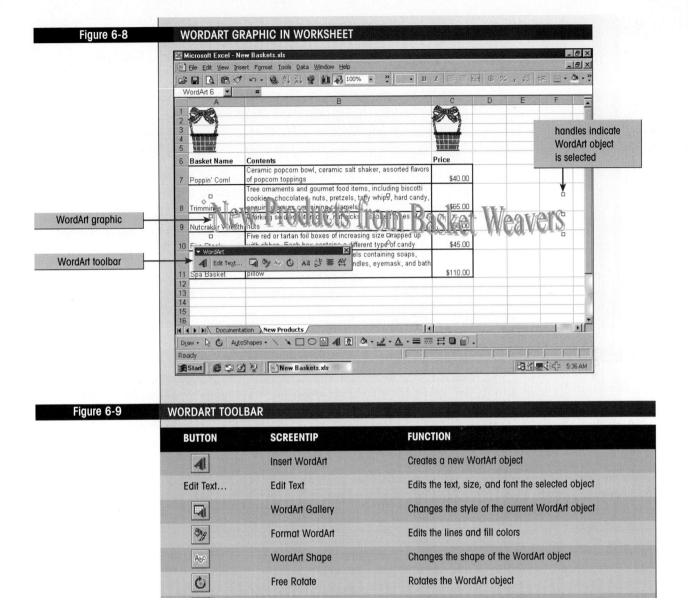

Figure 6-9	**WORDART TOOLBAR**

BUTTON	SCREENTIP	FUNCTION
	Insert WordArt	Creates a new WortArt object
Edit Text...	Edit Text	Edits the text, size, and font the selected object
	WordArt Gallery	Changes the style of the current WordArt object
	Format WordArt	Edits the lines and fill colors
Abc	WordArt Shape	Changes the shape of the WordArt object
	Free Rotate	Rotates the WordArt object
Aa	WordArt Same Letter Heights	Makes all the letters the same height
	WordArt Vertical Text	Changes between vertical and horizontal text orientation
	WordArt Alignment	Changes the text alignment
AV	WordArt Character Spacing	Changes the spacing between letters

As you review the WordArt graphic object, you decide that the graphic is too large. You decide to change the point size from 36 to 16 points and apply a bold style to make the graphic stand out. To make these changes, you need to return to the WordArt program because when you insert WordArt into an Excel worksheet, the object is embedded. This means that in order to modify the object, you need access to the commands and features of its source program.

To change the font point size and style of the WordArt object:

1. Make sure the graphic object is selected, and then click the **Edit Text** button on the WordArt toolbar to return to the Edit WordArt Text dialog box.

2. Click the **Size** list arrow and click **16**, click the **Bold** button, and then click the **OK** button. You return to the New Products worksheet.

   Now move the graphic object above the new products table, and between the two logos.

3. Make sure the graphic object is selected, and then position the pointer over the graphic until the pointer changes to a four-headed arrow ⊕.

4. Click and drag the WordArt object to the top of row 2 in column B. As you drag the object, an outline of the object indicates its placement on the worksheet. Release the mouse button.

   TROUBLE? If the Basket Weavers logo moves instead of the WordArt object, click Undo, select the WordArt object, and repeat Steps 3 and 4.

5. Click anywhere outside the graphic so it is no longer selected. See Figure 6-10.

| Figure 6-10 | WORDART GRAPHIC AFTER BEING MOVED AND EDITED |

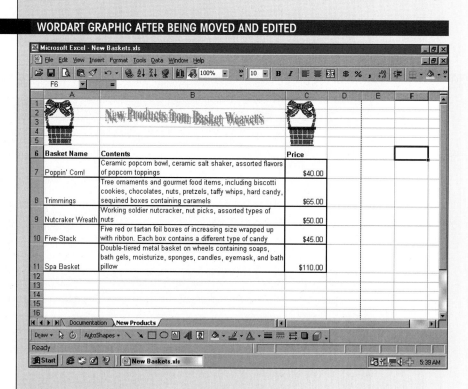

6. Save the worksheet.

7. Preview and print the worksheet for Karen.

8. Click the **Drawing** button on the Standard toolbar to remove the Drawing toolbar.

Karen wants to show Michael Flynn, the business manager for Basket Weavers, the flyer she designed. She attaches the flyer in an e-mail message she sends to him.

Mail a Workbook as an Attachment

Karen decided to take advantage of Excel's built-in features to use electronic mail. As long as Excel 2000 and one of the following e-mail programs: Outlook, Outlook Express, Microsoft Exchange Client, or Lotus cc:Mail is present, you can send or route workbooks or worksheets as attachments in e-mail messages.

REFERENCE WINDOW   **RW**

Mail a Workbook or Worksheet as an Attachment
- In Microsoft Excel, open the workbook or worksheet you want to send as an attachment.
- Click File on the menu bar, point to Send To, and then click Mail Recipient (as Attachment).
- In the To and Cc boxes, enter recipient names, separated by semicolons.
- Set the options you want for the message.
- Click Send.

If your computer has a mail program, you can use the Send To Recipient (as attachment) command to automatically attach a copy of the current workbook to an e-mail message. When the message is received, the recipient double-clicks the Excel icon in the mail message to open the workbook.

In his reply, Michael Flynn comments on the professional look that the company logo and WordArt lends to the worksheet. Karen is ready to print copies of the table, and distribute them as flyers at each store.

Linking an Excel Worksheet to a Word Document

Now Karen needs to link the new products table created in Excel and the customer letter created in Word. As you know, Karen maintains her new product and pricing information in an Excel workbook. She wants to include the new products table in a letter to her customers. Because the product and pricing information is always subject to change, the copy-and-paste method is not the appropriate method to integrate these documents. Recall that pasting only allows you to change or modify the pasted object in the destination program. Karen wants the most current pricing information to appear both in the original source file (the new products worksheet) and the destination document (the customer letter). Therefore, a better solution is to create a link between the data copied from Excel to Word. By creating a link, if the data changes in the source document, these changes automatically appear in the destination document. For example, Karen believes that the price of gift baskets will most likely change when she receives a signed quote from her supplier of baskets. It's possible that she won't receive this quote until right before she plans to send out the letter. Therefore, you'll link the table from the New Products worksheet to the Customer Letter document so that you can make changes to the Excel new products table and have these changes automatically reflected in the Word document.

REFERENCE WINDOW   `RW`

Linking an Object

- Start the source program, open the file containing the object to be linked, select the object or information you want to link to the destination program, and then click the Copy button on the Standard toolbar.
- Start the destination program, open the file that will contain the link to the copied object, position the insertion point where you want the linked object to appear, click Edit, and then click Paste Special.
- Click the Paste link option button, select the option you want in the As list box, and then click the OK button.

Karen has given you the Word file containing her letter. You need to link the new products table to the customer letter. First you need to select the new products table, which is the Excel object to be linked.

To link the new products table to the customer letter:

1. Make sure the New Products worksheet is the active sheet. Select the range of cells **A6:C11** to select the new products table.

2. Click the **Copy** button on the Standard toolbar to copy the data to the Clipboard.

Now, you need to start Word, and then open the customer letter document.

To start Word and open the customer letter document:

1. Make sure your Data Disk is in the appropriate disk drive. Click the **Start** button on the taskbar, point to **Programs**, and then click **Microsoft Word** to start this program.

2. Open the **Letter** document, which is located in the Tutorial folder for Tutorial.06 on your Data Disk. Karen's letter to the Basket Weavers' customers appears in the document window in print layout view. See Figure 6-11.

   TROUBLE? If your document does not show the nonprinting characters, click the Show/Hide button 🔏 on the Standard toolbar.

   Next you'll save the file with a new name. That way, the original letter remains intact on your Data Disk, in case you want to start the tutorial again.

Figure 6-11	BEGINNING OF CUSTOMER LETTER

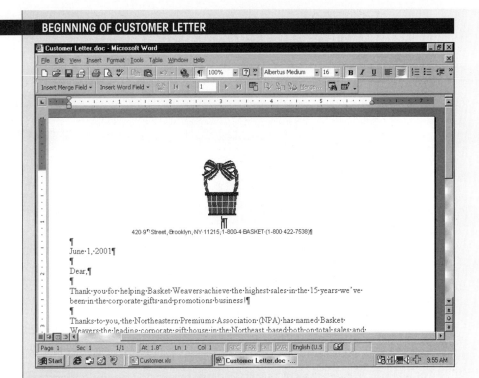

3. Use the **Save As** command to save the file as **Customer Letter** in the Tutorial folder for Tutorial.06 on your Data Disk.

Now link the Excel new products table to the customer letter.

4. Scroll the document and position the insertion point to the left of the paragraph mark above the paragraph that begins, "You will receive..." This is where you want the product and pricing data to appear. See Figure 6-12.

Figure 6-12	PLACEMENT OF NEW PRODUCTS TABLE IN CUSTOMER LETTER

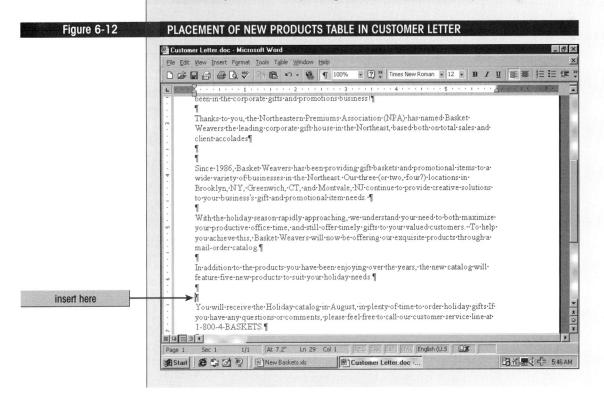

5. Click **Edit** on the menu bar, and then click **Paste Special**. The Paste Special dialog box opens. See Figure 6-13.

Figure 6-13	PASTE SPECIAL DIALOG BOX

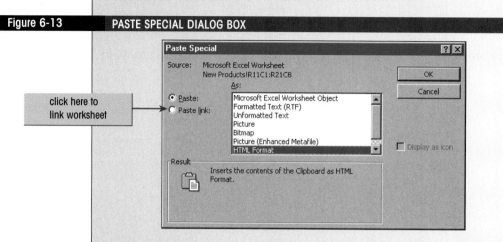

click here to link worksheet

6. In the Paste Special dialog box, click the **Paste link** option button to select this option, and then click **Microsoft Excel Worksheet Object** in the As list box.

The Paste link option specifies that the table will be linked.

7. Click the **OK** button to close the Paste Special dialog box and link the Excel worksheet to the customer letter. See Figure 6-14.

Figure 6-14	NEW PRODUCTS TABLE IN WORD DOCUMENT

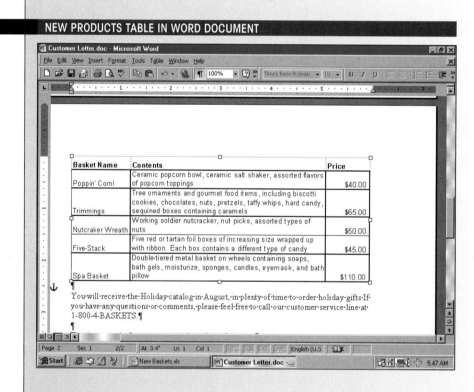

8. Click the **Save** button on the Word Standard toolbar to save the customer letter.

Karen has just received the signed quote from her basket supplier. As she expected, some of the prices have changed. She would now like you to update the new products table.

Updating **Linked Objects**

Now that you have linked the new products table from Excel to the customer letter, when you make changes to the source document, the Excel new products table, the changes will automatically be reflected in the destination file. When making changes, you can have one or both files open.

To update the new products table in Excel:

1. Click the **Microsoft Excel** button on the taskbar to switch to the New Baskets workbook. Make sure the New Products sheet is the active sheet.

2. Click any cell to deselect the table and press the **Esc** key to remove the data from the Clipboard.

   The price of Trimmings basket has changed from $65.00 to $70.00 each.

3. Enter **70** in cell C8.

   Now check to see if this change is reflected in the customer letter.

4. Click the **Microsoft Word** button on the taskbar to switch to the customer letter and view the price of Trimmings basket. Because you linked the table from Excel to Word, the change you just made to the price of Trimmings basket also appears in the destination document. See Figure 6-15.

| Figure 6-15 | CUSTOMER LETTER WITH UPDATED PRICE |

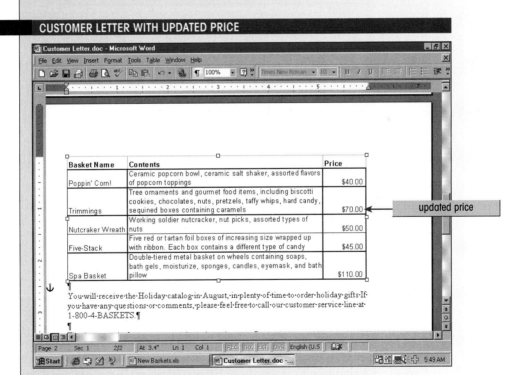

5. Click the **Save** button on the Word Standard toolbar to save the customer letter.

What would happen if you were working on the new products table in Excel without the Word document open? Would the information still be updated in the customer letter? To find out, make the remaining changes to the prices for gift baskets with the customer letter closed. You can then reopen the customer letter to ensure that the changes appear there as well.

To change the linked object with the Word document closed:

1. Click **File** on the Word menu bar, and then click **Close** to close the Customer Letter document.

2. Click the **Microsoft Excel** button on the taskbar to switch to the New Baskets workbook.

3. Enter **53** in cell C9, and then enter **47** in cell C10.

4. Click the **Save** button on the Excel Standard toolbar.

5. Close the Excel workbook.

   Now reopen the customer letter to confirm that the prices have been updated in the linked new baskets table.

6. Click the **Microsoft Word** button on the taskbar. Click **File** on the menu bar, and then open the **Customer Letter** file.

7. Scroll the document to view the linked table. Notice that the new basket prices appear in the linked table in Word. See Figure 6-16.

| Figure 6-16 | LINKED TABLE AFTER ALL PRICES UPDATED |

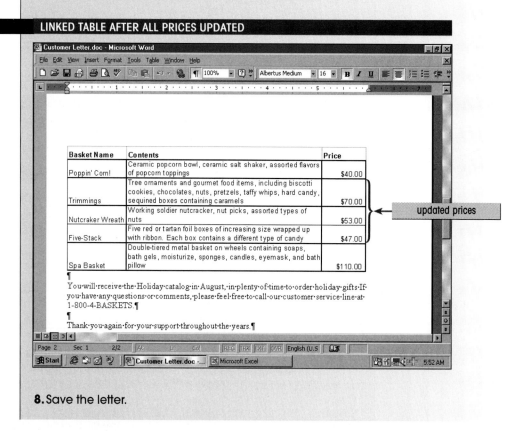

8. Save the letter.

The customer letter is almost complete. Now Karen just needs you to add the NPA pie chart.

Embedding **an Excel Chart in a Word Document**

Karen wants her letter to include the pie chart from the NPA workbook showing Basket Weavers as the top seller in the area. Karen knows the data for the chart will not change, so there is no need for her to link the pie chart in her Word letter to the source file. Therefore, she decides to embed it. That way, if the pie chart needs to be resized or moved once it is in the customer letter, she can make these changes using Excel chart commands. (Recall that when you embed an object, you automatically have access to the commands and features of the source program to manipulate it in the destination program.)

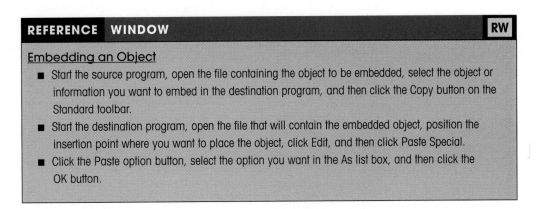

REFERENCE WINDOW   **RW**

Embedding an Object

■ Start the source program, open the file containing the object to be embedded, select the object or information you want to embed in the destination program, and then click the Copy button on the Standard toolbar.

■ Start the destination program, open the file that will contain the embedded object, position the insertion point where you want to place the object, click Edit, and then click Paste Special.

■ Click the Paste option button, select the option you want in the As list box, and then click the OK button.

Now you can embed the pie chart in the customer letter.

To embed the Excel chart in the Word document:

1. Click the **Microsoft Excel** button on the taskbar to switch to Excel. Open the **NPA** workbook, which is located in the Tutorial folder for Tutorial.06 on your Data Disk. The workbook appears in the worksheet window. See Figure 6-17.

Figure 6-17	NPA PIE CHART

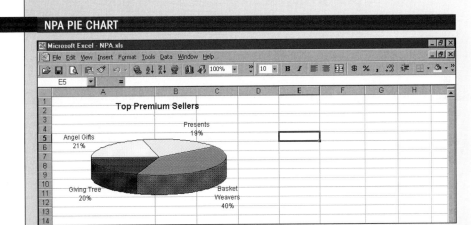

2. If necessary, click the **chart area** (the white area around the pie) to select the chart. When the chart is selected, handles appear on the chart area.

3. Click **Edit** on the menu bar, then click **Copy** to copy the chart to the Clipboard. The chart now appears with a rotating dashed line around its frame, indicating that it has been copied.

4. Click the **Microsoft Word** button on the taskbar to return to the Customer Letter document.

5. Scroll to page 1 of the Customer Letter document, and then click to the left of the paragraph mark immediately above the paragraph that begins "Since 1986, Basket Weavers..." to position the insertion point where you need to embed the pie chart. See Figure 6-18.

| Figure 6-18 | PLACEMENT OF PIE CHART IN CUSTOMER LETTER |

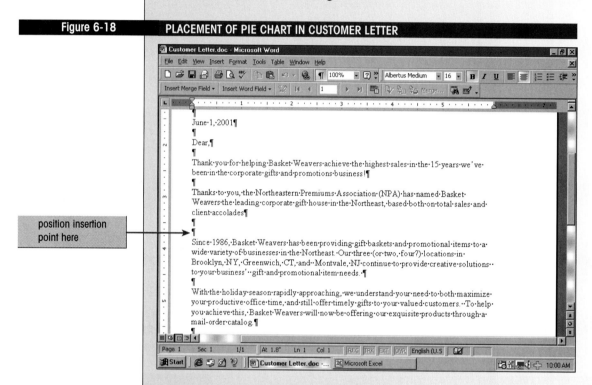

6. Click **Edit**, and then click **Paste Special**. The Paste Special dialog box opens. See Figure 6-19.

| Figure 6-19 | PASTE SPECIAL DIALOG BOX WITH SETTING FOR PASTE |

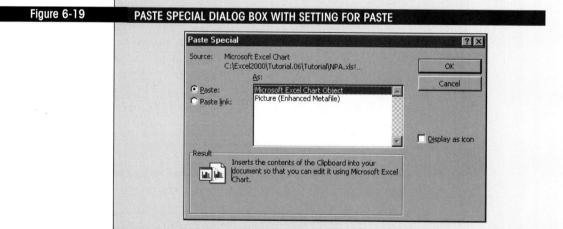

7. Make sure the Paste option button is selected. This option will embed the chart.

8. In the As list box, make sure Microsoft Excel Chart Object is selected as the object to be embedded.

TROUBLE? If the Microsoft Excel Chart Object option does not appear in the As list box, you might not have selected and copied the chart correctly. Click the Cancel button, and then repeat Steps 1 through 8, making sure that when you select the chart, handles appear around the chart area, and that when you copy the chart, a rotating dashed line appears around the chart area.

9. Click the **OK** button. The Paste Special dialog box closes, and the Excel pie chart appears embedded in the letter. See Figure 6-20.

| Figure 6-20 | CUSTOMER LETTER WITH EMBEDDED PIE CHART |

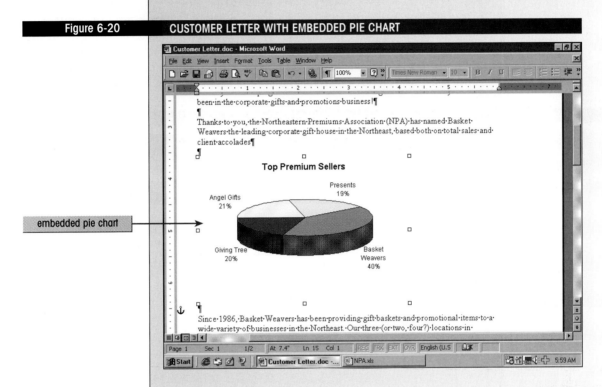

embedded pie chart

10. Click the **Save** button on the Word Standard toolbar to save the letter with the embedded chart.

11. Click the **Microsoft Excel** button on the taskbar, click any cell outside of the chart area to deselect the chart, and then close the NPA workbook.

TROUBLE? If a dialog box opens asking if you would like to save changes to the file before closing it, click the No button.

After reviewing the letter with the embedded pie chart, Karen decides that the Basket Weavers slice should be "exploded" and rotated to the front so the reader's attention is drawn to the fact that Basket Weavers' percentage of the market is the greatest among the competitors. Because you embedded the chart (as opposed to just copying and pasting it), you can use Excel chart commands from within the Word document to modify the chart.

Modifying an Embedded Object

When you make changes to an embedded object within the destination program, the changes are made to the embedded object only; the original object in the source program is not affected. When you select an embedded object, the menu commands on the menu bar of the destination program change to include the menu commands of the embedded object's source program. You can then use these commands to modify the embedded object.

Now that you have embedded the pie chart in Word, you can modify it by exploding the Basket Weavers pie slice.

To edit the pie chart from within Word:

1. Click the **Microsoft Word** button on the taskbar.

2. Double-click the **chart** to select it. After a moment, a thick border appears around the chart, and the Excel chart menu appears at the top of the Word window. See Figure 6-21. Notice that the embedded object appears within the Excel worksheet borders. You can now edit this object in place using Excel commands. Thus, you have access to all of the Excel features while you are in Word.

| Figure 6-21 | EMBEDDED OBJECT SELECTED FOR EDITING |

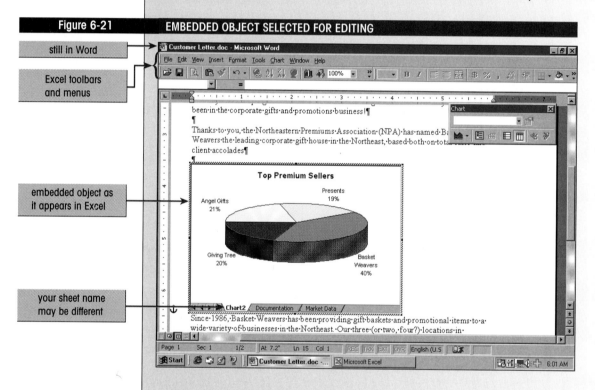

Now you can modify the chart.

3. Click anywhere within the **chart** to select it, and then click the **Basket Weavers slice** to select it. Selection handles now appear on only this slice.

TROUBLE? If the floating Chart toolbar appears, click its Close button to close it.

4. With the pointer on the selected slice, click and drag the Basket Weavers slice down and to the right, and then release the mouse button. The Basket Weavers slice is exploded.

5. Click **Chart** on the menu bar, and then click **3-D View** to open the 3-D View dialog box.

6. Click the **clockwise rotation arrow** button until the Rotation box shows 75, then click **OK**.

7. Click outside of the chart area to deselect the chart and return the window to the display of Word commands and features only. See Figure 6-22.

Figure 6-22   **PIE CHART IN WORD DOCUMENT AFTER SLICE EXPLODED AND ROTATED**

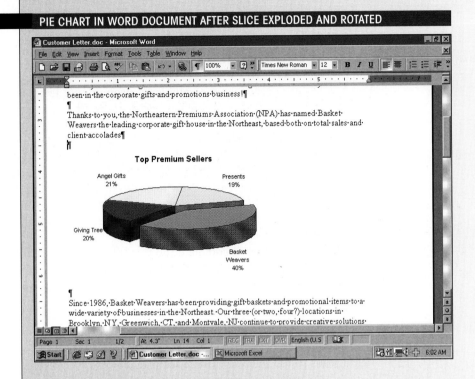

8. Click the **Save** button on the Word Standard toolbar to save the Customer Letter document.

Session 6.1 QUICK CHECK

1. OLE stands for _____.

2. If two documents are _____ using OLE, changing the source document will automatically change the destination document.

3. Updating an embedded object (does, does not) affect the original source object.

4. When you _____ an object, that object is now part of the new document, and can only be altered from within that document's program.

5. You should _____ an object if you plan to use the same data in several documents and need to ensure that the data will be identical in each document.

6. You can create special text effects using _____.

7. When linking objects, you use the _____ command on the Edit menu.

8. You have embedded a range of cells in a Word document. Describe what happens when you double-click the embedded object.

Now that you have completed the body of the customer letter, Karen is ready for you to send it to her New Jersey customers. You can do this through a mail merge. You will do this in Session 6.2.

SESSION 6.2

In this session you will plan and complete a mail merge by inserting merge fields into a form letter that links to data in an Excel list.

Customizing a Form Letter Using an Excel List

Karen is ready to send out the completed promotional letter announcing the new mail-order catalog and introducing the new gift baskets. She has decided to customize the customer letter by inserting the customer's name and address into each letter. Using her customer list, which is maintained in Excel, she plans separate mailings to coincide with promotional events at each of her company's three stores. For instance, the store in Montvalle, New Jersey has an open house planned next month, and Karen wants to send the letter to only those customers in New Jersey so that they receive the letter in advance of the open house. Later, she will do a separate mailing for Connecticut customers to coincide with a winter festival, and then a mailing to New York customers to coincide with the Brooklyn store's participation in a holiday carnival.

In this section you will complete the customer letter for Karen by merging it with the names and addresses of Basket Weavers' New Jersey customers. This data is stored as an Excel list. Therefore, you will again be integrating Excel data with a Word document.

Planning the Form Letter

Karen plans to use the Mail Merge feature of Word to send the customer letter you completed in the previous session to each Basket Weavers customer in New Jersey. She will be sending the same letter, a form letter, to each customer; only the name and address will change. A **form letter** is a Word document that contains standard paragraphs of text and a minimum of variable text, usually just the names and addresses of the letter recipients. The **main document** of a form letter contains the text that stays the same in each letter, as well as the **merge fields** that tell Word where to insert the variable information into each letter. The variable information, the information that changes from letter to letter, is contained in a **data source**, which can be another Word document, an Excel list, an Access database, or some other source. The main document and the data source work together—when you merge the main document with the data source, Word replaces the merge fields with the corresponding field values from the data source. The process of merging the main document with the data source is called a **mail merge**.

In this case, Karen's customer letter will be the main document, and a customer list maintained in Excel containing the names and addresses of Basket Weavers customers will be the data source. Figure 6-23 shows Karen's plan for the form letter.

Figure 6-23   KAREN'S PLAN FOR THE FORM LETTER

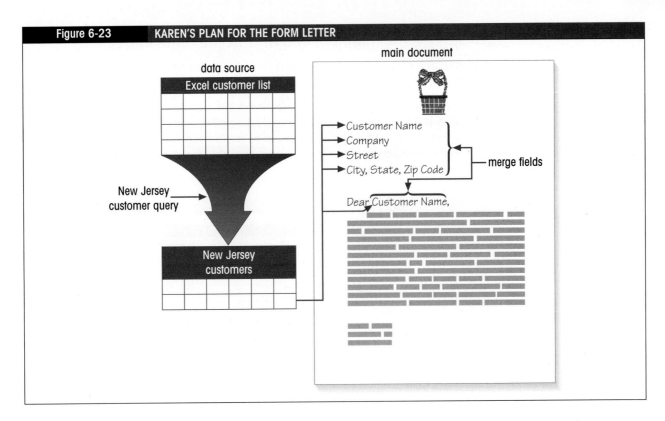

Note that the data source contains all Basket Weavers customers. Karen first wants to send the letter to only the New Jersey customers.

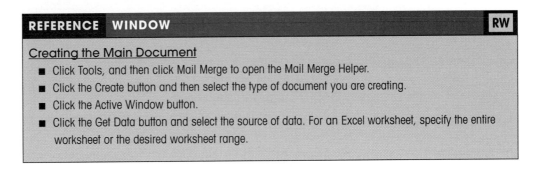

REFERENCE WINDOW   RW

Creating the Main Document
- Click Tools, and then click Mail Merge to open the Mail Merge Helper.
- Click the Create button and then select the type of document you are creating.
- Click the Active Window button.
- Click the Get Data button and select the source of data. For an Excel worksheet, specify the entire worksheet or the desired worksheet range.

To help simplify the mail-merge process, you will use the Word Mail Merge Helper, which guides you through the steps of the mail merge.

Specifying a Main Document and a Data Source

A mail-merged main document can be a new or existing Word document. In this case, the main document is Karen's customer letter.

Now you need to specify the customer letter as the main document and the Excel customer list as the data source.

To specify the main document and the data source:

1. If you took a break after the last session, make sure that Excel and Word are running, and the Customer Letter document is open and visible on your screen.

2. Scroll to the top of the letter, click **Tools** on the menu bar, and then click **Mail Merge**. The Mail Merge Helper dialog box opens. See Figure 6-24. The dialog box displays the three tasks you need to perform: creating the main document, creating or getting a data source, and merging the main document with the data source.

Figure 6-24 | **MAIL MERGE HELPER DIALOG BOX**

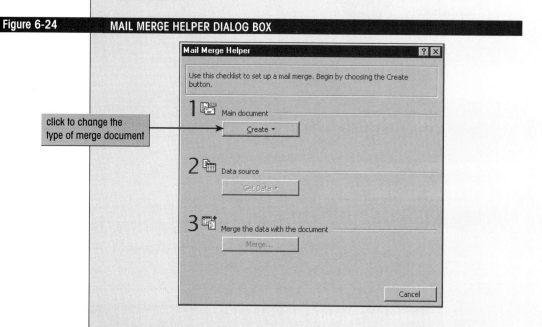

click to change the
type of merge document

The type of merge document you need to create is a form letter.

3. Click the **Create** button in the Main document section to display the list of main document types. Click **Form Letters**. A message box appears asking whether you want to use the active window as the main document or create a new main document. In this case, you want to use the open document, Customer Letter, as the main document.

4. Click the **Active Window** button. The area below the Create button now indicates the type of mail merge (Form Letters) and the file path (drive and folder) and name of the main document (Customer Letter).

You have now established Customer Letter as the main document. Next you need to specify the data source, the source of the variable information that will be inserted into the main document during the merge process. The data source is an Excel workbook named Customers.

5. Click the **Get Data** button in the Data source section of the Mail Merge Helper dialog box, and then click **Open Data Source**. The Open Data Source dialog box opens.

The Customers workbook is located in the Tutorial folder for Tutorial.06 on your Data Disk.

6. Make sure that the Tutorial folder appears in the Look in list box.

Because the dialog box currently shows only the Word documents in the selected folder, you need to change the entry in the Files of type list box to show the Excel files.

7. Click the **Files of type** list arrow, and then click **MS Excel Worksheets**. The dialog box now shows a list of all the Excel files in the Tutorial.06 folder on your Data Disk.

8. Click **Customer** and then click the **Open** button. A Microsoft Excel dialog box opens, in which you can choose the data source—either the entire spreadsheet or the range containing the customer list. In this case, you need to specify the range Customers. See Figure 6-25.

Figure 6-25   **CHOOSE DATA SOURCE**

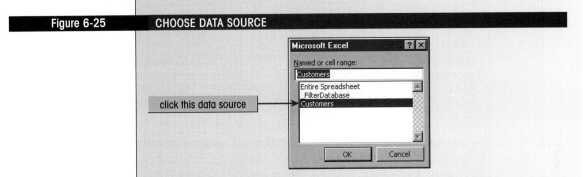

9. Click **Customers** in the list box, and then click the **OK** button. A message box appears indicating that your main document does not contain merge fields.

Your next step will be to insert the merge fields into the main document, the customer letter, so you need to edit the main document.

10. Click the **Edit Main Document** button. The Mail Merge Helper dialog box closes and the Mail Merge toolbar appears on the screen. See Figure 6-26.

Figure 6-26   **TOP OF MAIN DOCUMENT**

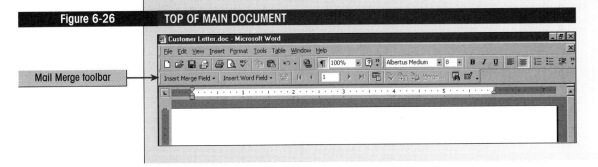

Inserting the Merge Fields

Because you now have a data source to use with the main document, you can go back to the main document and identify which fields in the Excel list to pull into the document as well as where to place each field. This process is called **inserting merge fields**. As noted earlier, a merge field is a special instruction that tells Word where to insert the variable information from the data source into a form letter.

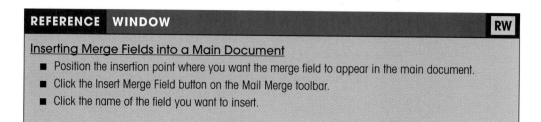

REFERENCE WINDOW   RW

Inserting Merge Fields into a Main Document
- Position the insertion point where you want the merge field to appear in the main document.
- Click the Insert Merge Field button on the Mail Merge toolbar.
- Click the name of the field you want to insert.

To complete Karen's form letter, you need to insert seven merge fields, one for each of the following pieces of information: customer name, company name (if any), street, city, state, and zip code—all for the inside address—and customer name again in the salutation of the letter.

To insert the merge fields into the customer letter document:

1. Scroll the document window and position the insertion point in the blank paragraph directly above the salutation ("Dear,"). This is where the customer's name and address will appear.

2. Press the **Enter** key to insert a blank line, and then click the **Insert Merge Field** button on the Mail Merge toolbar. A list of the available merge fields appears. See Figure 6-27.

| Figure 6-27 | INSERTING MERGE FIELDS INTO MAIN DOCUMENT |

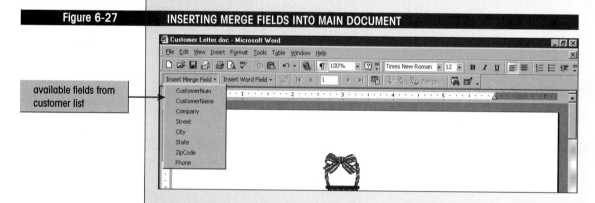

available fields from
customer list

3. Click **CustomerName** to select this field. See Figure 6-28. Word inserts the field name into the document, enclosed in chevron symbols (<< >>). The chevrons distinguish the merge fields from the rest of the text in the main document.

| Figure 6-28 | MAIN DOCUMENT AFTER ONE MERGE FIELD INSERTED |

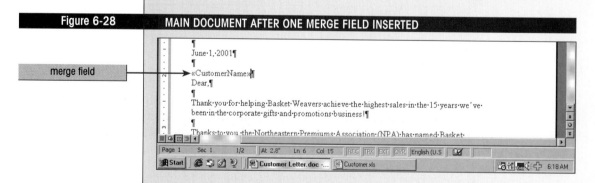

merge field

The company name (if any) should appear on the line below the customer name.

4. Press the **Enter** key to move the insertion point to the next line, click the **Insert Merge Field** button on the Mail Merge toolbar, and then click **Company**. The Company merge field is now in the document.

5. Repeat Step 4 to insert the **Street** field on the third line of the inside address.

6. Repeat Step 4 to insert the **City** field on the fourth line of the inside address.

   The State and ZipCode fields must appear on the same line as the City field, with a comma and a space separating the city and state, and a space separating the state and zip code.

7. Type **,** (a comma), press the **Spacebar**, click the **Insert Merge Field** button on the Mail Merge toolbar, and then click **State**.

8. Press the **Spacebar**, click the **Insert Merge Field** button on the Mail Merge toolbar, and then click **ZipCode**.

9. Press the **Enter** key to insert a blank line between the inside address and the salutation. The final merge field you need to insert is the CustomerName field again, after the word "Dear" in the salutation of the letter.

10. Position the insertion point between the "r" in the word "Dear" and the comma following it, press the **Spacebar**, click the **Insert Merge Field** button on the Mail Merge toolbar, and then click **CustomerName**. The merge fields are now complete. See Figure 6-29.

Figure 6-29	ALL MERGE FIELDS INSERTED INTO MAIN DOCUMENT

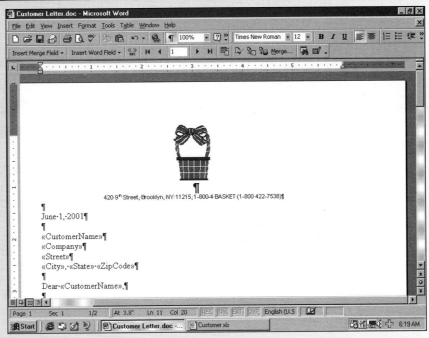

TROUBLE? Compare your screen with Figure 6-29 and make sure there are no extra spaces or punctuation around the merge fields. If you need to delete a merge field, highlight the entire field, and then press the Delete key.

11. Click the **Save** button on the Word Standard toolbar to save the letter.

Performing the Mail Merge

With the main document and merge fields in place, you're ready to merge the main document with the data source—the Excel customer list—to produce the customized letter.

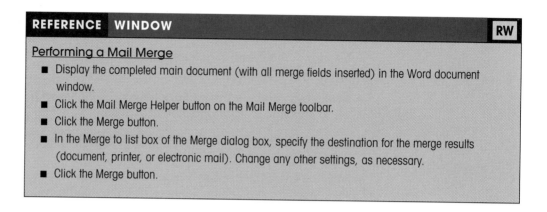

REFERENCE WINDOW RW

Performing a Mail Merge

- Display the completed main document (with all merge fields inserted) in the Word document window.
- Click the Mail Merge Helper button on the Mail Merge toolbar.
- Click the Merge button.
- In the Merge to list box of the Merge dialog box, specify the destination for the merge results (document, printer, or electronic mail). Change any other settings, as necessary.
- Click the Merge button.

In this case, Karen wants the merge results placed in a new document, so that she can check the merged form letters before printing them. First she needs to specify the records that are to be included in the mail merge—customers in New Jersey.

To specify selection criteria for records to retrieve from the data source:

1. Click the **Mail Merge Helper** button ▦ on the Mail Merge toolbar. The Mail Merge Helper dialog box opens.

2. Click the **Merge** button to display the Merge dialog box. See Figure 6-30.

Figure 6-30 MERGE DIALOG BOX

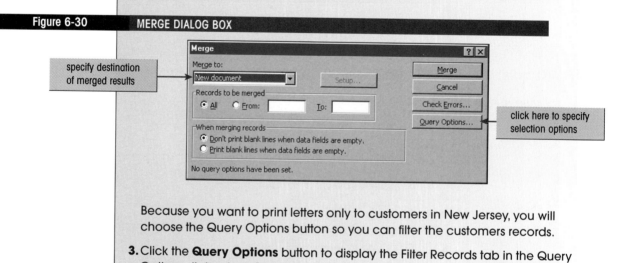

specify destination of merged results

click here to specify selection options

Because you want to print letters only to customers in New Jersey, you will choose the Query Options button so you can filter the customers records.

3. Click the **Query Options** button to display the Filter Records tab in the Query Options dialog box. See Figure 6-31.

Figure 6-31	QUERY OPTIONS DIALOG BOX

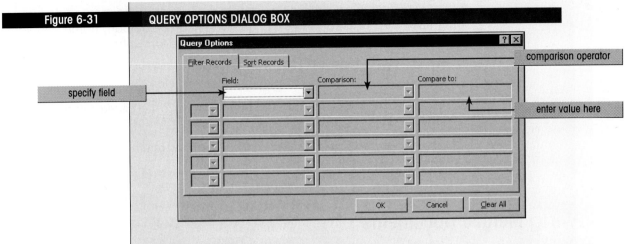

4. Click the **Field** list arrow to display the list of fields from the customer list. Scroll the list until the State field appears. Click **State** to select the field on which you want to base your selection. Notice that the Comparison operator box now displays the default operator—Equal to. Accept the default comparison operator and enter a value to compare to the State field.

5. Make sure the insertion point is in the Compare to text box and then type **NJ**.

6. Click the **OK** button to return to the Merge dialog box.

You are now ready to merge the data with the letter. You can merge the data to a new document, or merge directly to the printer, electronic mail, or fax. Karen wants to check the merged document before printing, so you will merge to a new document.

7. Click the **Merge** button. The Excel data is merged with the Word form letter and placed in a new document named Form Letters1 (the default name supplied by Word). The form letter for each of the five New Jersey customers is contained in the merged document, each separated by a section break.

8. Scroll the document until you can see the first merged address. Word replaced each merge field with the appropriate Excel data. See Figure 6-32.

Figure 6-32	MERGED RESULTS IN NEW DOCUMENT

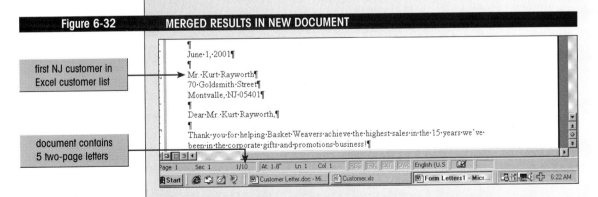

Notice that the merged document contains 10 pages. Each letter is two pages long, and there are five letters in all.

9. Use the buttons in the vertical scroll bar to page through the merged document. Notice that in addresses that do not include a company name, the blank line is suppressed. Also, notice that each two-page form letter is separated from the others by a section break.

Now you'll save the merged document and then close it.

10. Save the document as **Merged Customer Letters** in the Tutorial folder for Tutorial.06 on your Data Disk.

11. Close the Merged Customer Letters document. You return to the main document, the customer letter.

Viewing **Merged Documents**

When you're working with mail-merge documents, you don't have to open the document containing the merge results in order to view them. You can view the merged documents right from the main document.

The View Merged Data button on the Mail Merge toolbar lets you check the merge results quickly. When you click this button, information from the first data record appears in place of the merge fields. You can then use the navigation buttons on the Mail Merge toolbar to view the results for other data records. You'll practice using the navigation buttons to view the merge results.

To view the merge results from the main document:

1. Click the **View Merged Data** button on the Mail Merge toolbar. See Figure 6-33. The information from the first merged letter appears in place of the merge fields.

| Figure 6-33 | VIEWING MERGED RESULTS FROM MAIN DOCUMENT |

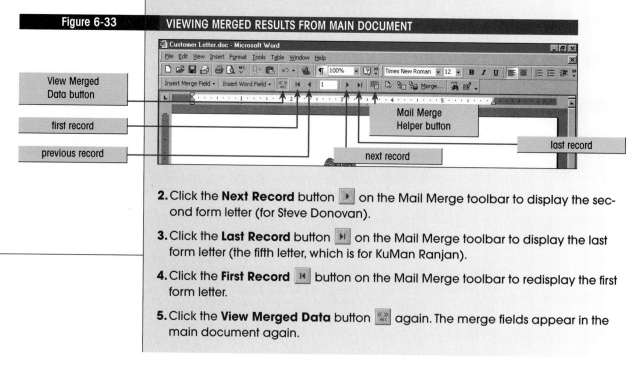

2. Click the **Next Record** button on the Mail Merge toolbar to display the second form letter (for Steve Donovan).

3. Click the **Last Record** button on the Mail Merge toolbar to display the last form letter (the fifth letter, which is for KuMan Ranjan).

4. Click the **First Record** button on the Mail Merge toolbar to redisplay the first form letter.

5. Click the **View Merged Data** button again. The merge fields appear in the main document again.

Karen has just learned that one of her customers, Wilson Gift Store, has moved to a different location. She asks you to enter the new address for this customer in Excel and then re-merge the Word document with the data.

To change the address and then re-merge the document:

1. Click the **Microsoft Excel** button on the taskbar to switch to Excel.

2. Use the data form to locate Wilson Gift Store (customer number 192) and change the Street entry to **10 Main Street**.

3. Click the **Microsoft Word** button on the taskbar to switch back to Word.

4. Click the **View Merged Data** [icon] button on the Mail Merge toolbar. The information from the first merged letter appears.

   The record for Wilson Gift Store is the second record (in the mail merge).

5. Click the **Next Record** button [icon] on the Mail Merge toolbar to select the next record. The record for Wilson Gift Store appears. Note that the data has been updated to show the new street address (10 Main Street).

   Although the main document now shows the updated record data, the document containing the merge results—Merged Customer Letters—still contains the old address, because it contains only the results of the previous merge. In order to update the Merged Customer Letters document, you need to re-merge the main document with the data source and then save the updated merge results.

6. Click the **Mail Merge Helper** button [icon] on the Mail Merge toolbar. The Mail Merge Helper dialog box opens.

7. Click the **Merge** button to open the Merge dialog box, and then click the **Merge** button. The mail merge results appear in a new document window.

8. Scroll through the results until you find the address for Wilson Gift Store. Note that it now includes the updated street data.

   Now you need to save the merge results as Merged Customer Letters to overwrite the existing document.

9. Use the Save As command to save the document containing the merge results as **Merged Customer Letters**, answer **Yes** to the prompt for replacing the existing file, and then close the Merged Customer Letters document. You return to the main document, which still displays the data for Wilson Gift Store.

After viewing the merged documents, Karen decides to print just one of the letters to check its appearance and layout before printing all the letters.

Previewing and Printing a Merged Document

You can preview and print a merged document in the same way that you do any Word document—using the Print Preview and Print buttons on the Standard toolbar. For the sample letter Karen wants to print, she decides that it would be best to print one that includes a company name in the address. This will allow her to make sure that the additional line for the company name does not cause a bad page break across the two pages of the letter. Because the main document already displays the data for Wilson Gift Store, which includes the company name, you can preview and print this merged letter.

To preview and print the merged letter for Wilson Gift Store:

1. Click the **Print Preview** button on the Standard toolbar. Both pages of the letter appear in Print Preview. See Figure 6-34.

Figure 6-34	MERGED LETTER FOR WILSON GIFT STORE IN PRINT PREVIEW

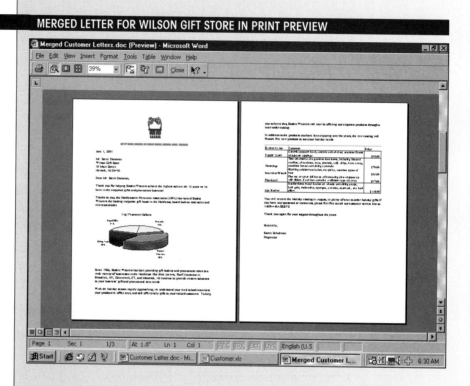

TROUBLE? If only one page appears, click the Multiple Pages button on the Print Preview toolbar, and then drag to select 1 x 2 pages.

Karen approves of the layout and pagination of the letter, and she asks you to print one copy of it and then close it.

2. Click the **Print** button on the Standard toolbar. One copy of the current merged letter (for Wilson Gift Store) prints.

3. Click the **Close** button on the Print Preview toolbar to return to the main document. Before saving and closing the document, you need to redisplay the merge fields so that they will appear instead of the address data the next time the main letter document is opened.

4. Click the **View Merged Data** button ⟨⟨⟩⟩ on the Mail Merge toolbar to redisplay the merge fields.

5. Save and close the customer letter. The Customers workbook automatically closes. Click the **Yes** button to save the changes you made to the Customers workbook.

6. Exit Word.

Karen plans on reviewing the printed letter with her assistants to make sure everyone approves of it before she prints and mails all the form letters.

Session 6.2 QUICK CHECK

1. The _____ document of a form letter contains the text that stays the same, as well as the _____.

2. A _____ contains the variable information in a form letter.

3. How do you insert merge fields into a main document?

4. How do you view merged documents directly from the main document?

5. During the mail-merge process you updated the customer list in Excel. After re-merging, you observed the updated address in the merged customer letter. That process illustrates _____.

Karen is pleased with her finished letter, which integrates her Excel data. She is confident that it will contribute to the successful promotion of Basket Weavers.

SESSION 6.3

In this session you will create hyperlinks between documents so that you can easily access other information from a single document. You will learn how to navigate a series of hyperlinks using the Web toolbar. You will also learn how to convert an Excel worksheet to HTML format so you can display Excel data as a Web document.

Creating Hyperlinks to Connect Files

In Sessions 6.1 and 6.2, you worked with several files from two different programs, Excel and Word, that contained related information. To do this, you opened each program and then navigated between the two using their program buttons on the taskbar. With Excel 2000, you can now insert links to documents created using Microsoft Office programs. These links allow you to easily navigate to different documents created in different programs, without having to launch each program first.

To link various documents, you can use a hyperlink. A **hyperlink** is an object (computer file pathname or address, text, or graphic) in a document that you can click to access information in other locations in that document or in other documents. This system of linked information is called **hypertext**. A hyperlink can be a filename, a word, a phrase, or a graphic that has been assigned an address to a file located elsewhere. If the hyperlink is a filename or text, the hyperlink will appear in color and as underlined text. If the hyperlink is a graphic, there is no visual cue until you position your mouse over the graphic. Then the mouse pointer changes to a pointing hand and displays the location of the link's destination. When you click a hyperlink, the destination document is brought into memory and appears on the screen. This hyperlink may reference

- a document created in Word, Excel, PowerPoint, or Access
- a section farther down in the same document
- a document on the World Wide Web

Hyperlinks offer a new way of making information available. Files containing hyperlinks are called **hyperlink documents**. Using the hyperlinks available to you in a hyperlink document, you are able to jump from one topic to the next in whatever order you want, regardless of where they reside.

As more hyperlinks are added between and within various documents, a structure emerges that you can navigate, traveling from hyperlink to hyperlink, following a path of information and ideas. You have already worked with such a structure when you accessed the Excel online Help system. By clicking a keyword or phrase, you were able to access additional information on the topic you were interested in. The Excel online Help system is an example of a series of hyperlink documents.

Inserting a Hyperlink

Karen asks you to place a hyperlink in the New Baskets workbook to the Merged Customer Letters (Word file) and to the Customers workbook (Excel file). With the files connected, she can easily jump to the other files if she wants to recall specific information. For instance, by including links to the customer list and the merged customer letter, she can check a customer's name or make sure she sent a letter to an important new client while working in the New Baskets workbook.

REFERENCE WINDOW   **RW**

Inserting a Hyperlink
- Select the text, graphic, or cell in which you want to insert the hyperlink, and then click the Insert Hyperlink button on the Standard toolbar to open the Insert Hyperlink dialog box.
- Type the address of the Web page or file you want to jump to. If you are not sure of the filename, click the Browse button to display the Link to File dialog box. Find and select the file you want to link to.
- If you want to jump to a particular location within the file, enter the location in the Named location in file text box.
- Click the Use relative path for hyperlink check box if you want the Excel destination's relative file address.

To insert a hyperlink into an Excel worksheet:

1. If you took a break after the last session, make sure Excel is running and your Data Disk is in the appropriate disk drive.

2. Open the **New Baskets** workbook located in the Tutorial folder for Tutorial.06 on your Data Disk.

3. Make sure the Documentation sheet is active, and then click cell **A10**. The Documentation sheet is where you want to insert the hyperlinks to the other files Karen works with when using this workbook.

4. Type **Cross-Reference to Related Documents**, and then press the **Enter** key.

5. Click cell **A10**, and then click the **Bold** button on the Formatting toolbar.

   Enter the text you want to use as a reference.

6. Click cell **A11**, type **Merged Customer Letters**, and press the **Enter** key.

7. In cell A12, type **Customer List**, and then press the **Enter** key.

   Now you need to specify the location of the destination file for each hyperlink. You do this using the Insert Hyperlink button on the Standard toolbar.

8. Click cell **A11** and then click the **Insert Hyperlink** button 🖳 on the Standard toolbar to open the Insert Hyperlink dialog box. See Figure 6-35.

TROUBLE? If the message "You should save this document before creating a hyperlink..." appears, click the Yes button and save the document before inserting the link.

| Figure 6-35 | INSERT HYPERLINK DIALOG BOX |

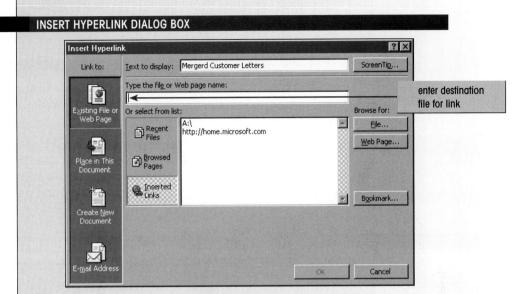

Enter the address of the merged customer letter, which is its filename.

9. Click the **File** button in the Browse for section to open the Link to File dialog box. Make sure your Data Disk is in the appropriate disk drive, and the Tutorial folder is specified in the Look in list box.

10. Click **Merged Customer Letters** and then click the **OK** button.

11. Click the **OK** button to close the dialog box. Notice that the hyperlink text is colored and underlined, which indicates the text is a hyperlink.

12. Click cell **A12** and repeat Steps 8–12 to create a hyperlink to the Customer workbook. See Figure 6-36.

| Figure 6-36 | HYPERLINKS INSERTED INTO DOCUMENTATION SHEET |

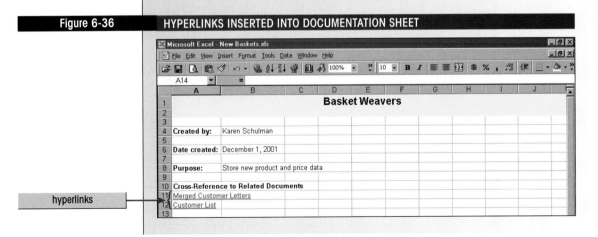

Now that you have created the hyperlinks, you should test them.

Testing Hyperlinks

Now that you have created the hyperlinks, you decide to test them to make sure each one links to the correct location. Recall that by clicking a hyperlink you jump to the referenced location. First, test the hyperlink to the merged customer letters.

To test the Merged Customer Letters hyperlink:

1. Position the pointer over the text **Merged Customer Letters** in cell A11. The pointer changes to a pointing hand 🖑, and a ScreenTip showing the address of the linked document appears.

2. Click the **Merged Customer Letters** hyperlink. Word launches and the Merged Customer Letters document opens on your screen. See Figure 6-37. Notice that the Web toolbar also appears on your screen. Figure 6-38 describes the function of each button on the Web toolbar in navigating between documents that contain hyperlinks.

Figure 6-37 | MERGED CUSTOMER LETTERS DOCUMENT OPENED FROM HYPERLINK

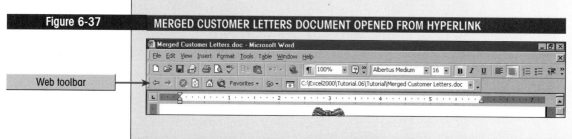

Web toolbar

Figure 6-38 | FUNCTION OF BUTTONS ON WEB TOOLBAR

ICON	BUTTON NAME	DESCRIPTION
⇦	Back	Displays the previous hyperlink document
⇨	Forward	Displays the next hyperlink document
⊗	Stop Current Jump	Terminates a jump
⟳	Refresh Current Page	Updates the information on a page
⌂	Start Page	Displays the home page of the current site
⊘	Search the Web	Uses the Internet Explorer to search the Web
Favorites ▾	Favorites	Adds sites to a Favorites folder for easy reference
Go ▾	Go	Displays a list of all commands on the toolbar
⬆	Show Only Web toolbar	Hides other toolbars
N/A	Address	Shows a history of documents and sites visited

Navigating Between the Hyperlink Documents

After reviewing the letter, you are ready to return to Excel. Instead of using the program button on the taskbar use the navigational buttons on the Web toolbar to move forward and backward between the hyperlink documents.

To move forward and backward between hyperlink documents:

1. Click the **Back** button ⇦ on the Web toolbar to return to the Documentation sheet for the New Baskets workbook. Notice that the hyperlink reference has changed color, indicating that you have used the hyperlink at least once to jump to the linked document.

2. Click the **Customer List** hyperlink. The Customers workbook opens.

3. Click the **Back** button ⇦ on the Web toolbar to return to the New Baskets workbook.

   TROUBLE? If the Web toolbar does not appear, click View on the menu bar, click Toolbars, and then click Web. Repeat Step 3.

4. Click the **Forward** button ⇨ on the Web toolbar to jump to the Customers workbook again.

5. Click the **Back** button ⇦ on the Web toolbar to return to the New Baskets workbook.

6. Save the New Baskets workbook. Close the Customer workbook. Remove the Web toolbar.

7. Switch to Word, close the Word document without saving it, and then exit Word.

Karen is pleased to have the hyperlinks in place for navigating between these related Basket Weavers documents.

Publishing Excel Data on a Web Page

The **World Wide Web (WWW)**, commonly called the Web, is a structure of documents connected electronically over the **Internet**, which is a large computer network made up of smaller networks and computers all connected electronically. Each document on the Web is called a **Web document** or **Web page**. These documents store different types of information, including text, graphics, sound, animation, and video. A Web page often includes hypertext links to other Web documents. These hypertext links point to other Web pages and allow you to follow related information by jumping from computer to computer to retrieve the desired information. Each Web page or document has a specific address, called its **Uniform Resource Locator**, or more commonly, **URL**. The URL indicates where the Web document is stored on the Web.

As a progressive businessperson, Karen recognized early the potential marketing power of the Internet. Understanding this potential, she hired a small firm to develop her company's documents to be placed on the Web. This provides Karen with another means to inform her customers of new gift baskets and events, in addition to the customer letter and the in-store flyers.

Now, she plans to develop an additional Web page showing her new gift baskets list. Fortunately, Karen can use her existing New Products worksheet to create this Web page.

Saving Excel Data as a Web Page

When people access the World Wide Web, they use a software program, called a **Web browser**, that enables them to access, view, and navigate all the Web documents on the Web. Web browsers recognize files that are in the HTML format. Therefore, any document that's on the Web needs to be in this HTML format. **HTML**, short for **HyperText Markup Language**, is the language in which your data needs to be formatted in order to be accessible on the Web. In order to display your Excel data on the Web, you need to convert it to HTML format. Excel workbook data can easily be converted to HTML format. You can put text, numbers, PivotTable reports, charts, graphics, and other items from a worksheet on a Web page. By using the publishing and saving features in Excel 2000, you can save an Excel workbook or some part of it in HTML format and make it available as a Web page that users can access with a Web browser.

Excel data can be saved in either *interactive* or *noninteractive* format. In interactive format, a person using a Web browser can work with the data and make changes to it. For example, a mortgage calculation worksheet can be published in an interactive format so users can enter their own information and determine their monthly mortgage payments. When you save data in a noninteractive format, users can only view the data. No changes to worksheet values are possible. For example, if you want to report your company's financial condition for the past year and do not want or expect users to change the data in any way, then a non-interactive approach is appropriate.

REFERENCE WINDOW	RW

Insert Noninteractive Excel Data into a Web Page
- Click **File** on the menu bar, click **Save as Web Page**.
- Click **Publish**.
- In the **Choose** list, click the type of data you want to publish, and in the box or list below that, specify the item you want.
- Make sure the **Add interactivity with** check box is cleared.
- To add a title to the published section, click **Change**, type the title you want, and then click **OK**.
- In the **File name** box, click **Browse**, and locate the drive, folder, Web folder, Web server, or FTP location where you want to save or publish your Web page.
- Click **Publish**.

Karen wants users accessing the New Baskets Web page to view the product and price list, but not edit it. Therefore, she asks you to put the product and price list worksheet data on a Web page in a noninteractive format.

First, Karen wants to see how the worksheet will look as a Web page before saving it in HTML format.

To preview the workbook as a Web page:

1. Make sure the New Baskets workbook is open and the New Products worksheet is selected. Click **File** on the menu bar, and then click **Web Page Preview** to open your Web browser. Excel opens the Internet Explorer (or the Web browser installed on your computer) and displays the workbook as a file. See Figure 6-39. Note, this preview shows all data in the workbook in noninteractive form.

Figure 6-39	PREVIEW OF WEB PAGE

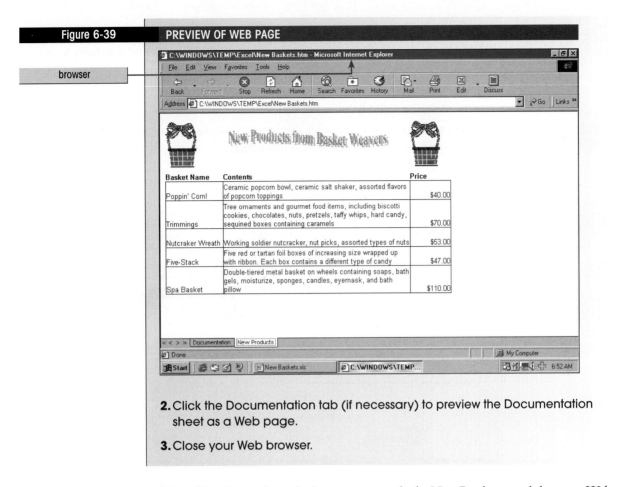

2. Click the Documentation tab (if necessary) to preview the Documentation sheet as a Web page.

3. Close your Web browser.

Karen likes the results and asks you to save only the New Products worksheet as a Web page.

To save a worksheet as a noninteractive Web page:

1. Click **File** on the menu bar, and then click **Save as Web Page** to open the Save As dialog box.

2. Click **Publish** to open the Publish as Web Page dialog box. See Figure 6-40.

Figure 6-40	PUBLISH AS WEB PAGE DIALOG BOX

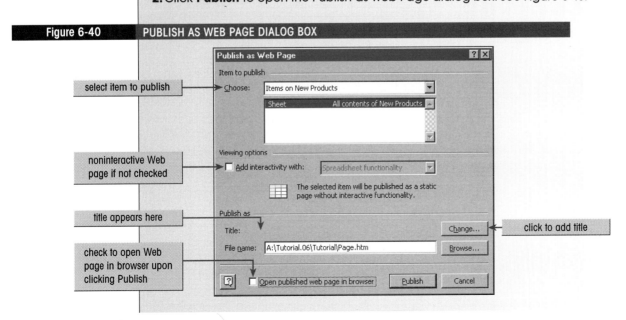

3. Make sure the Choose list displays Items on New Products.

4. To create a noninteractive Web page, make sure the **Add interactivity with** box is cleared.

5. Now you are ready to add a title to the top of the Web page. Click the **Change** button to open the Set Title dialog box.

6. Type **Price List**, and then click **OK** to return to the Publish as Web Page dialog box. The title appears next to the Title label.

7. In the File name box, select just the filename, **Page.htm**, and replace it with **BWPRICE.htm**.

8. Click to select the **Open published Web page in browser** check box.

9. Click **Publish** to open the New Products Sheet in your Web browser. See Figure 6-41.

Figure 6-41	WEB PAGE OPEN IN BROWSER

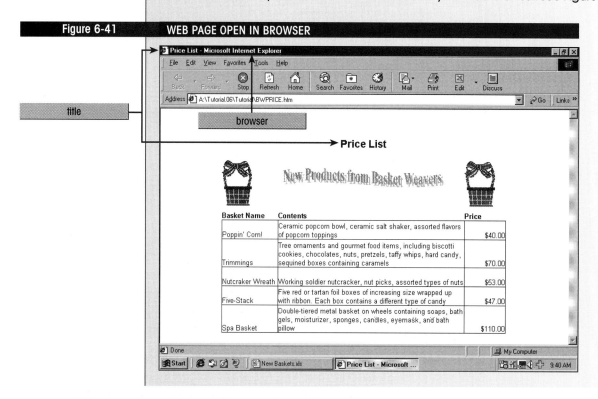

Karen is very pleased with the New Baskets Web page.

You have completed the Web page and it is now saved on your Data Disk as BWPRICE.htm. The file extension .htm indicates that it is in HTML format, and therefore readable using a Web browser. It is ready to be added to the series of Web documents Basket Weavers currently has available on the World Wide Web. Now close the Web browser and exit Excel.

To close the Web browser and exit Excel.

1. Click the **Close** button on the Web browser.

2. Click any cell to deselect the range. Press **Ctrl + Home** to make cell A1 the active cell.

3. Save the workbook.

4. Exit Excel.

Karen is very pleased to have informed her customers of the new baskets using a variety of methods—distributing flyers, mailing customized letters, and creating a Web document to be viewed on the World Wide Web.

Session 6.3 QUICK CHECK

1. A hyperlink can be a _____, _____, or _____.

2. You can jump to a document by clicking a _____.

3. The _____ button on the Standard toolbar is used to insert a hyperlink.

4. You use the _____ and the _____ buttons on the _____ toolbar to move forward and backward between hyperlink documents.

5. A software program called a _____ enables you to access Web documents.

6. _____ is the language used to present documents on the World Wide Web.

7. To convert Excel data to HTML format, you can use the _____ command.

8. The file extension _____ indicates that the file is in HTML format.

REVIEW ASSIGNMENTS

Karen is ready to send the merged customer letter to the Connecticut Basket Weavers customers. She also wants to add the NPA pie chart to a Web page to be viewable online. Finally, she needs to inform her advisory board, a group of local business professionals, about the company's new gift baskets and the NPA recognition. Help Karen with these tasks.

Do the following:

1. Start Word and open the document **CustLtr2** in the Review folder for Tutorial.06 and save it as **Customer Letter 2**.

2. Use the Merge Mail Helper to modify the selection criteria so only the Connecticut customers are selected. Merge the letter with the modified criteria. Close the Form Letters 1 document without saving it. (Note: The document Customer Letter 2 is still open.)

3. Print the letter for Ronald Kooienga.

4. Return to the customer list in Excel and change the street address of Ronald Kooienga (Customer Number 133) to 20 Freedom Trail. Print the revised letter. Save Customer Letter 2 and exit Word.

5. Open the workbook **NPA** in the Review folder for Tutorial.06. This workbook contains a pie chart comparing sales of the top premium sellers in the Northeast. Karen wants to add this chart as a new page on her Web site. Save the chart as a Web page named **NPA.htm**. Open your Web browser and view the Web document. Print the Web page from your browser.

6. Open the workbook **NewBask2** and save it as **New Baskets 2**. Use this workbook to answer Questions 7 through 11.

7. Activate the **New Products** worksheet. Use WordArt to create your own graphic. The text of the graphic is "New Baskets & Prices." Place the graphic above the new baskets list. Experiment with some of the features on the WordArt and Drawing toolbar. Save the workbook. Print the worksheet with the graphic.

8. Activate the Documentation sheet and add a hyperlink to the NPA workbook in cell A14. Instead of using a word or phrase as the hyperlink, use the file address of the NPA workbook in the Review folder for Tutorial.06 as the hyperlink.

Explore

9. In cell A15, create a hyperlink to a Gift, Premiums, and Stationery home page on the WWW. Its URL is **http://www.tdc.org.hk/prodmag/gifts/gifts.htm**. The hyperlink text should be "Gifts, Premiums & Stationery."

10. In cells A17:A18, create a WordArt object with the text "Store Sales." Use the WordArt graphic as a hyperlink to the MonSales workbook (located in the Review folder for Tutorial.06).

11. Save the **New Baskets 2** workbook. Print the Documentation worksheet. Close the workbook.

12. Karen has written a letter to her advisory board telling them of the Basket Weavers new baskets and their sales. Open the letter **AdvLetr** in the Review folder for Tutorial.06 and save it as **Advisory Board Letter**. Open the workbook **MonSales** in the Review folder for Tutorial.06 and save it as **MonSales2**. Link the **MonSales2** worksheet to the Word document **Advisory Board Letter**. Print the letter.

13. Add the sales for Connecticut (Figure 6-42) to the worksheet and print the advisory board letter again. Save and close both the letter and the workbook.

Figure 6-42

PRODUCT	CT
Poppin' Corn!	300
Trimmings	200
Nutcracker Wreath	1000
Five-Stack	750
Spa Basket	400

14. Open the letter **AdvLetr** in the Review folder for Tutorial.06 and save it as **Advisory Board Letter2**. Open the workbook **MonSales** in the Review folder for Tutorial.06 and embed it in the **Advisory Board Letter2**. Add the sales for Connecticut (Figure 6-42) to the worksheet in the Word document. Save and print the letter. Close Word.

15. Use Windows Explorer to compare the file size of the two Word documents: Advisory Board Letter and Advisory Board Letter2 in the Review folder for Tutorial.06. What is the file size of each file in bytes? Explain the difference in file sizes.

16. Close all open windows.

CASE PROBLEMS

Case 1. Reporting Sales for Toy World   Fred Galt, the manager of the local Toy World store, must report to the regional manager each week. He faxes a memo each week to the regional sales office indicating his recommendations regarding any special sales or promotions he feels will be needed, based on the summary sales information he includes in the report. Fred maintains a worksheet that summarizes sales in units and dollars for each day of the week. This sales summary is included in his weekly report, and on the company's Web page. Do the following:

1. If necessary, start Excel and make sure your Data Disk is in the appropriate drive. Open **ToyStore.xls** in the Cases folder for Tutorial.06. This is Fred's partially completed worksheet. Save it as **Toy Store Sales**.

2. Complete the worksheet by computing total sales in dollars for each day (including the formula for Saturday) by multiplying the number of units sold of each product by the price per unit (the price table is in the upper-right corner of the worksheet). Also, compute total sales for each product and the total sales for the store. (*Hint*: Check number for Monday through Friday: Total store sales = $87,654.20.)

3. Save the worksheet.

4. Start Word and open the document **ToyLtr** and save it as **Toy Memo**.

5. Link the worksheet range A1:F15 to the memo. Print the memo.

6. Saturday evening, Fred faxes the memo to the regional manager, indicating that sales are on target for the week and no special promotions are necessary at this time. Update store sales for Saturday using the following data: 20, 5, 19, 16. Save the workbook.

7. Print the memo.

8. Save the memo and exit Word.

9. Create a Web page named **ToySales.htm** which includes the range A7:F15. Open your Web browser and view the Web document. Print the page from your Web browser.

10. Use WordArt to replace the title "Store Analysis" with the title "Toy World Sales." Print the worksheet excluding the Product Price Table.

11. Save and close the workbook.

Case 2. Quarterly Sales at Happy Morning Farms   Casandra Owens is product manager for a line of breakfast cereals at Happy Morning Farms. Casandra is waiting for one figure so that she can complete her Sales Report—Summarized by State for next week's Operations Management Team (OMT) meeting. As she is working on the report, she receives an urgent call from one of her sales representatives indicating that he needs Casandra in Denver immediately to deal with a customer problem that requires management attention. Casandra realizes that she will not be able to make the next OMT meeting, so she plans to complete her report on the road. She will get the last figure she needs, finish the report, and then fax it to John Styles, who will represent her at the meeting. Before she leaves the office, Casandra decides to embed her data in a memo. Do the following:

1. If necessary, start Excel and make sure your Data Disk is in the appropriate drive. Open the workbook **StSales** in the Cases folder for Tutorial.06.

2. Open the Word document **StMemo** in the Cases folder for Tutorial.06 and save it as **State Sales Memo**.

3. Embed the **StSales** worksheet in the Word document, **State Sales Memo**, which can be found in the Cases folder for Tutorial.06.

4. Save the Word document with the embedded worksheet.

5. Print the memo with the embedded worksheet.

6. After arriving in Denver, Casandra gets a call with the missing sales figure—sales in Iowa this quarter were $42. Update the Word document by entering the Iowa sales number in the embedded worksheet.

7. Save the Word document and print the memo again. Close the Word document.

8. Print the source worksheet, **StSales**. Comment on the sales data in the source worksheet versus the sales data in the Word document.

9. Now repeat the process using a different approach. Activate the workbook **StSales** in the Cases folder for Tutorial.06 and save it as **State Sales**.

10. Open the Word document **StMemo1** in the Cases folder for Tutorial.06 and save the document as **State Sales Memo1**.

11. Link cell D49 in the State Sales workbook to the end of the first sentence in the State Sales Memo1 Word document. (*Hint*: For the best placement of the linked object, use the Unformatted text option instead of Microsoft Excel Worksheet object when you link the object.) Save the document. Print the letter.

12. Update the **State Sales** workbook by entering the Iowa sales number ($42).

13. Save and print **State Sales Memo1**.

14. At the bottom of the State Sales Memo1 document, add the line "Details for Sales are in the State Sales workbook." Create a hyperlink in the Word document to the State Sales workbook. The hyperlink text should be "State Sales workbook." Save the Word document. Test the hyperlink.

15. Save and close any open documents.

Case 3. Horizons State Alumni Office   Charlene Goodwin, director of alumni affairs, has been planning a marketing "blitz" in which she will use three methods to reach Horizons' alumni. For campus visitors, she will develop a flyer inviting friends of HSU to visit the campus store to view its new line of Horizons affinity products. For World Wide Web users, she plans to create a Web page highlighting these products. For all alumni, she plans a letter announcing the affinity products that alums can order using a mail-order form. Help her get these jobs completed. Do the following:

1. If necessary, start Excel and make sure your Data Disk is in the appropriate drive. Open the workbook **AlumProd** in the Cases folder for Tutorial.06, and save it as **Alumni Products**. This is the product list.

2. Open the Word document **Alumltr** in the Cases folder for Tutorial.06 and save it as **Alumni Letter**. Link the product list from the Alumni Products workbook beginning at the line [insert price list here]. Remember to remove the note [insert price list here]. Print the letter with the linked object.

3. You notice an error in the product list—the price of item 3 should be $80. Return to Excel and correct the error in the worksheet. Print the letter. Save and close the Word document.

4. Create a logo for Horizons State using WordArt. Insert it at the top of the product list in the Alumni Products workbook. Save the workbook and print the price list with your graphic.

5. Create a Web page for the product list in the Alumni Products workbook. Name the page **HorzPrc.htm**. View the page using your Web browser. Print the Web page using your Web browser.

6. Create a Documentation sheet with appropriate information to describe the workbook. Print the Documentation sheet.

7. In the Documentation sheet, insert a hyperlink to the Word document Alumni Letter.

8. In the Documentation sheet, insert a hyperlink to your institution's Web page.

9. Save and close any open files.

Case 4. *Inwood Design Group of Japan* Spurred by the Japanese passion for the sport, golf enjoys unprecedented popularity in Japan. Inwood Design Group plans to build a world-class golf course, and one of the four sites under consideration is Chiba Prefecture, Japan. Other possible sites are Kauai, Hawaii; Edmonton, Canada; and Scottsdale, Arizona. You and Mike Nagochi are members of the site selection team for Inwood Design Group. The team is responsible for collecting information on the sites, evaluating that information, and recommending the best site for the new golf course.

Your team identified five factors likely to determine the success of a golf course: climate, competition, market size, topography, and transportation. The team has collected information on these factors for all of the four potential golf course sites.

Mike created a worksheet that the team can use to evaluate the four sites. He brought the completed worksheet to the group's meeting so that the team could analyze the information and recommend a site to management.

Prepare a memo to the site selection committee with your team's findings. Do the following:

1. If necessary, start Excel and make sure your Data Disk is in the appropriate drive. Open the workbook **Inwood** in the Cases folder for Tutorial.06. Save the workbook as **Inwood 1**. Review the worksheet.

2. Open Word and write a brief memo to the site selection committee. State your recommendation for a site selection and reason(s). Support your narrative by referencing the Weighted Score section of the Inwood worksheet. Paste the Weighted Score section of the worksheet into your memo.

3. Save the Word document as **Inwood Memo** in the Cases folder for Tutorial.06.

4. Print the memo. Close Word.

5. Explain why pasting rather than linking or embedding is appropriate in this situation.

6. In the Inwood 1 workbook, activate the Documentation sheet and insert a hyperlink to the Inwood Memo. Test the hyperlink.

7. Use your Web browser to access one of the following sites: **www.yahoo.com**, or **www.excite.com**. Use the information at these Web sites to locate an interesting golf-related Web site. In the Inwood 1 workbook, below the hyperlink to the Inwood Memo, insert a hyperlink to this site.

8. Replace the Inwood Design Group title in the Documentation sheet with a WordArt image with the same text.

9. Save the **Inwood 1** workbook, print the Documentation sheet, then close and exit the workbook.

INTERNET ASSIGNMENTS

The purpose of the Internet Assignments is to challenge you to find information on the Internet that you can use to create effective spreadsheets. The actual assignments are updated and maintained on the Course Technology Web site. Log on to the Internet and use your Web browser to go to the Student Online Companion to accompany this text at **www.course.com/NewPerspectives/office2000**. Click the Excel link, and then click the link for Tutorial 6.

QUICK CHECK ANSWERS

Session 6.1

1. Object Linking and Embedding
2. linked
3. does not
4. embed
5. link
6. WordArt
7. Paste Special
8. The Excel menus and toolbars replace the menus and toolbar in the Word window. The embedded object now has column and row headings and the sheet tabs appear. Excel becomes the active program.

Session 6.2

1. main, merge fields
2. merge field
3. Position the insertion point where you want the merge field; click the Insert Merge Field button, and then click the name of the field you want to insert.
4. Click the View Merged data button on the Mail Merge toolbar
5. linking

Session 6.3

1. file address, text, graphic image
2. hyperlink
3. Insert Hyperlink
4. Forward, Back, Web
5. Web browser
6. HTML or Hypertext Markup Language
7. Save As Web Page
8. .htm

OBJECTIVES

In this tutorial you will:

- Arrange a worksheet in sections

- Assign data validation rules to a cell

- Assign and use range names

- Use IF and FV functions in formulas

- Create a series using AutoFill

- Protect worksheets

- Delete unnecessary sheets from a workbook

- Plan and record Excel macros

- Run a macro using menu commands, a shortcut key, and a button object

- View Visual Basic for Applications code

DEVELOPING AN EXCEL APPLICATION

Employee 401(k) Planning at CableScan

CASE

CableScan

CableScan intends to implement a 401(k) plan this year, and Mary Kincaid, benefits administrator, will travel to the company's three sites to present the plan and its features to all of the employees. A 401(k) plan is a retirement savings program that allows employees to deduct funds from their monthly pay, before taxes, provided that they invest them directly into various options within the 401(k) plan.

To introduce the 401(k) plan, Mary will hold formal meetings at each company location. At the meetings, she will give employees an audio-visual presentation that includes an overview of the plan, the administrative procedures, and the investment options. Currently, no other retirement plans are available to the employees other than personal savings, and the company wants to be sure that there is high participation in the 401(k) plan. Management has set a goal of 80% participation in the plan for all eligible employees. To help ensure this high rate of participation, the company will match, dollar for dollar, whatever the employee contributes, up to 4% of the employee's salary. Additionally, employees can contribute up to a total of 20% of their salaries.

Mary has asked you to work with individual employees after each of the formal presentations by answering any questions they may have. She also wants to provide an Excel workbook that can be used by employees to determine the appropriate amount they can contribute to the plan, and see how different contribution amounts will affect their retirement savings over the next five to 30 years. Employees can use this workbook to conduct their own what-if analyses on their retirement plans.

SESSION 7.1

In this tutorial you will develop a more complex workbook than you have in any previous tutorial. You'll build it in three sessions. In this session you will start the process by dividing your worksheet into separate sections for input and calculations. You'll use the Excel data validation feature to specify the type of data that a cell can store. You'll assign names to cells and use these names instead of cell addresses to build the formulas in your worksheet. Finally, you'll use the IF function to build formulas where the value you store in a cell depends on the result of a condition.

Planning the 401(k) Workbook Application

You have been asked to develop a simple investment model that will allow each CableScan employee to see the effect (dollar accumulation) of investing a percentage of his or her current salary each year at an annual return on investment over a 30-year period. You can use Excel to create a workbook that the employees can use to make these calculations and plan their retirement funding.

You realize that many of the employees at CableScan are familiar with Excel and will have no trouble using a 401(k) planning workbook. However, there are others who will require assistance in using the workbook, and you will be working on a one-on-one basis with those employees after Mary presents the plan. Because the CableScan employees using the workbook will have varying amounts of experience with Excel and computers in general, you want the workbook to be as easy to use as possible. It needs to produce valuable information clearly, while being nearly foolproof to use.

Figures 7-1 and 7-2 show the planning analysis sheet and the sketch that Mary has created to assist you in completing the workbook. You can see from the planning analysis sheet that the formulas to be used in the workbook are somewhat complex. Fortunately, Excel provides a few means of simplifying complex formulas. Mary also wants you to build the worksheet so that employees enter only valid data in the correct cells in the worksheet. Note in the sketch in Figure 7-2 that the worksheet will be divided into manageable sections—sections where the employee provides (inputs) information and sections containing information produced from calculating the input to produce output. Also note that the workbook allows the employee to view and analyze the information numerically and graphically, by including a line chart.

Figure 7-1	PLANNING ANALYSIS SHEET

Planning Analysis Sheet

My Goal
To develop a simple investment planing worksheet

What information do I need?
Name of Employee
Current salary
Percent of salary invested—enter a percent of salary. NOTE: The maximum percent an
employee can contribute is 20 percent.
Annual rate of return—enter as a percent

What calculations do I need to perform?
Employee contributions— monthly = current salary* percent of salary invested/12
Employer contributions— monthly = monthly employee contribution
NOTE: Remember that for every dollar employee contribution, employer invests a dollar,
up to 4% of employee's salary: employer invests nothing above 4% of employee's salary
Total monthly contributions = monthly employee contribution + monthly employer
contribution
Value of investment at 5, 10, 15, 20, 25, and 30 years. NOTE: use
=FV(monthly rate of return, number of periods, total monthly contribution) to compute
future value of investment

What output do I want to see?
Table showing future of investment at 5, 10, 15, 20, 25, and 30 years
Line chart displaying future value of investment

Figure 7-2	SKETCH OF WORKSHEET PLAN

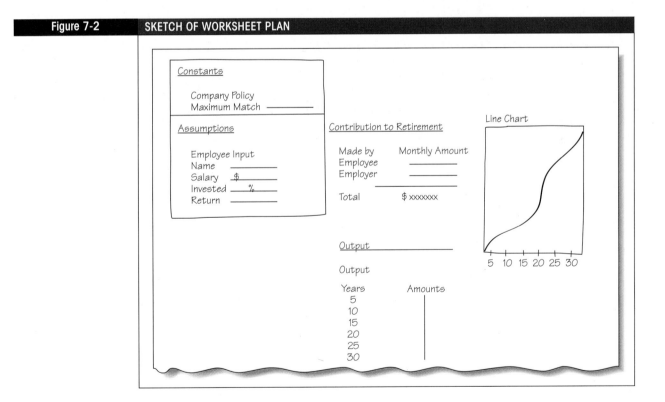

Use these planning documents to build the worksheet for Mary. She has already started
to create the workbook.

Open the 401k file and examine the work Mary has done so far.

To open the 401k workbook and save the workbook as 401kPlan:

1. Start Excel. Make sure your Data Disk is in the appropriate disk drive, open the workbook 401k in the Tutorial folder for Tutorial.07 on your Data Disk, and immediately save it as **401kPlan**.

2. Click the **401kPlan** sheet tab. In the 401kPlan worksheet, the labels and column headings have already been entered. See Figure 7-3.

Figure 7-3 **INITIAL 401KPLAN WORKSHEET**

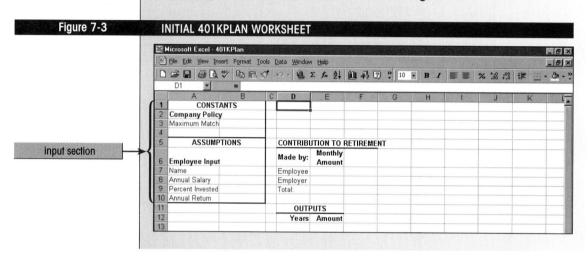

Arranging a Worksheet in Sections

Because many people will be using the worksheet, and will want to change assumptions such as current salary, percentage of salary invested, and annual return on investment, Mary has divided her worksheet into two sections: input and calculation/output. The input section contains the data values used in formulas. Sometimes the input section is said to contain the worksheet's initial conditions and assumptions because the results of the worksheet are based on the values in the input section. A second section, the calculation/output section, performs the calculations and displays the results of the model. The formulas in this section do not contain constants; instead they reference cells in the input section. For example, the formula to calculate the monthly employee contribution to the 401(k) plan (cell E7) will reference cells B8 and B9 in the input section, which contain values for the employee's salary and the percentage of salary the employee invests in the 401(k) plan, rather than constants, such as 30000 and .05.

Dividing the worksheet into sections has the following benefits:

■ The user knows exactly where to enter and change values—in the input area. Changes to the worksheet are made only to values in the input area.

■ The user clearly sees what factors affect the results of the worksheet.

■ The user doesn't have to change specific values in formulas to reflect new assumptions.

Entering Initial Values

Now that you have examined the current status of the workbook, it's time for you to continue creating the 401(k) application. Because the labels and headings have already been entered, you'll begin by entering and formatting the values shown in Figure 7-4.

Figure 7-4   INITIAL ASSUMPTIONS

CELL	VALUE	FORMATTING
B3	.04	Percent style
B7	Mike Tobey	
B8	30000	Currency style, no decimal place
B9	.05	Percent style
B10	.08	Percent style

To enter and format the input values:

1. Click cell **B3**, type **.04**, and press the **Enter** key. Return to cell B3 and click the **Percent style** button ![%] on the Formatting toolbar.

2. Click cell **B7** and enter the remaining values and formatting shown in Figure 7-4. When you're finished entering the data, your input section of the worksheet should look like Figure 7-5.

Figure 7-5   INPUT SECTION AFTER VALUES ENTERED

input section

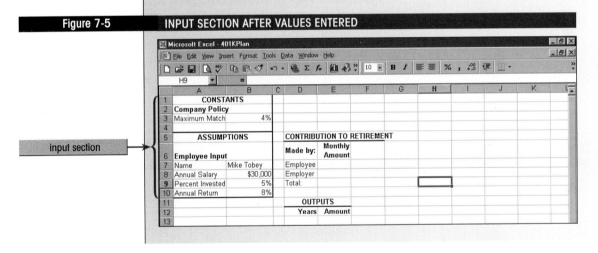

Mary is concerned that an employee may accidentally enter invalid data into the worksheet, which will result in output that is not correct. For example, employees are not allowed to invest more than 20% of their salary in the 401(k) plan. If an employee entered a value greater than 20% of his or her salary, the value of future investments would be inaccurate, because the plan does not allow for this level of investment.

You can use the Excel data validation feature to prevent a user from entering an invalid value. This will allow you to minimize errors introduced by the workbook user.

Validating Data Entry

One way to make sure the correct data is entered in a cell or range is to use the Excel data validation feature to restrict the information being entered in the worksheet. For instance, you can specify the type of data (whole numbers, dates, time, or text) allowed in a cell, as well as the range of acceptable values (for example, numbers between 1 and 100). If you wish, you can display an input message that appears when a user enters data in a given cell, reminding the user of valid entries for this cell. You can also display an error message when the user enters an invalid entry. Because the maximum percentage of salary an employee can invest is 20, Mary asks you to establish a validation rule so that a user cannot exceed this limit.

Specifying Data Type and Acceptable Values

The first step in using the data validation feature is to specify the type of data as well as the acceptable values allowed in a cell or range of cells. You need to specify that in cell B9 only decimal values less than or equal to .2 (or 20%) are permitted.

To specify a data type and acceptable values:

1. Click cell **B9**, the cell where you want to apply data validation.

2. Click **Data** on the menu bar, and then click **Validation** to open the Data Validation dialog box. See Figure 7-6. This dialog box allows you to specify the parameters for the validation, the message that appears as the user inputs a value, and an error alert message that appears if the user enters an invalid value.

Figure 7-6	SETTINGS TAB OF DATA VALIDATION DIALOG BOX

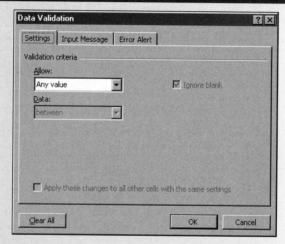

3. Make sure the **Settings** tab is selected, click the **Allow** list arrow, and then click **Decimal** from the list of allowable data types. Notice the number of text boxes in the dialog box changed to reflect the selection you made in the Allow list box.

Next, specify the range of values you will allow.

4. Click the **Data** list arrow, and then click **less than or equal to**. Notice that when you select this data operator, the number of text boxes in the dialog box change so that you can further specify the appropriate criteria for validation.

5. In the Maximum text box, type **.2**. The data validation rule of a value of less than or equal to 20% is now specified.

TROUBLE? If you accidentally pressed the Enter key or clicked the OK button and the Data Validation dialog box closed, you can reopen the dialog box by clicking Data on the menu bar, and then clicking Validation.

Next, establish a prompt that will appear when users select that cell, indicating the type of data they can enter into the cell.

Specifying an Input Message

Now create an input prompt that informs the user what kind of data is allowed in the selected cell. The message will appear as a ScreenTip beside the cell when the user selects it. Although the input message is optional, Mary asks you to include the input message—"Percent of salary invested by employee cannot exceed 20%," as an aid to the user during data entry.

To enter a data validation input message:

1. In the Data Validation dialog box, click the **Input Message** tab. See Figure 7-7.

| Figure 7-7 | INPUT MESSAGE TAB OF DATA VALIDATION DIALOG BOX |

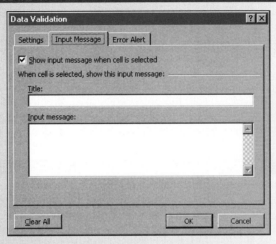

2. Make sure the Show input message when cell is selected check box is checked. This will ensure that the message will appear when the user selects the cell.

3. Click the **Title** text box, and then type **Valid Data**. This title will be at the top of the input message when it appears.

4. Click the **Input message** text box, and then type **Percent of salary invested by employee cannot exceed 20%**. This message will appear as a ScreenTip whenever the user selects cell B9.

The input message that you have entered will help minimize the chances of employees entering an invalid percentage of salary value. However, if users still enter a value above 20%, then you want them to be prompted to reenter a correct percentage.

Specifying an Error Alert Style and Message

You can also use the Data Validation dialog box to establish an error alert message, which is a message that appears if an invalid entry is typed in the cell. This message should inform the user of the error and identify a means to correct the error and enter a valid value.

Now create an appropriate error alert message for this cell.

To enter the error alert message:

1. In the Data Validation dialog box, click the **Error Alert** tab. See Figure 7-8.

Figure 7-8	ERROR ALERT TAB OF DATA VALIDATION DIALOG BOX

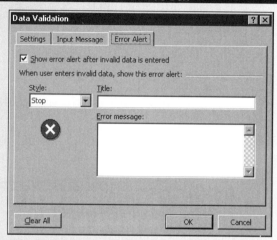

2. Make sure the Show error alert after invalid data is entered check box is checked. Now select the message style: Stop, Warning, or Information. Figure 7-9 describes the function of each style.

Figure 7-9	ERROR MESSAGE ALERT STYLE

ICON	TYPE OF ALERT	LABEL ON BUTTON	ACTION IF BUTTON CLICKED
⚠	Warning	Continue Yes Continue No Cancel	Value entered in cell; processing continues. Value entered in cell; Excel stops, waiting for you to enter another value. Value not entered in cell.
ⓘ	Information	OK Cancel	Value entered in cell; processing continues. Value not entered in cell.
⊗	Stop	Retry Cancel	Value remains in cell; Excel stops, waiting for you to enter another value. Value not entered in cell.

You decide to use the Stop style, because you don't want to continue data entry until the percentage invested is 20% or less.

3. If necessary, click the **Style** list arrow, and then click **Stop**.

Now specify the error alert message.

4. In the Title text box, type **Invalid Data**.

5. In the Error message text box, type **You entered a value above 20%. A valid percentage is 20% or less.**

6. Click the **OK** button to close the Data Validation dialog box.

The data validation rule is complete. Now test the validation rule to make sure it is working correctly when invalid data is entered in the cell.

To test data validation:

1. If necessary, click cell **B9**. The input message for Valid Data appears. See Figure 7-10.

Figure 7-10	DISPLAY OF INPUT MESSAGE

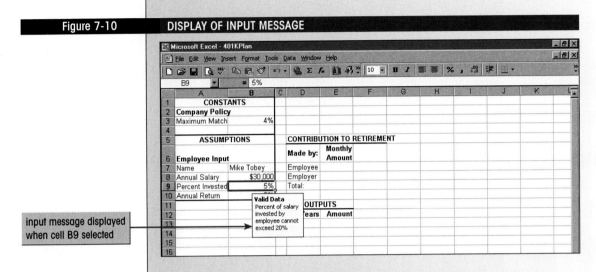

input message displayed
when cell B9 selected

Now attempt to enter an invalid value.

2. Type **.25** and press the **Enter** key. The error alert message for Invalid Data appears. See Figure 7-11. Your choices are to click Retry to correct the value or click Cancel. You decide to correct the value.

Figure 7-11	DISPLAY OF ERROR ALERT MESSAGE

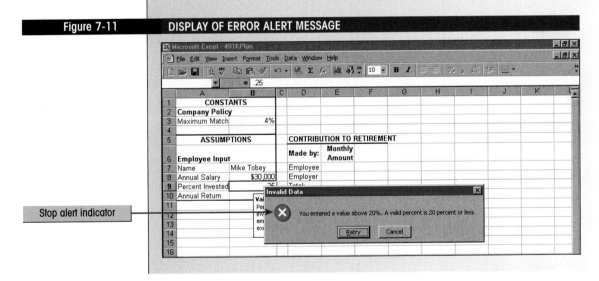

Stop alert indicator

3. Click the **Retry** button. Cell B9 is highlighted, and you can now enter a corrected value.

4. Type **.05** and press the **Enter** key. This entry is valid, so the cell pointer moves to the next cell, cell B10.

Now that you have made the data entry process easier and less error-prone for users, enter the formulas needed to perform the calculations in the workbook. Some of the formulas are complex. To avoid overwhelming users, you want to simplify the formulas a bit. This will also allow users to clearly see how the inputs are calculated to produce the output.

Using **Range Names**

So far in Excel you have always referred to cells by their addresses. Excel provides a valuable feature that allows you to assign a name to a cell or a range of cells so you don't have to remember the cell address. A **range name** is a descriptive name you assign to a cell or range of cells that can then be used to reference the cell or range of cells in formulas, print ranges, etc.

The ability to name a cell or range allows

- easier formula construction and entry
- improved documentation and clarification of the meaning of formulas
- navigation of large worksheets simply by using the Go To command to move the pointer to a named range
- specification of a print range

Range names must begin with a letter or the underscore character (_). After the first letter, any character, letter, number, or special symbol—except hyphens and spaces—is acceptable. You can assign names of up to 255 characters, although short, meaningful names of 5-15 characters are more practical.

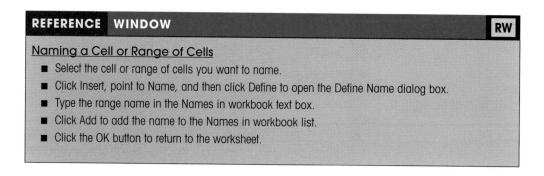

REFERENCE WINDOW | RW

Naming a Cell or Range of Cells
- Select the cell or range of cells you want to name.
- Click Insert, point to Name, and then click Define to open the Define Name dialog box.
- Type the range name in the Names in workbook text box.
- Click Add to add the name to the Names in workbook list.
- Click the OK button to return to the worksheet.

Defining a Range Name

You decide to assign range names to several cells in the input area. This will make it easier for you when you create the formulas to be used to calculate the output. Use the range name MaxMatch in cell B3, Salary in cell B8, Invested in cell B9, and Return in cell B10.

To define a range name:

1. Click cell **B8**, the cell for which you want to assign a range name.

2. Click **Insert** on the menu bar, point to Name, and then click **Define** to open the Define Name dialog box. See Figure 7-12. Notice that the name Annual_Salary already appears in the Names in workbook text box with the text label in the cell to the left of the selected cell. You can keep that name or change it by typing a new name in the text box. In this case, shorten the name to Salary.

Figure 7-12	DEFINE NAME DIALOG BOX

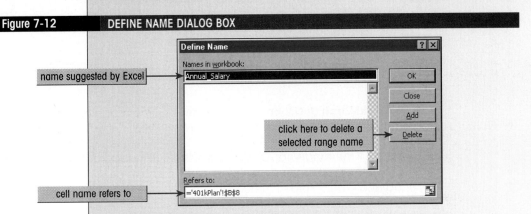

name suggested by Excel

click here to delete a selected range name

cell name refers to

3. Type **Salary** in the Names in workbook text box, and then click the **OK** button to close the dialog box. Notice that the range name of the cell appears in the Name box to the left of the formula bar.

4. Repeat Steps 2 and 3 to name cell B9 **Invested** and cell B10 **Return**.

As you have noticed, the range name of the selected cell appears in the Name box to the left of the formula bar. This Name box allows you to work with named ranges more easily.

Using the Name Box to Define a Range Name

You can also use the Name box as another means of assigning names to cells. You can use this Name box to define a range or to select and move to an already defined range. Assign the name MaxMatch to cell B3 using the Name box.

To assign a range name using the Name box:

1. Click cell **B3**, the cell you want to name.

2. Click the **Name** box to the left of the formula bar. See Figure 7-13.

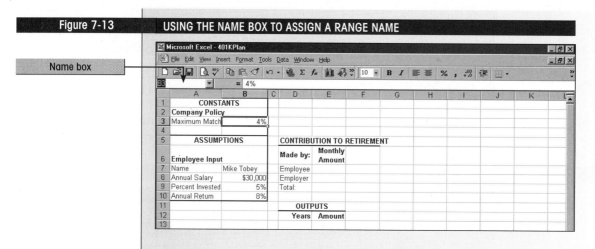

Figure 7-13   **USING THE NAME BOX TO ASSIGN A RANGE NAME**

Name box

3. Type **MaxMatch** and then press the **Enter** key. The range name has been assigned to cell B3 and appears in the Name box.

TROUBLE? If the range name appears in the cell instead of the Name box, press Esc if you haven't pressed the Enter key. If you have pressed the Enter key, click Undo and repeat Steps 1 through 3.

Now that you have assigned names to the input cells, you can use them as you create the formulas for the 401(k) investment model. First, calculate the amount the employee plans to invest each month.

Using a Range Name in a Formula

You can use the name of a cell or range in a formula instead of cell addresses as you enter your formulas into the worksheet. Rather than using the formula =B8*B9/12 to compute the amount the employee plans to invest each month, you can enter the formula using the range names =Salary*Invested/12. Now enter the formula to compute the monthly employee contribution.

To enter a formula using a range name:

1. Click cell **E7**, the cell where you calculate the monthly amount the employee contributes to the retirement plan.

2. Type **= Salary*Invested/12** and press the **Enter** key. Excel performs the calculations and displays the value 125.

3. Click cell **E7** and examine the formula in the formula bar. Notice that the range names appear in the formula instead of the cell addresses. See Figure 7-14.

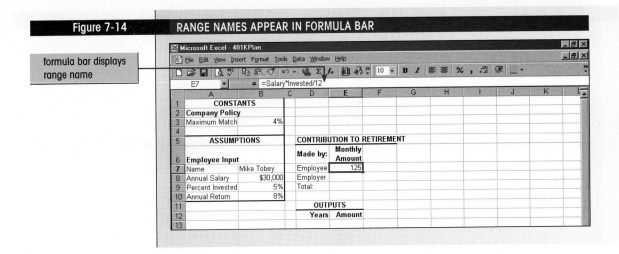

| Figure 7-14 | RANGE NAMES APPEAR IN FORMULA BAR |

formula bar displays range name

To delete a range name, you click Insert, point to Name and then click Define. Select the range name you want to remove, click the Delete button, and then click OK.

Next you need to enter a formula to calculate the amount of money the employer will contribute to the employee's 401(k) investment. The formula to calculate the employer's contribution is not as straightforward as the one for the employee's contribution. The amount the employer contributes depends on the percentage of salary the employee invests in the 401(k) plan. Recall that the company policy is to match dollar for dollar up to 4% of the employee's salary and nothing above 4% of the employee's salary. This calculation requires that you determine whether the employee is contributing more than 4%. If the employee is investing more than 4% of his or her salary, then the employer will only match 4% of the salary. On the other hand, if the employee is investing 4% or less, the employer will contribute an amount equal to the employee contribution.

Building a Conditional Formula Using the IF Function

There are many situations in which the value you store in a cell depends on certain conditions. For example:

- An employee's gross pay may depend on whether that employee worked overtime.
- A taxpayer's tax rate depends on his or her taxable income.
- A customer's charge depends on whether the size of the order entitles that customer to a discount.

In Excel, the IF function allows you to evaluate a specified condition, performing one action if the condition is true and another action if the condition is false. The IF function has the following format:

IF(logical_test, value_if_true, value_if_false)
where

- A logical_test evaluates a logical expression (condition) as either True or False.
- A value_if_true is the value returned if the logical_test is True.
- A value_if_false is the value returned if the logical_test is False.

An example may help illustrate how the IF function works. Suppose you need to determine whether an employee earns overtime pay, that is, whether he or she worked more than 40 hours in a week. Figure 7-15 illustrates the logic of this function.

Figure 7-15   FLOWCHART OF THE IF FUNCTION

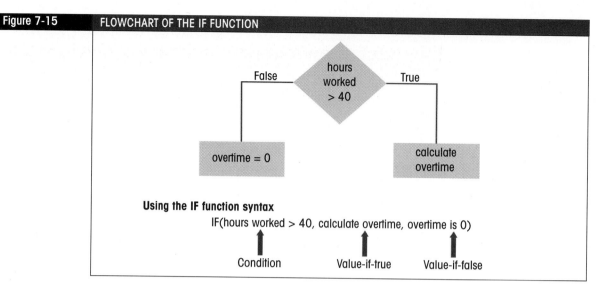

In this example, the condition is the comparison between the hours an employee works and 40 hours. The value_if_true is returned if an employee works more than 40 hours; then the condition is true and overtime pay is calculated. The value_if_false is returned if an employee works 40 hours or less; then the condition is false and overtime pay is 0.

The most common condition, a simple condition, is a comparison between two expressions. An **expression** may be a cell or range, a number, a label, a formula, or another function that represents a single value. For example, B5, B6*B7, and "West" are expressions. In addition to expressions, a condition contains a comparison operator. A **comparison operator** indicates a mathematical comparison, such as less than or greater than. Figure 7-16 shows the comparison operators allowed in Excel.

Figure 7-16   COMPARISON OPERATORS

TYPE OF COMPARISON	COMPARISON OPERATOR SYMBOL
Less than	<
Greater than	>
Less than or equal to	<=
Greater than or equal to	>=
Equal to	=
Not equal to	<>

A comparison operator is combined with an expression to form a condition. For example, say the hours worked value is stored in D10; then the condition "the number of hours worked is greater than 40" would be expressed in Excel as IF(D10>40...). Figure 7-17 illustrates several examples of conditional situations and how they can be expressed in Excel.

Figure 7-17   **EXAMPLES OF CONDITIONAL SITUATIONS**

CONDITIONAL SITUATION	EXCEL FORMULA

IF salesperson's sales are > 5000
   THEN return .1 (10% bonus)
   ELSE return 0.05 (5% bonus)
	=IF(B24>5000,0.10,0.05)
	NOTE: cell B24 stores salesperson's sales

IF company's region code equals 3
   THEN return the label East
   ELSE return the label Other
	=IF(N7=3,"East","Other")
	NOTE: cell N7 stores code for region

IF person's age is 65 or less
   THEN amount X 65 or under rate
   ELSE amount X over 65 rate
	=IF(A21<=65,B21*C21,B21*D21)
	NOTE: cell A21 stores person's age; cell B21 stores amount;
	cell C21 stores 65 or under rate; and cell D21 stores over 65 rate

Mary developed a flowchart to establish the logic behind the formula needed to calculate the employer's matching contribution to the 401(k) plan. See Figure 7-18.

Figure 7-18   **FLOWCHART OF EMPLOYER'S MONTHLY MATCHING CONTRIBUTION**

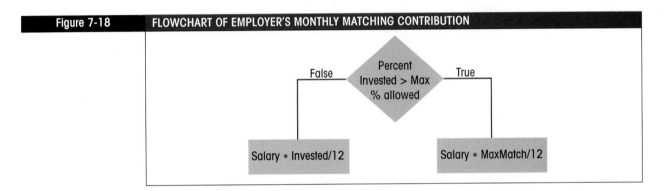

Now enter the IF function needed to calculate the employer's monthly matching contribution to the 401(k) plan.

To enter the IF function:

1. Click cell **E8** to select the cell where you want to enter the IF function.

2. Click the **Paste Function** button f_x on the Standard toolbar to open the Paste Function dialog box. Click **Logical** in the Function category list box, click **IF** in the Function name list box, and then click the **OK** button to open the IF function dialog box.

   TROUBLE? If the Office Assistant opens and offers Help on this feature, click the No button.

   Now enter the condition.

3. In the Logical_test text box, type **Invested>MaxMatch**.

4. Click the **Value_if_true** text box, and then type **Salary*MaxMatch/12**, the value to be returned if the condition is true. Because you're already in cell E8, you do not have to reference the cell again (do not enter E8= Salary* MaxMatch/12).

5. Click the **Value_if_false** text box, and then type **Salary*Invested/12**, the value to be returned if the condition is false. See Figure 7-19. Note again that you do not have to reference cell E8.

IF FUNCTION DIALOG BOX AFTER ARGUMENTS ENTERED

formula developed by
Excel based on your
entries in the IF function
dialog box

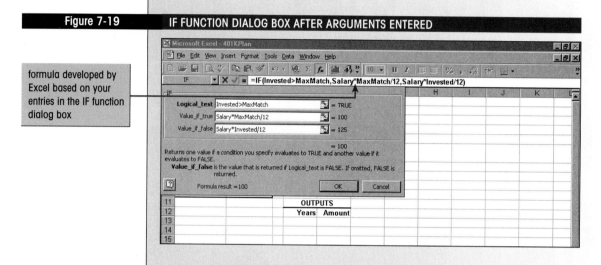

6. Click the **OK** button. Excel places the IF function in the worksheet. Because the condition in this case is True, the value 100 appears in cell E8. Notice that the formula =IF(Invested>MaxMatch,Salary*MaxMatch/12,Salary*Invested/12) appears in the formula bar.

Now compute the total amount invested each month, which is the sum of the employee and employer contributions.

To calculate the total contribution:

1. Click cell **E9**, click the **AutoSum** button Σ, and press the **Enter** key. The total amount invested is 225.

Now name cell E9 TotContribution.

2. Return to cell **E9**, click the **Name** box, type **TotContribution**, and press the **Enter** key.

TROUBLE? If the label TotContribution appears in cell E9, click the Undo button on the Standard toolbar, and then click the Name box, type TotContribution, and press the Enter key.

3. Format the range E7:E9 using the Currency style and zero decimal places.

4. Click any cell to deselect the range.

5. Save the workbook.

Session 7.1 QUICK CHECK

1. During data validation, the error alert message appears _____.

2. When you restrict the information being placed in a particular cell, you are applying _____.

3. During data validation, the input message appears when you _____.

4. Which of the following are invalid range names?
   a. Annual_Total
   b. 3rdQtr
   c. Qtr3
   d. Annual total

5. When you select a named cell or range, the name appears in the _____.

6. Rather than enter constants in formulas, you should reference values from a separate section of your worksheet referred to as the _____.

7. When the value you store in a cell depends on certain conditions, you should consider using a(n) _____ in your formula.

8. The symbol <= is an example of a _____.

You have completed the input section of the 401kPlan worksheet. By applying data validation rules, defining range names, and using range names and IF functions to create formulas, you have made the worksheet both easier for you to develop and for the numerous CableScan employees to use. In Session 7.2 you will complete the worksheet's calculation/output section.

SESSION 7.2

In this session you will finish the 401(k) planning workbook by entering the remaining formulas using the Excel AutoFill feature and FV function, creating a line chart, and protecting worksheet cells.

Computing the Retirement Fund

The last set of calculations will determine the dollars accumulated over time, or the total retirement fund, often called the "retirement nest egg." The values 5, 10, 15, 20, 25, 30—representing the years left until retirement—need to be entered in the first column, range D13:D18. Although you can type these numbers, there is an easier approach you can use when the values represent a series.

Creating a Series Using AutoFill

When working in Excel, you sometimes need to enter a series of data. If you enter one or two initial values in a series of numbers, dates, or text, the **AutoFill** feature of Excel completes the series for you. Figure 7-20 shows several series that AutoFill recognizes and automatically completes. You can quickly enter the series of data with the assistance of the fill handle. Enter the series 5, 10, 15, 20, 25, and 30 to represent the number of years left until retirement.

Figure 7-20   EXAMPLES OF SERIES COMPLETED USING AUTOFILL

INITIAL VALUE	REMAINING SERIES
Sunday	Monday, Tuesday, Wednesday, ...
1/10/2001	1/11/01, 1/12/01, 1/13/01
Qtr1	Qtr2, Qtr3, Qtr4
January	February, March, April, May, ...

To generate a series using AutoFill:

1. If you took a break after the last session, make sure Excel is running, the 401kPlan workbook is open, and the 401kPlan sheet is active.

2. In cell D13, enter **'5**. In cell D14, enter **'10**. Notice the values are left-aligned and stored as text, as a result of typing the apostrophe ahead of the value.

3. Select the range **D13:D14**.

4. Click and drag the fill handle in cell D14 through cells **D15:D18**. Notice that a ScreenTip displays each number in the series as you drag the mouse pointer. Release the mouse button. Excel has created the series, using the specified interval (5) between the two selected values.

5. Click any cell to deselect the range. See Figure 7-21.

Figure 7-21   SERIES CREATED USING AUTOFILL

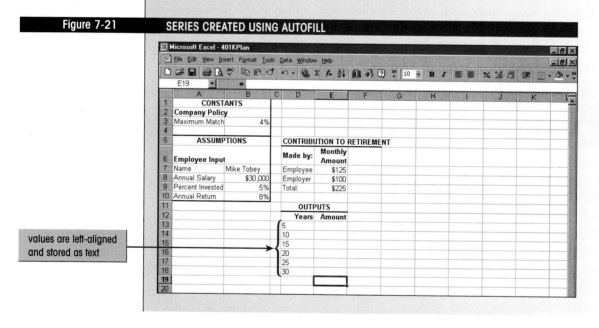

values are left-aligned and stored as text

Inserting the FV Function

Now enter the formula to calculate the future value of the investment, the retirement nest egg. The future value of an investment is its value at some future date based on a series of payments of equal amounts made over a number of periods earning a constant interest rate. You will use the financial function FV to compute the future value of the investment. The FV function has the following format:

FV(*rate, nper, pmt*)
where

- *rate* is the interest rate per period
- *nper* is the number of periods in which payments will be made
- *pmt* is the payments made each period. It cannot change over the life of the investment

This is one of several financial functions available in Excel. Figure 7-22 lists some of the other Excel financial functions.

Figure 7-22	SELECTED FINANCIAL FUNCTIONS

FUNCTION NAME	DESCRIPTION
PV	Computes the present value of a series of equal payments
PMT	Computes the periodic payment required to amortize a loan over a specified number of periods
RATE	Computes the rate of return of an investment that generates a series of equal periodic payments
DDB	Computes an asset's depreciation using the double-declining balance method
IRR	Computes an internal rate of return for a series of periodic cash flows

Now enter the future value formula, using the Paste Function button on the Standard toolbar.

To enter the future value formula:

1. Click cell **E13** to select the cell where you want to enter the FV function.

2. Click the **Paste Function** button [fx] on the Standard toolbar to open the Paste Function dialog box. Click **Financial** in the Function category list box, click **FV** in the Function name list box, and then click the **OK** button to open the FV function dialog box. See Figure 7-23.

   TROUBLE? If the Office Assistant opens offering Help on this feature, click the No button.

| Figure 7-23 | FV FUNCTION DIALOG BOX |

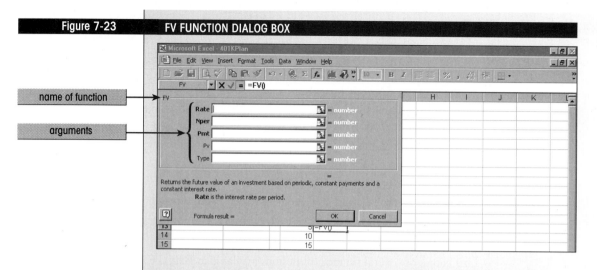

Now enter the arguments for this function. First, calculate the monthly return on the investment by dividing the annual return by 12.

3. In the **Rate** text box, type **Return/12**. Notice that the monthly return of .006666667 appears to the right of the Rate text box.

Next, calculate the number of monthly payments during the life of the investment.

4. In the **Nper** (number of periods) text box, type **D13*12**. Notice that 60, the number of months in five years, appears to the right of the Nper text box.

Now, enter the total amount invested each month.

5. In the **Pmt** text box, type **TotContribution** and press the **Enter** key. The value ($16,532.29) appears as a red negative value in cell E13. See Figure 7-24. This value, ($16,532.29), means that if an investment of $225 is made each month for 60 months and earns interest at a rate of 0.67% per month, you will have accumulated $16,532.29 in five years. By default, Excel shows this value as a negative number (in parentheses). You think the employees will be confused if they see the value of their investment as a negative number, so edit the formula and place a minus sign in front of the function name in order to display the future value as a positive number.

Figure 7-24   **FUTURE VALUE COMPUTATION FOR FIVE YEARS**

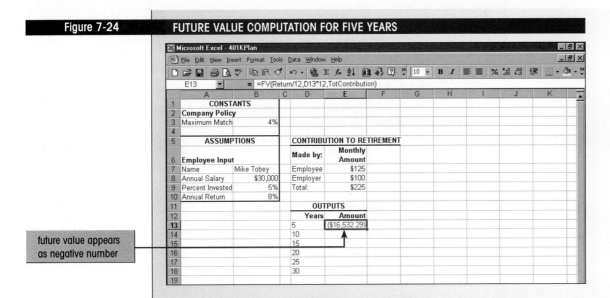

future value appears
as negative number

6. Double-click cell **E13**. Position the insertion point to the right of the equal sign (=) and type **-** (negative), and then press the **Enter** key. The value appears as a positive number.

7. Copy the formula in cell E13 to cells **E14:E18**.

TROUBLE? If the width of column E is too narrow, increase the column width to display the value.

8. Click any cell to deselect the range. See Figure 7-25.

Figure 7-25   **FUTURE VALUE COMPUTATION OVER 30-YEAR PERIOD IN FIVE-YEAR INCREMENTS**

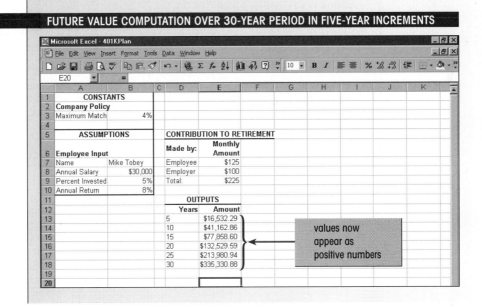

values now
appear as
positive numbers

The output table showing the dollars accumulated over 30 years is complete. Now display this information as a line chart showing the accumulation of dollars over the 30-year period.

To create the line chart:

1. Select the range **D13:E18**.

2. Click the **Chart Wizard** button 📊 on the Standard toolbar to open the Chart Wizard - Step 1 of 4 - Chart Type dialog box.

3. Click the **Line** chart type. Seven line chart sub-types appear. Click the **Line chart** sub-type (the first sub-type).

4. Click the **Next** button to open the Chart Wizard - Step 2 of 4 - Chart Source Data dialog box. On the Data tab, make sure the Data range box displays ='401kPlan'!$D$13:$E$18.

5. Click the **Next** button to open the Chart Wizard - Step 3 of 4 - Chart Options dialog box.

   TROUBLE? If the Category (X) axis is not labeled 5–30, click **Cancel** to exit the Chart Wizard. The values in D13:D18 were not entered correctly. Go back to page 7.18 and reenter the data in range D13:D18. Then return to this page to check the line chart.

   Next, add a title to the chart.

6. If necessary, click the **Titles** tab, click the **Chart title** text box, and type **Retirement Nest Egg** for the chart title. Click the **Category (X) axis** title box, and then type **Years in future**. Click the **Value (Y) axis** title box, and then type **Dollars**.

   Because there is only one data series, remove the legend; it is not needed.

7. Click the **Legend** tab and then click the **Show Legend** check box to remove the check and deselect that option.

8. Click the **Next** button to open the Chart Wizard - Step 4 of 4 - Chart Location dialog box. Embed the chart in the 401kPlan worksheet (the default option).

9. Click the **Finish** button to complete the chart and display it in the 401kPlan worksheet. See Figure 7-26. Note that the scale on your y-axis may appear different than shown here.

Figure 7-26   COMPLETED LINE CHART

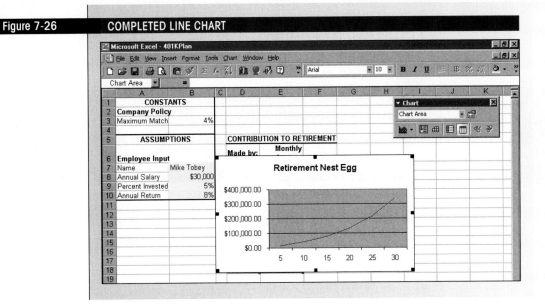

You need to move and resize the chart to improve its appearance.

To change the size and position of the chart:

1. Move and resize the chart object so it appears in the range **F6:K18**. See Figure 7-27.

Figure 7-27   LINE CHART AFTER BEING MOVED AND RESIZED

floating Chart toolbar may appear in a different location of your screen

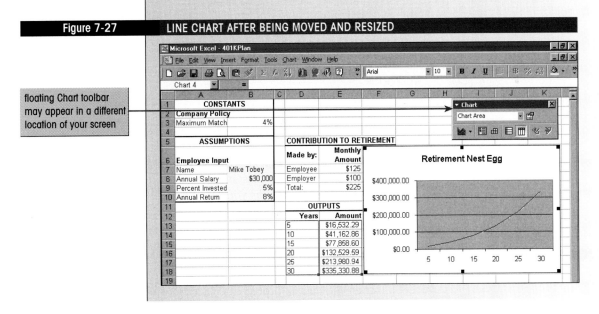

Now enhance the chart's appearance.

To improve the appearance of the chart:

1. Double-click the **Series 1** (Line object) to open the Format Data Series dialog box. On the Patterns tab, click the **Weight** list arrow, select the **thickest** line weight, and then click the **OK** button.

2. Click the **Numbers** tab, click Number in the Category list and change the number of decimal places to **0**, and then click the **OK** button.

3. Click anywhere outside the chart area to deselect the chart. See Figure 7-28.

Figure 7-28	FINAL VERSION OF LINE CHART

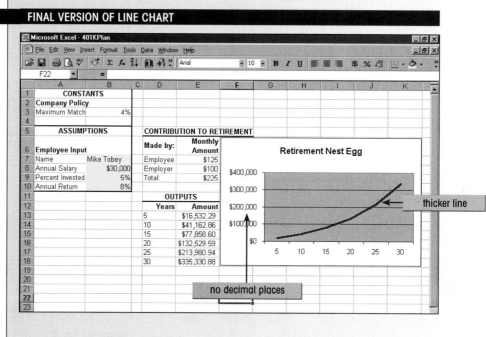

4. Save the workbook.

Now that all the components of the worksheet are complete, you still need to make a few enhancements to make the worksheet less susceptible to user error. Mary realizes that others will use the worksheet to explore what-if alternatives, and she worries about a user accidentally deleting the formatting or formulas in the calculation/output section of the worksheet. To preserve your work, Mary asks you to protect all the cells in the worksheet except the cells in the input section.

Protecting Cells in a Worksheet

When you **protect** a worksheet, data in protected cells cannot be changed. Once you have protected worksheet cells, the data in these cells can be viewed, but not edited or modified. Once you protect a worksheet, you cannot enter data, insert or delete rows, or change cell formats or column widths. Only the values in unprotected cells can be changed.

Unlocking Individual Cells

Most of the time you will not want to lock every cell in a worksheet. For example, in a worksheet that you share with others, you might want to protect the formulas and formatting, but leave particular cells unprotected so that necessary data may be entered. When you want to protect some but not all worksheet cells, you implement protection by following a two-step process. By default all cells in a worksheet have the locked property turned on, which means the cell is capable of being protected. First you need to identify the cells you want unprotected and turn off the "lock" associated with each of these cells. Once you have "unlocked" the selected cells, you activate the protection command to "turn on" protection for the remaining cells. Figure 7-29 illustrates this process.

Figure 7-29	PROCESS OF PROTECTING WORKSHEET CELLS

Default Status

By default, every cell in the worksheet has a locked property turned on, which means each cell has the capability of being protected, but at this step no cell is protected. You can enter data in any cell.

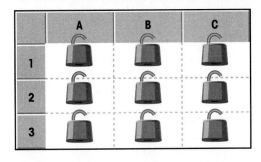

Step 1

The worksheet after some cells have their locks removed (locked property turned off). At this step no cell is protected. You can enter data in any cell.

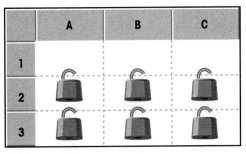

Step 2

The worksheet after the Protect Sheet command has been activated. The cells in the bottom two rows are protected—no data may be entered in these cells. You can still enter data in the first row.

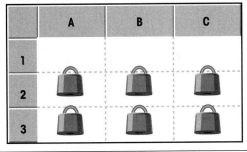

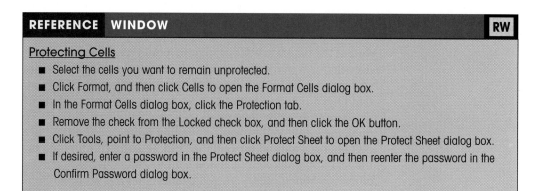

REFERENCE WINDOW   **RW**

Protecting Cells

- Select the cells you want to remain unprotected.
- Click Format, and then click Cells to open the Format Cells dialog box.
- In the Format Cells dialog box, click the Protection tab.
- Remove the check from the Locked check box, and then click the OK button.
- Click Tools, point to Protection, and then click Protect Sheet to open the Protect Sheet dialog box.
- If desired, enter a password in the Protect Sheet dialog box, and then reenter the password in the Confirm Password dialog box.

You start by unlocking the range of cells where the user can enter data, which in this case would be the input area of the 401kPlan worksheet. Then activate the protection for the rest of the worksheet, which will protect the data and formulas you do not want the employees to change.

To unlock the cells for data entry:

1. Click cell **A5** to make it the active cell, so you can view the input section.

2. Select the range **B7:B10**, the cells the user can change and therefore do not require protection.

3. Click **Format** on the menu bar, and then click **Cells** to open the Format Cells dialog box.

4. Click the **Protection** tab. By default, the Locked check box contains a check. See Figure 7-30.

Figure 7-30	PROTECTION TAB OF FORMAT CELLS DIALOG BOX

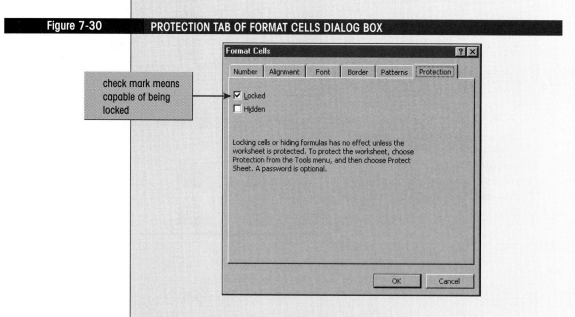

check mark means capable of being locked

5. Click the **Locked** check box to remove the check.

6. Click the **OK** button. Nothing visible happens to the worksheet to show that cells are unlocked.

Because Excel does not provide any on-screen indication of the protection status of individual cells, you decide to change the background color of the unlocked cells to distinguish them from the protected cells. This will be a nice visual cue for the employees using the worksheet, indicating which cells they should use to input their investment information.

To change the fill color of unprotected cells:

1. If necessary, select cells **B7:B10**.

2. Click the **Fill** color button list arrow on the Formatting toolbar to display the Color palette.

3. Click **Yellow** in the fourth row, third column of the Color palette.

4. Click any cell to view the yellow color applied to the unprotected cells.

Protecting the Worksheet

Now that you have unlocked the cells for data entry, you will turn on protection for the entire worksheet to protect every cell that you didn't unlock.

When you protect the worksheet, Excel lets you enter a password that must be used to unprotect the worksheet. If you specify a password, you must make sure to remember it so you can unprotect the worksheet in the future. Unless you are working on confidential material, it's probably easier not to use a password at all.

To turn protection on:

1. Click **Tools** on the menu bar, point to Protection, and then click **Protect Sheet** to open the Protect Sheet dialog box. See Figure 7-31. The Password text box lets you enter a password of your choice. The Contents check box locks the cells in the sheet. The Objects check box prevents changes to charts or graphical objects, and the Scenarios check box locks any scenario you've created.

| Figure 7-31 | OPTIONS FOR PROTECTING A WORKSHEET |

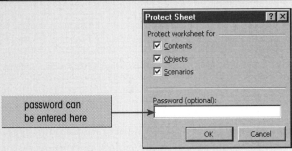

2. Click the **OK** button. If you had entered a password, a Confirm Password dialog box would open and you would be asked to retype the same password to make sure you remember it and that you entered it correctly the first time.

Testing Cell Protection

After protection is enabled, you cannot change a locked cell. Before you distribute the workbook to the employees to use, you decide to test the worksheet to assure yourself that protection has been implemented successfully.

To test worksheet protection:

1. Click cell **E13**, and then try typing **40000**. A message indicating that this cell is locked and cannot be changed appears. See Figure 7-32.

Figure 7-32   **MESSAGE DISPLAYED WHEN YOU ATTEMPT TO CHANGE A PROTECTED CELL**

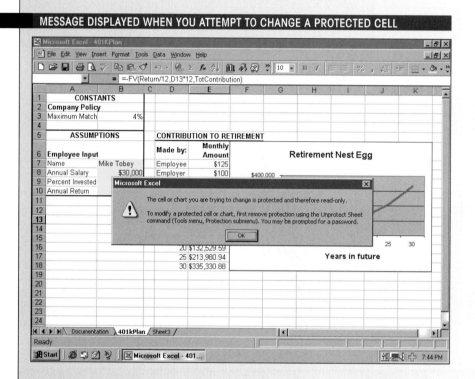

2. Click the **OK** button to continue.

   Now enter a value in a cell that is unlocked.

3. Click cell **B8**, type **40000**, and press the **Enter** key. Notice that the calculation and outputs changed.

Now that you are done creating the workbook, and have customized it so it is user friendly and appropriate for use by all CableScan employees, you give it to Mary to review. She is very pleased with the finished workbook. Her only suggestion is to further simplify the workbook by removing any unnecessary sheets. She thinks this will eliminate any possibility of people trying to enter data in the wrong area of the workbook.

Deleting **Unnecessary Worksheets**

If you want to remove an empty worksheet or a worksheet you no longer need, you can delete it. You decide to delete Sheet3 because it is not used in the 401(k) application.

To delete a worksheet:

1. Click the **Sheet3** tab to activate the Sheet3 worksheet.

2. Click **Edit**, and then click **Delete Sheet**. A message appears letting you know that the selected sheet will be permanently deleted.

3. Click the **OK** button. Notice that Sheet3 has been deleted from the workbook.

4. Save the workbook.

Session 7.2 QUICK CHECK

1. You can use the Excel _____ feature to complete a series of numbers, dates, or text values.

2. The FV function stands for _____. This function is found in the _____ category.

3. How does cell protection differ from data validation?

4. What happens when you try to enter a value in a protected cell?

5. Protecting a worksheet is a two-step process. You _____ and then you _____.

6. Why were the unprotected cells filled with color?

You have now completed the worksheet. In this next section you will create two macros that will simplify some of the tasks a user performs when using this workbook.

SESSION 7.3

In this session you will learn what macros are and how they can be used to automate tasks in a workbook for the user. You will also plan and create two macros using the Excel macro recorder.

Automating **Tasks Using Macros**

Typically macros are used to automate repetitive tasks. A **macro** is a series of commands and functions that you can initiate whenever you want to perform a particular task. That is, you create them to automatically perform a series of Excel operations, such as menu selections, dialog box selections, range selections, or keystrokes. They carry out repetitive tasks more quickly than you can yourself, making your work more productive and helping you make fewer errors. For example, you can create macros to automate the following tasks:

- move through a large worksheet quickly
- add a date and time stamp to a cell in the current worksheet

- extract data from an Excel list and create a chart
- print several reports from a worksheet, each with different print specifications
- apply a common set of formats to any sheet in a workbook

Macros simplify the use of workbooks for both experienced and novice users. In reviewing the 401kPlan workbook with Mary, you realize that macros would be useful to include. You know that all users will need to clear the input section after completing the worksheet so the next user doesn't see confidential financial information. You also know that people will most likely want to have a hard copy of some or all of the worksheet. Therefore, printing is another task that would be good to simplify.

Creating Macros

You can create a macro in two ways: you can use the macro recorder to record your keystrokes and mouse actions as you perform them (recording the selection of ranges, menu commands, dialog box options, etc.), or you can write your own macros by entering a series of commands in the **Visual Basic for Applications (VBA)** programming language, which tells Excel how to do a particular task.

The easiest way to create a macro in Excel is to use the macro recorder. When you record a macro, your keystrokes and mouse actions are automatically translated into Visual Basic instructions (code) that you can play back, or run, whenever you want to repeat those particular keystrokes and tasks. Your actions are recorded and then translated into a series of instructions in VBA. When you run the macro, the instructions are read and executed in sequence, thereby duplicating the actions you performed when you recorded the macro.

In this section you will create two macros using the macro recorder. The first will be a ClearInputs macro that will automate the task of clearing values from the input section of the workbook, so the user can enter new data. The second macro you will create will be a Print macro, which will simplify the printing process.

Planning Macros

As with most complex projects, you need to plan your macro. Decide what you want to accomplish and the best way to go about doing it. Once you know the purpose of the macro, you should carry out the keystrokes or mouse actions before you actually record them. Going through each step before recording a macro might seem like extra work, but it reduces the chances of error when you actually create the macro.

Mary realizes that many different employees will use the worksheet and will enter different sets of input assumptions. She wants you to create a macro that will automatically clear the values in the input section and place the cell pointer in cell B7—ready for the user to enter a new set of data.

She sits down at her computer and goes through the steps to include in the macro before you actually record them. This way you will be familiar with the steps to include in the macro, and the chances for errors in the macro are fewer. Figure 7-33 lists the steps Mary plans to include in the macro.

Figure 7-33   **PLANNING THE CLEARINPUTS MACRO**

ACTION	RESULT
Select the range B7:B10	Highlights the range you want to clear of data
Press the Delete key	Clears the contents of the selected range
Click cell B7	Makes cell B7 the active cell

Recording the ClearInputs Macro

After planning the macro, you are ready to record it. There are several actions you need to take before actually recording the macro. First, you want to decide on an appropriate name for the macro. For example, the first macro Mary asked you to create is for clearing the input section of any values, so a good name for this macro would be ClearInputs. A macro name can be up to 255 characters long; it must begin with a letter, and it can contain only letters, numbers, and the underscore character. No spaces or other punctuation marks are permitted. For multiple-word macros such as Clear Inputs, you can use initial caps (ClearInputs) or the underscore (Clear_Inputs).

When you record a macro, every keystroke and mouse click is stored by Excel. Therefore, your second task before you can record the macro is to specify where you want the macro stored. The macro is stored in the form of a VBA program, and its storage location plays a part in how you will be able to access and use the macro once it is created. There are three possible locations you can choose to store the macro. By default, the recorded macro is stored as part of the current workbook—in a hidden module that is part of the workbook. Macros stored in a workbook are available only when the workbook is open. If a workbook is closed, the macros stored within the workbook can't be used. Use this storage option to store macros that you plan to use only within this workbook.

If you use some macros on a regular basis, you may want to make them available at all times. In that case, you would choose to store the macros in the Personal Macro workbook. With this option, the macro is stored in a special workbook file named Personal Macro. When you start Excel, this workbook is opened and hidden automatically, making the macros in it available to any open workbook.

You can also store the macro in a new workbook file. In this case, another workbook opens to store the recorded macro. To use macros stored in another workbook, you need to open both the workbook with the macros as well as the workbook containing the application.

In addition to considering where you want to store your macro, before you record a macro you also need to make sure your worksheet is set up exactly as you want it to exist at the time you play back the recorded macro. This may involve opening a specific workbook, activating a specific sheet in which you want the macro to run, and moving to the location where you want to start recording. Otherwise the macro may not work as planned, and you may have to record it again.

When you record a macro, you name and describe it. You can also set up a shortcut key to run the macro, and specify the workbook in which to store the macro.

To record a macro to clear a range of cells:

1. If you took a break after the last session, make sure Excel is running, the 401kPlan workbook is open, and the 401kPlan sheet is active. If necessary, press **Ctrl + Home** to make cell A1 the active cell.

    Now start the macro recorder.

2. Click **Tools** on the menu bar, point to Macro, and then click **Record New Macro** to open the Record Macro dialog box. See Figure 7-34.

Figure 7-34   RECORD MACRO DIALOG BOX

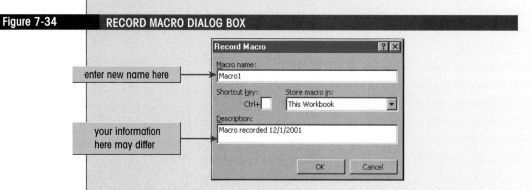

enter new name here

your information here may differ

Excel proposes a default name for the macro. This default macro name consists of the word "Macro" and a number corresponding to the number of macros you have recorded in the workbook in the current work session. You should change the macro name to a name more descriptive of what the macro will do. Name the macro ClearInputs.

3. Type **ClearInputs** in the Macro name text box.

Now specify the location of your macro. You want the macro to be accessible only to this workbook, and when this workbook is open. Therefore, you want to store the macro as part of this workbook.

4. Make sure the option This Workbook is selected in the Store macro in list box.

Notice the brief description indicating the date the macro is being recorded. You can add additional comments to explain the purpose of the macro.

5. Click anywhere within the **Description** text box. If the insertion point is not at the end of the default description, move it there. Press the **Enter** key to start a new line. Type **Clear the values from the input section**. See Figure 7-35.

Figure 7-35	COMPLETED RECORD MACRO DIALOG BOX

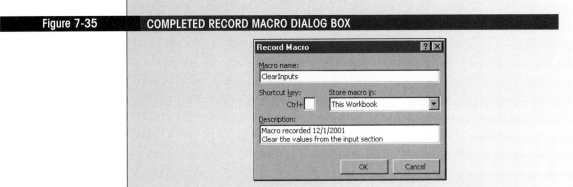

6. Click the **OK** button to start recording the macro. See Figure 7-36. Excel returns to the worksheet and the message "Recording" appears in the status bar at the bottom of the screen. You are now in Record mode and all keystrokes and mouse clicks will be recorded until you stop the macro recorder.

Figure 7-36	STOP RECORDING TOOLBAR

click here to stop recording of macro

relative reference button

status bar indicates macro is being recorded

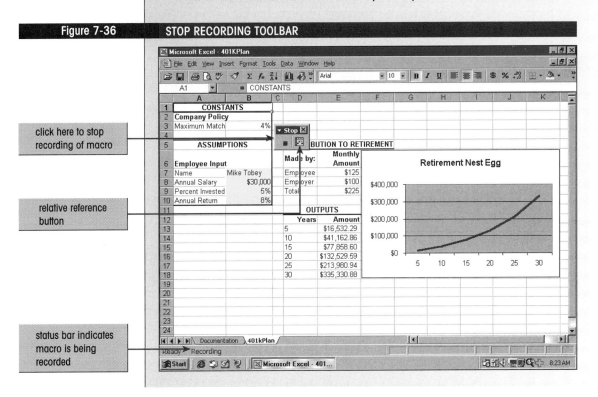

Notice that the Stop Recording toolbar also appears. This toolbar contains two buttons, the Stop Recording button and the Relative Reference button. By default Excel uses absolute references while recording macros. If you wanted a macro to select cells regardless of the position of the cell pointer in the worksheet when you run the macro, then you would click the Relative Reference button to record macros using relative references. When you have finished entering all tasks, you can use the Stop Recording button to stop the macro recorder.

TROUBLE? If a warning message appears indicating that the macro name already exists, click the Yes button and proceed to record the tasks in your macro. The existing macro is replaced with whatever you now record.

Now perform the tasks you want recorded.

To perform the steps to be recorded:

1. Select the range **B7:B10**.

2. Press the **Delete** key. The input section is now cleared.

3. Click cell **B7** to make it the active cell.

   You have completed the actions that you want recorded. Next, you will stop the macro recorder.

4. Click the **Stop Recording** button ■ on the Stop Recording toolbar or click **Tools**, point to Macro, and then click **Stop Recording** to stop the recording process. Notice that the message "Recording" no longer appears in the status bar and the Stop Recording toolbar disappears.

   TROUBLE? If you forget to turn off the macro recorder, it continues to record all of your actions. If this happens to you, you may need to delete the macro and record it again. To delete the macro, click Tools on the menu bar, point to Macro, and then click Macros in the Macros dialog box, select ClearInputs in the Macro Name list, and then click the Delete button. Click the Yes button to verify you want to delete the macro.

You have completed recording your first macro. Now test the macro by running it.

Running the ClearInputs Macro from the Tools Menu

After recording a macro, you can play it back, or run it, at any time. When you run a macro, you are telling Excel to execute the previously recorded instructions contained within the macro. It is a good idea to run the macro directly after you create it as a test to ensure that it works correctly. If it doesn't work correctly, you can:

- re-record the macro using the same macro name
- delete the recorded macro and then record the macro again
- edit the incorrect macro by opening the Visual Basic Editor

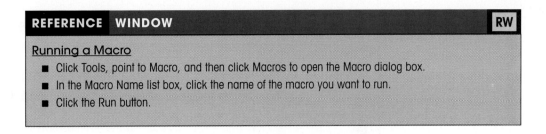

Running a Macro

- Click Tools, point to Macro, and then click Macros to open the Macro dialog box.
- In the Macro Name list box, click the name of the macro you want to run.
- Click the Run button.

The first time you run the macro, you are testing it to determine whether it works as expected. Run the macro you just created to see if it automatically clears the values from the input section. To do this, you need to first enter values in the section so they can be cleared.

To run a macro using the Macro command on the Tools menu:

1. Enter a new set of input values in cells B7:B10. Enter **Mary Higgins, 45000, .02, .06**.

2. Press **Ctrl + Home** to move to cell A1.

   Now save the workbook before running the macro for the first time in case anything goes wrong while running it.

3. Click the **Save** button 🖫 on the Standard toolbar to save the workbook.

4. Use the ClearInputs macro to erase the input values.

5. Click **Tools** on the menu bar, point to Macro, and then click **Macros** to open the Macro dialog box. See Figure 7-37. A list of all macros found in all open workbooks appears in the Macro Name list box.

Figure 7-37   **MACRO DIALOG BOX**

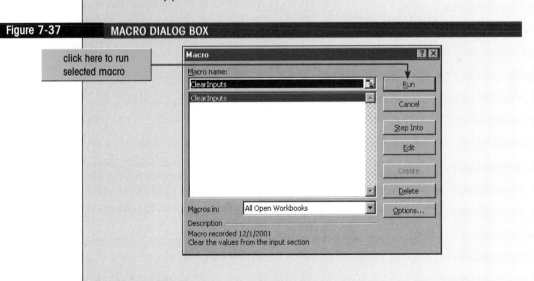

Select the name of the macro you want to run.

6. If necessary, click **ClearInputs** to display ClearInputs in the Macro name text box, and then click the **Run** button. The ClearInputs macro runs and clears the values in cells B7:B10. See Figure 7-38.

Figure 7-38   WORKSHEET AFTER MACRO RUN

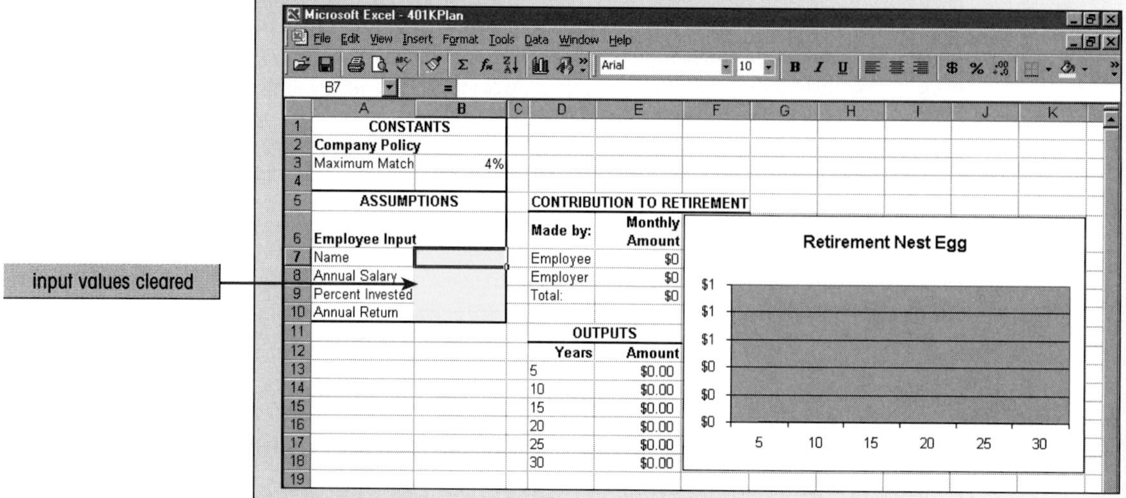

input values cleared

The macro ran successfully. Now that you know the macro works, you want to make it easy for users to run. There are several ways to do this.

Creating a Macro Shortcut Key

You can use the Macro command on the Tools menu to run macros that you execute infrequently, but this approach is inconvenient if you need to run the macro often. There are several ways to make it easier to run a macro. You can assign the macro to a:

- shortcut key that enables you to run the macro by using a combination of the Ctrl key and a letter key
- command that appears on one of the Excel menus
- button on a toolbar
- drawing object

A quick way to run a macro is to assign it to a shortcut key, a key you press along with the Ctrl key to run the macro. The shortcut key is a single uppercase or lowercase letter. If you use this option, you can run the macro by holding down the Ctrl key and pressing the shortcut key. Normally you assign a shortcut key when you first record a macro; however, if you didn't create a shortcut key at the time you recorded the macro, you can still assign one to the macro.

Mary asks you to create a shortcut key to execute the ClearInputs macro. She wants users to type Ctrl + c to execute the macro.

To assign a shortcut key to the macro:

1. Click **Tools** on the menu bar, point to Macro, and then click **Macros** to open the Macro dialog box.

2. If necessary, click **ClearInputs**, and then click the **Options** button to open the Macro Options dialog box. See Figure 7-39.

Figure 7-39	MACRO OPTIONS DIALOG BOX

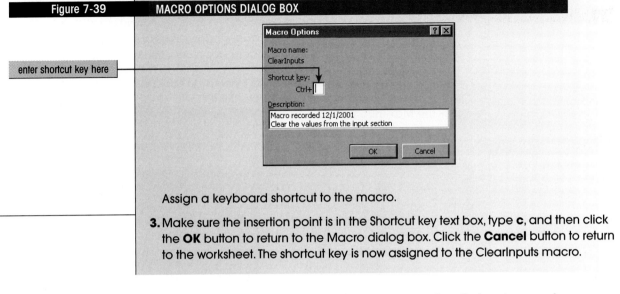

enter shortcut key here

Assign a keyboard shortcut to the macro.

3. Make sure the insertion point is in the Shortcut key text box, type **c**, and then click the **OK** button to return to the Macro dialog box. Click the **Cancel** button to return to the worksheet. The shortcut key is now assigned to the ClearInputs macro.

Now test the shortcut key to see if the macro runs when Ctrl + c is pressed.

To test the shortcut key:

1. In cells B7:B10, enter **FJ Miles, 50000, .05, .05**, to enter a new set of input values.

2. Press **Ctrl + c** to run the macro. The input values are erased and B7 is the active cell.

   Note that shortcut keys are case-sensitive, so if a user types Ctrl + Shift C, the shortcut will not run the ClearInputs macro.

The shortcut key successfully ran the macro. Now let's take a look at the code behind the ClearInputs macro.

Viewing **the ClearInputs Macro Code**

As you may have realized, you can successfully record and run a macro without looking at or understanding the instructions underlying it. For simple macros this approach is fine. There will be times, however, when you may welcome the greater flexibility that comes from understanding the commands underlying the recorded macro.

As Excel records your actions, it translates them into a series of instructions in the Visual Basic for Applications programming language. To view or edit the macro, you need to open the **Visual Basic Editor**, a separate application that works with Excel.

To view the Visual Basic code:

1. Click **Tools** on the Menu bar, point to Macro, and then click **Macros** to open the Macro dialog box.

2. Click **ClearInputs** in the Macro name list box, and then click the **Edit** button. The Visual Basic Editor opens as a separate application consisting of several windows. One of the windows, the Code window, contains the Visual Basic Code generated while your ClearInputs macro was recorded. See Figure 7-40.

TROUBLE? The number of windows that open may vary depending on your system. We will focus on the Code window. If the Code window is not maximized, click the Maximize button.

Figure 7-40	VISUAL BASIC EDITOR DISPLAYS VISUAL BASIC CODE FOR CLEARINPUTS MACRO

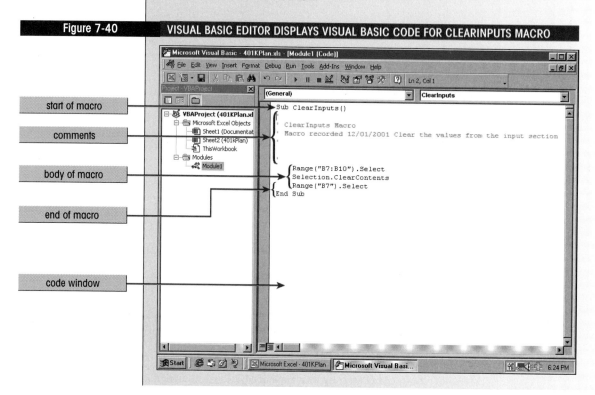

Visual Basic for Applications Code

The Visual Basic for Applications code shown in Figure 7-40 has the following components: **Sub/End Sub** are keywords that mark the beginning and end of a macro. The keyword Sub in the statement

Sub ClearInputs()

signals the start of the macro. It is followed by the macro name ClearInputs and then by left and right parentheses. The keywords End Sub signal the end of the macro. **Comments** are statements that explain or document what is happening in the macro. Any line of the code that is preceded by an apostrophe is a comment and is ignored when the macro is run. In Figure 7-40, the comments are the macro name, the date recorded, and the description you entered in the Record Macro dialog box.

The **body of the macro** is the series of statements between Sub and End Sub representing the VBA translation of the actions you performed while recording the macro. In Figure 7-40 the statement

Range("B7:B10").Select

is the VBA equivalent of selecting the range B7:B10.
The next statement

Selection.ClearContents

is the VBA equivalent of pressing the Delete key to clear the contents of the selected range. The last statement

Range("B7").Select

is the VBA equivalent of clicking B7 to make it the active cell.

Now that you have viewed the code behind the macro, you're ready to create your next macro, a macro to print a portion of the 401kPlan worksheet. First, close the Visual Basic Editor.

To close the Visual Basic Editor:

1. Click **File** on Visual Basic Editor menu bar, and then click **Close and Return to Microsoft Excel**. The Visual Basic Editor closes and the 401kPlan worksheet appears.

Recording the Print401k Macro

Because your worksheets may be large, containing input sections, data, tables, reports, charts, etc., you may want to use a macro to help you simplify the steps for printing different parts of a worksheet. Also, the addition of one or more print macros will make the printing process much easier for other users.

After an employee has made changes to certain input values and viewed the revised table and chart, Mary wants the employee to be able to print a hard copy of the worksheet for his or her records. Some employees may only want to print the table and chart from the 401k worksheet. Instead of the user having to establish print settings to get the output of just the table and chart, for example, you could create a macro to print just these sections of the worksheet. You would need to specify the print area for the portion of the worksheet you are printing. Mary also wants the user's output to automatically have informative headers and footers. Before printing, the user should also be able to view the output in the Print Preview window. Figure 7-41 shows the planning for this macro. Using this planning sheet, record the macro for Mary. Mary suggests that you name the macro Print401k and that it be stored just in this workbook. Now, set up the worksheet just the way you want it before you begin the macro recorder.

Figure 7-41	PLANNING THE PRINT401K MACRO

ACTION	RESULT
Click File, click Page Setup	Opens the Page Setup dialog box
Click the Sheet tab, click Print area, type D5:L18	Defines print area
Click Margins, click Horizontally check box	Horizontally centers output
Click Header/Footer tab, click Custom Header, click the Tab Name button, click OK	Defines custom header
Click Custom Footer, type Prepared by [enter your name], click OK	Defines custom footer
Click Print Preview	Displays output in Print Preview window
Click Close	Closes Print Preview window
Click cell A5	Makes cell A5 the active cell

To record the Print401k macro:

1. Enter **Tammy Beach, 25000, .04, .10** in the appropriate cells in range B7:B10 to input new values. Click cell **A1**.

   Now start the macro recorder.

2. Click **Tools** on the menu bar, point to Macro, and then click **Record New Macro** to open the Record Macro dialog box.

   The name Macro2 automatically appears because this is the second macro you have recorded during this work session. Change the name of the macro to Print401k.

3. Type **Print401k** in the Macro name text box.

   Now add a shortcut key.

4. Click the **Shortcut key** text box, and then type **p**.

   Add an additional comment to explain the purpose of the macro.

5. Place the insertion point at the end of the default description. Press the **Enter** key and type **Print preview output table and chart**.

6. Click the **OK** button to start the macro recorder.

7. Click **File** on the menu bar, and then click **Page Setup** to open the Page Setup dialog box.

   By default, the entire worksheet prints. To print only a part of the worksheet, you must specify the part you want.

8. Click the **Sheet** tab of the Page Setup dialog box, click the **Print area** text box, and then type **D5:K18**.

   Now specify the print settings so the output is centered horizontally.

9. Click the **Margins** tab, and then check the **Horizontally** check box to select it.

10. Click the **Header/Footer** tab, and then click the **Custom Header** button. In the center section, click the **Tab Name** button (last button), and then click the **OK** button.

11. Click the **Custom Footer** button, type **Prepared by (enter your name)** in the Right section, and then click the **OK** button.

    Review the output in the Print Preview window.

12. Click the **Print Preview** button on the right side of the dialog box to preview the output. See Figure 7-42.

Figure 7-42	PRINT PREVIEW AS A RESULT OF RECORDING THE MACRO

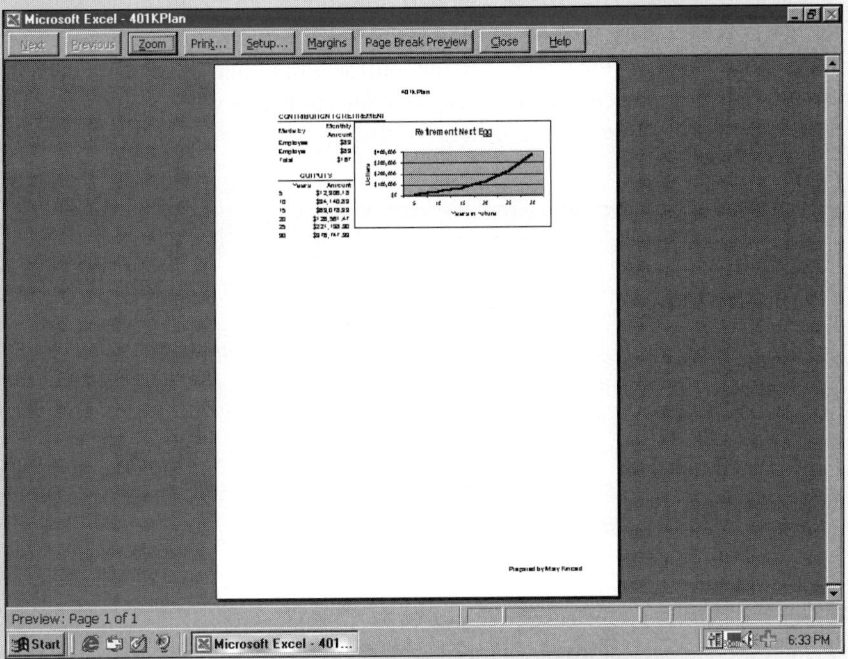

13. Click the **Close** button to close the Print Preview window and return to the 401kPlan sheet. Note that you cannot stop the macro until you leave the Print Preview window.

14. Click cell **A5** to make it the active cell.

You have completed the tasks for the macro; now turn off the macro recorder.

15. Click the **Stop Recording** button ▪ on the Stop Recording toolbar to stop recording the macro.

Now test the Print401k macro using the shortcut key.

To test the macro using the shortcut key:

1. Save the workbook.

2. Press **Ctrl + p** to run the macro. The output table and chart appear in the Print Preview window.

3. If you want a hard copy, click the **Print** button on the Print Preview toolbar, and then click the **OK** button in the Print dialog box; otherwise click the **Close** button.

The shortcut key successfully ran the print macro. However, Mary thinks it may be easier for a user to run the print macro by clicking a button placed on the worksheet. Mary asks you to create this button.

Assigning the Print401k Macro to a Button on the Worksheet

Another way to run a macro is to assign it to a button. You place the button on a worksheet, assign the macro to the button, and then run the macro by clicking the button. This approach makes the macro easier to use. It will speed up your own work, as well as make the macro easier for others to run.

REFERENCE WINDOW   **RW**

Assigning a Macro to a Button on a Worksheet

- Click the Button button on the Forms toolbar.
- Position the mouse pointer where you want the button, and then click and drag the mouse pointer until the button is the size and shape you want.
- Release the mouse button. The button appears on the worksheet with a label, and the Assign Macro dialog box opens.
- Select the name of the macro that you want to assign to the button from the Macro Name list box.
- Click the OK button.

Because the workbook is still protected, you need to turn protection off in order to make any changes to the worksheet (except in unlocked cells), such as placing a button on the worksheet.

To turn protection off:

1. Click **Tools** on the menu bar, point to Protection, and then click **Unprotect Sheet**. The worksheet is unprotected. If you had password-protected the worksheet, the Unprotect Sheet dialog box would open so that you could enter the password.

Now place a button on the worksheet.

To place a button on the worksheet and assign a macro to the button:

1. Click cell **D2**.

   Next, display the Forms toolbar, which contains the tools you need to place the button on the worksheet.

2. Click **View** on the menu bar, point to Toolbars, and then click **Forms** to display the Forms toolbar. If necessary, drag the Forms toolbar out of the way. See Figure 7-43.

Figure 7-43	FORMS TOOLBAR DISPLAY IN WORKSHEET WINDOW

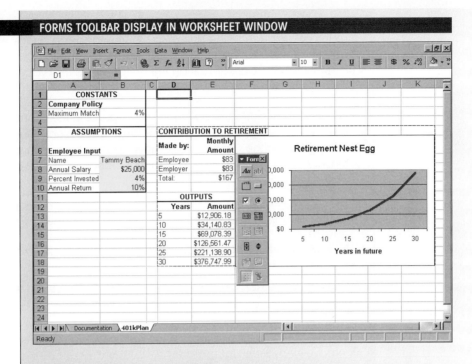

3. Click the **Button** button ▭ on the Forms toolbar. Now position the mouse pointer in the worksheet where you want the button to appear.

4. Position the mouse pointer in the upper-left corner of cell D2. The pointer shape changes to +. Click and drag the mouse pointer until the box covers the range **D2:E3**. When you release the mouse button, the Assign Macro dialog box opens. See Figure 7-44. Here you select the macro that will be run when the user clicks this button. This is referred to as assigning a macro to a button.

Figure 7-44	BUTTON AND ASSIGN MACRO DIALOG BOX

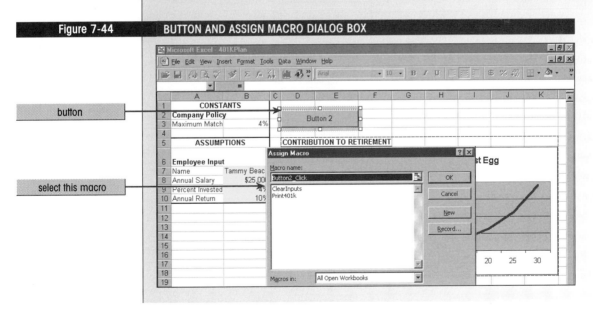

button

select this macro

5. Click **Print401k** in the Macro Name list box, and then click the **OK** button. The macro is assigned to the button. The button appears on the worksheet. It is selected (selection handles appear around the button), and the default name Button 2 appears as a label on the button. Note that your button number may differ.

TROUBLE? If the button is too small, too large, or in the wrong location, you can resize or move it just as you move or resize any object. If the button is not selected, press the Ctrl key while moving the mouse pointer on top of the button, and then click the mouse. Selection handles appear around the button, indicating that you can move or resize it.

TROUBLE? If the Forms toolbar is in the way, click and drag it to move it out of the way, or click the Forms toolbar Close button to remove it from the screen.

Now change the name on the button to one that indicates the function of the macro assigned to it.

6. Highlight the label on the button and type **Print 401k Report**.

7. Click anywhere in the worksheet to deselect the button.

8. If you haven't already removed the Forms toolbar, click its **Close** button to remove it now. See Figure 7-45.

Figure 7-45   **BUTTON TO RUN PRINT401K MACRO**

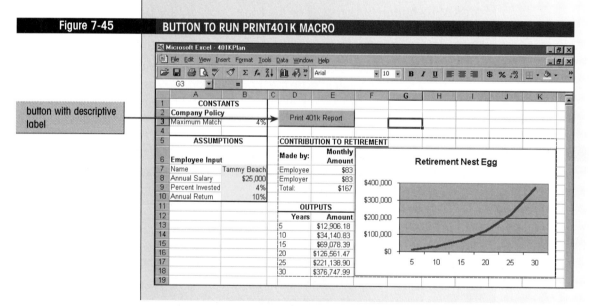

button with descriptive label

Now test the command button to make sure it runs the macro.

To test the Print401k macro using the command button:

1. Type **.08** in cell B10 and press the **Enter** key.

2. Click the **Print 401k Report** button. The output and chart appears in the Print Preview window.

3. If you want a hard copy, click the **Print** button and then click the **OK** button in the Print dialog box; otherwise click the **Close** button.

Your Print401k macro worked successfully using the button. Now protect the worksheet again.

4. Click **Tools**, point to **Protection**, click **Protect Sheet**, and then click **OK**.

5. Save the workbook, and then close it and exit Excel.

You have created a workbook for the CableScan employees that will allow them to easily and efficiently plan and establish 401(k) plans.

Session 7.3 QUICK CHECK

1. A _____ automates repetitive tasks.

2. You can create a macro by _____ or _____.

3. A recorded macro stores instructions in the _____ programming language.

4. Print Chart is a valid macro name. (True/False)

5. Macros are stored in a(n) _____, _____, or _____.

6. To stop recording a macro, you _____.

7. Name three ways to run a macro.

8. What is the purpose of a shortcut key?

REVIEW ASSIGNMENTS

After the presentation at the first CableScan site, you received feedback from the employees on how to improve the usability of the 401kPlan workbook. Do the following:

1. If necessary, start Excel and make sure your Data Disk is in the appropriate disk drive. Open the workbook **401kPlan2** in the Review folder for Tutorial.07 and save it as **401kPlan3**. A message appears informing you that this workbook contains macros. Click the Enable Macros button to continue.

2. Remove cell protection from 401kPlan3 worksheet.

3. Specify a data validation rule for the Salary value, cell B8. You want to allow integer values between 5000 and 150000.

4. Test the data validation. Enter a salary of 200000. What happens?

5. Modify the data validation you just assigned in cell B8 to include an input message. The message should state "Valid salary values are between 5000 and 150000" and have the title Valid Data.

6. Modify the data validation you assigned in cell B8 to include an error alert message. The error message should have the title Invalid Data, and the message should state "You entered a value less than $5000 or greater than $150,000." Use the Warning style in defining the error alert.

7. Test the data validation again. Enter a value of 200000. What happens?

8. Change the error alert style to Information. Enter 200000 as the current salary. What happens?

9. Assign the name Contributions to the range E7:E8. Replace the formula in cell E9 with the formula =Sum(Contributions). What value appears in E9?

10. The FV function in cell E13 assumes that payments are made at the end of the month. A more realistic assumption is that payments are made at the beginning of the month. Use the Paste Function button on the Standard toolbar to modify the FV function in cell E13 by placing a 1 in the Type argument. Copy the modified formula to the other cells in the output table. Use the Print 401k Report button to print the worksheet.

Explore 11. Modify the IF function in cell E8 so the condition is expressed Invested <=MaxMatch instead of Invested > MaxMatch. Modify the other arguments of the IF function so you get the same results as in the tutorial. What formula did you enter in cell E8?

12. Plan and create a macro to print preview the entire worksheet except the range A1:B4. Name the macro PrintWorksheet. Include the label "CableScan 401k Plan" as a custom header in the center setting and change the page orientation to Landscape. Assign a shortcut key to the macro. Place a button on the worksheet next to the Print 401k Report button. Label the button Print Worksheet. Test your macro twice, using the Print Worksheet button and the shortcut key. (Note: By default, the macro button does not print.)

13. Delete Sheet3 from the workbook, and then save and close the workbook.

Explore 14. Open a new workbook and use AutoFill to create the series
   a. Q197,Q297,Q397,Q497,Q198,Q298,...,Q199,...,Q499. Print the series.
   b. What values must be entered in the worksheet in order for Excel to recognize the pattern and create this series?
   c. What value appears after Q499?
   d. Save the workbook as **AutoFill Exercise** in the Review folder for Tutorial.07 on your Data Disk.

Explore 15. Open a new workbook and create two macros that are identical, except that in the first case you'll record the macro using absolute references and in the second, you'll record the macro using relative references. Both macros enter a company's name and address into three worksheet cells. Figure 7-46 describes the steps required for each macro.

Figure 7-46

Name of Macro: NameAddress1 Shortcut key: x Description: using absolute references
Click cell A1
Type Adobe Development Corporation
In cell A2, type 101 Terra Way
In cell A3, type Tucson, AZ

Name of Macro: NameAddress2 Shortcut key: y Description: using relative references
Click Relative Reference button
Click cell A1
Type Adobe Development Corporation
In cell A2, type 101 Terra Way
In cell A3, type Tucson, AZ
Click Relative Reference button

Do the following:
   a. Record the NameAddress1 macro, as described in Figure 7-46.

b. Before you record the second macro, clear the contents of cells A1:A3, and then make A3 the active cell.

c. Record the Name Address2 macro described in Figure 7-46.

d. Activate Sheet2.

e. Click cell D5 and run the NameAddress1 macro using the shortcut key.

f. Click cell D12 and run the NameAddress2 macro using the shortcut key.

g. Activate Sheet3.

h. Click cell D5 and run the NameAddress1 macro.

i. Click cell D12 and run the NameAddress2 macro.

j. Save the workbook as **Relative vs. Absolute** in the Review folder for Tutorial.07. Close the workbook.

Comment on the differences between the two macros.

CASE PROBLEMS

Case 1. Travel Expense Worksheet for Tax Purposes Jack Conners, an accountant for a manufacturing company, has been preparing tax returns on weekends for several years to earn extra income. Although Jack uses a commercial tax package to prepare tax returns, he has discovered that it doesn't provide assistance in determining the portion of a business trip that is tax deductible. Jack has asked you to develop a worksheet to determine deductible travel expenses that he can use with a client who travels on business.

The IRS rules state that a taxpayer can deduct travel expenses incurred while pursuing a business purpose. Those travel expenses include transportation, lodging, incidentals, and 50% of meals. Incidentals are items such as local transportation, laundry, and similar small items that are necessary while traveling. Sometimes a trip may involve both business and personal activities. If fewer than 50% of the travel days are devoted to business, none of the transportation expenses are deductible; otherwise the transportation expenses are fully deductible. The costs for lodging, meals, and incidentals are deductible to the extent that they are related specifically to business activities. Only 50% of meals associated with business travel, are deductible.

Figure 7-47 incorporates the information you need to complete the travel expense worksheet.

Figure 7-47

```
Inputs
        Name of taxpayer
        Dates of travel
        Destination
        Purpose
        Number of business travel days
        Number of personal travel days
        Transportation (total cost)
        Lodging (cost per day)
        Meals (cost per day)
        Incidentals (cost per day)

Calculations
        Transportation =  IF Number of business travel days is greater than Number of personal travel days THEN
                                Transportation = (total cost)
                           ELSE
                                Transportation = 0
                           END IF
        Lodging = Number of business travel days × Lodging (cost per day)
        Meals = Number of business travel days × Meals (cost per day) x 50%
        Incidentals = Number of business travel days × Incidentals (cost per day)
        Total deductible travel expense = Transportation + Lodging + Meals + Incidentals
```

Do the following:

1. If necessary, start Excel and make sure your Data Disk is in the appropriate disk drive.

2. Prepare a travel expense worksheet based on the information in Figure 7-47. Name the sheet **Travel**.

3. Divide the worksheet into two sections: input and calculation/output. As you develop the input section, assign range names to each cell.

4. The IRS guideline limits the deduction for meals to $75 per day, unless the taxpayer has receipts to justify a higher expense. Set up a data validation rule in the input section to comply with this guideline. You should include an input message and determine appropriate text for the message. Also, include an error alert message using the Warning style. You determine the text of the error alert message. Test the data validation.

5. Use the range names to build the formulas in the calculation section of your worksheet.

6. Improve the appearance of the worksheet, so you have a professional-looking report you can output.

7. Print the worksheet using Taxpayer 1 data from Figure 7-48.

Figure 7-48

INPUT FIELD	TAXPAYER 1	TAXPAYER 2
Name of taxpayer	Ken Tuner	Ellen Wymer
Dates of travel	Jan 5-12	April 21-28
Destination	Austin, Tx	San Antonio, Tx
Purpose	Sales call	Consulting
Number of business travel days	3	5
Number of personal travel days	5	3
Transportation (total cost)	300	375
Lodging (cost per day)	125	110
Meals (cost per day)	60	70
Incidentals (cost per day)	20	15

8. Save the worksheet as **Travel Expense** in the Cases folder for Tutorial.07 on your Data Disk.

9. Print the formulas for the worksheet. Include row and column headers. Output the formulas on one page.

10. Create macros to clear the input section and print the worksheet. Assign each macro to a button. Use Taxpayer 2 data from Figure 7-48 to test your macros.

11. Apply cell protection to all cells in the worksheet except cells in the input section. Test the cell protection. Assign a color to identify the range that is unprotected.

12. Delete any unused worksheets in the workbook, then save and close the workbook.

(Note: If you get a Runtime error message box when testing a macro, click the End button to return to the worksheet. Review the steps in your macro and re-record the macro using the same name.)

Case 2. Sales Agreement Application for Desert Dreams   Desert Dreams, a self-contained community, is being developed in New Mexico by Adobe Sun Corporation as an environment to appeal to people of all ages. Desert Dreams offers lifestyle features such as an 18-hole golf course, state-of-the-art fitness center, swimming and tennis center, and hiking and bike paths. In addition, the floor plans for the houses in the development are winners of numerous architectural awards.

Interest in the community has been abundant. To assist the sales associates, you have been asked to develop a Sales Agreement worksheet to use with potential home buyers as they finalize the sale of a home.

The worksheet should summarize the total purchase price, which consists of the cost of the lot, the base price of the home, and the cost of extras (options). In addition, the worksheet should lay out the payment schedule for two alternative financing schedules: a cash plan and a mortgage payment plan. Figure 7-49 shows the information you need to include in your worksheet.

Do the following:

1. If necessary, start Excel and make sure your Data Disk is in the appropriate disk drive.

2. Design the worksheet with the two users in mind. Make it useful to sales associates as they enter data but also attractive and easy to follow for home buyers, who will receive a copy of the sales agreement. Consider dividing the worksheet into input and calculation/output sections. In your calculation/output section include a payment schedule for both the mortgage and cash financing plans. Use the information in Figure 7-49 as you build your worksheet. Name the sheet **Sales Agreement**.

Figure 7-49

Input
      Name of buyer
      Lot cost
      Base price of home
      Cost of options

Calculations
      Purchase Price = Lot cost + Base price of home + Cost of options

Financing Plan – Mortgage payment

1	Deposit at signing sales agreement	$7500
2	Down payment at start of construction	18% × purchase price
3	Final payment at closing	Purchase price less (down payment + deposit)
4	Total cash paid out	Sum of 3 payments

Financing Plan – Cash payments

1	Deposit at signing sales agreement	$15000
2	Down payment at start of construction	30% × purchase price
3	Payment at start of framing	35% × purchase price
4	Final payment at closing	Purchase price less (sum of 3 payments + cash discount)
5	Cash discount	2.5% of base price
6	Total cash paid out	Sum of payments (1 – 4)

---

3. Apply the following data validation rules:

    ■ Base price of home does not exceed $300,000.

    ■ Lot prices are between $20,000 and $100,000.

    ■ For each rule you should include an appropriate input and error alert message.

4. Create and use range names as you build formulas and in any other way you see fit. (*Hint:* Values in the input section and selected calculations are the most useful choices for range names.)

5. Format an attractive sales agreement worksheet, using features you have learned throughout the tutorials.

6. Save your workbook as **Sales Agreement** in the Cases folder for Tutorial.07 on your Data Disk.

7. Enter the data in Figure 7-50, and then print the worksheet.

Name of buyer	Helen Chomas
Lot cost	30000
Base price	160000
Options	12500

8. Develop macros to:

   a. clear input values from your input section. Name this macro ClearInputs and assign it to a button.
   b. print the portion of the worksheet that includes inputs and costs of both financing plans. Name this macro PrintData, and assign it to a button.

9. Helen Chomas has just selected some additional options which increased the options cost to $15,000. Make this change to the input section of your worksheet and use your PrintData macro to print a new output of the financing plans.

10. Create a Documentation sheet. Print the Documentation sheet.

Explore 11. Use the Index tab in the Help dialog box to learn how to "paste" range names and their associated addresses into your worksheet. Create a section in your Documentation sheet to include all range name information in your worksheet. Print the modified Documentation sheet.

12. Protect all cells in your worksheet except the cells where a user enters input values.

13. Save your worksheet, and then print the worksheet formulas. Remember to include row and column headers in your output.

Explore 14. Modify the Financing Plan - Mortgage to include a line for the monthly mortgage payment. Assume 8% annual interest, 25 years, and amount borrowed (use final payment at closing). Read Appendix 1 or use the Office Assistant to learn about the PMT function. Use your print macro to output the Sales Agreement worksheet.

15. Save and close the workbook.

Case 3. Customer Billing for Apex Auto Rental

Apex Auto Rental is the only car rental company in a midwest city. The company has been in business for two years. John Prescott, president and founder of Apex, has asked you to help him computerize the bills he gives to his customers.

Apex rents two types of cars: compact and luxury. The current rental rates are shown in Figure 7-51.

Figure 7-51

TYPE	CHARGE/DAY	CHARGE/MILE
Compact	$40	$0.25
Luxury	$50	$0.35

1. If necessary, start Excel and make sure your Data Disk is in the appropriate disk drive.

2. Develop a worksheet that calculates and prints customer bills. Divide your workbook into the following sheets:

   ■ A Documentation sheet that includes a title, your name, date developed, file-name, and purpose.

   ■ A worksheet for the customer bill. Name the worksheet **Customer Bill**. The customer bill should include the information shown in Figure 7-52. Divide your worksheet into input, calculation, and output sections. Use the layout in Figure 7-53 to design your output section. As you create your input and calculation sections, assign range names to these cells.

Figure 7-52

Assumptions
  Rental rate information (Figure 7-51)

Rental Inputs
  Customer name
  Type of car (compact or luxury)
  Number of days rented
  Number of miles driven

Calculations
  Charge per day (depends on type of car rented, which is entered in input section. Get charge from rental rate information)

  Charge per mile (depends on type of car rented, which is entered in input section. Get charge from rental rate information)

  Amount due = (days driven × charge per day) + (miles driven × charge per mile)

Figure 7-53

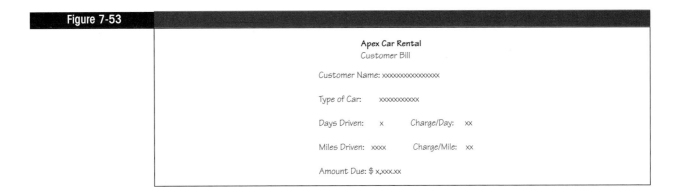

Apex Car Rental
Customer Bill

Customer Name: xxxxxxxxxxxxxx

Type of Car: xxxxxxxxxx

Days Driven: x   Charge/Day: xx

Miles Driven: xxxx   Charge/Mile: xx

Amount Due: $ x,xxx.xx

Explore   3. Apply the data validation rules from Figure 7-54 to the input section. You decide on appropriate input and error alert messages.

Figure 7-54

FIELD	RULE
Number of Days	<30
Number of miles	<5000
Type of car	List (use values from rental rate information)

4. Use the range names as you build the formulas for the customer bill.

5. Improve the appearance of your worksheet.

6. Save your worksheet as **Apex Rental** in the Cases folder for Tutorial.07.

7. Enter the Customer 1 data from Figure 7-55 into the input section of your worksheet. Print the entire worksheet.

Figure 7-55

INPUT FIELD	CUSTOMER 1	CUSTOMER 2
Customer name	Marisa Flowers	Henry Bibbs
Type of car	Compact	Luxury
Days driven	3	8
Miles driven	225	1150

8. Create macros to:
   a. clear the rental input section. Name this macro ClearInputs and assign the macro to a button.
   b. print only the customer bill. Name this macro PrintBill and assign it to a button.
   c. use the Customer 2 data from Figure 7-55 to test your macros.

9. Print the formulas (include row and column headers).

10. Apply cell protection to the worksheet cells, while permitting the user to enter data in the input section. Use color or shading to identify the unprotected area.

Case 4. Aging Invoices at Duchess Pools   MaryAnn Kodakci works in the accounting department of Duchess Pools. She has several reports to prepare for the monthly meeting and plans to use Excel to analyze the data. She's downloaded data on outstanding sales invoices and asks you to do the following:

1   Start Excel, open the file **Invoices** in the Tutorial folder for Tutorial.07 and save it as **Sales Invoices**.

2. Freeze the pane so the column headings and Invoice No field don't scroll off the screen as you navigate the sales Invoice list.

3. Compute the Number of days outstanding for each invoice.

   a. Place the label "Age as of" in cell A1 and "10/1/99" in cell B1. Assign the range name "AsOfDate" to cell B1.

   b. Subtract the Invoice date for each invoice from the Age as of date (cell B1) and place the result in the Days Outstanding column. (Note: when you subtract dates the displayed values may appear in a dd/mm/yy format. If this occurs, format the values using the General format so the values appear as numbers.)

4. Assign the Amount Owed to one of four columns (30 days or less, 31–60 days, 61–90 days, and Over 90 days.) Use the Days Outstanding, computed in Question 3, to determine which column to assign the Amount Owed to.

   (*Hint:* The amount owed for each invoice can only appear in one of the four columns; the other three should be equal to zero. You may want to read Appendix 1 or use Office Assistant to learn about the AND function.)

5. Prepare a macro to sort the Invoice list by Customer number and within customer number by Invoice date (earliest date first). Name the macro CustSort. Assign the macro to a button and place the button in rows 2 to 3 above the Cust No field in the Invoice list. Change the label on the button to read "Sort by customer". Test the macro.

Explore 6. Prepare a macro that goes to the last record in the list. Name the macro LastRecord (cell A100). Assign the macro to a button and place the button in rows 2 to 3. Change the label on the button to "Last Record". Test the macro.

7. Prepare a macro that goes to first record in the list. Name the macro FirstRecord (cell A5). Assign the macro to a button and place the button in rows 2 to 3. Change the label on the button to "First Record". Test the macro.

8. Prepare a macro that previews (Print Preview) invoices that have an Amount Owed greater than zero. This report should sort so the largest amount owed appears first. The page setup for the output should include a custom header with the sheet name and a custom footer with your name; landscape orientation, scaled to fit 1 page wide, and centered horizontally on the page. Name the macro AmtOwed. Assign the macro to a button on the worksheet and place the button in rows 2 to 3 above the Amount Owed field name in the Invoice list. Change the label on the button to read "Who Owes". Tasks on this macro include (1) filtering records, (2) sorting the filtered records, (3) setting Page Setup, (4) print previewing the filtered list, and (5) removing the filter arrows after closing the Print Preview window. Test the AmtOwed macro. Print the AmtOwed report.

   (*Note:* If you get a Runtime error Message box when you attempt to run the macro, click the End button to return to the worksheet. Review the steps in the macro and re-record the macro using the same name to replace the current macro.)

9. Save the workbook.

INTERNET ASSIGNMENTS

The purpose of the Internet Assignments is to challenge you to find information on the Internet that you can use to create effective spreadsheets. The actual assignments are updated and maintained on the Course Technology Web site. Log on to the Internet and use your Web browser to go to the Student Online Companion to accompany this text at **www.course.com/NewPerspectives/office2000**. Click the Excel link, and then click the link for Tutorial 7.

QUICK | CHECK ANSWERS

Session 7.1

1. if you enter a value that violates the validation rule
2. data validation
3. click on a cell
4. b and d
5. Name box
6. input section
7. IF Function
8. comparison operator

Session 7.2

1. AutoFill
2. Future Value; Financial
3. Cell protection prevents you from entering any data in a protected cell. Assuming a cell is unprotected, data validation allows you to specify what values users are allowed to enter in the cell.
4. A message box appears informing you that the cell is protected.
5. remove the Locked property from cells you want to be able to enter into, activate the Protect Sheet command
6. To help users identify them

Session 7.3

1. macro
2. recording, or entering Visual Basic code
3. Visual Basic for Applications or VBA
4. False. Macro names cannot contain spaces. Use an underscore.
5. current workbook, another workbook, or Personal Macro workbook
6. Click the Stop Recording button
7. Shortcut key (Ctrl + letter), command button object, Run button from Macro dialog box
8. provides a quick way to run a macro

OBJECTIVES

In this tutorial you will:

■ Insert, name, and move worksheets

■ Create worksheet groups

■ Edit multiple worksheets at the same time

■ Consolidate information from multiple worksheets and workbooks

■ Create a workbook template

■ Learn how to store templates

■ Create a lookup table and use Excel's lookup function

■ Create and use an Excel workspace

WORKING
WITH MULTIPLE WORKSHEETS AND WORKBOOKS

Creating Grading Sheets at MidWest University

CASE

MidWest University

Professor Karen White teaches calculus in the mathematics department at MidWest University, a liberal arts school that draws students from the Midwest and from across the United States. Her Calculus 223 course is one of the most popular courses in the department. Because her calculus course is required for computer science, as well as several other majors at the university, Professor White's lecture is filled with over 200 students each semester. Students attend Professor White's weekly lecture, as well as smaller biweekly discussion sections with a teaching assistant (TA) to receive extra instruction, discuss special topics, and work on problems. In addition to leading discussion sections, the four TAs assigned to Professor White's lecture are responsible for grading all the homework assignments, midterm exams, and final exams of the students in their sections. Professor White's TAs teach three discussion sections, each with about 20 students per section.

In the past, Professor White and her TAs have used handwritten grading sheets to keep track of homework and exam scores and to calculate final grades. Professor White feels that the accuracy and efficiency of record-keeping for her calculus course could be greatly improved if the TAs used Microsoft Excel 2000 for these tasks instead of the grading sheets currently used. She also thinks automating the record-keeping process would save time for her TAs, who carry full course loads in addition to their assistantships.

Professor White has asked you to use Excel to create a grading workbook that her TAs can use to both record the progress of their students and to give her an overall picture of how well all the classes, and each of her assistants, is doing. For each TA's sections, the workbook must be able to calculate the average of the homework and exam results, weigh each one according to the values determined by Professor White, and automatically assign a final letter grade. Professor White would also like to be able to combine the results from each TA's workbook into a single summary workbook, so she can combine and compare the information to evaluate TA performance. In addition, she would like to use Excel to automatically assign grades based on students' numeric scores.

As you plan a spreadsheet solution that meets Professor White's needs, you review her requirements. You know that you will need a worksheet that can display both the detail and summary information clearly, that can be readily distributed to the TAs, and that will have a consistent format so you can easily combine the results. To meet these goals, you explore the possibility of using multiple worksheets with Excel.

SESSION 8.1

In this session you will learn how to work with multiple worksheets, including inserting and moving worksheets. You'll learn how to work with groups of worksheets at the same time. Finally, you'll be introduced to 3-D cell references that allow you to summarize data from several worksheets.

Why Use Multiple Worksheets?

One of the most useful ways to organize information in your workbooks is to use multiple worksheets. Using multiple worksheets makes it easier for you to group your information. For example, a company with branches located in different regions could place sales information for each region on a separate worksheet. Users could then view regional sales information by clicking a sheet in the workbook, rather than scrolling through a large and complicated worksheet.

By using multiple worksheets, you can also more easily hide information that might not be of interest to all users. For example, if your director is only interested in the bottom line, the first worksheet could contain your conclusions and summary data, with more detailed information available on separate worksheets.

You can also use separate worksheets to organize your reports, because it is easier to print a single worksheet than it is to select and define a print area within a large worksheet and then print it.

Finally, if individual worksheets in a single workbook contain the same type of data and formatting (which is often true of documents like regional sales reports), Excel allows you to edit several worksheets simultaneously and to easily combine the results of several worksheets, saving you time.

Whenever you use multiple worksheets, it's important to plan the content and organization carefully.

Planning a Multiple-Sheet Workbook

Before creating a workbook with multiple worksheets, you should consider how you will organize the sheets to create a coherent and easy-to-use document. Proper organization is particularly important if other people will be using your workbook. One way of organizing your workbook is to create a Documentation sheet, data sheets, and a summary sheet.

As you know, a **Documentation sheet** describes the content, structure, and purpose of the workbook. Sometimes called a **Title sheet**, it is usually the first worksheet in a workbook. The Documentation sheet should include any information that you think would help other people who might use your workbook. It should list the source of the data, the assumptions you used in creating the workbook, and any conclusions you've derived from analyzing the workbook data. The Documentation sheet should enable anyone who opens your workbook to use it without additional assistance from you. Although the Excel File Properties dialog box and cell notes are useful tools for documenting worksheets, every well-designed workbook also should contain a Documentation sheet.

After the Documentation sheet, use a separate worksheet for each group you plan on including in the worksheet. These **data sheets** could contain data on different sales regions, departments, or areas of production. They can contain both data and charts.

Finally, if the information from each of the data sheets can be summarized, you should place this information in a **summary worksheet**. In the sales example, the summary worksheet could contain total sales figures for all the individual regions. You can place the summary sheet either at the start of the workbook after the Documentation sheet, or at the end. If you, or the people who will use the workbook, are more interested in the overall picture than in the details, place the summary worksheet at the beginning of the workbook. On the other hand, if you want your workbook to tell a "story" to the user, where the details are just as important as the final product, place the summary worksheet at the end of the workbook.

Professor White has sketched out the workbook structure she envisions, shown in Figure 8-1. The workbook will have a Documentation sheet that will include the TA's name, contact information, office hours, and class times for each of his or her sections. You'll place grades for each section on a separate worksheet. Because you know Professor White is as interested in the details as in the summary information, you'll place a summary of the discussion section grades on a summary sheet at the end of the workbook. Later on, you'll summarize the information on these summary sheets from each TA's workbook into a single workbook for Professor White to use.

| Figure 8-1 | PROPOSED STRUCTURE OF THE GRADING WORKBOOK EACH TA WILL USE |

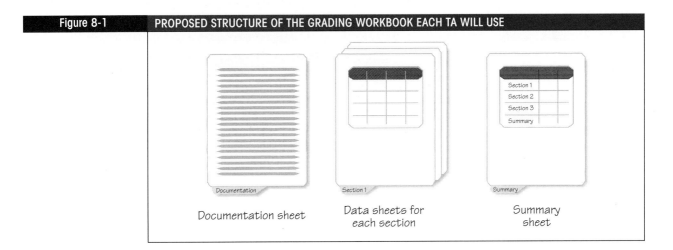

Documentation sheet   Data sheets for   Summary
                              each section   sheet

Inserting a Worksheet

To create Professor White's grading workbook, you begin by starting Excel, saving the new workbook, and creating a Documentation sheet and separate sheets for each of the sections. Because you are the author of this workbook and the person who will be responsible for maintaining it, you will also add your name and the date that the workbook was created.

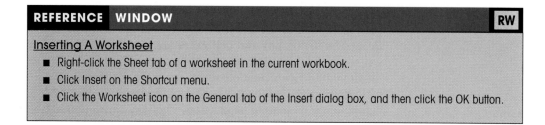

REFERENCE WINDOW **RW**

Inserting A Worksheet
- Right-click the Sheet tab of a worksheet in the current workbook.
- Click Insert on the Shortcut menu.
- Click the Worksheet icon on the General tab of the Insert dialog box, and then click the OK button.

First you'll create a new workbook and practice adding a new sheet to that workbook.

To create the new workbook and insert a new worksheet:

1. Start Excel as usual, and make sure your Data Disk is in the appropriate drive.

2. Open a new workbook and save as **Grades** in the Tutorial folder in Tutorial.08 folder on your Data Disk.

3. Right-click the **Sheet1** sheet tab, and then click **Insert** on the Shortcut menu to open the Insert dialog box.

   You could also have modified one of the blank sheets, turning it into the Documentation sheet. This approach however gives you a chance to practice inserting new sheets into your workbook.

4. Click the **Worksheet** icon, as shown in Figure 8-2, and then click the **OK** button.

| Figure 8-2 | INSERT DIALOG BOX |

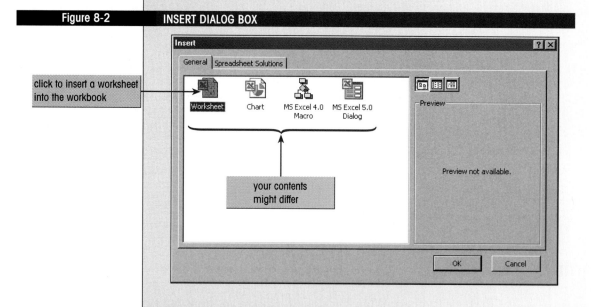

click to insert a worksheet into the workbook

your contents might differ

5. Double-click the new worksheet's sheet tab, type **Documentation**, and then press the **Enter** key.

Next, you'll enter Documentation sheet information.

To set up the Documentation sheet:

1. Enter the following titles in the Documentation worksheet:

   Cell A1: **TA Name**
   Cell A2: **Office**
   Cell A3: **Phone #**
   Cell A4: **Office Hours**
   Cell A6: **Section 1**
   Cell A7: **Section 2**
   Cell A8: **Section 3**
   Cell A10: **Purpose:**
   Cell A13: **Workbook:**
   Cell A14: **Created by:**
   Cell A15: **Date Created:**
   Cell B5: **Section Times**
   Cell C5: **Location**

   Now enter the purpose of the worksheet.

2. Click cell **B10**, type **To record the grades for Section 1 - Section 3** and then press the **Enter** key.

3. In cell B11, enter the following text: **discussion groups of Prof. White's Calculus 223 lecture**.

4. Type **Grades** in cell B13.

5. Enter [*Your Name*] and the date in cells B14 and B15, respectively.

6. Apply the boldface style to the ranges A1:A15 and B5:C5. Adjust the width of column A to make the column fit its content, resize columns B and C to 25 characters, and then press **Ctrl + Home** to return to cell A1. See Figure 8-3.

Figure 8-3	COMPLETED DOCUMENTATION SHEET

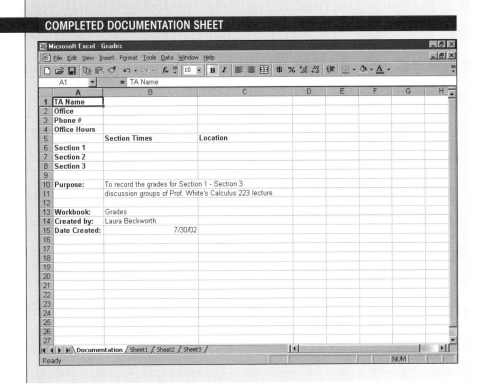

You'll leave the rest of the Documentation sheet to be completed by the TAs when they start using your workbook. Next you'll set up the individual grading sheets.

Moving **Worksheets**

Now that you have created a Documentation sheet, you'll create the grading sheet for each discussion section. Each of Professor White's four TAs teaches three discussion sections, so you'll be inserting three grading sheets into the workbook.

As you saw when you created the Documentation sheet, Excel places new worksheets directly to the left of the currently selected sheet. You want the Documentation sheet to be the first sheet in the workbook, so you'll have to move the new grading sheet directly to the right of the Documentation sheet. You can do this using drag and drop.

REFERENCE **WINDOW**   **RW**

Moving or Copying A Worksheet
- Click the tab of the worksheet you want to move.
- Drag the sheet tab along the row of sheet tabs until the small arrow is in the desired location.
- Release the mouse button.
- To create a copy of the worksheet, hold down the Ctrl key as you drag the sheet tab to the desired location.

Try moving the first grading sheet now.

To insert and move the first grading sheet:

1. Right-click the **Documentation** sheet tab, and then click **Insert** on the Shortcut menu.

2. Make sure the Worksheet icon is selected, and then click the **OK** button.

3. Double-click the tab of the new worksheet, type **Section 1**, and then press the **Enter** key.

4. Click the **Section 1** tab, and then hold down the mouse button so that your pointer changes to ⬚, and drag it directly to the right of the Documentation sheet.

5. Release the mouse button.

6. Repeat the technique from Steps 1 through 5 to insert two additional worksheets named **Section 2** and **Section 3**, placed after the Section 1 worksheet. See Figure 8-4.

Figure 8-4	GRADES WORKBOOK WITH THREE GRADING SHEETS

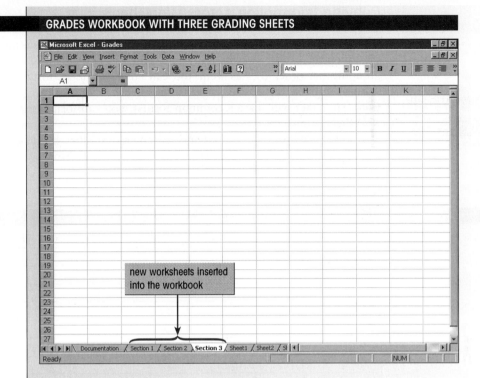

Your workbook now contains the Documentation sheet and the grading sheets you need. Next you'll remove the extra worksheets from the workbook, which you can do in one step by creating a worksheet group.

Working **with Worksheet Groups**

When you start the Excel program, it opens a new workbook with three blank worksheets (although your version of Excel might be set up to display a different number of worksheets). You don't need these additional sheets in Professor White's workbook, so you can delete them. You could delete the sheets one at a time, but it's more efficient to select the entire group of worksheets and delete them all at once.

To group and delete the worksheets:

1. Click the **Sheet1** sheet tab.

2. Press and hold down the **Shift** key and click the rightmost worksheet in the workbook (you might have to click the Last Worksheet button to see it.) All three sheet tabs become white, indicating that they are selected.

3. Right-click any one of the selected sheets, and then click **Delete** on the Shortcut menu.

4. Click the **OK** button to confirm the deletion. The blank worksheets are deleted from your workbook.

Your workbook is now set up according to Professor White's sketch. Next you'll add column titles to the Section 1 grading worksheet, which you can then copy to the other worksheets.

Copying Information Across Worksheets

The process you used to select multiple worksheets for deletion is called **grouping**. Grouping the blank worksheets in the Grading workbook made it easy to delete them, but grouping has other uses as well. You can enter formulas, format and copy values into a worksheet group, or create range names for each sheet in the group. If you have several worksheets that will share a common format, you can format them all at once by using a worksheet group.

Professor White hands you a handwritten grading sheet from a previous semester, shown in Figure 8-5. She would like the grading sheets in your workbook to have the same structure as this sheet.

Figure 8-5

PROFESSOR WHITE'S GRADING SHEET

Student ID	Homework 1	Homework 2	Homework 3	Homework 4	Exam 1	Exam 2	Final	Overall	Grade
1001	90	95	92	88	96	89	91	90	A
1002	81	88	85	70	88	72	80	81	B
1003	85	85	90	95	86	92	95	93	A
1004	81	78	65	75	80	72	76	75	BC
1005	99	65	100	99	100	100	95	95	A
1006	81	90	92	85	88	85	86	86	AB
1007	70	100	72	75	75	70	71	74	BC
1008	95	95	95	90	91	92	88	88	AB
1009	94	100	100	81	100	91	93	96	A
1010	100	95	81	96	96	84	89	88	AB
1011	100	100	100	100	100	100	98	98	A
1012	95	94	92	96	95	93	97	97	A
1013	100	100	92	96	100	91	94	98	A
1014	70	75	70	72	76	69	78	77	BC
1015	85	92	81	88	91	84	87	86	B
1016	81	68	75	60	81	65	71	70	C
1017	88	92	84	87	90	65	85	87	AB
1018	75	72	71	75	73	81	71	70	C
1019	92	81	84	85	87	65	87	86	B
1020	94	96	93	90	95	84	91	90	AB

Professor White scores homework and exams on a 100-point scale. She then calculates an overall average of each student's scores and assigns a letter grade based on the average. Professor White uses the traditional ABC grading system with grades of AB and BC assigned to intermediate grades. Because she gives the same assignments and tests for every section, you can create column titles for the Section 1 grading sheet and then copy them to the Section 2 and Section 3 worksheets.

To add column titles to the Section 1 worksheet:

1. Click the **Section 1** sheet tab.

2. Type **ID** in cell A1, and then press the **Tab** key.

3. Type **Home1** in cell B1, and then press the **Tab** key.

4. Continue entering the following column titles in the first row of the worksheet: **Home2**, **Home3**, **Home4**, **Exam1**, **Exam2**, and **Final**. See Figure 8-6.

| Figure 8-6 | COLUMN TITLES FOR THE SECTION 1 GRADING WORKSHEET |

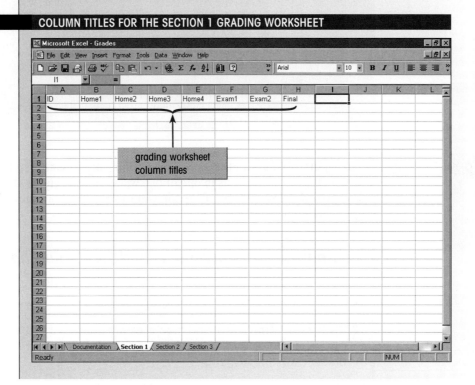

With the column titles in place, you'll group the worksheets and use the Excel Fill Across Worksheets command to copy the titles to the other two grading sheets.

To copy the Section 1 column titles:

1. Select the range **A1:H1**.

2. Press and hold down the **Shift** key and click the **Section 3** tab, and then release the **Shift** key.

3. Click **Edit** on the menu bar, point to **Fill**, and then click **Across Worksheets**.

4. Click the **All** option button, and then click the **OK** button.

The Fill Across Worksheets command only copies the cells that you've selected. When you use the Fill Across Worksheets command, you can copy the contents of the selected cells only, the formats, or both. In the preceding steps, you copied both the cell contents and formats.

REFERENCE   WINDOW   **RW**

Grouping And Ungrouping Worksheets

- Click the sheet tab of the first worksheet in the group, press and hold down the Shift key, and then click the sheet tab of the last sheet in the group.
- To select non-consecutive worksheets, press and hold down the Ctrl key, and then click the sheet tab of each worksheet you want to include.
- To ungroup worksheets, either click the sheet tab of a worksheet not in the group, or right-click the tab of one of the sheets in the group, and select Ungroup Sheets on the Shortcut menu.

To begin working with the individual grading sheets again, you must first ungroup them. You can ungroup worksheets in one of two ways: You can click a sheet in the workbook that is not part of the worksheet group, or you can use the Ungroup Sheets command on the worksheet's Shortcut menu.

To ungroup the worksheets and view your changes:

1. Right-click the sheet tab of any of the selected sheets.

2. Click **Ungroup Sheets** on the Shortcut menu.

3. Click the **Section 2** tab, and then click the **Section 3** tab. You can see that the titles you entered on the Section 1 worksheet are copied into both the Section 2 and Section 3 worksheets.

   With the basic structure of the grading sheets in place, your next task will be to enter formulas that summarize the students' test scores. This information is available in another workbook.

4. Click the **Documentation** sheet tab, and then press **Ctrl + Home** to return to cell A1.

5. Save and close the Grades workbook, leaving Excel running.

You're now ready to work with some sample data.

Entering Text and Formulas into a Worksheet Group

Professor White has given you the scores of former students in her class from a previous semester. This data has been placed in the Grades2 workbook. Open and view this workbook now.

To view Professor White's workbook of previous grades:

1. Open the **Grades2** workbook in the Tutorial folder for Tutorial.08 on your Data Disk and save the workbook as **Grades3**.

2. Enter **Grades3** in cell B13 of the Documentation sheet along with (*Your Name*) and the data in cells B14:B15.

3. Click the **Section 1** sheet tab. The Section 1 worksheet displays scores for all the homework assignments, exams, and the final exam for each of 20 students. See Figure 8-7.

| Figure 8-7 | SAMPLE STUDENT SCORES IN THE SECTION 1 WORKSHEET |

Microsoft Excel - Grades3

File Edit View Insert Format Tools Data Window Help

Arial   10   **B** *I* U

A1   = ID

	A	B	C	D	E	F	G	H	I	J	K	L
1	ID	Home1	Home2	Home3	Home4	Exam1	Exam2	Final				
2	1101	64	77	63	97	72	98	62				
3	1102	86	86	85	81	84	87	68				
4	1103	67	69	51	75	86	72	54				
5	1104	91	94	94	88	90	94	91				
6	1105	83	55	72	77	82	64	54				
7	1106	82	83	73	86	92	70	87				
8	1107	97	93	97	94	95	94	97				
9	1108	64	49	65	72	63	28	65				
10	1109	71	23	52	61	69	39	21				
11	1110	80	79	92	100	92	88	94				
12	1111	93	83	92	90	93	90	89				
13	1112	98	98	98	97	97	97	96				
14	1113	83	82	49	57	46	70	85				
15	1114	58	73	60	66	73	77	75				
16	1115	78	66	47	70	46	54	66				
17	1116	85	85	93	89	85	71	86				
18	1117	64	65	63	108	46	55	69				
19	1118	90	94	93	95	100	86	83				
20	1119	66	40	63	82	64	70	79				
21	1120	80	92	88	84	92	97	82				
22												
23												
24												
25												
26												
27												

Documentation **Section 1** Section 2 Section 3

Ready   NUM

4. Look at the Section 2 and Section 3 worksheets, and verify that they also contain sample scores, and then return to the Section 1 worksheet.

As you look over the grading sheets, you realize that you still have to create a column for each student's overall score. In Professor White's grading system, the average homework grade is worth 20%, the average of the two midterm exams is worth 40%, and the final exam counts for 40% of the final grade. To create this column for all three grading sheets, you could add a column to the Section 1 grading sheet that calculates this weighted average and then use the Fill Across Worksheets command to transfer the formula to the remaining sheets. Another option, which will save you a step, is to group the three grading sheets together and enter the formula simultaneously in all three sheets. You'll try this method now.

To add the weighted average to all grading sheets:

1. With the Section 1 tab still selected, press and hold down the **Shift** key and click the **Section 3** tab to group the worksheets. Notice that the word "(Group)" appears in the title bar, indicating that a group is selected.

2. Click cell **I1**, type **Overall**, and then press the **Enter** key. Now you'll enter the formula for the weighted averages.

3. In cell I2, type **=20%*AVERAGE(B2:E2)+40%*AVERAGE(F2:G2)+40%*H2** and then press the **Enter** key. The first student's average score of 73.85 appears in cell I2, this being the sum of the weighted averages of the student's grades (20%), midterm exams (40%), and final exam (40%.) Now you'll copy the formula to calculate the averages for the rest of the students.

4. Click cell **I2** and then click and drag the fill handle down to cell **I21**.

The weighted average scores for the Section 1 worksheet are shown in Figure 8-8.

Figure 8-8 **WEIGHTED AVERAGES FOR SAMPLE STUDENT SCORES IN SECTION 1**

title bar shows that a worksheet group is selected

weighted average formula

Microsoft Excel - Grades3 [Group]

I2 = =20%*AVERAGE(B2:E2)+40%*AVERAGE(F2:G2)+40%*H2

ID	Home1	Home2	Home3	Home4	Exam1	Exam2	Final	Overall
1101	64	77	63	97	72	98	62	73.85
1102	86	86	85	81	84	87	68	78.3
1103	67	69	51	75	86	72	54	66.3
1104	91	94	94	88	90	94	91	91.55
1105	83	55	72	77	82	64	54	65.15
1106	82	83	73	86	92	70	87	83.4
1107	97	93	97	94	95	94	97	95.65
1108	64	49	65	72	63	28	65	56.7
1109	71	23	52	61	69	39	21	40.35
1110	80	79	92	100	92	88	94	91.15
1111	93	83	92	90	93	90	89	90.1
1112	98	98	98	97	97	97	96	96.75
1113	83	82	49	57	46	70	85	70.75
1114	58	73	60	66	73	77	75	72.85
1115	78	66	47	70	46	54	66	59.45
1116	85	85	93	89	85	71	86	83.2
1117	64	65	63	108	46	55	69	62.8
1118	90	94	93	95	100	86	83	89
1119	66	40	63	82	64	70	79	70.95
1120	80	92	88	84	92	97	82	87.8

weighted averages

worksheet group is selected

Documentation / **Section 1** / Section 2 / Section 3

Ready   Sum=1526.05   NUM

Because you have grouped the worksheets, the formulas you entered in the Section 1 worksheet should also have been entered in the corresponding cells on the other worksheets in the group.

5. Click the **Section 2** sheet tab. The worksheet displays the new column of weighted averages shown in Figure 8-9.

Figure 8-9 **WEIGHTED AVERAGES FOR SAMPLE STUDENT SCORES IN SECTION 2**

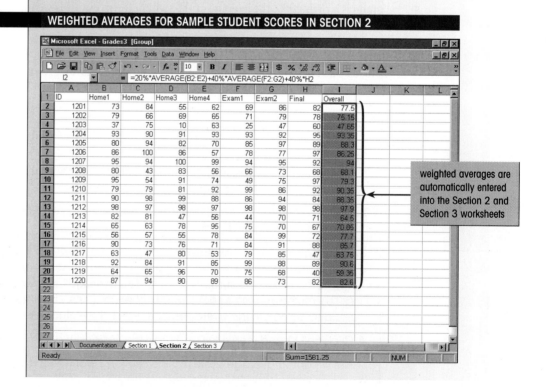

Microsoft Excel - Grades3 [Group]

I2 = =20%*AVERAGE(B2:E2)+40%*AVERAGE(F2:G2)+40%*H2

ID	Home1	Home2	Home3	Home4	Exam1	Exam2	Final	Overall
1201	73	84	55	62	69	86	82	77.5
1202	79	66	69	65	71	79	78	75.15
1203	37	75	10	63	25	47	60	47.65
1204	93	90	91	93	93	92	95	93.35
1205	80	94	82	70	85	97	89	88.3
1206	86	100	86	57	78	77	97	86.25
1207	95	94	100	99	94	95	92	94
1208	80	43	83	56	66	73	68	68.1
1209	95	54	91	74	49	75	97	79.3
1210	79	79	81	92	99	86	92	90.35
1211	90	98	99	88	86	94	84	88.35
1212	98	97	98	97	98	98	98	97.9
1213	82	81	47	56	44	70	71	64.5
1214	65	63	78	95	75	70	67	70.85
1215	56	57	55	78	84	99	72	77.7
1216	90	73	76	71	84	91	88	85.7
1217	63	47	80	53	79	85	47	63.75
1218	92	84	91	85	99	88	89	90.6
1219	64	65	96	70	75	68	40	59.35
1220	87	94	90	89	86	73	82	82.6

weighted averages are automatically entered into the Section 2 and Section 3 worksheets

Documentation / Section 1 \ **Section 2** / Section 3

Ready   Sum=1581.25   NUM

6. View the sample scores for the Section 3 worksheet, and then return to the Section 1 worksheet, leaving the sheets grouped.

Although Professor White's grading sheet from last semester included only the individual scores for each test and the weighted average for each student, it would probably be helpful for her and her TAs to see the section average for each homework assignment and exam. Then they could quickly see how the whole section scored on an exam or homework assignment. To create section averages, you will add an additional row to each grading sheet that averages the scores entered into the columns.

To insert a formula calculating homework and exam averages:

1. Click cell A22, type **Average**, and then press the **Tab** key.

2. In cell B22, type **=AVERAGE(B2:B21)** and then press the **Tab** key. The value 79 appears in cell B22.

3. Click cell **B22** and then drag the fill handle to cell **I22**.

Figure 8-10 displays the Section 1 averages for homework assignments and exams.

Figure 8-10	SECTION 1 AVERAGES FOR HOMEWORK ASSIGNMENTS AND EXAMS

Microsoft Excel - Grades3 [Group]

File Edit View Insert Format Tools Data Window Help

B22   =   =AVERAGE(B2:B21)

	A	B	C	D	E	F	G	H	I	J	K	L
1	ID	Home1	Home2	Home3	Home4	Exam1	Exam2	Final	Overall			
2	1101	64	77	63	97	72	98	62	73.85			
3	1102	86	86	85	81	84	87	68	78.3			
4	1103	67	69	51	75	86	72	54	66.3			
5	1104	91	94	94	88	90	94	91	91.55			
6	1105	83	55	72	77	82	64	54	65.15			
7	1106	82	83	73	86	92	70	87	83.4			
8	1107	97	93	97	94	95	94	97	95.65			
9	1108	64	49	65	72	63	28	65	56.7			
10	1109	71	23	52	61	69	39	21	40.35			
11	1110	80	79	92	100	92	88	94	91.15			
12	1111	93	83	92	90	93	90	89	90.1			
13	1112	98	98	98	97	97	97	96	96.75			
14	1113	83	82	49	57	46	70	85	70.75			
15	1114	58	73	60	66	73	77	75	72.85			
16	1115	78	66	47	70	46	54	66	59.45			
17	1116	85	85	93	89	85	71	86	83.2			
18	1117	64	65	63	108	46	55	69	62.8			
19	1118	90	94	93	95	100	86	83	89			
20	1119	66	40	63	82	64	70	79	70.95			
21	1120	80	92	88	84	92	97	82	87.8			
22	Average	79	74.3	74.5	83.45	78.35	75.05	75.15	76.3025			
23												
24												
25												
26												
27												

Documentation \ Section 1 / Section 2 / Section 3

Ready   Sum=616.1025   NUM

Because the three grading sheets are still grouped together, the formulas in the Section 1 worksheet are also entered into the Section 2 and Section 3 worksheets.

Now that you have entered the formulas that will calculate the section averages Professor White and her TAs need, you'll format the worksheet to make it attractive and readable.

Formatting a Worksheet Group

You have used worksheet groups to insert formulas and text into more than one worksheet at once. You can also use groups to simultaneously format the appearance of multiple worksheets. You decide to format the test scores, and use one of the Excel built-in worksheet designs to format the column titles.

To format the column averages, totals, and scores:

1. Make sure the Section 1 worksheet is selected, and that the three section worksheets are still grouped.

2. Select the range **I2:I21**, and then click the **Increase Decimal** button on the Excel toolbar.

3. Select the range **B22:I22**, and then click three times.

   Now both the overall totals and averages appear to three decimal place accuracy. Next you'll format the appearance of the values.

4. Select the range **A1:I22**, click **Format** on the menu bar, and then click **AutoFormat**.

5. Click **Classic 3** from the Table format list, and then click the **OK** button.

6. Press **Ctrl + Home** to return to cell A1.

7. The worksheet is now formatted with the Classic 3 AutoFormat. See Figure 8-11.

Figure 8-11	FORMATTED SECTION 1 WORKSHEET

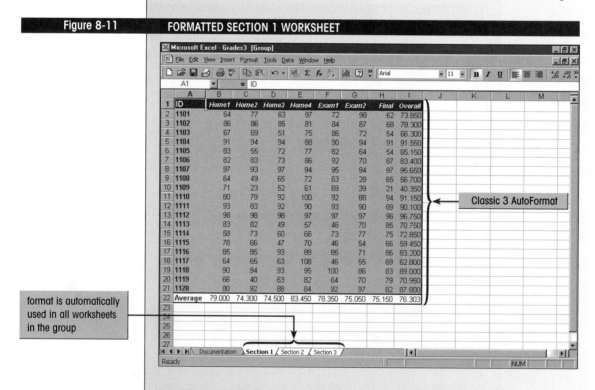

format is automatically used in all worksheets in the group

Classic 3 AutoFormat

8. View the Section 2 and Section 3 worksheets to verify that the format has been applied to all three sheets, then click the **Section 1** sheet tab.

9. Right-click the **Section 1** tab, and then click **Ungroup Sheets** on the Shortcut menu to ungroup the worksheets.

Creating a Summary Worksheet

Now that you have used sample scores in your workbook to calculate student and section averages and formatted the worksheets, you'll summarize the data from the three sections into a single worksheet. Using the summary worksheet, the TAs can get a quick comparison of the different sections.

First, you'll create the summary worksheet, then you can use the techniques you've learned so far to copy the format of the grading sheets into the new summary worksheet.

To create and format the summary sheet:

1. Insert a blank worksheet at the end of the workbook named **Summary**.

2. Group together the Section 3 and Summary worksheets.

   TROUBLE? If you have not ungrouped the Section 1 - Section 3 sheets, you should do so now.

3. Select the cell range **A1:I22** on the Section 3 worksheet.

4. Click **Edit** on the menu bar, point to **Fill**, and then click **Across Worksheets**.

   The Fill Across Worksheets dialog box opens, asking if you want to fill the contents, formats, or both.

5. Click the **Formats** option button, and then click the **OK** button.

   Now, you'll copy the column titles to the Summary worksheet.

6. Select the cell range **A1:I1**, click **Edit** on the menu bar, point to **Fill**, and then click **Across Worksheets**.

7. Click the **Contents** option button, and then click the **OK** button.

The grading sheet that you used to create the Summary sheet contains information for 20 students. Because the Summary sheet will summarize the results from only three sections, you'll have to remove the unnecessary rows from the table.

To complete the Summary worksheet:

1. Ungroup the worksheets and then select the Summary sheet.

2. Select the cell range **A5:I21**, click **Edit** on the menu bar, and then click **Delete**.

3. Click the **Shift cells up** option button, and then click the **OK** button.

4. Click cell **A1**, type **Section**, and then press the **Enter** key.

5. Enter the following in column A:

   Cell A2: **1**
   Cell A3: **2**
   Cell A4: **3**
   Cell A5: **All**

6. Press **Ctrl + Home** to return to cell A1.

   Figure 8-12 shows the final layout of the Summary sheet.

Figure 8-12   **SUMMARY WORKSHEET**

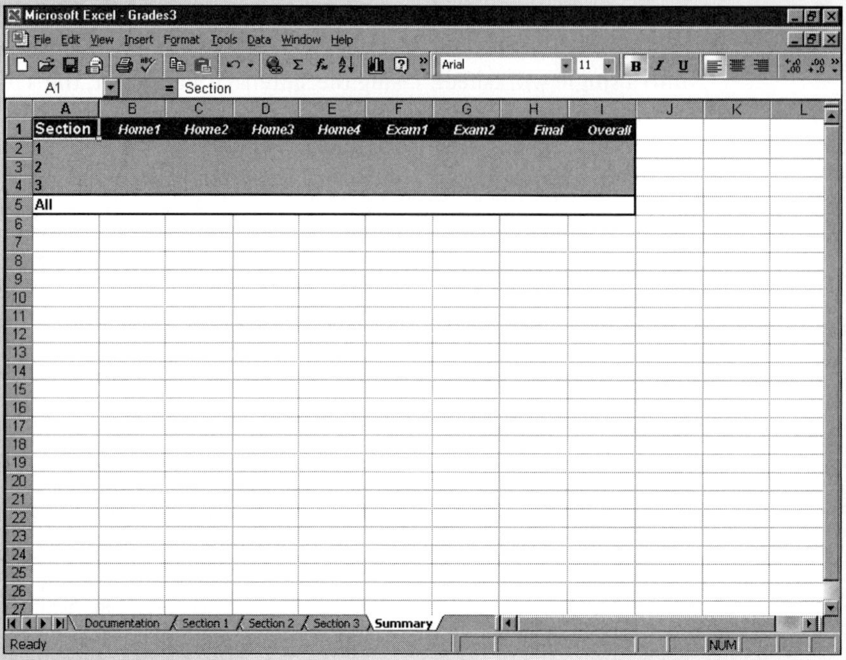

Having set up the Summary sheet, you are ready to start consolidating the information from the individual sections.

Consolidating Data with 3-D References

When you consolidate worksheet data, you use formulas that summarize the results contained in several worksheets (or workbooks) into a single cell. For example, consolidation formulas can total sales figures from several regional sales worksheets, or simply report the values from several regions, in one easy-to-read table. In your grading workbook, you want the Summary worksheet to consolidate grading information from the individual sections, showing the section averages for each homework assignment and exam. You'll then use this information to calculate an overall average, pooling information from all the sections that the TA is teaching. Figure 8-13 shows a diagram of the consolidation you'll be creating.

Figure 8-13 | **CONSOLIDATING THE SECTION WORKSHEETS**

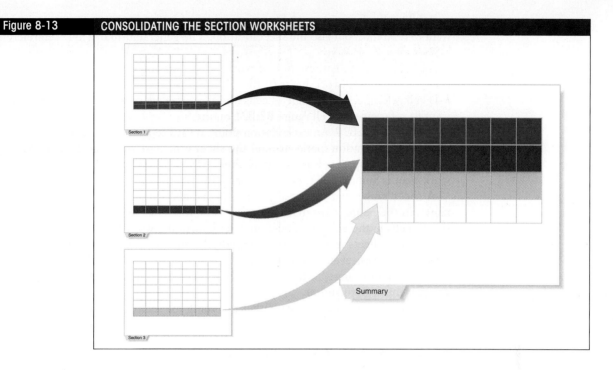

To consolidate data in a workbook, you need to know some of the basic rules for referencing cells in other worksheets. Cell references that specify cells in other worksheets are called 3-D cell references. As shown in Figure 8-14, you can consider the rows and columns as representing two dimensions. The worksheets themselves comprise the third dimension.

Figure 8-14 | **THE THREE DIMENSIONS OF A WORKBOOK**

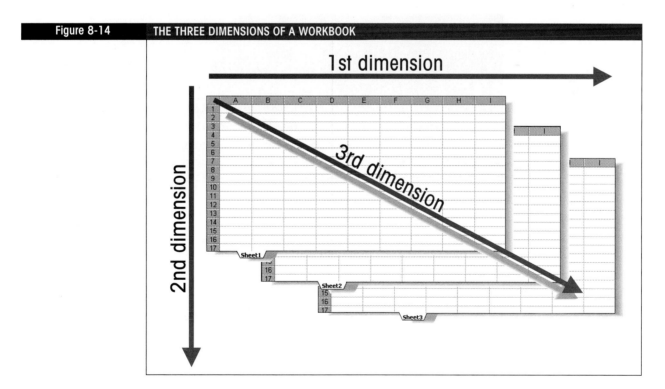

A 3-D cell reference must include not only the rows and columns that contain the data you want to reference, but also the sheet location. The general form of a 3-D cell reference is:

Sheet Range!Cell Range

The sheet range is the range of worksheets that you're referencing. It can be a single sheet or a group of worksheets (if the group is contiguous). The cell range portion of the 3-D cell reference is the range of cells on the worksheet or worksheets. For example, if you want to reference the cell range B2:B21 on the Section 1 worksheet, the 3-D cell reference is 'Section 1'!B2:B21. An exclamation point always separates the sheet range from the cell range. The quotation marks around the sheet range are only necessary if the sheet name contains blank spaces. For example, the 3-D cell reference to cell B1 on the Summary worksheet is Summary!B1, not 'Summary'!B1.

A sheet range that covers a group of worksheets must include the first and last sheet names in the range, separated by a colon. The reference 'Section 1:Section 3'!A1, refers to the A1 cells in the Section 1, Section 2, and Section 3 worksheets. When you are including several worksheets in the sheet range, you do not enclose each worksheet name in single quotation marks, even if the sheet name contains spaces—just the sheet range. In other words, the sheet range 'Section 1:Section 3' is correct, but 'Section 1':'Section 3' will cause an error message to appear.

You enter 3-D cell references either by typing the reference or by selecting the appropriate cells with the mouse as you enter the formula. If you are using the mouse, you must first select the sheet range, followed by the cell range.

A note of caution: Calculations or charts based on data on a worksheet might become inaccurate if you move the worksheet. Similarly, if you move a new worksheet into the middle of a sheet range referred to elsewhere by a 3-D formula reference, the data on the new worksheet might be included in the calculation. It's generally a good idea NOT to move worksheets around in your workbook if they contain 3-D cell references.

REFERENCE WINDOW   **RW**

<u>Inserting A Formula Using A 3-D Cell Reference</u>
- Select the cell where you want the formula to appear.
- Type = and the function name, if any.
- Click the sheet tab for the sheet containing the cell (or cells) that you want to reference.
- To reference a range of worksheets, press and hold down the Shift key, and then click the tab of the last sheet in the range.
- Click the cell range you want to reference.
- Finish the formula and then press the Enter key.

You'll use 3-D cell references to calculate the average scores from each of the three sections taught by the TA. You can begin by consolidating the exam and homework averages from Section 1 into the Summary worksheet.

To insert the Section 1 averages into the Summary worksheet:

1. Click cell **B2** on the Summary worksheet.

2. Type **=**

3. Click the **Section 1** sheet tab (you might have to scroll through the sheet tabs to see it.)

4. Click cell **B22** and then press the **Enter** key.

The value 79 appears in the Summary sheet in cell B2. Now go back and view the formula.

5. Click cell **B2** and see that the formula ='Section 1'!B22 appears in the formula bar. Now that you know the formula is correct, you'll copy it to the other summary cells for Section 1.

6. Drag the fill handle from cell B2 to cell **I2** and release the mouse button.

Each exam and homework average score for Section 1 now appears in the range B2:I2. See Figure 8-15.

Figure 8-15	SUMMARY SCORES FOR SECTION 1

3-D cell reference

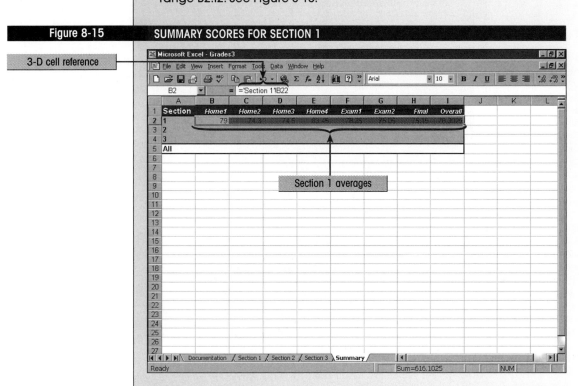

Section 1 averages

7. Repeat this technique to create references to the exam and homework averages in the range B3:I3 for Section 2 and in the range B4:I4 for Section 3.

8. Figure 8-16 shows the Summary sheet with average scores from each section.

Figure 8-16

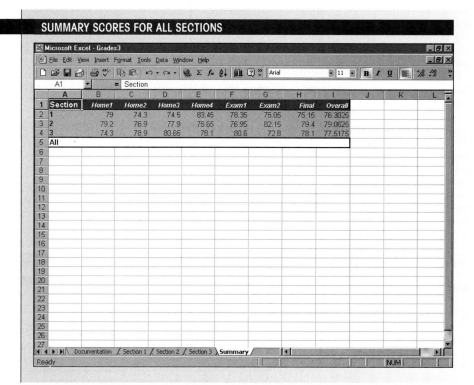

SUMMARY SCORES FOR ALL SECTIONS

Now you'll complete the final part of the Summary worksheet, the average scores across all sections for homework assignments and exams.

To insert overall averages:

1. With the Summary sheet still selected, click cell **B5**.

2. Type **=AVERAGE(** to begin the function.

3. Click the **Section 1** sheet tab, press and hold down the **Shift** key and click the **Section 3** tab. The formula bar shows that the worksheet range for the three sections has been entered into the function.

4. Click cell **B22**, type **)** (a closing parenthesis), and then press the **Enter** key.

   Excel inserts the formula, "=AVERAGE('Section 1:Section 3'!B22)" into cell B5, displaying the value 77.500.

5. Click **B5** and drag the fill handle to cell **I5**. The overall averages for all tests for all sections appear in the All row.

6. Select the range **B2:I5** and then click the **Increase Decimal** button on the Formatting toolbar three times. All the numbers in the table should now appear with three decimal place accuracy.

7. Press **Ctrl + Home** to return to cell A1.

   Figure 8-17 shows the completed Summary sheet.

Figure 8-17   **COMPLETED SUMMARY WORKSHEET**

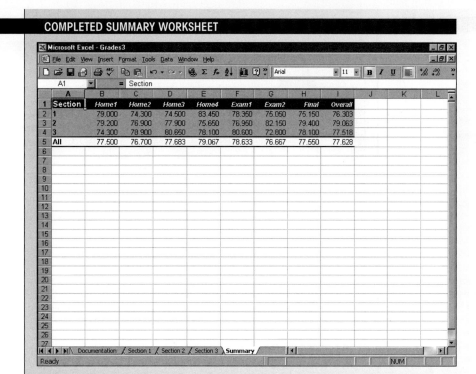

The summary table you've just created will be automatically updated whenever sample scores in the individual grading sheets are added or changed. To test this feature, you decide to change one of the sample scores in the Section 1 worksheet. First, notice that the current overall average for Section 1 is 76.303 and the average across all three sections is 77.628.

To change one of the values in the Section 1 worksheet:

1. Click the **Section 1** sheet tab.

2. Click cell **H2**, type **92**, and then press the **Enter** key.

3. Click the **Summary** sheet tab.

   Figure 8-18 shows the revised values in the Summary worksheet.

| Figure 8-18 | REVISED SUMMARY WORKSHEET |

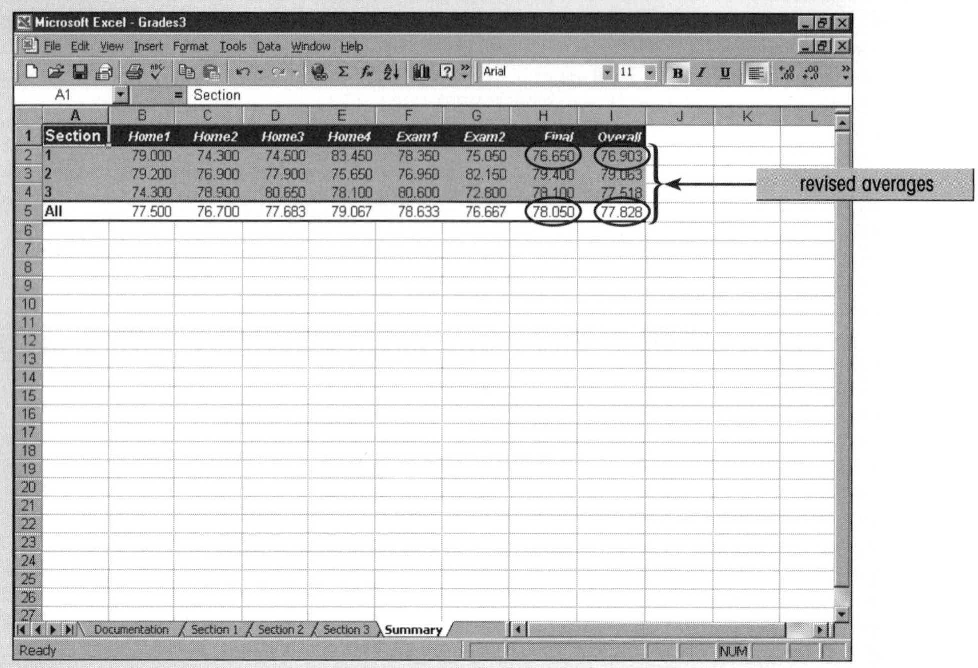

revised averages

By changing the value of the score in cell H2 of the Section 1 worksheet from 62 to 92, the overall average for Section 1 is increased from 76.303 to 76.903 and the overall average for all sections is automatically increased from 77.628 to 77.828.

Now that you've completed your grading worksheets, you can print them using worksheet groups.

Printing Worksheet Groups

Now that you've completed the grading workbook, you decide to print it, but first you'll set up the pages. You can set up your pages individually, or you can quickly format all the worksheets by using the Page Setup command to apply to all the worksheets in the group. You decide to print the grading sheets and the Summary sheet centered on the page both vertically and horizontally, with the worksheet name in the page header and the workbook name in the page footer.

To print the grading sheets and the Summary sheet:

1. Group the range of worksheets from Section 1 to Summary.

2. Click **File** on the menu bar, and then click **Page Setup**.

3. Click the **Margins** tab and then select the **Center on page Horizontally** and **Vertically** check boxes.

4. Click the **Header/Footer** tab, click **Section 1** in the Header list box and then click **Grades3** in the Footer list box to place the worksheet name in the header and the workbook name in the footer for all the worksheets in the group.

> TROUBLE? If Section 1 does not appear in your list box but Summary does, this just means you clicked the Summary tab first when you selected the range. Click Cancel, reselect the group, then reopen the dialog box and continue. If you see "Grades3.xls" instead of "Grades3" in the footer list box, use that instead.

5. Click the **Print Preview** button and verify that the same page setup has been used for all sheets in the worksheet group, using the Next and Previous buttons at the top of the Preview window to view each sheet. Figure 8-19 displays the Section 1 worksheet in Print Preview.

Figure 8-19   **PRINT PREVIEW OF THE SECTION 1 WORKSHEET**

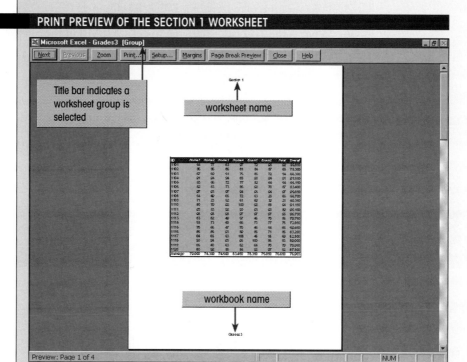

6. Click the **Print** button on the Print Preview toolbar, and then click the **OK** button to print the selected worksheets.

7. Click the **Documentation** tab so that the next time this worksheet is opened, the user sees the Documentation sheet.

8. Save and close the **Grades3** workbook.

Using a worksheet group has made it possible to format and print all the grading worksheets at the same time.

Session 8.1 QUICK | CHECK

1. Explain how to insert a new worksheet directly to the right of the active sheet.

2. What is a worksheet group?

3. How do you select and deselect a worksheet group?

4. How do you copy text and formulas from one worksheet into a range of worksheets?

5. What are the two parts of a 3-D cell reference?

6. What is the 3-D cell reference to cells A1:A10 in the Section 1 worksheet?

7. What is the 3-D cell reference to cells A1:A10 in the Sheet1 through Sheet10 worksheets?

You have created a workbook with multiple worksheets, inserted and moved worksheets, created worksheet groups, and combined data from separate worksheets into a consolidation worksheet that TAs can use to compare the performance of their discussion sections. In the next session you will see how templates can help Professor White and the TAs share the workbook you have created.

SESSION 8.2

In this session you will create and use Excel templates. You'll learn how Excel organizes templates on your computer and how to use some of the built-in templates Excel provides.

Using Templates

In the last session you created a workbook that the TAs in Professor White's calculus lecture will use to maintain grading records for their discussion sections. But how should you make the new workbook available to them? One possibility is to simply give a copy of the workbook to each user. However, there is a potential problem with this approach: Once the file leaves your hands, you have no way of controlling the changes the TAs will make to it. You would like to have a single workbook file that will be available to them but that will always retain the format you created. One way of doing this is to create a template.

A **template** is an Excel document that contains specific content and formatting that you can use as a model for Excel workbooks. A template can include standardized text such as page headers and row and column labels, as well as formulas, macros, and customized menus and toolbars. When you open a template, Excel opens a blank workbook with content and formatting identical to the template. You then add data to the blank workbook and save it as an Excel file with any name you choose. The original template will retain its original design and formats for the next time you or another user need to create another workbook based on it. This is very useful if you want several users to maintain a workbook containing the same types of information. The original workbook design will always be available to them because they will only save files based on the template. The template itself will remain unchanged.

Excel has several templates that are automatically installed on your hard disk when you install the program. In fact, whenever you start Excel and see the blank workbook called Book1, you are actually using a workbook that's based on a template known as the **default template**. Excel also includes several specialized templates that you can use for specific tasks, such as creating an accounting ledger or sales worksheet.

Opening a Workbook Based on a Template

To see how templates work, you'll create a new workbook based on one of the built-in Excel templates.

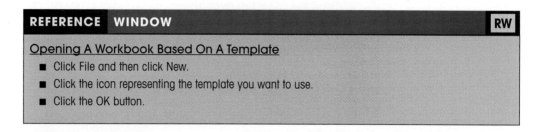

REFERENCE WINDOW   **RW**

Opening A Workbook Based On A Template
- Click File and then click New.
- Click the icon representing the template you want to use.
- Click the OK button.

You'll open an Excel Invoice template, so you can get an idea of how the grading template you'll create for Professor White will look when the TAs open it.

To open a built-in template:

1. If you took a break at the end of the last session, make sure Excel is running.

2. Click **File** on the menu bar, and then click **New**. The New dialog box opens.

TROUBLE? If a new, blank workbook opened instead of the New dialog box, you probably clicked the New button on the Standard toolbar. In order to open a template, you must use the New command from the File menu, not the New button on the toolbar.

3. Click the **Spreadsheet Solutions** tab.

The tab displays icons representing templates, shown in Figure 8-20.

Figure 8-20	BUILT-IN TEMPLATES PROVIDED BY EXCEL

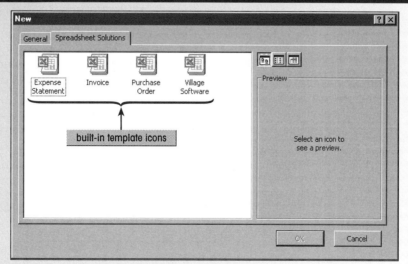

TROUBLE? Depending upon how Office 2000 or Excel 2000 was installed on your system, you might see different workbook templates. If you don't see the Invoice template, open any other template.

Next, you'll open a blank workbook based on the Invoice template.

4. Click the **Invoice** icon and then click the **OK** button.

TROUBLE? You may be asked to insert the Office 2000 CD to use this feature. If so, insert the CD if you have it, and follow the instructions to install the Invoice template. If the CD is not available or if you have other problems, talk to your instructor.

5. Click the **Enable Macros** option button to enable the macros that are included with the Invoice template.

Excel opens the workbook shown in Figure 8-21.

Figure 8-21	THE INVOICE TEMPLATE

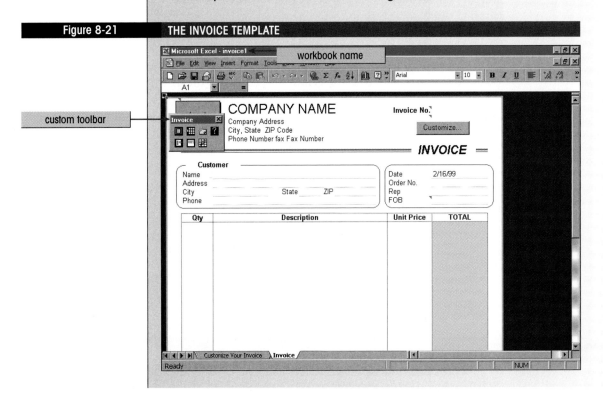

Figure 8-21 displays a workbook based on the Invoice template. Notice that the name in the title bar is not Invoice but Invoice1. Just as the blank workbooks you see when you first open Excel have the sequential names Book1, Book2 and so forth, a workbook based on a template always displays the name of the template, followed by a sequential number. Any additions you make to this workbook will only affect the new document you are creating and will not affect the Invoice template itself. However if you want to save your changes, you would save the Invoice1 workbook in the same way you save the Book1 workbook that you see when you first start Excel. The next time you create a new workbook based on this template, you'll be presented with the same workbook and workbook features.

Having seen how to create a workbook based on a template, you can close the Invoice1 workbook. You do not need to save your changes.

To close the Invoice1 workbook:

1. Click **File** on the menu bar, and then click **Close**.
2. Click the **No** button when prompted to save your changes.

Now that you've seen how to access a template, you can see how useful a template would be for Professor White's TAs. You can make your grading sheet into a template, make it available to the TAs, and they can create grading sheet documents based on your template. At regular intervals, they can submit their sheets to you or Professor White, who can easily consolidate the information because it will have the same structure and format on all the worksheets.

Next you'll learn how to save your workbook as a template and learn about storing templates in the correct folder, so it is available to those who need it.

Creating **and Storing a Workbook Template**

To create a template, you simply save an Excel workbook as a template file using the Save As command. Excel will then automatically convert the workbook to a template file. You decide to try this with the grading workbook you created in the last session.

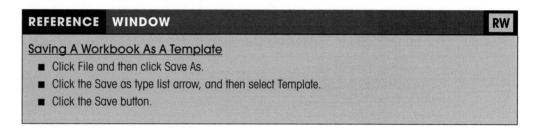

REFERENCE WINDOW   **RW**

<u>Saving A Workbook As A Template</u>
- Click File and then click Save As.
- Click the Save as type list arrow, and then select Template.
- Click the Save button.

The Grades4 workbook in the Tutorial folder for Tutorial.08 on your Data Disk contains many of the same formulas and formats that you created in the last session. The main difference is that the sample data has been removed to allow teachers to enter fresh data. You'll open the Grades4 workbook and save it as a template file now.

To save the Grades4 workbook as a template file:

1. Open the **Grades4** workbook in the Tutorial folder for Tutorial.08 on your Data Disk. Notice that it has the same structure as the previous workbook. Now you'll save it as a template.
2. Click **File** on the menu bar, and then click **Save As** to open the Save As dialog box.
3. Type **Grading Sheet** in the File name text box, and then press the **Tab** key.
4. Click the **Save as type** list arrow, and click **Template** in the Save as Type list box.
5. In the Save in list box, locate the Tutorial folder for Tutorial.08 on your Data Disk.

   TROUBLE? When you select the Template file type, Excel automatically opens a folder named "Template." As you'll see, Excel is preset to put all template files in this folder. But because you might not have access to your computer network's Template folder, you should save the template file to your Data Disk.

> **6.** Click the **Save** button. Excel saves the Grades4 workbook as a template file named "Grading Sheet" on your Data Disk.
>
> **7.** Close the Grading Sheet template.

Once you've converted a workbook to a template, you have to make the template accessible to other users. To do this, you have to understand how Excel stores templates.

Using the Templates Folder

To use a template file like the one you just created, the template must be placed in the Templates folder that is in the Microsoft Office folder on your computer or network. You cannot create a workbook based on your template unless it's in the Templates folder. As you've seen, Excel will try to save any template files you create to that folder by default.

Depending on your computer environment, you might not be able to modify the contents of your Templates folder. If Excel and Microsoft Office are installed on a computer network, it may be that only a limited group of people has access to the folder. For that reason, the material that follows is provided for you to review, but you might not be able to perform the steps on your system. If you would like to work with the Templates folder yourself but are not sure if you have access to it, ask your instructor or the technical support person in your computer lab.

The exact location of the Templates folder depends on how Microsoft Office was installed on your computer. For example, in Microsoft Office 2000, the Templates folder is located in the C:\WINDOWS\Application Data\Microsoft\Templates folder. Figure 8-22 shows the location of the Templates folder as shown in Windows Explorer.

Figure 8-22   SAMPLE CONTENTS OF THE TEMPLATES FOLDER

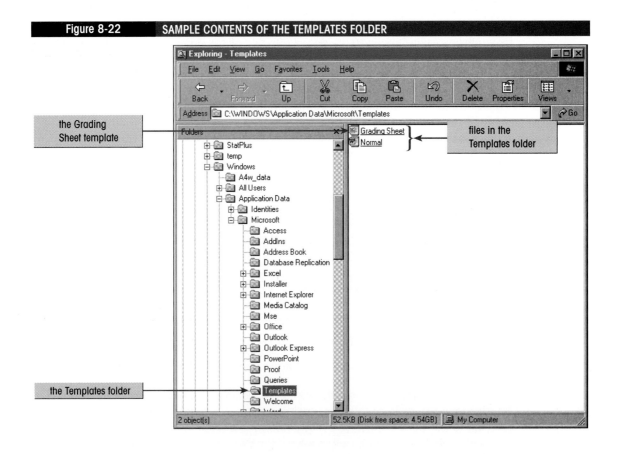

If you did have access to the Templates directory, the Grading Sheet template would be stored as shown in Figure 8-22. Excel workbooks are shown with a 📄 icon and Excel templates with a 📄 icon. Template files created in other Office 2000 applications (in this case, Word) appear in this folder as well.

When a template is placed in the Templates folder, its icon will appear on the General tab in the New dialog box. Figure 8-23 shows the Excel New dialog box that corresponds to the Templates folder from Figure 8-22. It displays your Grading Sheet template but not other Office 2000 template files because you are viewing it from within Excel.

Figure 8-23	NEW DIALOG BOX CONTAINING THE GRADING SHEET TEMPLATE

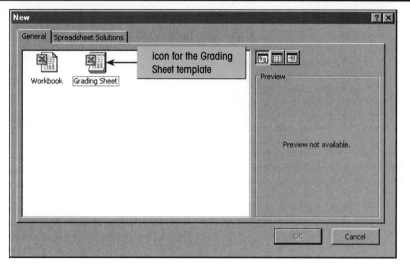

The Templates folder can include subfolders used to organize your different Office 2000 template files. The Templates folder shown in Figure 8-24 contains a single subfolder named "Classroom" into which the Grading sheet template has been placed.

Figure 8-24	CLASSROOM SUBFOLDER OF THE TEMPLATES FOLDER

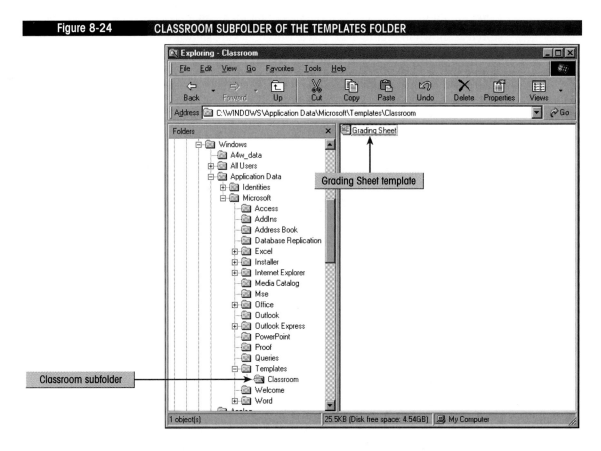

Subfolders containing Excel template files will then appear as dialog tabs in Excel's New dialog box. For example, the Classroom subfolder from Figure 8-24 appears as the Classroom dialog tab shown in Figure 8-25.

Figure 8-25	CLASSROOM TAB IN THE NEW DIALOG BOX

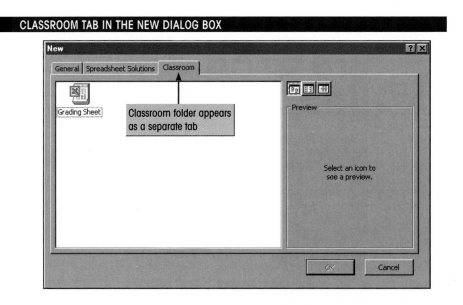

Because MidWest University has installed Office 2000 on the campus network, your Grading Sheet template would be readily available to Professor White's four TAs, as shown in Figure 8-26. If you decide to make changes to the template, you can place the updated template file on the network. The TAs could then easily create new workbooks based on your revised template.

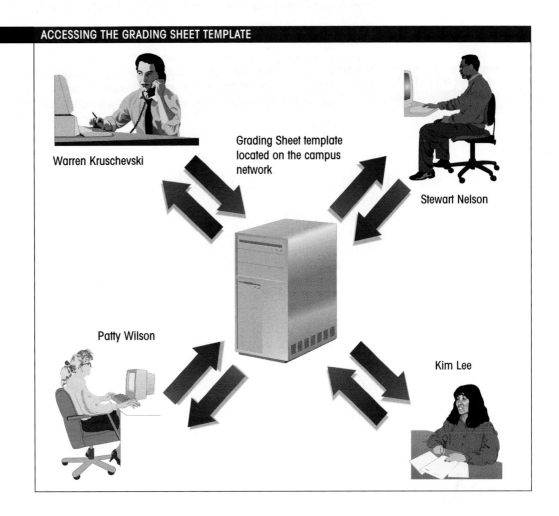

Figure 8-26 | **ACCESSING THE GRADING SHEET TEMPLATE**

Warren Kruschevski

Grading Sheet template located on the campus network

Stewart Nelson

Patty Wilson

Kim Lee

If your template was indeed placed on the university network, TAs would then use it to create their grading workbooks, which they would then turn in to you or Professor White. You'll use their workbooks created from your template to help you design the next version of the Grading Sheet workbook.

Session 8.2 QUICK CHECK

1. What is a template?

2. What are two advantages of using a template instead of simply distributing a workbook file?

3. What is the default workbook template?

4. How do you save a file as a template?

5. Where must you store your templates?

6. How would you place a template into its own tab in the New dialog box?

You have created the grading workbook template and learned about the Template folder. In the next session you will learn how to consolidate information from the TAs' completed workbooks into a single workbook that Professor White will use to evaluate all the sections of her Calculus 223 course.

SESSION 8.3

In this session you will learn how to consolidate data from several workbooks. You'll learn how to use Excel to retrieve and update that information. You'll also learn how to create a lookup table and how to use lookup functions to retrieve information from the table. Finally, you'll create an Excel workspace file to access several workbooks at once.

Summarizing **Data from Several Workbooks**

In the last session you saved your grading sheet as a template. Since then, the template has been made available to Professor White's four TAs. They have used the template to create a workbook containing the grades they assigned to students in their sections. Professor White would like you to create a workbook that consolidates the data from the TAs' workbooks into a single file. She'll use the consolidated file to monitor the performance of the students and the TAs as the semester progresses.

A workbook has been created for you, with the name "White." It has a Documentation sheet and a consolidation worksheet in which you'll place the summary grades from each TA. To do this, you'll have to create a 3-D cell reference to each TA's workbook.

Creating 3-D Cell References to Other Workbooks

A 3-D cell reference to a workbook is similar to the 3-D cell references you created earlier in Session 8.1. The difference is that you'll include the name of the workbook in the reference, in addition to the name of a worksheet. The general form of a 3-D cell reference that includes the workbook is:

Location[Workbook name]Sheet Range!Cell Range

The location is the drive and folder that contains the workbook to which you are creating the reference. For example, assume you want to create a reference to the cell range B5:E5 on the "Summary Info" worksheet of the Sales.xls workbook, and the workbook is located in the Business folder on drive E of your computer. In this case, the 3-D cell reference is:

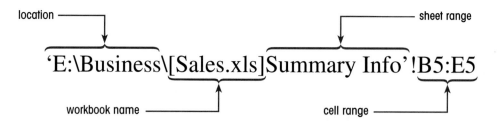

As you did earlier when you used sheet references with the sample data, you enclose the Location[Workbook name]Sheet Range portion of the 3-D cell reference in single quotation marks if there are any blank spaces in the location, workbook, or worksheet names. For example, 'E:\Business\[Sales.xls]Summary Info' needs quotation marks, but E:\Business\[Sales.xls]Summary does not.

If you are referring to workbooks located in the same folder as the active workbook, you do not need to include the location information in your cell reference. Excel will assume that if you do not specify a location, you want to use workbooks located in the folder of the active workbook, and it will add the location information for you automatically.

The four TAs assigned to Professor White's lecture have stored their grading sheets in the following files: TA1, TA2, TA3, and TA4. Because each TA has created his or her workbook from the template you created earlier, you know where the relevant information has been stored. For example, you know that the name of each TA should be entered on the Documentation sheet of each workbook in cell B1 (recall Figure 8-3). With that in mind, you can create a reference to that cell in Professor White's Summary Grades workbook.

To open the workbook and add a reference to each TA's name:

1. If you took a break after the last session, restart Excel.

2. Open the **White** workbook in the Tutorial folder for Tutorial.08 of your Data Disk.

3. Enter [**Your Name**] and the date in cells B14 and B15. Enter **Summary Grades** in cell B13.

4. Save the workbook as **Summary Grades**.

5. Click the **Summary** tab.

   Now you'll enter the 3-D cell reference that will enter the name of the first TA in cell A2.

6. Click cell **A2** and type **=[TA1]Documentation!B1** and then press the **Enter** key. The name "Stewart Nelson" appears in cell A2.

7. Click the **A2** cell again and notice that Excel has automatically inserted the path indicating the location of the TA1 workbook file into the cell reference.

Next you'll continue entering the references to the remaining TA names. You'll use a reference to the TA2 workbook to enter Patty Wilson's name in cell A3, TA3 to enter Kim Lee's name in A4, and TA4 to enter Warren Kruschevski's in A5.

To complete the column of TA names:

1. Click cell **A3**.

2. Type **=[TA2]Documentation!B1** and then press the **Enter** key. Patty Wilson's name appears in cell A3.

3. In cell A4, enter **=[TA3]Documentation!B1**. Kim Lee's name appears.

4. In cell A5 enter **=[TA4]Documentation!B1**. Warren Kruschevski's name appears.

   Figure 8-27 displays the completed column of TA names.

Figure 8-27	TA NAMES PULLED FROM THE GRADING SHEET WORKBOOKS

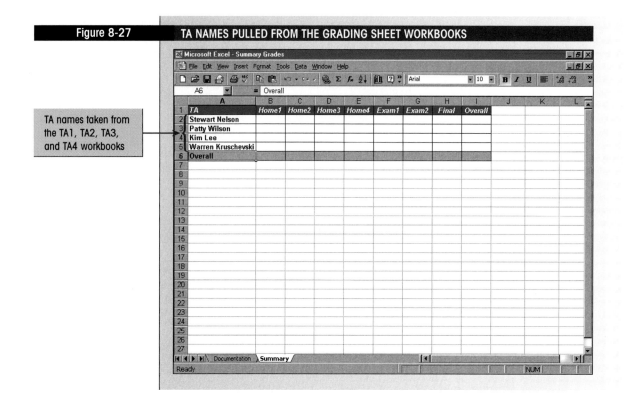

TA names taken from the TA1, TA2, TA3, and TA4 workbooks

Next you'll need to reference the average scores that are recorded on the Summary sheet of each TA's workbook in cells B5:I5 (see Figure 8-17). As with the column of TA names, you can create columns of homework and exam averages, but here you can use the Fill Right command because the structure of the Summary sheet from Figure 8-17 is identical to the Summary sheet in the Summary Grades workbook. Start with the grades for Stewart Nelson's discussion sections row 2 drawn from the TA1 workbook.

To create a reference to Stewart Nelson's grading averages:

1. Click cell **B2** and type **=[TA1]Summary!B5** and then press the **Enter** key. The value 77.50 appears in cell B2.

2. Click cell **B2** and drag the fill handle to **I2** and release the mouse button.

3. Click cell **A1**.

   As shown in Figure 8-28, Excel has filled in the average scores for homework and exams for Stewart Nelson's discussion sections from the TA1 workbook. See Figure 8-28.

Figure 8-28 **SUMMARY SCORES FROM THE TA1 WORKBOOK**

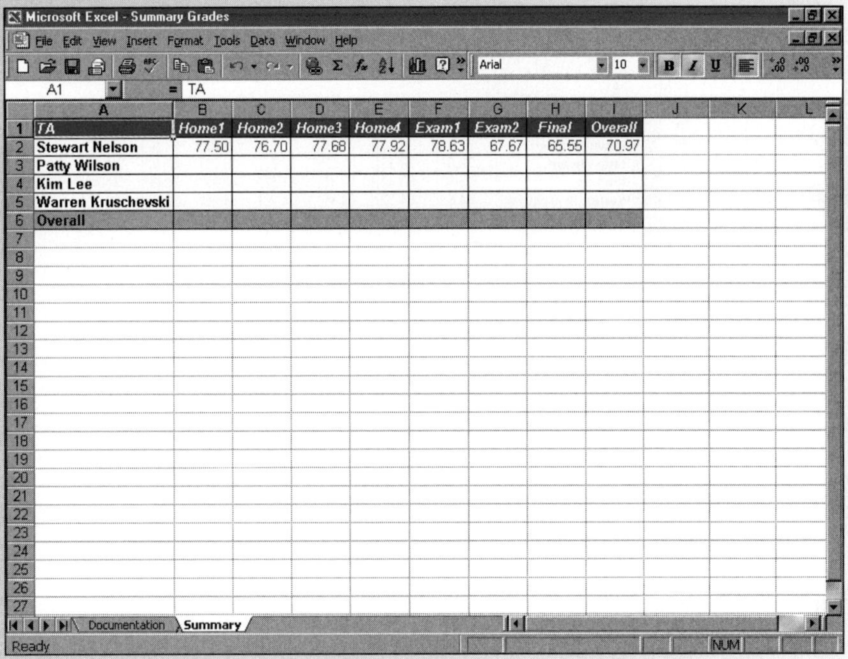

	A	B	C	D	E	F	G	H	I
1	TA	Home1	Home2	Home3	Home4	Exam1	Exam2	Final	Overall
2	Stewart Nelson	77.50	76.70	77.68	77.92	78.63	67.67	65.55	70.97
3	Patty Wilson								
4	Kim Lee								
5	Warren Kruschevski								
6	Overall								

Next you'll fill in the scores for the other TAs. Patty Wilson's scores are in the TA2 workbook, Kim Lee's are in TA3, and Warren Kruschevski's are in TA4.

To add references to the rest of the TA workbooks:

1. Click cell **B3** and type **=[TA2]Summary!B5**, and then press the **Enter** key. The value 79.07 appears in cell B3.
2. Type **=[TA3]Summary!B5** in cell B4.
3. Type **=[TA4]Summary!B5** in cell B5.
4. Select the range **B3:B5** and drag the fill handle to the range **I3:I5**.

   Note that you can use the keyboard shortcut Ctrl + R in place of the Edit, Fill, and Right commands.
5. Click **A1**.

   Your screen should display all the average scores for each TA, as shown in Figure 8-29.

Figure 8-29   SUMMARY SCORES FROM THE TA1–TA4 WORKBOOKS

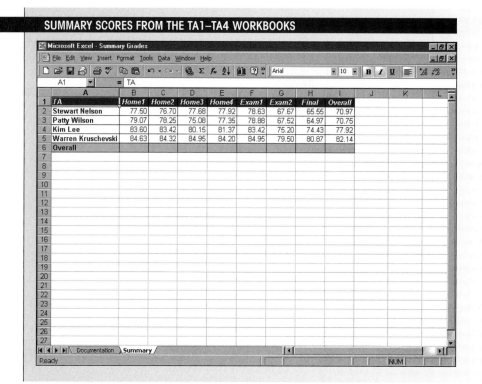

Finally, Professor White would like you to calculate the overall average scores for the four TAs. You can place these values in row 6.

To calculate the average of the TA grades:

1. Click cell **B6** and type the formula **=AVERAGE(B2:B5)**. The value 81.20 appears in cell B6.

2. Click cell **B6** and drag the fill handle to cell **I6**.

3. Click cell **A1**.

   The average scores for each TA appear in row 6 of the Summary worksheet. See Figure 8-30.

Figure 8-30	COMPLETED SUMMARY WORKSHEET

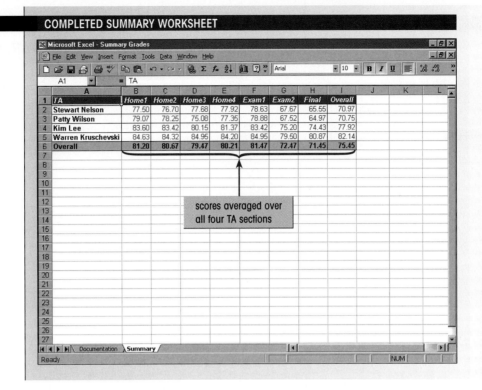

scores averaged over
all four TA sections

From your Summary sheet, Professor White will be able to see that two of the TAs, Stewart Nelson and Patty Wilson, have section averages well below the other two. She will most likely want to look into the reasons for this.

When you created the 3-D references in Professor White's Summary Grades workbook, you actually created a link between the Summary workbook and the four TA workbooks. You'll learn how to examine these links in the next section.

Working with Linked Workbooks

When you create a 3-D cell reference to another workbook, you are also creating a link, or a "live" connection, between workbooks. Because the workbooks are linked (recall the earlier discussion of linked files in Tutorial 6), changing a score in one TA's workbook causes a change in the Summary workbook. You've already seen this principle in action within a workbook when a changed value in one of the worksheets resulted in a changed value in a summary worksheet.

Professor White has talked to a student who feels that an answer was incorrectly marked wrong on her final exam. After reviewing the problem, Professor White decides that the student is right, which will increase her final exam score from 85 to 95. The student's ID number is 1107, and she is in Stewart Nelson's first discussion section. If Professor White wants to update the grading sheet, how will she know which workbook to access? She can view the list of linked workbooks.

To view the list of links:

1. Click **Edit** on the menu bar, and then click **Links**.

Figure 8-31 shows the list of workbooks linked to the Summary Grades workbook.

Figure 8-31   **FILES LINKED TO THE SUMMARY GRADES WORKBOOK**

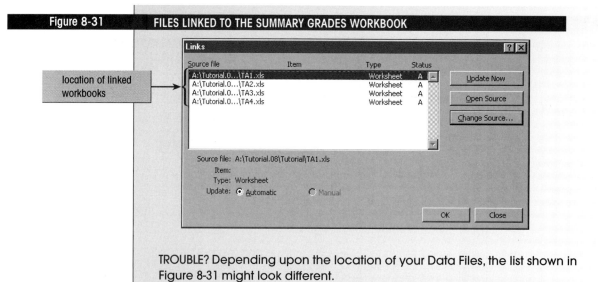

location of linked
workbooks

TROUBLE? Depending upon the location of your Data Files, the list shown in
Figure 8-31 might look different.

Professor White knows that because Stewart Nelson covers the first set of discussion sections, his grades will be in the TA1 workbook.

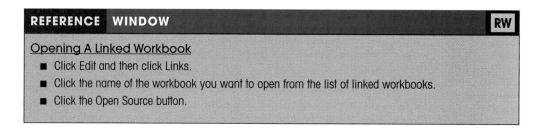

REFERENCE WINDOW   **RW**

Opening A Linked Workbook
■ Click Edit and then click Links.
■ Click the name of the workbook you want to open from the list of linked workbooks.
■ Click the Open Source button.

Professor White can open Stewart Nelson's workbook through the Links dialog box. Try
this now.

To open the TA1 workbook:

1. Click **TA1.xls** in the Source file list box.

2. Click the **Open Source** button.

   Excel opens the TA1 workbook.

3. Click the **Section 1** tab, type **95** in cell H8, and then press the **Enter** key. Figure 8-32
   shows the new values.

Figure 8-32	REVISED SCORE IN THE SECTION 1 WORKSHEET OF THE TA1 WORKBOOK

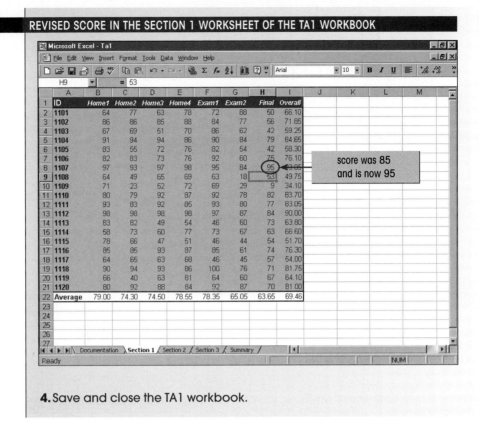

4. Save and close the TA1 workbook.

After changing the student's final exam grade, the average final exam grade in Stewart Nelson's discussion sections, in cell H2 of the Summary worksheet, has increased from 65.55 to 65.72 and the average of his overall scores in cell I2 has increased from 70.97 to 71.04.

Opening and changing a source file in this way will automatically update the formulas to which it is linked in the workbook. If the Summary workbook is closed when you change the source, when you reopen it Excel will ask you if you want to update links to other files. If you click the Yes button, Excel retrieves any new or updated data. This guarantees that the workbook contains accurate and timely information.

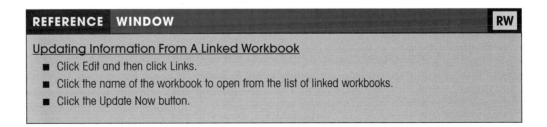

REFERENCE WINDOW   **RW**

Updating Information From A Linked Workbook
- Click Edit and then click Links.
- Click the name of the workbook to open from the list of linked workbooks.
- Click the Update Now button.

Professor White would like to know what would happen if one of her TAs makes changes to the linked file while she is working on the Summary Grades workbook. You explain that when this happens, she can manually update the link to that workbook. For example, what if, while she was changing the grade of the student in Stewart Nelson's discussion section, Kim Lee was making changes in her grading sheet workbook? In that case, Professor White could retrieve the new information from Kim's source file by manually updating the link. You show her how to update the link to Kim Lee's grading sheet, located in the TA3 workbook.

To update information from the TA3 workbook:

1. Click **Edit** on the menu bar, and then click **Links**.

2. Click **TA3.xls** in the Source file list box.

3. Click the **Update Now** button.

4. Click the **OK** button to close the Links dialog box.

Any changes that Kim may have saved to her TA3.xls workbook will now be incorporated into the Summary Grades workbook. Because the end of the semester is approaching, Professor White turns her attention to assigning final letter grades to each of her students, which she will do by using lookup tables.

Using Lookup Tables

Professor White has reviewed each of the grades her TAs recorded. She has noted the overall average scores and has opened the workbooks containing the individual scores. Based on what she has seen, she has decided on a grading scale that determines the letter grades she wants to assign to each score category. Figure 8-33 shows the grading scale and the letter grades she has created.

Figure 8-33	PROFESSOR WHITE'S GRADING SCALE

OVERALL SCORE	GRADE	GRADE POINT
0 - < 30	F	0.0
30 - < 50	D	1.0
50 - < 60	C	2.0
60 - < 70	BC	2.5
70 - < 77	B	3.0
77 - < 84	AB	3.5
84 - 100	A	4.0

compare values →

Professor White could just give this table to her TAs and have them manually enter each student's letter grade, but it would be much more efficient to have the letter grades automatically entered into the grading sheet workbooks using a lookup table. A **lookup table** consists of rows and columns of information organized into separate categories. For example, the table in Figure 8-33 displays seven different categories in the overall score column. If you knew what a student's score was, you could determine the student's letter grade or grade point from the table by finding the appropriate row in the table and then looking in the letter grade or grade point column. You'll enter Professor White's grading scale as an Excel lookup table.

The categories for the lookup table are usually located in the table's first row or column and are called **compare values**, because an individual student's score is compared to each category to determine the grade. The value that is sent to the table is called the **lookup value**. In Figure 8-33, the first column contains compare values and each student's score is the lookup value.

A lookup table can have many different columns or rows to incorporate more pieces of information. Professor White's grading table displays both the letter grade and the corresponding grade point. To use this lookup table, you have to specify both the lookup value (the student's test score) and whether you're interested in retrieving the student's grade or grade point. See Figure 8-34.

Figure 8-34	USING A LOOKUP TABLE

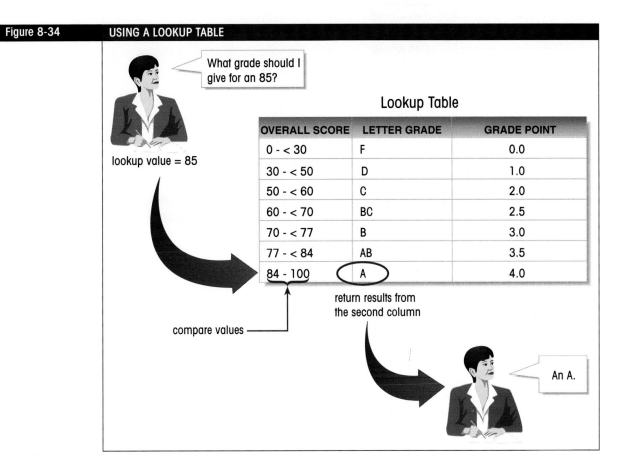

Professor White wants you to enter the values from Figure 8-33 into the Summary Grades workbook. Because of the way Excel works with lookup tables, you'll only insert the lowest value that a student needs to receive a particular letter grade in the compare values column of the table. For example, in the lookup table you'll type the value "84" rather than "84 – 100" for As; or "70" rather than "70 – < 77" for Bs. This point will become clearer when you learn about lookup functions later in the tutorial.

To create the lookup table:

1. Insert a worksheet named **Grading Scale** to the right of the Summary sheet.

2. Enter the following values on the Grading Scale worksheet:

   Cell A1: **Score**
   Cell B1: **Grade**
   Cell C1: **Grade Point**
   Cell A2: **0**
   Cell A3: **30**
   Cell A4: **50**
   Cell A5: **60**
   Cell A6: **70**
   Cell A7: **77**
   Cell A8: **84**

3. Enter the remaining grades and grade points from the table in Figure 8-33 to columns B and C in the Grading scale worksheet.

4. Click **A1**. The final table is shown in Figure 8-35.

Figure 8-35	GRADING SCALE LOOKUP TABLE

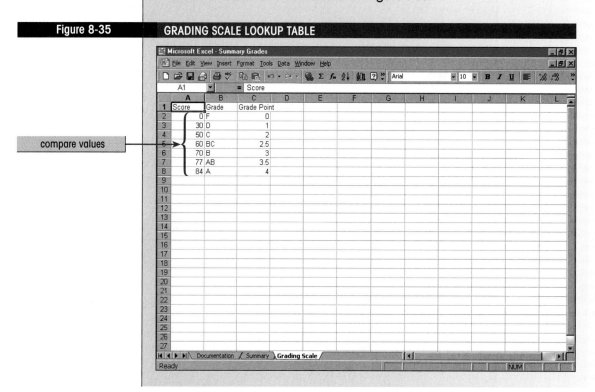

compare values

Finally, you should give a range name to your lookup table. Although this is not necessary in creating a lookup table, a range name will make it easier for functions to refer to values in the table, because the function would only have to include the range name and not the cell reference.

To name the lookup table:

1. Select the range **A1:C8**.

2. Click **Insert** on the menu bar, point to **Name**, and then click **Define**.

3. Type **Grade_Scale** in the Names in workbook text box, and click the **OK** button.

4. Save your changes and close the Summary Grades workbook.

Now that you've created the lookup table, you'll see how Professor White's TAs can use it to calculate letter grades for each of their students.

Using **Lookup Functions**

To retrieve a value, in this case a letter grade, from a lookup table, you'll use one of Excel's lookup functions. In a lookup function, you specify the location of the lookup table, the lookup value, and the column or row that contains the values you want retrieved from the table. Excel has two lookup functions: the VLOOKUP function and the HLOOKUP function. The VLOOKUP (or vertical lookup) function is used for lookup tables in which the compare values are placed into the first column of the table, and the HLOOKUP (or horizontal lookup) function assumes that the compare values are located in the table's first row. With the lookup table you created in Professor White's workbook, you'll use the VLOOKUP function because the compare values (the scores) were placed in the table's first column. The form of the VLOOKUP function is:

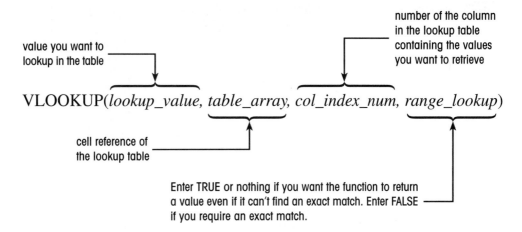

The VLOOKUP formula can look imposing, but once you examine each piece of the function, you'll find it easier to understand. The first argument in the function is the **lookup value**, this is the value you want to compare with other values in the table. For example, the lookup value shown in the example from Figure 8-34 is 85. For your VLOOKUP function, you'll enter references to the cells that contain the student scores rather than the scores themselves. The second argument is the **table_array**, which is the cell reference that specifies the location of the lookup table. In the lookup table you just created, the table_array would be '[Summary Grades]Grading Scale'!A1:C8, or if you use the range name you created, '[Summary Grades]'!Grade_Scale (note that you don't need to specify the worksheet name if you use a range name.) The **col_index_num** is the column number that contains the information you want to retrieve. For example, a col_index_num of 1 returns the value in the first column of the lookup table, a col_index_num of 2 returns the value from the second column and so forth. You'll want your VLOOKUP function to look at column 2, the letter grade column, and retrieve the appropriate grade.

The **range_lookup** is a logical value that can be either TRUE or FALSE. It tells VLOOKUP how to match the compare values in the first column of the table with your lookup value. If the range_lookup value is FALSE, the function will look for only exact matches to your lookup value. For example, if you are trying to retrieve values for a particular student, you would want an exact match to that student's ID number. If the VLOOKUP function fails to find an exact match, an #N/A error value is generated.

If the range_lookup value is TRUE or omitted, the situation is a little more complicated. In this case, Excel uses the largest compare value that is less than the lookup value. To see how this works examine Figure 8-36. Recall that when you created the lookup table, you entered the lower end of the range for each letter grade in the compare values column. Now you'll see why. If you want to see what letter grade is given for a score of 65, the VLOOKUP function moves down the Score column until it locates the highest score value that is less than 65. In this case that is 60, and the function returns a letter grade of BC. Based on the table, you can determine that any score greater than or equal to 60 and less than 70 will return a grade of BC, which is what you want based on the table shown from Figure 8-34.

Figure 8-36	RETURNING A VALUE WITH THE RANGE_ LOOKUP VALUE SET TO TRUE

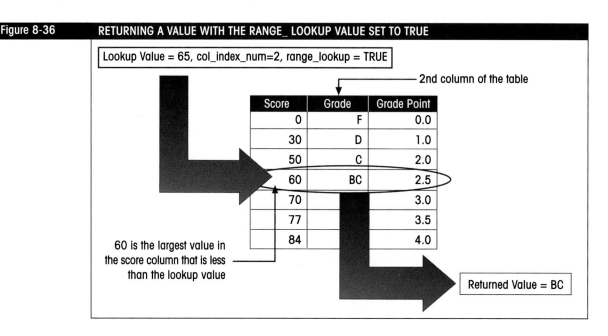

This example brings up an important point. If the range_lookup value is TRUE or omitted, the lookup table *must* be sorted in ascending order of the compare values. If it isn't, the VLOOKUP function will either return an incorrect value or an error.

Because the VLOOKUP function seems to be just what you need to automatically generate letter grades, you'll add the function to Stewart Nelson's grading sheet in the TA1 workbook. In this tutorial, you'll only add the function to TA1; you can add it to TA2, TA3, and TA4 at another time.

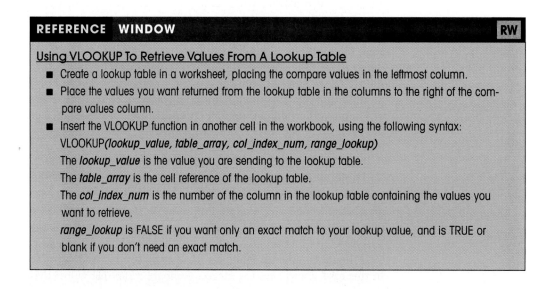

REFERENCE WINDOW   **RW**

Using VLOOKUP To Retrieve Values From A Lookup Table
- Create a lookup table in a worksheet, placing the compare values in the leftmost column.
- Place the values you want returned from the lookup table in the columns to the right of the compare values column.
- Insert the VLOOKUP function in another cell in the workbook, using the following syntax:
  VLOOKUP(*lookup_value, table_array, col_index_num, range_lookup*)
  The *lookup_value* is the value you are sending to the lookup table.
  The *table_array* is the cell reference of the lookup table.
  The *col_index_num* is the number of the column in the lookup table containing the values you want to retrieve.
  range_lookup is FALSE if you want only an exact match to your lookup value, and is TRUE or blank if you don't need an exact match.

You'll begin by opening the TA1 workbook and entering the lookup function in a new Grades column that you'll add to each of the section worksheets.

To add a column of final grades to the worksheet:

1. Open the **TA1** workbook from the Tutorial folder for Tutorial.08 on your Data Disk.

2. Enter (*Your Name*) and the date in cells B14:B15 of the Documentation worksheet. Type **TA1Lookup** in cell B13.

3. Save the workbook as **TA1Lookup**.

4. Group the Section 1 through Section 3 worksheets. Click the **Section 1** worksheet tab.

5. In cell J2, type **=VLOOKUP(I2,'Summary Grades'!Grade_Scale,2)** and then press **Enter**.

   You have instructed Excel to use the value in cell I2 to retrieve the corresponding letter grade located in the second column of the lookup table named "Grade_Scale" in the Summary Grades workbook.

   TROUBLE? If you receive an error message stating that Excel cannot find the Summary Grades workbook, verify that you've typed the name of the file correctly. The Summary Grades workbook should be in the same folder as the current workbook you're editing.

6. Click cell **J2** and drag the fill handle down to cell **J21**.

7. Click cell **A1**.

   Figure 8-37 shows the final version of the table. Because you've grouped the three grading sheets, the VLOOKUP formula and cell formats have been added to all three worksheets. A quick glance at the grades assigned to the students indicates a fairly even mix of letter grades.

| Figure 8-37 | GRADES FOR THE STUDENTS IN THE TA1 WORKBOOK |

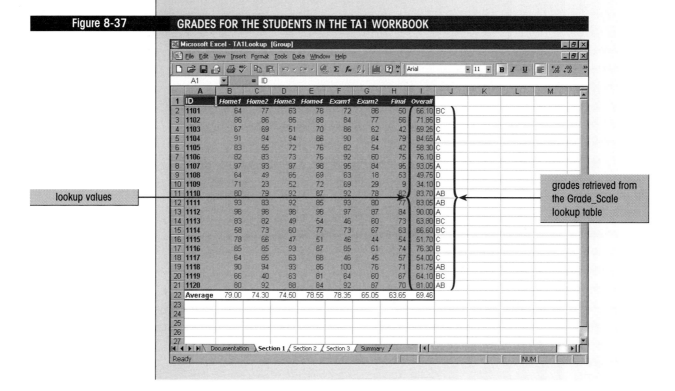

lookup values

grades retrieved from the Grade_Scale lookup table

8. Check to see if appropriate letter grades have been entered into the Section 2 and Section 3 worksheets.

9. Select the Documentation sheet and then save and close your workbook.

With the lookup table in place, if Stewart makes a change in one of his student's homework or exam scores, or if Professor White revises her grading scale, the grades in column J can be automatically updated. This is much more accurate and efficient than simply entering the grades by hand. In the future, you can use this technique in all of the TA workbooks.

Creating **an Excel Workspace**

Professor White now has five different workbooks to keep track of grades in her course: the four TA workbooks and the Summary Grades workbook. Most of the time, she'll need to access only one workbook at a time, but there will be those occasions (such as at the end of the term) when she'll have all five opened simultaneously. It would be a great help for Professor White if she could open all those workbooks at once. For one thing, it would save time; but more importantly, it would save her the trouble of remembering all those filenames and their folder locations.

To do this, you'll create a workspace. A **workspace** is an Excel file that saves information about all of the currently opened workbooks, such as their locations, their window sizes, and screen positions. The workspace does not contain the workbooks themselves—only information about them. That is enough however. You can open all of the workbooks for the Calculus 223 lecture and then create the workspace file based on those workbooks. To open that set of workbooks again, Professor White can simply open the workspace file and the five workbooks will be opened as well.

REFERENCE WINDOW	RW

Creating And Using An Excel Workspace
- Open only those workbooks you want to include in the workspace.
- Click Save Workspace from the File menu.
- Assign a name for your workspace file and click the Save button.
- To access the workspace later, open the workspace file from the Open command in the File menu. All workbooks related to your workspace will be automatically opened.

To create the Calculus223 workspace file:

1. Open the **TA1**, **TA2**, **TA3**, **TA4** and **Summary Grades** workbooks from the Tutorial folder for Tutorial.08 on your Data Disk. Click **Yes** if you are prompted to update any links.

2. Click **Summary Grades** from the Windows menu so that the Summary Grades workbook appears in the document window.

3. Click **Save Workspace** from the File menu.

4. Type **Calc223** in the File Name box, verify that "Workspaces" is selected in the Save As Type list box and that the Tutorial folder for Tutorial.08 appears in the Save In box.

5. Click the **Save** button.

The Calc223 workspace file is created on your Data Disk.

TROUBLE? If Excel prompts you to save changes to one of your workbooks, click the Yes button.

Now that you've created the workspace file, your next step is to open it to confirm that it opens all five of Professor White's grading workbooks.

To test the Calc223 workspace:

1. Close all five of the grading workbooks contained in the Calc223 workspace.

2. Click **Open** from the File menu.

3. Select **Calc223** from the Tutorial folder for Tutorial.08 and click the **Open** button. See Figure 8-38. Click **Yes** if you are prompted to update any links.

Figure 8-38 | OPENING THE CALC223 WORKSPACE FILE

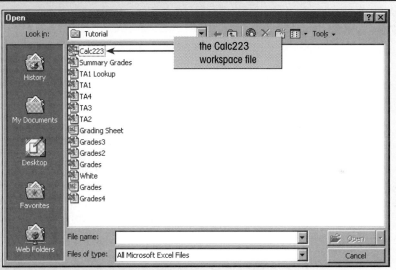

The five workbooks in the Calc223 workspace are open.

4. Close all of the Calc223 workbooks. You don't need to save any changes because you haven't modified the document.

5. Exit Excel.

You display the workspace file to Professor White. She's very happy with it and realizes that she can create a separate workspace file for each of her courses. She teaches several classes, and a workspace is an excellent way of organizing all of those workbooks. That's a job for the future, for now you've completed your work for Professor White.

Session 8.3 QUICK CHECK

1. What is the 3-D cell reference for the A1:A10 cell range on the Sales Info worksheet in the Product Report workbook located in the Reports folder on drive D?

2. How does a 3-D cell reference to a workbook differ from a 3-D reference to a worksheet?

3. How would you view a list of links to other workbooks in your current workbook?

4. Define lookup table, lookup value, and compare value.

5. What are two of the functions that Excel uses to retrieve values from a lookup table?

6. What is the range_lookup value? What does a value of TRUE mean for the range_lookup value?

7. What is a workspace file? Explain how workspace files can help you organize your work.

In this tutorial, you have worked with multiple worksheets and workbooks, learned about templates, and used the Excel VLOOKUP function. Professor White is pleased with the grading sheets you've created. She'll look over your work and let you know if she has any changes.

REVIEW ASSIGNMENTS

Professor White has looked over the grading workbooks you've created. Based on her suggestions, you've made some formatting changes to the documents. She has a couple of items that she wants you to add to her new Summary Grades workbook and to each of her TA's grading sheet workbooks. In her Summary Grades workbook, she would like you to add a worksheet containing contact information for each TA retrieved from the TA1–TA4 workbooks, and she would like you to add a column with the student's grade point to each TA's grading sheet. To make Professor White's modifications, do the following:

1. If necessary, start Excel, and make sure your Data Disk is in the appropriate drive. Open the **Calc223** workbook in the Review folder for Tutorial.08, and save it as **Calc223 Grades**. When you are asked if you want to update links, click the Yes button.

2. On the Documentation worksheet, enter the new workbook name, [**Your Name**], and the date in cells B13:B15.

3. Insert a new worksheet between the Documentation sheet and the Summary worksheet, and name it **TA Info**.

4. Enter the following column titles:

   Cell A1:   "Sections 1-3"
   Cell B1:   "Sections 4-6"
   Cell C1:   "Sections 7-9"
   Cell D1:   "Sections 10-12"

5. Increase the size of columns A through D to 20 characters.

6. Type a 3-D cell reference in cell A2 referring to cell B1 in the Documentation sheet of the TA1 workbook.

7. Drag the fill handle from cell A2 to A5 to fill in the complete TA information for Sections 1–3.

8. Repeat the last two steps on columns B through D, referencing the TA information for Patty Wilson, Kim Lee, and Warren Kruschevski located in the TA2, TA3, and TA4 workbooks.

9. Save your changes to the workbook. Print the TA Info worksheet and then close the document.

10. Open the **TA1** workbook from the Review folder for Tutorial.08, and then save it as **SNelson**.

11. On the Documentation sheet, enter the new workbook name, your name and the date in cells B13:B15.

12. Group the three section grading sheets, select the cells in the table, and copy the format from the Section 1 worksheet into the Section 2 and Section 3 worksheets.

13. In column J, use the VLOOKUP function to add the grade point for each student to each of the three grading sheets using the grading table found in the Calc223 Grades workbook. (*Hint*: The lookup table in the Calc223 Grades workbook has the range name, Grade_Scale. Grade point values are located in the third column of the table.)

14. Calculate the average grade point for the three sections in the SNelson workbook. What are the three grade point averages?

15. Print the three grouped grading sheets with a common page setup format: Center the table of scores and grades on the page, place your name in the page header and the date in the page footer.

16. Ungroup the worksheets and save your changes.

17. Reopen the **Calc223 Grades** workbook you created in previous steps and close all other workbooks aside from it and the SNelson workbook. Create a workspace file named **Calc223 Workbooks** that contains information about these two documents.

CASE PROBLEMS

Case 1. Consolidating Copier Sales at DOC-Centric   DOC-Centric makes six brands of copiers. They track sales information from four sales regions—North, South, East and West—in a sales workbook. You've been asked by your supervisor, Peter Mitchell, to format the workbook and to create a summary worksheet that will sum up the sales information from all four regions. To do this, you'll use the Excel worksheet grouping feature and 3-D cell references. Do the following:

1. If necessary, start Excel, and make sure your Data Disk is in the appropriate drive. Open the Copiers workbook in the Cases folder for Tutorial.08, and save it as Copier Sales.

2. Enter the workbook name, [**Your Name**], and the date in cells B5, B6 and B7 of the Documentation sheet worksheet.

3. Insert a new sheet in the workbook titled **Total Sales** at the end of the workbook.

4. Using the Edit, Fill Across Sheets command, copy the row titles and column titles from the East worksheet into the Total Sales worksheet.

5. In cells B3:F9 of the Total Sales worksheet, insert the sum of the sales in the corresponding cells in the North–East worksheets. (Be sure to ungroup the worksheets first.)

6. Format the numbers in the North–Total Sales worksheets with the Comma style, reducing the number of decimal places shown to 0.

7. Format the tables in the North–Total Sales worksheets using the Classic 2 AutoFormat table style.

8. Ungroup the worksheets and print the Total Sales worksheet.

9. Save your changes.

10. Remove the sales data, but not any summary formulas, from the four region sales worksheets and remove the workbook name, your name and the date from the Documentation sheet.

11. Save the empty workbook as a template with the name **Copier Sales Form** in the Cases folder for Tutorial.08 on your Data Disk.

12. Print the template and close the template file.

Case 2. Examining Sales Information at Kitchen WareHouse   Jaya Torres tracks the sales of kitchen appliances at Kitchen WareHouse. Kitchen WareHouse has stores in five regions. Jaya has recorded the monthly sales of refrigerators, microwaves, ovens, and dishwashers for each region in a workbook titled Kitchen located in the Cases folder for Tutorial.08 on your Data Disk. Jaya would like to include a worksheet that consolidates the sales information from the five regions. She would also like to take advantage of the Excel lookup feature to allow users to quickly retrieve the total sales of a particular product in a specific month.

Jaya has already placed an empty worksheet in her workbook that will be the summary sheet. The worksheet's title is All Regions. She wants you to add formulas to the table that sum the sales for each product in each month across the five sales regions.

She has also included a worksheet entitled Sales Results, in which she wants you to use the VLOOKUP function to allow a user to enter the month number and the product ID code, and have the total sales appear in a cell labeled Units Sold.

Do the following:

1. If necessary, start Excel, open the **Kitchen** workbook in the Cases folder for Tutorial.08 on your Data Disk, and then save it as **Kitchen WareHouse**.

2. Enter the new workbook name, your name, and the date in cells B3, B4, and B5 of the Documentation sheet.

3. In cells B4:N8 of the Summary worksheet, enter a formula that sums the values in the corresponding cells from the Region 1 to Region 5 worksheets.

4. Print the Summary worksheet.

5. Assign the range name Total_Sales to cells A3:N8 in the Summary worksheet. This will be the lookup table used in the following step.

Explore   6. In cell B5 of the Sales Results worksheet, create a lookup formula with the VLOOKUP function that will display sales figures based on the Month Number entered into cell B3 and the Product Number entered into cell B4 (*Hint*: Use the Product Number as your lookup value. Retrieve sales figures from the column in the lookup table corresponding to the Month Number plus one. The function should only look for exact matches.)

7. Test the lookup function by using it to answer the following questions:

   a. How many refrigerators were sold in all regions in January?
   b. How many dishwashers were sold in all regions over the entire year?
   c. How many appliances were sold in all regions in March?
   d. How many ovens were sold in all regions in June?

8. Print and save the final version of the Kitchen WareHouse workbook.

Case 3. Using the MATCH Function to Create a Stock Index Reporter   Kelly Watkins is an investment counselor at Davis and Burns. Some of the many kinds of information that she refers to in her job are the daily stock indices on the New York Stock Exchange (NYSE). The indices are measures of changes in the market value of NYSE common stocks, adjusted to eliminate the effects of new stock listings and deleted stock listings. There are four subgroup indices—Industrial, Transportation, Utility, and Finance—and a Composite index combining the values of the other four. Kelly is constructing a workbook that contains long-term historical data on the NYSE. Kelly would like to be able to find the closing value of any of these subgroups on any particular day from her historical data. As a starting point in constructing her historical workbook, she has some raw data for the 1990 NYSE. She would like you to help her create a simple workbook in which she would only need to enter the date from that year and the name of the subgroup and have Excel tell her the closing value. In the future, she'll build on this simple model to include more years and more stock information.

Do the following:

1. Open the **Index** workbook in the Cases folder for Tutorial.08 of your Data Disk, and save it as **NYSE Index**.

2. Enter your name, the date, and the workbook name in the Documentation sheet.

3. In the Index Data worksheet, name the range A1:F254 "Closing_Values".

4. In the Reporter worksheet, insert a VLOOKUP in cell C6 that displays the closing value based on the date entered into cell C4 and an Index number entered into cell C5 (*Hint*: The date is your lookup value, the Index number represents the column from the Closing Values table—2 = Composite, 3 = Industrial, 4 = Transport, 5 = Utility and 6 = Finance. Use only exact matches to the date.)

5. Test your function with the following set of dates and index values:
   a. Date = 10/4/90, Index = 2
   b. Date = 10/4/90, Index = 3
   c. Date = 3/14/90, Index = 4

6. Print the Reporter sheet with the results of the last lookup and save your changes to the NYSE Index workbook.

   Kelly has viewed the workbook. She wants this "index reporter" to be friendly and easy to use because she plans on sharing it with other people who might not be experienced computer users. So she wants you to remove the code numbers for each stock index and instead allow users to type in the name of the index itself.

   You'll use the MATCH function to solve this problem. The MATCH function operates like the lookup functions, except that it indicates the location of matching values in a list of values. For example, in matching the word *Utility* to the list—Date, Composite, Industrial, Transport, Utility, Finance—the MATCH function would return the value "5" because Utility is the fifth item in the list. You can use the MATCH function in place of the index number in the VLOOKUP function. Instead of having the user indicate the column number from a lookup table, the user can enter the index name and have the MATCH function determine the column number. The syntax of the MATCH function is

   MATCH(*lookup_value,lookup_array,match_type*)

   where *lookup_value* is the value you want to find, *lookup_array* is the column or row containing the values, and *match_type* is a variable that determines the type of match you want. Set match_type to 0 for exact matches. For more information, see the Excel Office

Assistant Help file on the MATCH function. Now that you've seen how the MATCH function works, you can modify your VLOOKUP function to take advantage of it.

7. Return to the Documentation sheet of the NYSE Index workbook and enter "NYSE Index 2" into cell C3. Save the workbook as **NYSE Index 2** in the Cases folder for Tutorial.08.

8. In the Index Data worksheet, name the range A1:F1 as "Index_Groups".

Explore 9. Go to the Reporter worksheet. Edit the VLOOKUP function in cell C6, replacing the column index parameter (which currently is the cell reference, C5) with the following formula: "MATCH(C5,Index_Groups,0)".

10. Test your new function using the following parameters:
    a. Date = 10/4/90, Index = Composite
    b. Date = 10/4/90, Index = Industrial
    c. Date = 3/14/90, Index = Transport

11. Print the Reporter sheet with the results of the last lookup, and then save and close the NYSE Index 2 workbook.

Case 4. *Projected Income Statement for the Bread Bakery* Your supervisor, David Keyes, has asked you to prepare the annual projected income statement for The Bread Bakery—a company specializing in fine baked breads. You've been given workbooks from three regions in the country. Each workbook has quarterly projected income statements for three of the company's products: French baguettes, sourdough wheat bread, and sourdough white bread. David wants you to summarize each workbook for him, reporting the annual totals for Earnings Before Tax in a new worksheet. Once you have added this information to each workbook, he wants you to consolidate the information from the three regional workbooks, reporting in a single workbook, the same information for the entire company.

Do the following:

1. Open each regional sales workbook, R1–R3, in the Cases folder for Tutorial.08 of your Data Disk and save **R1** as **North**, **R2** as **South** and **R3** as **Southwest**.

2. In each regional sales workbook, enter your name, the name of the workbook, and the date on the Documentation sheet.

3. Place a worksheet named **Summary** near the beginning of each regional sales workbook, right after the Documentation sheet. The Summary sheet should total all the Earnings Before Tax figures for each of the products for each of the four quarters. Also include summary values for the Earnings Before Tax figures across all four quarters and for all products.

4. Format the Summary sheet using any format you choose.

5. Create a new workbook named **Bread Bakery Report** in the Cases folder for Tutorial.08 of your Data Disk.

6. Create a documentation sheet in the Bread Bakery Report workbook containing the workbook name, [**Your Name**], and the date.

7. Create a summary worksheet in the Bread Bakery Report workbook. The sheet should contain the Earnings Before Tax values summarized over region, product, and quarter. Include summary totals over these ranges.

8. The format and design of the Bread Bakery Report workbook is up to you.

9. Print the Summary sheets from the four workbooks you've created.

10. Create a workspace named **Bread Bakery** for the four workbooks you created in this assignment.

INTERNET ASSIGNMENTS

The purpose of the Internet Assignments is to challenge you to find information on the Internet that you can use to create effective spreadsheets. The actual assignments are updated and maintained on the Course Technology Web site. Log on to the Internet and use your Web browser to go to the Student Online Companion to accompany this text at **www.course.com/NewPerspectives/office2000**. Click the Excel link, and then click the link for Tutorial 8.

QUICK CHECK ANSWERS

Session 8.1

1. Right-click the sheet tab of the active sheet, click Insert on the Shortcut menu, click the worksheet icon in the Insert dialog box, then click the OK button; click the sheet tab of the newly created worksheet, then drag it to the right of the previously active sheet.
2. A worksheet group is a collection of worksheets that have all been selected for editing and formatting.
3. Select the worksheet group by either pressing and holding down the Ctrl key and clicking the sheet tab of each worksheet in the grouping or if the worksheets occupy a contiguous range in the workbook, by clicking the first sheet tab in the range, pressing and holding down the Shift key, and clicking the sheet tab of the last sheet in the range. Deselect a worksheet group by either clicking the sheet tab of a worksheet not in the group or right-clicking one of the sheet tabs in the group and clicking Ungroup Sheets on the Shortcut menu.
4. Create a worksheet group consisting of the range of worksheets. In the first worksheet in the group, select the text and formulas you want to copy and click Edit, click Fill , then click Across Worksheets. Select whether you want to copy the contents, formulas, or both, then click the OK button.
5. the sheet range and the cell range
6. 'Section1'!A1:A10
7. Sheet 1:Sheet10!A1:A10

Session 8.2

1. A template is a workbook that contains specific content and formatting that you can use as a model for other similar workbooks.
2. A user can modify the contents of a workbook based on a template without changing the template file itself. The next time a workbook is created based on a template, it is opened with all the original properties intact.
3. the template used in creating the blank workbook you first see when starting a new Excel session
4. click File, Save As, click Template in the Save as type list box, then click the Save button
5. Templates folder (a subfolder of the Microsoft Office folder)
6. create a subfolder in the Templates folder, then move the template file into it

Section 8.3

1. 'D:\Reports\[Product Report]Sales Info'!A1:A10
2. It includes both the location and the name of the workbook.
3. click Edit, then click Links
4. A lookup table is a table in which rows and columns of information are organized into separate categories. The lookup value is the value that indicates the category in which you are looking. The categories for the lookup table are usually located in the table's first row or column and are called compare values.
5. VLOOKUP and HLOOKUP
6. The range_lookup value is a parameter in the VLOOKUP and HLOOKUP functions that tell Excel where to look for an exact match in a lookup table. A value of TRUE means that Excel does not have to find an exact match.
7. A workspace file is a file containing information about all of the currently opened workbooks, including their locations, window sizes, and screen positions. By opening a workspace file, you open all related workbooks. This helps you organize projects that may involve several workbooks because you don't have to keep a list of those filenames.

OBJECTIVES

In this appendix you will:

- Use PMT, PPMT, IPMT functions

- Use AND function

- Use nested IF function

- Use YEAR function

EXCEL FUNCTIONS

SESSION A1.1

In this session you will develop a loan calculator using the PMT function and an amortization schedule using the PPMT and IPMT functions.

Financial Functions

Many people need to make loans for expensive items such as automobiles, sound systems, or home improvements. Often, they may not have the cash on hand at one time to make such purchases. Asking for a loan may cause anxiety for people who do not understand the full picture of how loans and interest rates are calculated.

At a local financial institution, which makes such loans, Jerry Angelo wants to develop a loan calculator worksheet for the institution's customers. The loan calculator would be made available to potential customers so that they can begin some calculations before meeting with a loan officer. His plan will allow the customer to use a computer to experiment with different loan scenarios. The calculator would determine the customer's monthly payment using varying loan amounts, interest rates, and time periods. In addition, the worksheet would also display an amortization schedule, a report that shows the details of each monthly payment—how much of each payment goes to paying off the loan and how much applies to interest. Jerry believes this service will help educate the loan applicant and reduce some of the applicant's anxiety.

Jerry asks you to develop the loan calculator and amortization schedule worksheet using data from an old loan application. Use as an example a loan of $20,000 at 7% interest being paid off monthly over three years.

Introduction to Financial Functions

Excel has fifteen financial functions that are related to money. Figure A1-1 shows four financial functions used to analyze loans and annuities.

Figure A1-1	FINANCIAL FUNCTIONS USED TO ANALYZE LOANS AND ANNUITIES
FUNCTION AND ARGUMENTS	**DESCRIPTION**
PMT(rate,nper,pv)	Calculates the payment for a loan based on constant payments and a constant interest rate.
IPMT(rate,per,nper,pv)	Returns the interest payment for a given period for an investment based on periodic, constant payments and a constant interest rate.
PPMT(rate,per,nper,pv)	Returns the payment on the principal for a given period for an investment based on periodic, constant payments and a constant interest rate.
PV(rate,nper,pmt)	Returns the present value of an investment. The present value is the total amount that a series of future payments is worth now.

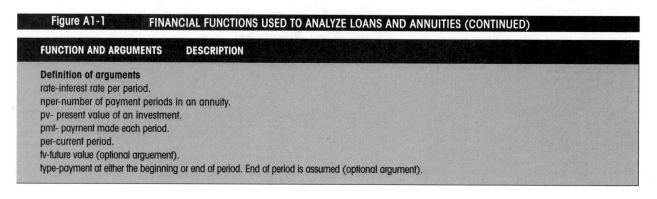

Figure A1-1	FINANCIAL FUNCTIONS USED TO ANALYZE LOANS AND ANNUITIES (CONTINUED)

FUNCTION AND ARGUMENTS   **DESCRIPTION**

Definition of arguments
rate-interest rate per period.
nper-number of payment periods in an annuity.
pv- present value of an investment.
pmt- payment made each period.
per-current period.
fv-future value (optional arguement).
type-payment at either the beginning or end of period. End of period is assumed (optional argument).

You will use the functions in Figure A1-1 to develop the loan calculator and amortization schedule.

Calculating a Loan Payment Using the PMT Function

The PMT function calculates the periodic payment of a loan assuming a constant interest rate and constant payments over the life of the loan. It is based on three factors: amount of the loan (principal), interest rate, and length of the loan (term). Now, develop the loan calculator section of the worksheet.

To develop the loan calculator:

1. Open the **Loan Analysis** workbook in the Tutorial folder for Appendix.01 and save it as **LoanCalculator**. Review the row and column labels.

   Enter the rate, term, and principal for the loan.

2. Type **7%** in cell B2, **3** in cell B3 and **20000** in cell B4 (Do not use the comma when typing 20000.)

   Enter the function to calculate the loan payment.

3. If necessary, click **B5**, click **Paste Function** $f_\ast$, click **Financial**, and then double-click **PMT** to open the PMT formula palette. See Figure A1-2.

Figure A1-2	PMT FORMULA PALETTE

PMT

Rate [   ] = number

Nper [   ] = number

Pv [   ] = number

Fv [   ] = number

Type [   ] = number

=

Calculates the payment for a loan based on constant payments and a constant interest rate.

Rate is the interest rate per period for the loan.

? Formula result =   [OK]   [Cancel]

4. In the Rate text box, type **B2/12**. The interest rate entered in cell B2 was an annual rate so you need to divide it by 12 to get the rate per month.

5. In the Nper (number of periods) text box, type **B3*12**. The entry in cell B3 is expressed in years, you need to multiply the years by 12 to compute the number of monthly payments.

6. In Pv text box, type **B4** and click **OK**. The monthly payment appears as a negative number ($617.54).

   Display the monthly payment as a positive number.

7. Double-click cell **B5**. Position the insertion point to the right of the equal sign (=), type **-**, and then press the **Enter** key. The monthly payment appears as $617.54.

8. Click cell **B5**. See Figure A1-3.

Figure A1-3	COMPLETED LOAN CALCULATOR

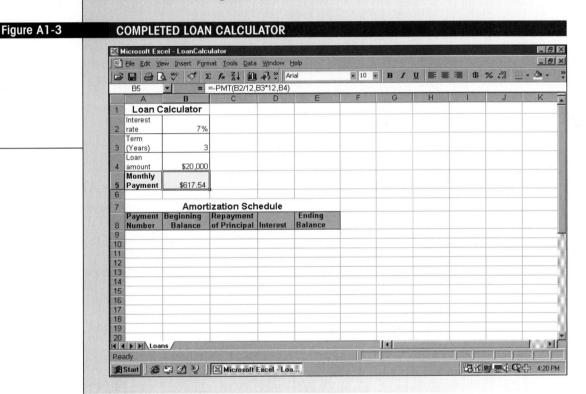

The loan calculator portion of the worksheet is complete.

Developing **the Loan Amortization Schedule**

Now prepare the **loan amortization schedule**, a report that shows the details of each loan payment. This schedule shows how much of each month's payment is applied to the repayment of principal, and how much is applied toward interest. The schedule also shows the ending loan balance after each loan payment. Figure A1-4 describes the calculations you'll use to prepare the amortization schedule.

Figure A1-4	CALCULATIONS FOR AMORTIZATION SCHEDULE

COLUMN IN AMORTIZATION SCHEDULE	NOTES ABOUT FORMULA
Payment number	In cells A9:A44 enter values 1 to 36
Beginning Balance	In cell B9, enter the amount of loan In cells B10:B44, enter ending loan balance from previous period
Repayment of Principal	In cells C9:C44, use PPMT function
Interest	In cells D9:D44, use IPMT function
Ending Balance	In cells E9:E44, use beginning balance less repayment of principal

Use Excel's AutoFill feature to enter the numbers 1 to 36 to represent the 36 payments.

To enter the numbers 1 to 36 using AutoFill:

1. Type **1** in cell A9 and **2** in cell A10.

2. Select **A9:A10** and use the AutoFill feature to complete the sequential series 3 to 36 in cells A11:A44.

Now, enter the beginning loan balance. Before the first payment is made, the beginning balance equals the amount of the loan.

To enter the beginning balance for period 1:

1. In cell B9, type **=B4**.

Calculating the Principal Paid in Each Period Using the PPMT Function

The column labeled Repayment of Principal in the amortization schedule shows the amount of the monthly payment that is applied to repaying the principal. This amount varies throughout the life of the loan and depends on the interest rate, total number of payments, amount of the loan, and the specific period. These are the arguments used with PPMT function to compute the principal paid for a specific period.

To calculate the repayment of principal using the PPMT function:

1. Click **C9**, click **Paste Function** *fx*, click **Financial**, and then double-click **PPMT** to open the PPMT formula palette. See Figure A1-5.

Figure A1-5   PPMT FORMULA PALETTE

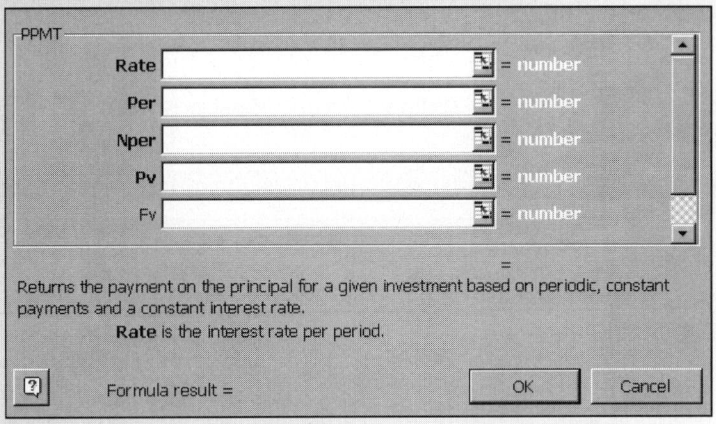

2. In the Rate text box, type **$B$2/12** to compute the monthly interest. Because you will be copying Rate to other rows in the amortization schedule, you add the dollar signs to the cell reference to make this portion of formula an absolute cell reference.

3. In the Per (current period) text box, type **A9.** Because this portion of the formula references the payment period it needs to vary as it is copied to other cells. Leave this portion of the formula as a relative cell reference.

4. In the Nper (number of periods) text box, type **$B$3*12** to determine the number of monthly payments.

5. In Pv text box, type **$B$4** and click **OK**. The repayment of principal amount appears as a negative number. Display this amount as a positive number. Double-click cell **C9**. Position the insertion point to the right of the equal sign (=), type -, and then press the **Enter** key. The repayment of principal for payment number 1 appears as $500.88. The formula in cell C9 is =-PPMT($B$2/12,A9,$B$3*12,$B$4).

Calculating the Interest Paid in Each Period Using the IPMT Function

The interest column in the amortization schedule shows the amount of the monthly payment that is applied toward interest for each period. The IPMT function is used to calculate this amount.

To calculate interest payment for a given period using IPMT function:

1. Click **D9**, click **Paste Function** 𝑓ₓ , click **Financial**, and then double-click **IPMT** to open the IPMT formula palette.

2. In the Rate text box, type **$B$2/12**.

3. In the Per text box, type **A9**.

4. In the Nper text box, type **$B$3*12**.

5. In Pv text box, type **$B$4** and click **OK**. The interest amount appears as a negative number. Double-click cell **D9**. Position the insertion point to the right of the equal sign (=), type -, and then press the **Enter** key. The interest appears as $116.67.

6. Click cell **D9** to view the interest payment formula. See Figure A1-6.

Figure A1-6	EARLY STAGES OF AMORTIZATION SCHEDULE

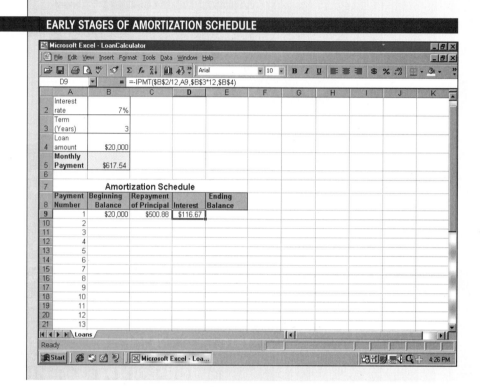

Now, complete the amortization schedule.

Completing the Amortization Schedule

First, compute the ending balance for the first month, this represents the amount of the principal that still needs to be repaid.

To complete the amortization schedule:

1. In cell E9, type **=B9-C9,** the formula to compute the ending balance. The amount is $19,499.12.

For the remaining payment periods, the ending balance for the current month is also the beginning balance for the next month.

2. In cell B10, type **=E9.**

Copy the formulas in C9:E9 down one row.

3. Select **C9:E9,** then click and drag the fill handle in cell **E9** down one row to row 10.

Now copy the formulas in row 10 to the other rows of the amortization schedule.

4. Select **B10:E10,** then click and drag the fill handle in cell **E10** to row 44.

5. When finished, your amortization schedule should look like Figure A1-7. Check that the ending balance in period 36 equals zero.

Figure A1-7

Figure A1-7 | **COMPLETED AMORTIZATION SCHEDULE**

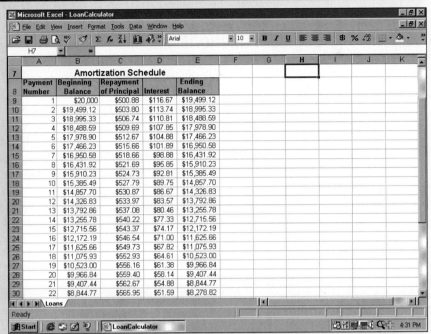

6. Change the input values (Interest rate, Term, and Loan amount) to see the effect on both the Monthly Payment and Amortization Schedule.

7. Save, then close the workbook.

The loan calculator and amortization schedule are complete and can now be used by the bank's customers.

SESSION A1.2

In this session you will learn to develop complex conditional formulas. You will nest the AND function within the IF function. You'll also learn how to nest IF functions.

AND, OR, NOT, and Nesting IF Functions*

Maria Abba, vice president of administration for Branco, Inc., is compiling Branco's budget estimates for two of Branco's employee benefits: costs for matching employee contributions to the 401(k) retirement plan and the cost of health insurance.

Maria provides you with information on each benefit program.

401(k) plan: Branco matches dollar-for-dollar up to 3% of an eligible employee's salary into the employee's 401(k) account. The company policy specifies that only *full-time regular* employees, employed for *one or more years* are eligible for the 401(k) plan.

*Before reading this section, you may find it helpful to review the IF function on page EX 7.13.

Health insurance costs: Branco pays 100% of the health insurance cost for all employees. The amount Branco pays per employee depends on the level of an employee's coverage: $5000 for family coverage, $4000 for individual coverage, and $0 if the employee has coverage elsewhere.

Maria asks you to help her develop these cost estimates for each employee.

Introduction to Logical Functions

In Tutorial 7 you were introduced to the IF function as a way of applying conditional logic to choose between two alternative formulas. The calculations for 401(k) and health insurance require more complex logic than the IF function alone is capable of handling. In the case of 401(k) plan, you have to test two conditions before you can determine the 401(k) cost; the IF function evaluates one condition. In the case of health insurance cost, you need to choose from three alternative formulas; the IF function only evaluates two alternative formulas. Each of these calculations requires a modification of the IF function in order to resolve the conditional logic.

Excel provides three logical functions (AND, OR, and NOT) that are typically used with the IF function to test more complex conditions. The AND and OR functions enable you to test multiple conditions, and the NOT function reverses a condition that returns true or false. Figure A1-8 describes the syntax of these functions.

Figure A1-8	SYNTAX OF AND, OR, AND NOT FUNCTIONS		
FUNCTION	**DESCRIPTION**	**EXAMPLE**	**RESULT**
AND(logical condition1, logical condition2, ...logical condition30)	Returns TRUE if all logical conditions (up to 30) are TRUE; returns FALSE if one or more logical condition is FALSE	IF(AND(B2>=10000,B2<=4000), B2*1.05,B2) Assume B2=30000 Assume B2=50000	31500 50000
OR(logical condition1, logical condition2, ...logical condition30)	Returns TRUE if any logical condition (up to 30) is TRUE; returns FALSE if all logical conditions are FALSE	IF(OR(C2="Finance",C2="Accounting"), "Eligible","Ineligible") Assume C2=Accounting Assume C2=Marketing	Eligible Ineligible
NOT(logical condition)	Reverse the value of its argument, if logical condition is FALSE, NOT(logical condition) returns TRUE, if logical condition is TRUE, NOT(logical condition) returns FALSE.	IF(NOT(A2="Married"),"Other","Joint") Assume A2=Sales Assume A2=Married	Other Joint

The AND, OR, and NOT functions are typically placed within the IF function to create a **nested function**, a function that is used as an argument within another function.

Using the AND Function to Compute the 401(k) Costs

First, review the company's 401(k) policy.

The company policy specifies that only full-time employees employed with the company for one or more years are eligible for a 401(k) plan. Both conditions must be met to be eligible for the plan. Maria developed a flowchart to represent the logic to calculate the 401(k) costs. See Figure A1-9.

Figure A1-9	FLOWCHART SHOWING EMPLOYEE ELIGIBILITY FOR 401(K) RETIREMENT PLAN

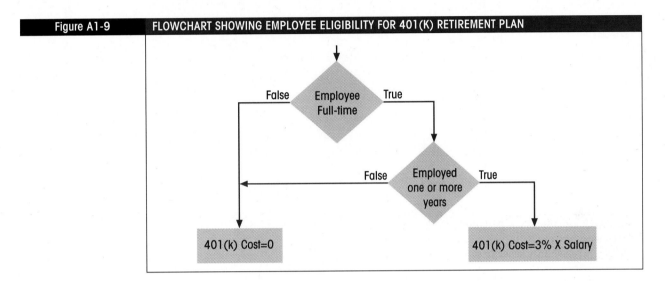

As you see in the flowchart, both conditions must be TRUE for an employee to be eligible for the 401(k) plan, in which case the company contributes 3% of the employee's salary; otherwise the employee is not eligible and the company's contribution is zero.

The IF function evaluates a single condition. To create the formula to determine the cost of the 401(k) plan for each employee, you use the AND function along with the IF function.

Now open the workbook that contains the employee data.

To open the Employee workbook:

1. Open the **Employee** workbook in the Tutorial folder for Appendix .01 and save it as **Employee Benefits**. See Figure A1-10.

    Data on each employee is stored in separate rows. There are seven fields for each employee. The Job Status codes for the employees' current status, are FT= full-time, PT= part-time, and CN= consultant. Heath Plan codes for type of coverage are F=family, I=individual, and N=no coverage. Notice two fields: 401(k) Cost and Health Insurance Cost have no values.

Figure A1-10   **EMPLOYEE DATA WORKSHEET**

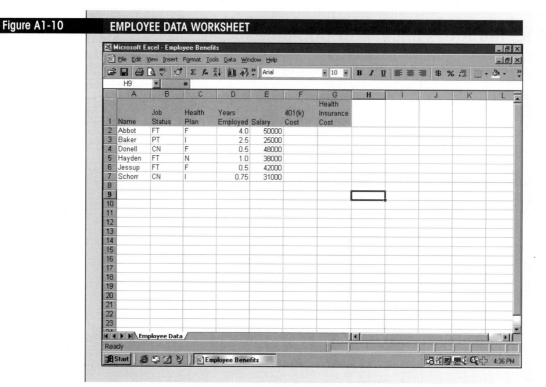

To create a formula to determine the cost of matching an employee's contribution to the 401(k) plan, you nest the AND function within the IF function. The Excel formula for the first employee has the following syntax

`=IF(AND(B2="FT",D2>=1),E2*0.03,0)`

`where red = condition, green = value-if-true, and blue = value-if-false.`

Now enter the formula for each employee.

> *To enter a formula using an AND function, nested within an IF function:*
>
> **1.** Click cell **F2** to make it the active cell.
>
> **2.** Type **=IF(AND(B2="FT",D2>=1),E2*0.03,0)** and press **Enter**. Notice, 1500 appears in cell F2.
>
> **3.** Copy the formula in cell **F2** to the range **F3:F7**.
>
> **4.** Click cell **F7**. When finished your output should be similar to Figure A1-11.

Figure A1-11	401(K) COST ESTIMATES COMPLETED

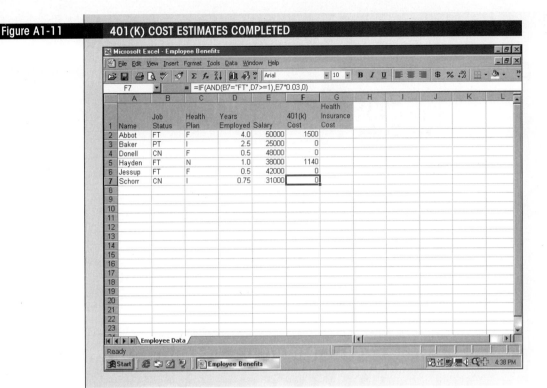

The formulas you created will calculate the 401(k) costs. Now build the formula to compute the health insurance costs.

Nesting IF Functions to Compute Health Insurance Costs

There are decisions in which the AND and OR functions cannot resolve the conditional logic for certain computations. In these cases, you may find that placing the IF function within another IF function, or *nesting* the IF function, creates a hierarchy of tests and is a good way to resolve the conditional logic. For example, determining the health insurance cost for each employee requires a formula to choose from among three cost options: $5000 for family coverage, $4000 for individual coverage, and $0 if the employee has coverage elsewhere. The employee database contains a Health Plan code that is used to determine the level of coverage. Figure A1-12 illustrates the logic to determine the health insurance cost.

Figure A1-12	FLOWCHART SHOWING HEALTH INSURANCE COST OPTIONS

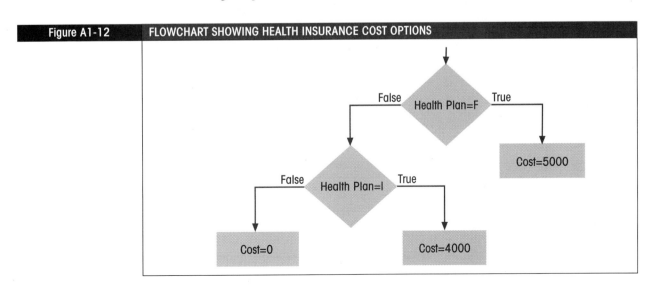

The nested IF function equivalent of the logic illustrated in the flowchart for the first employee shown in figure A1-13.

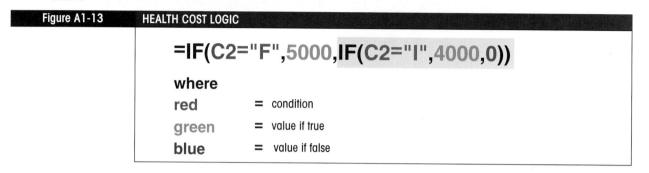

Figure A1-13 **HEALTH COST LOGIC**

=IF(C2="F",5000,IF(C2="I",4000,0))

where

red   = condition

green   = value if true

blue   = value if false

Now enter the nested IF function needed to calculate the cost of health insurance for each employee.

To enter the nested IF function:

1. Click cell **G2** to make it the active cell.

2. Type **=IF(C2="F",5000,IF(C2="I",4000,0))** and press **Enter**. The IF function returns 5000.

3. Copy the formula in cell **G2** to the range **G3:G7**.

4. Click cell **G7**. When finished, your output should be similar to Figure A1-14.

5. Save, then close the workbook.

Figure A1-14 **HEALTH INSURANCE COST ESTIMATE COMPLETED**

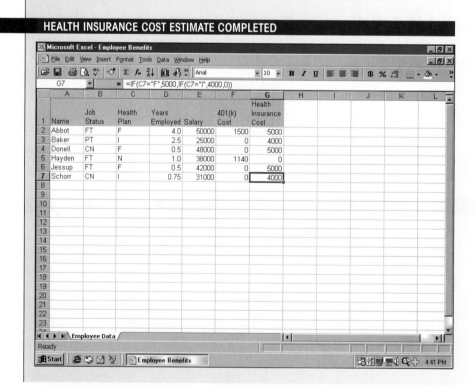

In this session you used the AND function within an IF function to develop the conditional logic needed to calculate the 401(k) costs. Then you nested IF functions to develop a conditional formula to calculate the health insurance cost.

SESSION A1.3

In this session you will learn how Excel stores date and time values and uses the YEAR function to calculate the number of years between dates.

Date and Time Functions

Century, Inc. recognizes employees for their longevity of employment by providing service awards at one-year, five-year, ten-year and twenty-year time intervals. Millie Fenton subtracts the employee's hire year from the current year to compute the number of years an employee has been employed. She uses this information to determine which employees receive service awards.

Introduction to Date and Time Values

Excel stores dates and times as values. Each date between January 1, 1900 and December 31, 2078 is stored as a sequential serial number. January 1, 1900 is assigned the value 1, January 2, 1900 is assigned the value 2, January 1, 1901 is 367, January 1, 2000 is the value 36526, and so on.

Excel works with time values as fractions of a 24-hour day. For instance, midnight is stored as 0.0, noon (12 PM), is stored as 0.5, and 6 PM is stored as 0.75. Time is treated as an extension of the serial number Excel uses with dates. So January 1, 2000 at 12 PM is represented by the value 36526.5.

Because dates are stored as serial numbers, you can perform calculations with dates (sometimes referred to as date arithmetic.) For example, you can add integers to dates or calculate the number of days between two dates. You can also perform arithmetic with time values. For example, you can calculate the number of hours between two times.

Excel has many functions to assist you with dates and times. Figure A1-15 lists some of these functions.

Figure A1-15	DATE AND TIME FUNCTIONS

FUNCTION	DESCRIPTION
TODAY() *Notice that although parentheses are included, no arguments are used in this function*	Returns the current date
NOW() *Notice that although parentheses are included, no arguments are used in this function*	Returns the current date and time
DATE(year, month, day)	Returns the date based on its three arguments: year, month, and day
DAY(date)	Extracts a day of the month from a date
MONTH(date)	Extracts a month number from a date
YEAR(date)	Extracts a year (yyyy) from a date
WEEKDAY(date)	Returns a day of the week (Sunday =1) from a date
DATEVALUE(date_text)	Converts a date from text to a date
DATEDIF(start_date, end_date, unit)	Calculates the number of days, months, or years between two dates. Units are entered as "Y" (complete years), "M" (complete months), or "D" (days).
HOUR(time)	Extracts the hour part from a time
MINUTE(time)	Extracts the minute part from a time
SECOND(time)	Extracts the second part from a time

Using the YEAR Function to Calculate Years Employed

Now calculate the number of years an employee has been employed at Century, Inc. The data Millie has about employees includes the date hired. You will extract the year from the date hired using the YEAR function so you can subtract the year hired from the current year.

To calculate years employed:

1. Open the **Service** workbook in the Tutorial folder for Appendix.01 and save it as **YearsEmployed**.

2. Enter the current year. Type **2001** in cell B1.

3. Type **=$B$1-YEAR(B4)** in cell C4. Notice the cell is formatted with date and time.

4. Return to cell C4, click **Format**, click **Cells**, and click **General** format in the **Numbers** tab. Click **OK**. 15 appears in cell C4.

5. Copy the formula to the cells in the range **C5:C7**.

Figure A1-16	CALCULATION OF YEARS EMPLOYED COMPLETED

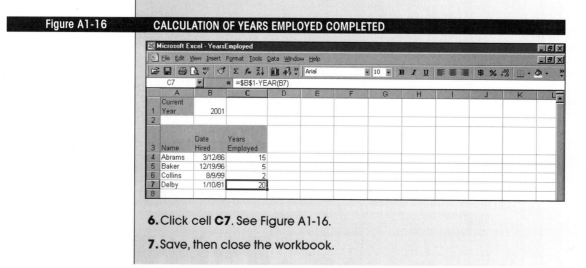

6. Click cell **C7**. See Figure A1-16.

7. Save, then close the workbook.

Text and Statistical Functions

Excel has several hundred functions that perform a wide range of calculations. Figure A1-17 lists a few text and statistical functions that you may find useful. For more information on these and other functions consult the online help system.

Figure A1-17	ADDITIONAL STATISTICAL AND TEXT FUNCTIONS		
FUNCTION	**DESCRIPTION**	**EXAMPLE USING FIG A1-18**	**RESULT**
COUNT(value1,value2,...)	Counts the number of values in a range.	=COUNT(A1:A6)	3
COUNTA(value1,value2,...)	Counts the number of nonblank characters in a range.	=COUNTA(A1:A6)	6
COUNTIF(range,criteria)	Counts the number of cells within a range that meet the given criteria.	=COUNTIF (A1:A6,"Rhode Island")	2
SUMIF(range,criteria,sum_range)	Adds the cells specified by a given criteria.	=SUMIF(A1:A6,">20")	56
LEFT(text,# of leftmost characters)	Returns leftmost characters of a string.	=LEFT(A1,5)	Rhode

Figure A1-17   ADDITIONAL STATISTICAL AND TEXT FUNCTIONS (CONTINUED)

FUNCTION	DESCRIPTION	EXAMPLE USING FIG A1-18	RESULT
MID(text,position of first character you want to extract, # of characters to extract)	Returns a specific number of characters from a text string starting at a position you specify.	=MID(A1,7,2)	Is
RIGHT(text, number of characters to extract)	Returns rightmost characters in text string.	=RIGHT(A1,4)	Land
LEN(text)	Returns the number of characters in a text string.	=LEN(A1)	12
CONCATENATE(text1,text2,...)	Joins several text strings into one text string.	=CONCATENATE(A3,A4)	Massachusetts24

Figure A1-18

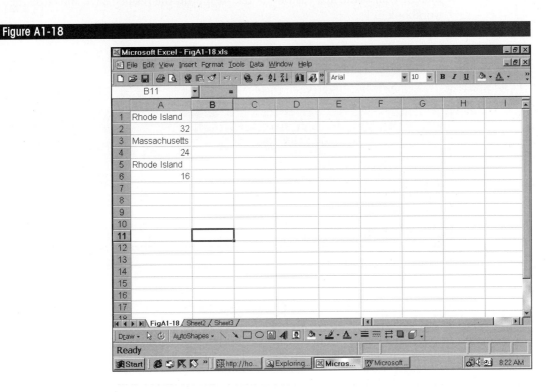

REVIEW ASSIGNMENTS

1. Open the **LoanAnalysis2** workbook in the Review folder of Appendix.01 and save it as **LoanAnalysis3**.

2. Change the interest rate to 8%. Print the results.

3. Insert two formulas to calculate total payments made during the entire loan (monthly payment times number of payments) and total interest (total payments – loan amount). Place the formula to calculate Total Payments in cell B6 and the formula to calculate Total interest in cell B7. Print only the loan calculator section of the worksheet.

Explore

4. In a separate sheet, develop a worksheet to determine the number of periods needed to pay off a loan assuming a potential borrower knows the interest rate, the loan amount, and the amount the borrower wants to repay each month. How many months will it take to pay off a $10,000, 9% loan paying $100 a month? (*Hint*: Look up the NPER function in Help. Enter the payment amount as a negative number.) Develop an attractive worksheet. Print the results.

5. Save and close the workbook.

6. Open the **Employee2** workbook in the Review folder of Appendix .01 and save it as **Employee3**.

Explore

7. a. The company is considering changing its 401(k) policy to include eligibility for all of its employees, both full-time and part-time, regardless of their years of service. Create a formula in column F to reflect these changes.

   b. Another possible revision to the plan specifies that both full-time and part-time employees employed with the company for one or more years are eligible for a 401(k) plan. Both conditions must be met to be eligible for the plan. Create a formula in column G to calculate 401(k) cost based on this new policy.

Explore

8. Develop the health insurance formula so you display the label "invalid code" in the Health Insurance Cost column if an invalid code is entered in the Job Status field.

9. Include your name in a custom footer, then print the results. Save and close the workbook.

10. Open a blank workbook and calculate how many days until you graduate. Follow the steps in Figure A1-19.

Figure A1-19	STEPS FOR CALCULATING DAYS UNTIL GRADUATION

CELL	ENTER
A1	Enter the label **Graduation Date**
B1	Enter your date of graduation
A2	Enter the label **Today's date**
B2	Enter a function to display today's date
A3	Enter the label **Number of days until graduation**
B3	Enter a formula to compute the number of days from today's date until you graduate

11. Print the results. Save the workbook as **GraduationDate**.

12. Microsoft has developed a rule to interpret dates entered with a two-digit year occurring in either the 20th or 21st century. For example, if you enter 4/24/99, does Excel store this date as 4/24/1999 or 4/24/2099? Determine how Excel treats dates entered using a two-digit year (mm/dd/yy instead of mm/dd/yyyy) by inputting the dates in Figure A1-20 into Sheet2. Format the six cells using the date format m/d/yyyy. Briefly explain how Excel treats dates entered with a two-digit year.

Figure A1-20	DATES TO INPUT

A2	7/1/00
A3	7/1/28
A4	7/1/29
A5	7/1/30
A6	7/1/31
A7	7/1/99

13. a. Open the **Service2** workbook in the Review folder of Appendix.01 and save it as **Service3**.

   b. Enter the TODAY function in cell B1 and then format that cell using the format type m/d/yyyy. Use the same format type to format cells B4:B7.

   c. Apply the DATEDIF function in cells C4:C7 to calculate the number of complete years of service. If necessary, use Help to learn more about the DATEDIF function.

   d. Print and save the workbook.

CASE PROBLEMS

Case 1. Depreciation at Imat   Helen Fayer is an accountant at Imat Corporation. One of her responsibilities is to maintain information about the assets that the company owns. This information is used to compute depreciation for the financial reports and identify new assets that need a property identification tag stamped on the asset.

1. Open the **Asset** workbook in the Cases folder for Appendix.01, and save it as **AssetData**. Notice data has been entered in all columns except the Depreciation and Needs Tag columns. You need to develop formulas for each of these columns.

2. Accountants use different methods to calculate depreciation. Excel provides functions that calculate depreciation for each of these depreciation methods. Figure A1-21 describes each function.
   Use the IF function to develop a formula to compute depreciation for each asset. Within the IF function test the depreciation method code (SLN is straight-line-code, SYD is sum-of-years-digits, DDB is double-declining balance) to determine the appropriate depreciation function to use to compute depreciation.

Figure A1-21	DESCRIPTION OF FUNCTIONS	
DEPRECIATION METHOD	**FUNCTION AND ARGUMENTS**	**DESCRIPTION**
Straight Line	SLN(cost,salvage,life)	The SLN function calculates straight-line depreciation for a single period. This method distributes the depreciation evenly over the life of the asset.
Double-declining balance	DDB(cost,salvage,life,period)	The DDB function uses the double-declining balance method to calculate the amount of depreciation for a specified period. This method computes depreciation at an accelerated rate. Depreciation is highest in earlier periods and decreases in successive periods.
Sum of years digits	SYD(cost,salvage,life,period)	The SYD function uses the sum-of-the-years'-digits method to calculate an asset's depreciation for a specified period. This method concentrates depreciation in earlier periods.
	where cost=purchase price of the asset salvage=value of the asset at end of useful life life=number of periods over which the asset is being depreciated period=period for which to calculate depreciation	

3. Print a report that includes the Asset description, Cost, Date purchased, and Depreciation.

4. In the Needs Tag column, enter a formula that displays "Yes" or "No" depending on whether the asset needs a property tag. The criteria for tagging is as follows:

- Asset purchased in current year. Use 2001 as the current year.
- Cost of asset is $3000 or more

Both criteria must be met to place "Yes" in the Needs Tag column, otherwise place "No".
First, enter the current year in cell B2 and the Tag cutoff amount in cell B3. Use the information in cell B2 and cell B3 to develop an IF function in the Needs Tag column.

5. Use the information in the Needs tag column to print only those assets that need to be tagged. Show only the columns Asset description, Date purchased, and Needs Tag on the printout.

6. Save and close the workbook.

Case 2. North State University Revisited Dean Long of the College of Business Administration has to prepare a summary report for a presentation to advisory council. She has prepared a sketch of the information to summarize from the faculty list. See Figure A1-22.

Figure A1-22	SKETCH OF SUMMARY REPORT

GROUP	NUMBER	TOTAL SALARY
All faculty		
Female faculty		
Full professor		

1. Start Excel and make sure your Data Disk is in the appropriate disk drive. Open the workbook **FacultyRevisited** in the Cases folder for Appendix.01, and then save it as **FacultySummary**.

2. Complete the summary report, cells A2:C5. Use the appropriate functions in Figure A1-17 to develop formulas for the summary report.

3. Print only the summary report. Remember to include your name in the custom footer.

Explore

4. North State University has changed servers for their email and every faculty, staff, and student has a new email address. The dean wants to include the new address in column M of the faculty list. The email address can be generated by using text functions. A new address consists of the following:

The user id portion of the email address is formed from the

- First letter of your first name, plus the
- First three letters of your last name, plus the
- Last four digits of your social security number, then
  add @nsu.edu to complete the address.

For example, Alicia Smith's social security number is 000-10-9999. Her email is ASMI9999@nsu.edu. (*Hint*: Review the CONCATENATE function.)

Print the faculty list.

5. Save the workbook.

TASK	PAGE #	RECOMMENDED METHOD
3-D cell reference, create	EX 8.18	(When entering a function into a worksheet cell) select a sheet or sheet range, then select the cell range within those worksheets.
AutoComplete, use	EX 1.15	To accept Excel's suggestion, press Enter. Otherwise, continue typing a new label.
AutoFill, create series	EX 7.17	Enter the first or first two values in a series. Select this range. Click and drag the fill handle over cells you want the series to fill.
AutoFilter	EX 5.19	Click any cell in the list. Click Data, point to Filter, then click AutoFilter. Click list arrow in column that contains the data you want to filter, then select the value with which you want to filter.
AutoFilter, custom	EX 5.22	Click any cell in list. Click Data, point to Filter, then click AutoFilter. Click list arrow in column that contains the data you want to filter. Click Custom then enter the criteria in Custom AutoFilter dialog box.
AutoFormat, use	EX 2.28	Select the range to format, click Format, then click AutoFormat. Select desired format from Table Format list, then click OK.
AutoSum button, use	EX 2.07	Click the cell where you want sum to appear. Click Σ. Make sure the range address in the formula is the same as the range you want to sum.
Border, apply	EX 3.21	*See* Reference Window: Adding a Border.
Cancel action	EX 2.26	Press Esc, or click Undo ↶.
Cell contents, clear	EX 1.29	Select the cells you want to clear, then press Delete.
Cell contents, copy using Copy command	EX 2.10	Select the cell or range you want to copy, then click 🗐.
Cell contents, copy using fill handle	EX 2.10	Click cell(s) with data or label to copy, then click and drag the fill handle to outline the cell(s) to which the data is to be copied.
Cell reference types, edit	EX 2.14	Double-click cell containing formula to be edited. Move insertion point to part of cell reference to be changed, then press F4 until reference type is correct, then press Enter.
Chart, activate	EX 4.11	Click anywhere within the chart border. Same as selecting.
Chart, add data labels	EX 4.17	Select the chart, then select a single data marker for the series. Click Chart, click Chart Options, then click Data Labels. Select the type of data labels you want, then click OK.
Chart, adjust size	EX 4.11	Select the chart and drag selection handles.
Chart, apply a pattern to a data marker	EX 4.20	*See* Reference Window: Selecting a Pattern for a Data Marker.
Chart, apply a texture	EX 4.32	Click Format Chart Area on Chart toolbar, click Patterns tab, click Fill Effects button, and then click the Texture tab. Select the desired texture.
Chart, create	EX 4.06	Select data to be charted. Click 📊, then complete the steps in the Chart Wizard dialog boxes.

TASK	PAGE #	RECOMMENDED METHOD
Chart, delete data series	EX 4.14	Select the chart, select the data series, then press Delete.
Chart, explode pie slice	EX 4.29	Select the pie chart, then click the slice to explode. Drag the selected slice away from center of pie.
Chart, format labels	EX 4.31	Select chart labels, then use Formatting toolbar to change font type, size, and style.
Chart, move	EX 4.11	Select the chart and drag it to a new location.
Chart, rotate a 3-D chart	EX 4.30	Select a 3-D chart. Click Chart, then 3-D View. Type the values you want in the Rotation and Elevation boxes.
Chart, select	EX 4.11	Click anywhere within the chart border. Same as activating.
Chart, update	EX 4.13	Enter new values in worksheet. Chart link to data is automatically updated.
Chart, use picture	EX 4.36	Create column or bar chart. Select all columns/bars to be filled with picture, then click Insert, point to Picture, then click From File. Select picture from Insert Picture dialog box, then click Insert.
Chart title, add or edit	EX 4.16	Select the chart. Click Chart, then click Chart Options. In the Titles tab, click one of the title text boxes, then type the desired title.
Chart Wizard, start	EX 4.07	Click 📊 .
Clipboard contents, paste into range	EX 2.15	Click 📋 .
Colors, apply to a range of cells	EX 3.24	*See* Reference Window: Applying Patterns and Color.
Column width, change	EX 2.23	*See* Reference Window: Changing Column Width.
Conditional formatting	EX 5.24	Select the cells you want to format. Click Format, then click Conditional Formatting. Specify the condition(s) in the Conditional Formatting dialog box. Click the Format button and select the formatting to apply if condition is true.
Copy formula, use copy-and-paste method	EX 2.14	Select the cell with the formula to be copied, click 📋 , click the cell you want the formula copied to, then click 📋 .
Data, validation	EX 7.05	Select the cell for data validation. Click Data, then click Validation. Use the tabs in the Data Validation dialog box to specify validation parameters (Settings tab), the input message (Input Message tab), and the error alert message (Error Alert tab).
Data form, add record	EX 5.14	Click any cell in list, click Data, then click Form. Click New button, type values for new record, then click Close.
Data form, delete record	EX 5.17	Click any cell in list, click Data, then click Form. Click Criteria button, enter criteria, then click Find Next. After finding record to delete, click Delete button.
Data form, search	EX 5.17	Click any cell in list, click Data, then click Form. Click Criteria button, enter criteria, then click Find Next.

TASK	PAGE #	RECOMMENDED METHOD
Embed, object	EX 6.16	In Excel, select object and click Copy button. Switch to another program and open document. Select location where document will appear and click Edit, click Paste Special. Click the Paste option button, click Microsoft Excel Worksheet Object, then click OK.
Excel, exit	EX 1.34	Click File, then click Exit, or click the Excel Close button.
Excel, start	EX 1.05	Click the Start button, point to Programs, if necessary click Microsoft Office, and then click Microsoft Excel.
Font, select	EX 3.17	Select the cell or range you want to format. Click Format, click Cells, and then click the Font tab. Select the desired font from the Font List box.
Font, select size	EX 3.16	Select the cell or range you want to format. Click Format, click Cells, and then click the Font tab. Select the desired font size from the Font List box.
Footer, add	EX 2.32	In the Print Preview window, click Setup, then click the Header/Footer tab in the Page Setup dialog box. Click Custom Footer and edit the existing footer in the Footer dialog box.
Format, apply to several worksheets at once	EX 8.14	Group worksheets to be formatted and then apply formatting commands. Ungroup the sheets after formatting.
Format, bold	EX 3.16	Select the cell or range you want to format, then click **B**, which toggles on and off.
Format, center in cell	EX 3.12	Select the cell or range you want to format. Click ▤, which toggles on and off.
Format, center text across columns	EX 3.14	Select the cell or range with text to center. Click Format, click Cells, then click the Alignment tab. Click the Horizontal Text alignment arrow and select Center Across Selection.
Format, comma	EX 3.11	Select the cell or range of cells you want to format, then click **,** .
Format, copy	EX 3.09	Select the cell or range of cells with the format you want to copy. Click ✏, then select the cell or range of cells you want to format.
Format, currency	EX 3.06	Select the cell or range of cells you want to format. Click Format, then click Cells. Click the Number tab, click Currency in the Category box, then click the desired options.
Format, font	EX 3.16	Select the cell or range you want to format. Click the Font arrow and select the desired font.
Format, indent text	EX 3.15	Select the cell or range you want to indent. Click ▤.
Format, italic	EX 3.18	Select the cell or range you want to format, then click *I*, which toggles on and off.
Format, percent	EX 3.11	Select the cell or range of cells you want to format, then click **%** .
Format, wrap text	EX 3.13	Select the cell or cells you want to format. Click Format, click Cells, then click the Alignment tab. Click the Wrap text check box.

TASK	PAGE #	RECOMMENDED METHOD
Formula, enter	EX 2.08	Click the cell in which you want the result to appear. Type = and then type the rest of the formula. For formulas that include cell references, type the cell reference or select each cell using the mouse or arrow keys. When the formula is complete, press Enter.
Formulas, display	EX 2.37	Click Tools, then click Options. Click the View tab, then click the Formulas check box.
Formulas, enter into several worksheets at once	EX 8.11	Group worksheets to contain formulas and then enter formulas. Ungroup the sheets after entering the formulas.
Freeze rows and columns	EX 5.06	Select the cell below and right of row or column you want to freeze. Click Window, then click Freeze Panes.
Function, enter	EX 1.18	Type = to begin the function. Type the name of the function in either uppercase or lowercase letters, followed by an opening parenthesis. Type the range of cells you want to calculate using the function, separating the first and last cells in the range with a colon, as in B9:B15, or drag the pointer to outline the cells you want to calculate. *See also* Paste Function button, activate.
Gridlines, add or remove	EX 3.32	Click Tools, click Options, then click View. Click the Gridlines check box.
Header, add	EX 2.32	In the Print Preview window, click Setup, then click Header/Footer tab in the Page Setup dialog box. Click the Custom Header button to add a header in the Header dialog box.
Help, activate	EX 1.26	*See* Reference Window: Using the Office Assistant, and Figure 1-23
Hyperlinks, insert	EX 6.24	Select text or graphic to serve as hyperlink, then click Insert Hyperlink button. Click File, Web Page or Bookmark, select the file you want to link to, and then click OK.
Labels, enter	EX 1.14	Select cell, then type text you want in cell.
Link, update	EX 6.15	In Excel, edit data. Switch to other program to view changes in destination document.
Linked Workbook, open	EX 8.38	Click Edit, click Links, click name of workbook from list of links and click Open.
Linked workbook, retrieve data from	EX 8.39	Click Edit, click Links, click name of workbook from list of links and click Update Now.
Links, objects	EX 6.11	In Excel, select object and click copy. Switch to another program and open document. Select location where object will appear and click Edit, and then click Paste Special. Click the Paste Link option button, click Microsoft Excel Worksheet Object, then click OK.
Links, view list of	EX 8.37	Click Edit and Links from Excel menu bar.
Lookup Tables, create	EX 8.44	Create a table on a worksheet. Insert compare values in first row or column of table. Insert values to be retrieved in rows or columns that follow.
Macro, assign shortcut key	EX 7.37	Click Tools, point to Macro, click Macros. Select name of macro, click Options, enter shortcut key letter in Shortcut key text box, click OK.

TASK	PAGE #	RECOMMENDED METHOD
Macro, assign to button	EX 7.43	*See* Reference Window: Assigning to a Button Object in a Worksheet.
Macro, recording	EX 7.31	Click Tools, point to Macro, then click Record New Macro. In Record Macro dialog box, enter a descriptive name in the Macro Name box, select location where you want to store macro, assign a shortcut key, click OK. Perform the tasks in the macro. Click Stop Recording button.
Macro, run from Tools menu	EX 7.35	Click Tools, point to Macro, then click Macros. Select the name of macro you want to run, then click Run button.
Macro, run using shortcut key	EX 7.38	Press Ctrl + shortcut key.
Non-adjacent ranges, select	EX 4.25	Click the first cell or range of cells to select, then press and hold the Ctrl key as you select the other cell or range of cells to be selected. Release the Ctrl key when all non-adjacent ranges are highlighted.
Numbers, enter	EX 1.15	Select the cell, then type the number.
Page Break, insert	EX 5.31	Click row selector button where you want to start new page. Click Insert, then click Page Break.
Paste, graphic object	EX 6.06	Select cell where you want to place object. Click Insert, point to Picture, then click from File. Select object, then click Insert.
Paste Function button, activate	EX 2.19	*See* Reference Window: Using the Paste Function button.
Patterns, apply to a range of cells	EX 3.24	*See* Reference Window: Applying Patterns and Color.
PivotTable, create	EX 5.34	Select any cell in list. Click Data, then click PivotTable and PivotChart Report. Identify source, location, layout of data, and placement of pivot table.
Print Preview window, open	EX 2.30	Click .
Printout, center	EX 2.31	In the Print Preview dialog box, click the Setup button. Click the Margins tab, then click the Horizontally and/or Vertically check boxes.
Printout, landscape orientation	EX 3.34	In the Print Preview window, click the Setup button. Click the Page tab in the Page Setup dialog box, then click the Landscape option button in the Orientation box.
Protection, cell	EX 7.25	Select cells you want to remain unprotected. Click Format, click Cells, click the Protection tab and remove check from Locked check box. Click Tools, point to protection, then click Protect Sheet. Click OK.
Range, highlight	EX 1.30	Position pointer on the first cell of the range. Press and hold the mouse button and drag the mouse through the cells you want, then release the mouse button.
Range, move	EX 2.27	Select the cell or range of cells you want to move. Place the mouse pointer over any edge of the selected range until the pointer changes to an arrow. Click and drag the outline of the range to the new worksheet location.

TASK	PAGE #	RECOMMENDED METHOD
Range, nonadjacent	EX 4.25	*See* Non-Adjacent ranges, select.
Range, select	EX 1.30	*See* Range, highlight.
Range name, defining	EX 7.10	Select the cell or range you want to name. Click Insert, point to Name, then click Define. Type the name in Names in workbook box, then click OK.
Row or column, delete	EX 2.26	Click the heading(s) of the row(s) or column(s) you want to delete, click Edit, then click Delete.
Row or column, insert	EX 2.24	Click any cell in the row/column above which you want to insert the new row/column. Click Insert and then click Rows/Columns for every row/column in the highlighted range.
Sheet, activate	EX 1.10	Click the sheet tab for the desired sheet.
Sheet tab, rename	EX 2.15	Double-click the sheet tab for the desired sheet.
Shortcut menu, activate	EX 3.10	Select the cells or objects to which you want to apply the command, click the right mouse button, then select the command you want.
Sort, more than one sort field	EX 5.12	Select any cell in list. Click Data, then click Sort. Specify sort fields and sort order, then click OK.
Sort, single sort field	EX 5.10	Select any cell in column you want to sort by. Click Sort Ascending or Sort Descending button on Standard toolbar.
Spell check	EX 2.22	Click Tools, click Spelling.
Subtotals, insert	EX 5.28	Sort the list on column you want to subtotal. Select any cell in list, then click Data, then click Subtotals. Specify the criteria for subtotals, click OK.
Templates, create	EX 8.27	Create a workbook. Click File and Save As. Enter template filename and select Template from Save As Type drop-down list box.
Templates, open	EX 8.25	Click File and New. Double-click icon of the template you want to open.
Text box, add	EX 3.27	Click [icon] on the Drawing toolbar. Position pointer where text box is to appear, then click and drag to outline desired size and shape. Type comment in box.
Toolbar, add or remove	EX 3.26	Click any toolbar with right mouse button. Click the name of the toolbar you want to use/remove from the shortcut menu.
Undo button, activate	EX 2.26	Click [icon].
WordArt, embedding	EX 6.07	Click [icon], then click [icon]. Select WordArt style, enter the text, specify font, then click OK.
Workbook, open	EX 1.10	Click [icon] (or click File, then click Open). Make sure the Look in box displays the name of the folder containing the workbook you want to open. Click the name of the workbook you want to open, then click Open.
Workbook, save with a new name	EX 1.21	Click File, then click Save As. Change the workbook name as necessary. Specify the folder in which to save workbook in the Save in box. Click Save.
Workbook, save with same name	EX 1.21	Click [icon].

TASK	PAGE #	RECOMMENDED METHOD
Worksheet, close	EX 1.33	Click File, then click Close, or click the worksheet Close button.
Worksheet, delete	EX 7.29	Click sheet tab of sheet you want to delete. Click Edit, click Delete Sheet, then click OK.
Worksheet, insert	EX 8.04	Right-click the Sheet tab of a worksheet in the workbook and click insert from the Shortcut menu. Double-click the Worksheet icon in the dialog box.
Worksheet, move	EX 8.06	Click the worksheet tab and drag the tab along the row of sheet tabs, dropping the tab at the desired location.
Worksheet, Print	EX 1.31	Click 🖨 to print without adjusting any print options. Use the Print command on the File menu to adjust options.
Worksheet labels, formula	EX 5.26	Use column headers and row labels in place of cell references to build formulas.
Worksheets, group	EX 8.10	For a contiguous sheet range: click the first sheet tab in the range, hold down the Shift key and click the last sheet tab in the range. For a noncontiguous sheet range: hold down the CTRL key and click the sheet tab of each sheet in the range.
Worksheets, ungroup	EX 8.10	Click a sheet tab of a sheet not in the group, or right-click the tab of a sheet in the group and click Ungroup Sheets from the Shortcut menu.
Workspace, create	EX 8.46	Open all of the workbooks in the workspace, click File and Save Workspace.
Workspace, open	EX 8.46	Click File and Open and click the Workspace file from the File Open dialog box.

Standardized Coding Number	Certification Skill Activity — Activity	Tutorial Pages	End-of-Tutorial Practice — End-of-Tutorial Pages	Exercise	Step Number
XL2000.1	**Working with cells**				
XL2000.1.1	Use Undo and Redo	2.24			
XL2000.1.2	Clear cell content	1.30–1.33	1.35	Review Assignment	6
			1.38	Case Problem 4	7
XL2000.1.3	Enter text, dates, and numbers	1.16–1.17	1.35	Review Assignment	5, 7
			1.36	Case Problem 1	3, 4
			1.36	Case Problem 2	3, 4
			1.37	Case Problem 3	3, 6, 7
			1.38	Case Problem 4	1, 2, 3, 4, 7
		2.04–2.07	2.37–2.38	Review Assignment	4, 10
			2.39	Case Problem 1	1, 5
			2.40	Case Problem 2	1
			2.42	Case Problem 4	1
		8.05	8.48	Review Assignment	2
XL2000.1.4	Edit cell content	1.23–1.24	1.35	Review Assignment	4
		1.26	1.37	Case Problem 2	7
XL2000.1.5	Go to a specific cell	1.08–1.09			
XL2000.1.6	Insert and delete selected cells	3.18			
XL2000.1.7	Cut, copy, paste, paste special and move selected cells, use the Office Clipboard	2.10–2.14 6.14	2.38	Review Assignment	12, 17
XL2000.1.8	Use Find and Replace	5.09			
XL2000.1.9	Clear cell formats	3.17	3.36	Review Assignment	12
XL2000.1.10	Work with series (AutoFill)	7.17–7.18	7.38	Review Assignment	1
XL2000.1.11	Create hyperlinks	6.33–6.37	6.42	Review Assignment	8, 9, 10
			6.44	Case Problem 2	14
			6.45	Case Problem 3	7, 8
			6.45	Case Problem 4	6
XL2000.2	**Working with files**				
XL2000.2.1	Use Save	1.34	1.37	Case Problem 2	5
			1.37	Case Problem 3	8
			1.38	Case Problem 4	5
		2.35	2.38	Review Assignment	14
			2.39	Case Problem 1	8
			2.40	Case Problem 2	7
			2.41	Case Problem 3	6
			2.42	Case Problem 4	6
			3.41	Case Problem 4	6

Standardized Coding Number	**Certification Skill Activity** Activity	Tutorial Pages	End-of-Tutorial Practice End-of-Tutorial Pages	Exercise	Step Number
XL2000.2.2	Use Save As (different name, location, format)	1.22–1.24	1.35	Review Assignment	2
			1.36	Case Problem 1	2
			1.36	Case Problem 2	1
			1.37	Case Problem 3	2
			1.38	Case Problem 4	5
			2.37	Review Assignment	3
			2.41	Case Problem 3	1
			3.36	Review Assignment	1
			3.37	Case Problem 1	1
			3.38–3.39	Case Problem 2	1, 8
			3.40	Case Problem 3	1
XL2000.2.3	Locate and open an existing workbook	1.11–1.12	1.35	Review Assignment	1
			1.36	Case Problem 1	1
			1.36	Case Problem 2	1
			1.37	Case Problem 3	1
XL2000.2.4	Create a folder	1.22			
XL2000.2.5	Use templates to create a new workbook	8.24–8.28	8.50	Case Problem 1	10, 11
XL2000.2.6	Save a worksheet/workbook as a Web Page	6.37–6.40	6.41	Review Assignment	5
			6.43	Case Problem 1	9
			6.45	Case Problem 3	5
XL2000.2.7	Send a workbook via email	6.11			
XL2000.2.8	Use the Office Assistant	1.27–1.29	1.35	Review Assignment	11
			2.38	Review Assignment	9, 16
			2.42	Case Problem 3	10
			4.40	Case Problem 1	11
XL2000.3	**Formatting worksheets**				
XL2000.3.1	Apply font styles (typeface, size, color and styles)	3.14–3.17 3.27	3.36	Review Assignment	3
			3.37	Case Problem 1	3
			3.38	Case Problem 2	4
			3.40	Case Problem 3	3
			3.41	Case Problem 4	3
XL2000.3.2	Apply number formats (currency, percent, dates, comma)	3.06–3.10	3.37	Case Problem 1	3
			3.38	Case Problem 2	4
			3.40	Case Problem 3	3
			3.41	Case Problem 4	3
		5.41–5.42 A1.14			

Standardized Coding Number	Certification Skill Activity — Activity	Tutorial Pages	End-of-Tutorial Practice — End-of-Tutorial Pages	Exercise	Step Number
XL2000.3.3	Modify size of rows and columns	2.22 3.24	3.36	Review Assignment	3
XL2000.3.4	Modify alignment of cell content	3.11–3.13	3.36 3.37 3.38 3.40 3.41	Review Assignment Case Problem 1 Case Problem 2 Case Problem 3 Case Problem 4	5 2 4 3 3
XL2000.3.5	Adjust the decimal place	3.09–3.10			
XL2000.3.6	Use the Format Painter	3.09			
XL2000.3.7	Apply autoformat	2.26–2.27	2.39 2.41 2.41 2.42	Case Problem 1 Case Problem 2 Case Problem 3 Case Problem 4	6 9 4 4
XL2000.3.8	Apply cell borders and shading	3.19–3.23			
XL2000.3.9	Merging cells	3.13	3.37	Review Assignment	14
XL2000.3.10	Rotate text and change indents	3.11–3.13	3.37	Review Assignment	14
XL2000.3.11	Define, apply, and remove a style	3.17			
XL2000.4	**Page setup and printing**				
XL2000.4.1	Preview and print worksheets & workbooks	1.32	1.35 1.36 1.37 1.37–1.38 1.38	Review Assignment Case Problem 1 Case Problem 2 Case Problem 3 Case Problem 4	9 6 6 9, 12 6, 8, 9
		2.28–2.30	2.38 2.41 2.41 2.43	Review Assignment Case Problem 2 Case Problem 3 Case Problem 4	15 8, 11 7 7
		3.31–3.34			
XL2000.4.2	Use Web Page Preview	6.38–6.40	6.43 6.45 6.45	Case Problem 1 Case Problem 3 Case Problem 4	9 5 7
XL2000.4.3	Print a selection	2.33	2.41	Case Problem 3	7
XL2000.4.4	Change page orientation and scaling	2.36 3.32–3.33			
XL2000.4.5	Set page margins and centering	2.29–2.30	2.40 2.41 2.41 2.43	Case Problem 1 Case Problem 2 Case Problem 3 Case Problem 4	9 11 7 7
		3.33			

Standardized Coding Number	Certification Skill Activity Activity	Tutorial Pages	End-of-Tutorial Practice		
			End-of-Tutorial Pages	Exercise	Step Number
XL2000.4.6	Insert and remove a page break	5.31–5.33	5.51	Review Assignment	16
			5.51	Case Problem 1	3
XL2000.4.7	Set print, and clear a print area	2.33	2.42	Case Problem 3	11
			4.41	Case Problem 3	7
XL2000.4.8	Set up headers and footers	2.30–2.32	2.40	Case Problem 1	9
			2.41	Case Problem 3	7
			2.43	Case Problem 4	7
		3.33	3.36	Review Assignment	7
			3.37	Case Problem 1	5
			3.38	Case Problem 3	5
			3.41	Case Problem 4	7
			4.40	Case Problem 2	5
XL2000.4.9	Set print titles and options (gridlines, print quality, row & column headings)	2.36	2.40	Case Problem 1	11
			2.41	Case Problem 2	8, 11
			2.41	Case Problem 3	7
		3.30–3.31 5.32–5.33			
XL2000.5	**Working with worksheets & workbooks**				
XL2000.5.1	Insert and delete rows and columns	2.22–2.24	2.38	Review Assignment	8, 9
			2.40	Case Problem 2	3, 4
XL2000.5.2	Hide and unhide rows and columns	3.34–3.35	5.51	Review Assignment	15
XL2000.5.3	Freeze and unfreeze rows and columns	5.06–5.07	5.51	Case Problem 1	2
			5.52	Case Problem 2	3
			5.53	Case Problem 3	2
XL2000.5.4	Change the zoom setting	5.08–5.09			
XL2000.5.5	Move between worksheets in a workbook	1.07 1.12	1.37 1.38	Case Problem 3 Case Problem 4	7 2
XL2000.5.6	Check spelling	2.21			
XL2000.5.7	Rename a worksheet	2.14	2.38	Review Assignment	5
			2.39	Case Problem 1	7
			2.40	Case Problem 2	6
XL2000.5.8	Insert and Delete worksheets	7.23–7.24 8.04–8.05	7.39 7.41	Review Assignment Case Problem 1	13 12
XL2000.5.9	Move and copy worksheets	8.06–8.07			
XL2000.5.10	Link worksheets & consolidate data using 3D References	6.03–6.05 8.32–8.40	8.48	Review Assignment	6
			8.49	Case Problem 1	5
			8.50	Case Problem 2	3, 4, 5, 6, 7
			8.52	Case Problem 4	3, 7

Standardized Coding Number	Certification Skill Activity		Tutorial Pages	End-of-Tutorial Practice		
	Activity			End-of-Tutorial Pages	Exercise	Step Number
XL2000.6	**Working with formulas & functions**					
XL2000.6.1	Enter a range within a formula by dragging		2.19–2.20	2.38	Review Assignment	12
XL2000.6.2	Enter formulas in a cell and using the formula bar		1.17–1.18	1.36	Case Problem 1	3
				1.36	Case Problem 2	2
				1.37	Case Problem 3	4, 5
				1.38	Case Problem 4	1
			2.07–2.08	2.38	Review Assignment	11
				2.39	Case Problem 1	2, 3, 4
				2.40	Case Problem 2	2, 3
				2.41	Case Problem 3	2
				2.42	Case Problem 4	2
XL2000.6.3	Revise formulas			2.41	Case Problem 3	9
XL2000.6.4	Use references (absolute and relative)		2.10–2.12	2.38	Review Assignment	8
				2.40	Case Problem 2	3
				2.41	Case Problem 3	2
XL2000.6.5	Use AutoSum		2.06–2.07	2.40	Case Problem 2	2
XL2000.6.6	Use Paste Function to insert a function		2.17–2.18	2.38	Review Assignment	13
XL2000.6.7	Use basic functions (AVERAGE, SUM, COUNT, MIN, MAX)		1.19–1.20			
			2.15–2.20	2.38	Review Assignment	13
				2.40	Case Problem 2	2
				2.41	Case Problem 3	3
				2.42	Case Problem 4	1
			5.40–5.41	5.50	Review Assignment	8
				5.52	Case Problem 2	3
XL2000.6.8	Enter functions using the formula palette		2.17–2.18			
XL2000.6.9	Use date functions (NOW and DATE)		A1.14–A1.15	A1.18	Review Assignment	10,11,12
XL2000.6.10	Use financial functions (FV and PMT)		7.19–7.21	7.51	Case Problem 2	4
			A1.02–A1.03	A1.17	Review Assignment	4
XL2000.6.11	Use logical functions (IF)		7.13–7.16	7.47	Review Assignment	11
				7.53	Case Problem 3	4
				7.54	Case Problem 4	4
			A1.08–A1.14	A1.18	Review Assignment	8, 9

Standardized Coding Number	Certification Skill Activity / Activity	Tutorial Pages	End-of-Tutorial Practice		
			End-of-Tutorial Pages	Exercise	Step Number
XL2000.7	**Using charts and objects**				
XL2000.7.1	Preview and print charts	4.23	4.39	Review Assignment	9
			4.40	Case Problem 1	7, 9, 11
			4.40	Case Problem 2	5, 7, 8
			4.41	Case Problem 3	7
			4.41	Case Problem 4	4
XL2000.7.2	Use Chart Wizard to create a chart	4.07–4.12	4.39	Review Assignment	5
		4.26	4.40	Case Problem 1	2, 8, 11
		4.36	4.40	Case Problem 2	2
			4.41	Case Problem 3	2, 3, 4
			4.41	Case Problem 4	2, 3, 4
		5.48–5.49			
		7.22–7.25			
XL2000.7.3	Modify charts	4.14–4.19	4.39	Review Assignment	6, 8, 10, 11, 12
		4.27–4.29	4.40	Case Problem 1	3, 4, 5, 6
			4.40	Case Problem 2	4
			4.41	Case Problem 3	2, 3, 4
			4.41	Case Problem 4	2, 3, 4
XL2000.7.4	Insert, move, and delete an object (picture)	4.36–4.38	4.39	Review Assignment	14b
XL2000.7.5	Create and modify lines and objects	4.19–4.21	4.39	Review Assignment	8

File Finder

Location in Tutorial	Name and Location of Data File	Student Saves File As...	Student Creates File
EXCEL LEVEL 1, DISK 1			
Tutorial 1			
Session 1.1	Tutorial.01\Tutorial\Inwood.xls		
Session 1.2	Tutorial.01\Tutorial\Inwood.xls	Tutorial.01\Tutorial\Inwood 2.xls	
Review Assignments	Tutorial.01\Review\Inwood 3.xls	Tutorial.01\Review\Inwood 4.xls	
Case Problem 1	Tutorial.01\Cases\Enroll.xls	Tutorial.01\Cases\Enrollment.xls	
Case Problem 2	Tutorial.01\Cases\Budget.xls	Tutorial.01\Cases\BudgetSol.xls	
Case Problem 3	Tutorial.01\Cases\Medical.xls	Tutorial.01\Cases\Medical 2.xls	
Case Problem 4			Tutorial.01\Cases\CashCounter.xls
Tutorial 2			
Session 2.1			Tutorial.02\Tutorial\MSI Sales Report.xls
Session 2.2	Tutorial.02\Tutorial\MSI Sales Report.xls *(Saved from Session 2.1)*	Tutorial.02\Tutorial\Report.xls MSI Sales Report.xls	
Review Assignments	Tutorial.02\Review\MSI 1.xls	Tutorial.02\Review\	MSI Sales Report 2.xls
Case Problem 1			Tutorial.02\Cases\MJ Income.xls
Case Problem 2			Tutorial.02\Cases\Airline.xls
Case Problem 3	Tutorial.02\Cases\Fresh.xls	Tutorial.02\Cases\Fresh Air Sales Incentives.xls	
Case Problem 4			Tutorial.02\Cases\Portfolio.xls
Tutorial 3			
Session 3.1	Tutorial.03\Tutorial\Pronto.xls	Tutorial.03\Tutorial\ Pronto Salsa Company.xls	
Session 3.2	Tutorial.03\Tutorial\ Pronto Salsa Company.xls *(Saved from Session 3.1)*	Tutorial.03\Tutorial\ Pronto Salsa Company.xls	
Review Assignments	Tutorial.03\Review\Pronto 2.xls Tutorial.03\Review\Explore3.xls	Tutorial.03\Review\Pronto 3.xls Tutorial.03\Review\Pronto 4.xls Tutorial.03\Review\Explore3 Solution.xls	
Case Problem 1	Tutorial.03\Cases\Running.xls	Tutorial.03\Cases\Running2.xls	
Case Problem 2	Tutorial.03\Cases\Recycle.xls	Tutorial.03\Cases\Recycle2.xls Tutorial.03\Cases\Recycle Data.xls Tutorial.03\Cases\Recycle3.xls	
Case Problem 3	Tutorial.03\Cases\StateGov.xls	Tutorial.03\Cases\State Government.xls	
Case Problem 4			Tutorial.03\Cases\Payroll.xls
Tutorial 4			
Session 4.1	Tutorial.04\Tutorial\Concepts.xls	Tutorial.04\Tutorial\Cast Iron Concepts.xls	
Session 4.2	Tutorial.04\Tutorial\Cast Iron Concepts.xls *(Saved from Session 4.1)* Tutorial.04\Tutorial\Stove.pcx		
Review Assignments	Tutorial.04\Review\Concept2.xls Tutorial.04\Review\ ElectronicFilings.xls	Tutorial.04\Review\Cast Iron Concepts 2.xls Tutorial.04\Review\Filing Solution.xls	
Case Problem 1	Tutorial.04\Cases\Tekstar.xls	Tutorial.04\Cases\TekStar Electronics.xls	
Case Problem 2	Tutorial.04\Cases\DowJones.xls	Tutorial.04\Cases\Dow Jones Chart.xls Tutorial.04\Cases\Dow Jones 2.xls	
Case Problem 3	Tutorial.04\Cases\California.xls	Tutorial.04\Cases\California Economic Data.xls	
Case Problem 4			Tutorial.04\Cases\ RealtorCharts.xls

File Finder

Location in Tutorial	Name and Location of Data File	Student Saves File As...	Student Creates File
Excel Level II			
Tutorial 5			
Session 5.1	Tutorial.05\Tutorial\Faculty.xls	CBA Faculty.xls	
Session 5.2			
Session 5.3			
Review Assignment	Tutorial.05\Review\Faculty2.xls	CBA Faculty 2.xls	
Case Problem 1	Tutorial.05\Cases\Office.xls	Office Supplies.xls	
Case Problem 2	Tutorial.05\Cases\Medical.xls	Med Tech.xls	
Case Problem 3	Tutorial.05\Cases\TeaHouse.xls	TeaHouse Revenue.xls	
Case Problem 4	Tutorial.05\Cases\NBA.xls	NBA Salaries.xls	
Tutorial 6			
Session 6.1	Tutorial.06\Tutorial\Baskets.xls Tutorial.06\Tutorial\Letter.doc Tutorial.06\Tutorial\NPA.xls	New Baskets.xls Customer Letter.doc	
Session 6.2	*(Continue from Session 6.1)*		
Session 6.3	Tutorial.06\Tutorial\New Baskets.xls	New Baskets.xls	
Review Assignment	Tutorial.06\Review\CustLtr2.doc Tutorial.06\Review\NPA.xls Tutorial.06\Review\NewBask2.xls Tutorial.06\Review\AdvLetr.doc Tutorial.06\Review\MonSales.xls Tutorial.06\Review\AdvLetr.doc Tutorial.06\Review\MonSales.xls	Customer Letter 2.doc NPA.htm New Baskets 2.xls Advisory Board Letter.doc MonSales2.xls Advisory Board Letter2.doc Advisory Board Letter2.xls	
Case Problem 1	Tutorial.06\Cases\ToyStore.xls Tutorial.06\Cases\ToyLtr.doc	Toy Store Sales.xls Toy Memo.doc	
Case Problem 2	Tutorial.06\Cases\StSales.xls Tutorial.06\Cases\StMemo.doc Tutorial.06\Cases\StMemo1.doc	State Sales Memo.doc State Sales Memo1.doc	
Case Problem 3	Tutorial.06\Cases\AlumProd.xls Tutorial.06\Cases\Alumltr.doc	Alumni Products.xls Alumni Letter.doc HorzPrc.htm	
Case Problem 4	Tutorial.06\Cases\Inwood.xls	Inwood 1.xls	Inwood Memo.doc
Tutorial 7			
Session 7.1	Tutorial.07\Tutorial\401k.xls	401kPlan.xls	
Session 7.2	*(Continue from Session 7.1)*		
Session 7.3	*(Continue from Session 7.2)*		
Review Assignment	Tutorial.07\Review\401kPlan2.xls	401kPlan3.xls	
Case Problem 1			Travel Expense.xls
Case Problem 2			Sales Agreement.xls
Case Problem 3			Apex Rental.xls
Case Problem 4	Tutorial.07\Cases\Invoices.xls	Sales Invoices.xls	
Tutorial 8			
Session 8.1	Tutorial.08\Tutorial\Grades2.xls Tutorial.08\Tutorial\Grades4.xls	Grades3.xls Grades4.dot	Grades.xls
Session 8.2	Tutorial.08\Tutorial\White.xls	Summary Grades.xls	
Session 8.3	Tutorial.08\Tutorial\TA1.xls	TA1Lookup.xls	
Review Assignment	Tutorial.08\Review\Calc223.xls	Calc223 Grades.xls	
Case Problem 1	Tutorial.08\Cases\Copiers	Copier Sales.xls	
Case Problem 2	Tutorial.08\Cases\Kitchen.xls	Kitchen Warehouse.xls	
Case Problem 3	Tutorial.08\Cases\Index.xls	NYSE Index.xls	
Case Problem 4	Tutorial.08\Cases\R1.xls Tutorial.08\Cases\R2.xls Tutorial.08\Cases\R3.xls	North.xls South.xls Southwest.xls	Bread Bakery